Managing Organizations in Developing Countries

Kumarian Press Library of Management for Development

New Directions
in
Development Management

Series Editor
Lawrence S. Graham
University of Texas at Austin

a series of books sponsored by
The National Association of Schools
of Public Affairs and Administration
(NASPAA)

Managing Organizations in Developing Countries

An Operational and Strategic Approach

Moses N. Kiggundu

KUMARIAN PRESS

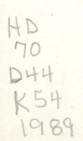

To my mother Juliet
whose generation epitomizes
the victims of underdevelopment,
but whose sagacious strategic parenting
symbolizes the glow of
hope for future generations

Copyright ©1989 Kumarian Press, Inc.
630 Oakwood Avenue, Suite 119, West Hartford, Connecticut, 06110-1505

Printed in the United States of America
93 92 91 90 89 5 4 3 2 1

Cover design by Marilyn Penrod
Typeset by The Type Galley, Boulder, Colorado

Library of Congress Cataloging-in-Publication Data

Kiggundu, Moses N., 1945-
    Managing organizations in developing countries :
an operational and strategic approach / by Moses N.
Kiggundu.
    p.   cm. — (Kumarian Press library of
management for development)
    Bibliography: p.
    Includes indexes.
    ISBN 0-931816-75-0. — ISBN 0-931816-42-4 (pbk.)
    1. Management—Developing countries.   2.
Developing countries—Economic policy.   I. Title.
   II. Series.
HD70.D44K54   1989
658'.009172'4—dc19   88-13422
                                                CIP

Contents

Figures

Tables

Series Foreword

New Directions in Development Management

This series is the most recent product of a decade of cooperation between the National Association of Schools of Public Affairs and Administration (NASPAA) and the Bureau for Science and Technology in the U.S. Agency for International Development (AID). During the second phase of this collaboration (1985–89), the primary funding mechanism for the NASPAA/ AID Cooperative Agreement has been the Performance Management Project. As a project focused on the improvement of managerial performance in the private and public sectors of developing countries, applied research and concern with the lessons learned from the technical services provided have constituted important underlying themes. Whereas the first series, under the editorship of Louis Picard, provided four state-of-the-art books, this series is intended to bring before the public new research and writing engaging the issues and concerns at the forefront of the development management field.

The first author in this new series, Moses N. Kiggundu, and his book, centering on management issues in the public and private sectors of developing countries, bring into focus an important shift in the management field and the way in which NASPAA's member schools and programs have cooperated in this project. As the project has proceeded, the issues confronted have become less and less ones concerning how best to render external technical assistance. Much more now we are addressing how to foment technical cooperation, with the goal of bringing together a pool of managerial talent and knowledge that links U.S. academic-based researchers and their institutions with their counterpart professionals and institutions in the developing world. As a consequence of grappling with practical issues and the management of development projects and programs, the concern with performance and managerial capacity within developing countries' organizations has led to a shift in attention away from the relative merits of public versus private initiatives in development toward the building of intersectoral linkages and the promotion of more effective interactions between the two sectors.

In initiating this series, the guiding concept has been how best to promote applied research on questions of performance management and capacity building in developing country organizations, both public and private. In addition to this book by Dr. Kiggundu, other projects will follow as faculty at NASPAA-member schools and others active in the network established under the Performance Management Project come together in specific activities sponsored by the project and related professional networks. A second project has been initiated, this time in cooperation with the Section on International and Comparative Administration (SICA) in the American Society for Public Administration (ASPA). The scholar in this second undertaking is Milton J. Esman; his research project entails taking stock of the development management field as a whole: what we have accomplished in promoting better theory and practice, and where we are headed as we move to the end of this century. Other projects have been initiated with scholars active in the Performance Management Project such as Richard Moore and Louise G. White. Additional professional involvement in the field of development management will be brought into play as vital parts of an endeavor to sustain new applied research and policy-relevant writing in development management.

Lawrence S. Graham, Series Editor
University of Texas at Austin

Foreword

Dr. Moses N. Kiggundu, a native of Uganda, personifies a gratifying trend of recent years. More and more, women and men from sub-Saharan African countries are providing internationally visible leadership in development organization and management. As managers and entrepreneurs, as teachers, trainers, and consultants, and as leaders of business and professional associations, they are fostering internal development and improving commercial links to their countries. They are also having an effect on the links between international development agencies and the countries they seek to assist. Donor agencies have considerable difficulty adapting their work to the differing environments of developing countries. People like Dr. Kiggundu, who have been managers in their own countries and who also understand the opportunities and costs that donor agencies represent, can be extremely valuable brokers in the process of international collaboration and assistance.

Dr. Kiggundu's contribution to international organization and management is especially noteworthy for its attention to framework and theory. The importance of this contribution should not be underestimated. In *Institutional Development: Incentives to Performance*, Arturo Israel of the World Bank characterized institutional development as an important, but "messy," area. He is quite right. Neither the concrete world of management incentives, structures, and action, nor the abstract world of analysis, with its prescriptions for action and "control," are distinguished by clear questions, let alone clear answers. If the questions can be better ordered, better answers will follow.

The analytical framework developed in *Managing Organizations in Developing Countries* spans private and public sectors, and facilitates valid and reliable inter-country comparisons. Starting with a reasonably parsimonious set of concepts, Dr. Kiggundu constructs a sturdy framework which he tests and elaborates with an impressive cut of the literature of the field. His unique combination of African and North American experience implicitly applies a valuable "reality test" to the applicability of the framework in different settings.

Given the multiple sources of his synthesis, readers should not expect to agree with every one of his interpretations and judgments. I hope they will agree that this work represents an unusually ambitious, important, and successful effort to bring more order and discipline to the analysis and understanding of a challenging area of social science. Nothing is more practical than good theory.

Kenneth L. Kornher, Chief
Institutional Development and Management Division
Office of Rural and Institutional Development
Bureau for Science and Technology
Agency for International Development

Acknowledgments

It is not possible to acknowledge all the support, advice, and criticism I have received during the development and preparation of this manuscript. I was fortunate to have done my doctoral work with leading organization scientists such as Bob House, Martin Evans, Harvey Kolodny, and Hugh Arnold of the University of Toronto from whom I benefited greatly during the earlier years of my academic training. I have also gained from the ideas of many pioneering thinkers, researchers, and practitioners in both organization science and development administration and many of these have been recognized in the appropriate parts of the book through extensive citations.

I was on the Faculty of Management at McGill University when I started paying attention to the study of administrative theory and practice in developing countries. When I arrived, two books—one by Jan J. Jorgensen on Uganda, and the other by Rabi Kanungo on work alienation—were in their final stages of completion. Working with these two researchers further stimulated my interest in development administration. Jan Jorgensen, Taieb Hafsi, and I have undertaken a five-year program of research in administrative theory and practice in developing countries, the results of which have appeared in *Administrative Science Quarterly*, the *Journal of Management Studies*, and the *Academy of Management Review*. My thinking about development administration was greatly helped by my association and friendship with these two incredibly creative thinkers. Others at McGill whose work has influenced me include Henry Mintzberg, Nancy Adler, and Al Jaeger.

In Ottawa, I have been fortunate to be associated with the international development community particularly through the Canadian International Development Agency (CIDA) and its Briefing Centre. Through this association, I have been able to meet hundreds of ordinary people from different parts of the world who are directly involved in various aspects of the development process either on the firing line, or in the board rooms of complex development organizations. Their different perspectives on development and underdevelopment have been instructive to me. The section on expatriate effectiveness has benefited from the work

Bernard Dasah and I have done for CIDA's Briefing Centre and other international organizations.

Carleton University, my present employer, provided more than the usual institutional support and intellectual freedom. The research for this book was done during the 1986–87 academic year when I was on sabbatical leave, and the offices of both the Dean of Social Science and the Director of the School of Business assisted in the typing and word processing of various revisions of the manuscript.

The National Association of Schools of Public Affairs and Administration (NASPAA), Washington, D.C., provided me with intellectual stimulation and support throughout the various stages of research and writing of this book. I am particularly grateful for advice and support from Edwin Connerley, Louis Picard, Richard Fehnel, Kenneth Kornher, and Jeanne North. Dr. Wendell Schaeffer deserves special thanks for his early appreciation of my work, for continuing support, confidence, and encouragement, and for broadening my perspectives on development administration.

This manuscript was formally reviewed by L. David Brown of the Institute for Development Research, Boston; Silvio de Franco, Professor at the Instituto Centroamericano de Administración de Empresas; Andrea L. Jones of the International Development Management Center, the University of Maryland, College Park; David K. Leonard, University of California, Berkeley; and Janet Poley of the Office of International Cooperation and Development, United States Department of Agriculture. The manuscript gained greatly from the extensive practical and research experiences of each of these people as they have all worked with organizations in different parts of the developing world. As is often the case, however, I was unable to incorporate all their insightful comments and suggestions into a single volume.

Finally, I owe special thanks and gratitude to my family, both nuclear and extended. My mother, to whom this book is dedicated, is responsible for directing me to an academic career. I hope that this book will make a positive contribution to the betterment of the human condition for her and other victims of underdevelopment. I thank my wife Eunice (Makula) for her love, and for managing a warm and supportive home that makes writing both possible and enjoyable. My two young children Andrew and Jacqueline have been wonderful and equally supportive. Although they are perplexed by the idea that I am writing a book when my den is full of books, they still give me the benefit of the doubt and keep their demands and interruptions to a minimum.

Preface

The intellectual genesis and the emotional commitment to this book date back to the early 1960s when I was growing up in Butambala, a small county in southern Uganda, where I was constantly confronted by the dualities and contradictions of development and underdevelopment side by side. I grew up in a business family and started several of my own businesses at a relatively early age. As a teenager, I served as a consultant by reading, writing and translating for the local "progressive farmers" who, with assistance from the government, were supposed to eliminate traditional farming practices and usher in a new era of modern commercial farming. No matter how hard they worked, and no matter how much the government agencies promised, the results were always well below expectations.

I was always struck by the gaps and inconsistencies between official government strategic plans and the hard realities of my clients' and family businesses. Official explanations, whenever attempted, were often incomplete and inadequate. At the university I soon realized that my clients were not alone. Working with more complex development organizations, I came to realize that the problems of implementation and sustainability of development initiatives are pervasive and persistent. It was with this background that I dedicated myself to the search for explanations that I and my clients would understand, accept, and do something about. Little did I know then how long and arduous the search would turn out to be. This book represents the first formal statement of my on-going inquiry.

This book concerns organization and management for economic development and social change. One of the greatest challenges of our times is the fight against underdevelopment and the creation of conditions for sustainable economic development and social justice. Although the world is experiencing the greatest technological advances in the history of civilization, and although it is enjoying the greatest wealth so generated, the challenges of underdevelopment continue to defy the best solutions the world has to offer. Consequently, an estimated three-quarters of the world population still lives under human conditions characterized by underdevelopment, deprivation, oppression, fear, and hunger, and faces challenging administrative problems in trying to survive.

Increasing global interdependence implies, among other things, that the burden and consequences of underdevelopment must be borne by all citizens of the world regardless of where they live or work. Experience over the last three decades has clearly shown that the constraints to development have little to do with overall availability of resources. Rather, the most serious constraints relate to the organization, management, and utilization of available resources and the opportunities for more balanced development. This book provides an organizational framework and practical techniques for more effective management and use of resources and opportunities for sustained economic development and social change.

The book is addressed to all those who care about, seek to understand, and have the capacity and opportunity to do something about underdevelopment by contributing positively to the development process. Specifically, it is addressed to the intellectual development community in both the developing and the industrialized countries. It seeks to speak to both the North and the South, as partners in development.

This is not a homogeneous audience, nor is it easy to delineate, but it includes the following groups. First, to students and active researchers in development administration and organization science who seek to understand the development process through systematic application of theories of organization and management, the book offers numerous opportunities for empirical research and hypothesis testing, especially because it is grounded in theory. Second, policy makers in both the developing countries and the international donor or funding communities who are responsible for the strategic management of the development enterprise, and whose decisions significantly affect resource availability, management, and use. To this audience, the book offers a framework and scope for well-informed strategic decisions for development. Third, the book offers practical implications and techniques for managers, administrators, officers, and all others responsible for the implementation of development initiatives once they have been determined by the policy makers. These include government departments, nongovernmental organizations, and private sector firms called upon to serve as executing agencies for the implementation of development projects. Finally, the book can be useful for the individual who seeks to understand the challenges and complexities of organizing and managing development, and who may be called upon to participate in the development process as technical specialist, advisor, consultant, trainer, counterpart, expatriate, or diplomat.

The book draws from and brings together the two disciplines of management and development. Although it is advantageous for the reader to have a working knowledge of at least one of these areas, the book can be read and understood with little or no such background. For classroom use, however, it is expected that students will have had at least one introductory course in management or administrative theory. The book should be helpful for courses in areas such as development administration, and international, comparative, and cross-cultural management. Universities in developing countries should find the book relevant for courses in organization theory, organization behavior, human resource management, business policy, general management and administration, and industrial and organizational sociology and psychology. The book should be particularly useful at the senior undergraduate and graduate levels.

The nine chapters of the text are divided into two parts. Part One, comprising the first four chapters, provides the theoretical organizational framework and discusses its relevancy for the development and management of organizations in both developing and industrialized countries. Chapter One discusses the role and importance of organizations for developing countries, and identifies ten common development challenges whose resolution requires the existence of strong organizations and effective management. The chapter concludes with a brief review of the current state of knowledge in development administration and organization science and calls for the integration of the two subdisciplines.

Chapters Two and Three describe how the organization works. Chapter Two focuses on the critical operating tasks (COTs), with illustrations from production and service organizations in developing countries. Chapter Three concentrates on strategic management tasks (SMATs), and outlines the basic steps for the development of these tasks and the ways in which they can be traced within an organization from the mission statement to individual employee behavior at work. The chapter concludes with a brief discussion of the role of the board of directors in facilitating the effective performance of both types of tasks.

Chapter Four details the integration of the two task subsystems (COTs and SMATs) into a total functioning purposive organization. The integrating mechanisms—routine, complex, and interorganizational—are also discussed. The chapter concludes with a detailed analysis of the concept of collaborative institutional arrangements (CIAs) and its potential usefulness in strengthening individual organizations through a network of mutually advantageous collaborative arrangements with other organizations.

Part Two presents selected topical applications of the framework and its organizational concepts introduced in Part One. These were included because of their relevancy for development administration, the management of organizations, and overall economic development of the developing countries. Some of the topics, such as human resource utilization, decentralization, technology transfer, and structural adjustment, are also relevant for organizations in the industrialized countries.

Chapter Five details human resource development and utilization. Although much emphasis is put on human resource development as a strategy for development, especially by the international donor community and newly independent countries, very little attention is paid to the successful utilization of these resources for effective organizational performance once personnel have been trained or otherwise developed.

Chapter Six provides a process model of the transfer of technology, knowledge, and expertise which links technology-producing and -supplying organizations with technology-importing and -implementing organizations right down to the level of the individual operator. The concept of local technological capacity (LTC) is applied to assess the extent to which the technology is acquired, utilized, modified, or exported to other organizations. The chapter concludes with a discussion of three special cases particularly relevant for developing countries. These are: (1) small-scale enterprises; (2) agricultural extension services; and (3) small and island states. Technology transfer is presented as a continuing organizational learning process.

Chapter Seven discusses the theory and practice of decentralization and concludes that, in spite of the pressures for decentralization, the evidence to date suggests that most organizations in developing countries, both public and private, have been unsuccessful in sustaining decentralized performance of their COTs or SMATs. They remain highly centralized.

Chapter Eight introduces the current topic of managing structural adjustments and public sector reform. It includes a discussion of state-owned enterprises (SOEs), privatization, and the role of the indigenous private sector organizations (IPSOs) in facilitating macroeconomic structural adjustments and reform. Structural adjustment is conceptualized as a form of collaborative institutional arrangements (CIAs) with domestic and international public and private sector organizations. The success of the reform program depends on the capacity of the participating organizations to initiate, manage, and sustain those collaborative institutional arrangements that facilitate the desired structural changes and internal performance improvements.

In general, topics are discussed starting with the micro individual level of analysis and intervention such as human resource development, and move to the more macro national or policy levels. The concept of organization is a useful one in dealing with the question of managing development at all strata. Chapter Nine provides an explicit link among these different levels or approaches to development administration. By introducing the concept of strategic organizations and strategic roles, it pulls together the previous discussions and illustrates their relevancy for managing development. Specifically, it emphasizes that effective management of development requires identifying and concentrating on strategic organizations and that the selection and utilization of diagnostic and intervention methods as well as other resources should be guided by the extent to which these bring about effective performance of the critical operating and strategic management tasks of the organizations. Two particularly important issues in development administration—those of leadership and sustainability—are briefly discussed.

This book recommends no quick fixes, no shortcuts, and no instant solutions to the complex problems of managing development and underdevelopment. Rather, it intends to improve understanding of the requirements for managing organizations for development and thus to facilitate more informed dialogue, choices, and realistic expectations for the long-term consequences of alternative courses of action. In sum, the book provides a fresh approach to the understanding of the causes of underdevelopment, and the effective management of the development process.

Moses N. Kiggundu
Ottawa, Ontario, Canada

PART ONE

A Conceptual Model for Understanding Organizations

CHAPTER 1

The Importance of Organizations for Developing Countries

I. The Role of Organization and Management in Development

For someone working or living in extreme conditions of underdevelopment, maldevelopment, and basic needs deprivation like those of the slums of Calcutta, the refugee camps of Ethiopia, or Uganda's Luwero Triangle, a call for strengthening organization and management of development initiatives may sound frivolous or even callous. For the official of a ministry of finance and planning grappling with problems of ever increasing budget deficits, public debt, and competing demands for limited foreign exchange reserves, for the Kenyan small-farm tea grower trying to save enough money for next year's fertilizers, school fees, taxes, and living expenses, and for the Filipino factory worker hardly making U.S. $1000 annual household income with a family of six, money and not organization seems to be the immediate and urgent solution to their problems. The concepts of organization, organization science, and development administration seem remote and almost irrelevant to their pressing needs.

Yet experience from developing and industrial countries shows that development initiatives have often fallen short of expectations partly because of their failure to identify and make available in usable form the required organization resources or the management of such resources. The argument being advanced in this chapter is that development initiatives by either the governments, international aid agencies, nongovernmental organizations, voluntary agencies, or the private sector will not make significant contributions to development unless serious attention is paid to developing and sustaining strong and effective organizations. In his introduction to the third edition of *Papers on the Science of Administration*, one of the classics in organization science, Luther Gulick—emphasizing the role organizations play in sustaining human civilization—wrote: "More and more throughout the world, thoughtful men are realizing that the development, if not the survival, of civilization depends on organization . . . that is, on the science and practice of administration" (1954: 3d ed.).

There is strong evidence from various developing countries in sup-

3

port of the view that lack of effective organizations is a serious bottleneck for development. The least developed low-income developing countries (GNP per capita less than U.S. $400 in 1983), where most of the modern sector systems do not work well and whose overall responses to development initiatives are quite modest, have very limited organizational and management capabilities and resources. Most World Bank reports emphasize the point that these countries do not have adequate capabilities effectively to manage development initiatives or to manage themselves out of current economic, social, and political difficulties. Hage and Finsterbusch (1987) take, as their starting point, the need to build and sustain effective and productive organizations as a prerequisite for achieving economic, social, and political development.

A recent USAID mission charged with the responsibility of evaluating the agency's training projects in Pakistan found that the country's organizational infrastructure was too weak to manage development initiatives. Headed by Richard A. Fehnel under contract from the National Association of Schools of Public Affairs and Administration (NASPAA), and including Harold Freeman, Alice Murray, and Louis Picard, the mission observed that: "By 1982 the Government of Pakistan recognized that government departments could not adequately identify, design and implement development projects, and that the improvement of management training programs and the institutions responsible for them was a critical factor in managing developmental activities more effectively" (Fehnel et al., 1985:22).

The mission report goes on to say that the limitations of managerial practices in Pakistan require structural reorganization and more effective utilization of resources. Although the mission team recommended that more training resources be made available to the Government of Pakistan, they concluded that "the institutional capacity to develop and deliver the kind of quality and amount of management training needed in the key development sectors does not exist, and its creation is a lengthy process" (Fehnel et al., 1985:27). Unfortunately, these observations apply to practically all developing countries, especially the low- and middle-income countries. In his recent book based largely on field experiences in East and Central Africa, Goran Hyden (1983) warns that there can be no shortcuts to development because these countries are essentially made up of pre-scientific, not yet organizational societies. Organizations in developing countries are sometimes difficult to discern. A Latin American specialist once told me that there are no organizations in Haiti; only piles of people in crowded warehouses overseen by officials who view their positions as privilege or entitlement, not as a duty to serve.

A comparison of the performances of developing countries seems to indicate that the strength of their organizational infrastructure is a major determinant of the success of their overall performance. In Africa, those countries considered to be doing better than others—such as the Côte d'Ivoire, Algeria, Malawi, and Zimbabwe—seem to have stronger and more effective organizations than do countries like Ghana, Uganda, Tanzania, the Sudan, Ethiopia, and Mozambique, which are experiencing very serious development problems.

In Asia, those countries making rapid economic progress, especially the members of the Association of South East Asian Nations (ASEAN) (Singapore, Thailand, Malaysia, Indonesia, the Philippines, and Borneo), Hong Kong, and South Korea, have developed effective indigenous organizations in comparison to countries like Bangladesh, Bhutan, Maldives, Nepal, and, as was mentioned above, Pakistan. In a 1984 publication, Yung Whee Rhee, Bruce Ross-Larsen, and Garry Pursell described how Korea managed to enter into world markets and expand its export business from less than $100 million per year in the 1960s to more than $20 billion per year in the early 1980s. They asked over 100 exporters what was important for their export businesses in the areas of institutional support, technological developments, and overseas marketing. Not surprisingly, these authors found a strong interaction between exporting and the effectiveness of a country's economic organizations in both the public and the private sectors. They also found that without effective organizations a country may not be able to implement successful policies for export promotion. The organizational weaknesses that Aaron Wildavsky (1972) found to explain failures in planning and plan implementation in Nepal—including costly and inappropriate organizational forms and administrative procedures, limited capacity to manage development on an ongoing basis, inadequate management information systems, and uncontrollable external or environmental forces—have also been documented in Tanzania (Moris, 1981; Hyden, 1983), Kenya (Dasah and Kiggundu, 1985; and Leonard, 1977), and Zambia (Chenoweth, 1986).

The Zambian study is particularly interesting because it almost replicates Wildavsky's Nepalese study fifteen years later. Florence A. Chenoweth, under contract from the Canadian International Development Agency (CIDA), undertook an appraisal of the organization, planning processes, and management of the Planning Division of the Ministry of Agriculture and Water Development of the Government of Zambia. Confirming the results of an earlier 1982 World Bank report, she found that the division was suffering from poor management procedures including lack of well-defined work programs, insufficient delegation, poor internal work coordination, poor supervision, and inadequate management information. These problems made it almost impossible for the division to reform its planning functions. Although she recommended reorganization and restructuring the division, she also noted that similar recommendations had been made by the previous World Bank report; however, the division has limited capacity for implementation.

As a country begins to make progress in its economic, technological, social, and political development, the need for organization and improved management becomes obvious and the constraints so imposed become more apparent and frustrating. India is unique among developing countries in at least three aspects. Despite the gross inequalities among its population of almost 800 million people, it has made rapid economic progress and stands out as one of the most successful developing countries. India is now about the world's seventh largest industrial economy and has moved from a position of mass starvation in the 1960s to a net exporter of food in the late 1980s. In addition, unlike many other developing countries, India has been active, since World War II, in studies of organization science. While foreign researchers like Rice (1958), with his studies of the application of sociotechnical systems in Ahmedabad textiles, McClelland and Winters (1969) with the applications of the need achievement theory to Indian entrepreneurs, and Hill and co-workers (1973), with the early institution building studies, provided the initial impetus and created the institutional settings, by far the majority of studies are being done by Indians working in Indian universities, management institutions, and institutes of public administration. The Indian Institute of Management, Vastrapur, Ahmedabad, is a leader in this regard.

The combination of these three factors—rapid economic progress, serious problems of inequality, and the availability of organization science knowledge about local organizations—has made it possible for the Indian leadership to become painfully aware of the limitations of organization and management for the country's future development. Addressing the Conference of Directors of National Laboratories of the Council of Scientific and Industrial Research meeting in New Delhi on May 28, 1986, the Prime Minister, Shri Rajiv Gandhi, reflecting on this problem said:

> Scientific administration must be a subject of its own. It cannot be borrowed from our general bureaucratic system because it is not going to work. At the same time, the answer is not to find the best scientists we have and put them in charge as administrators because then we lose a scientist. Perhaps, we do not even gain in administration. It is a very specialized task. We have not developed people in this area and we must see how we can develop this. (*Employment News*, Saturday, June 14, 1986, Vol. XI, No. 11, p. 32)

Improvements in organization and management in developing countries would also be beneficial to the United States and other industrialized countries. These are essentially trading nations and exports constitute a significant part of their overall economic performance. According to a recent Canadian Government report of the special joint committee on Canada's international relations chaired by Senator Jean-Maurice Simard and Tom Hockin (1986), some 39 percent of Japanese, 36 percent of U.S., 46 percent of European, and 10 percent of Canadian exports go to Asia, Africa, and Latin America. Each of these countries is individually involved in programs aimed at boosting its export performance. The Canadian government report contained a wide range of export promotion recommendations, many of which are specifically aimed at developing countries. In the United States, in 1980, the President's Export Council produced a two-volume report in which it warned that the country's trade deficit, growing since 1976, was undermining the country's economic base and that the "United States urgently needs a rapid and sustained expansion of its exports of goods and services" (The President's Export Council, 1(8):13, 1980).

An effective way for these countries to increase their exports is to increase trade with the developing countries. The only way developing countries can increase their trade activities on a sustainable basis is to increase their economic performance, especially, as has been illustrated with Korea, that of their own export sectors. This growth can come about only if they have strong effective organizations and improved management practices.

In addition to trade and commerce, industrialized countries have interests in developing countries which are best served under conditions of international economic and political tranquility. These interests cover the wider areas of international relations, world security including the control of terrorist activities, technology flows, direct investment, and population flows. The better organized and managed these developing countries are, the more likely they are to play a positive and constructive role in the complicated affairs of international relations, a role that would be of benefit to both industrialized and developing countries.

II. Organizations in Developing Countries

Studies show that organizations in developing countries share common structural and managerial attributes. These attributes differ from those typically found in North America, Europe, and Japan. Anant R. Negandhi's comparative study (1979) of 56 American subsidiaries and 55 comparable local firms in three Latin American (Argentina, Brazil, and Uruguay) and three Asian (India, Taiwan, and the Philippines) countries was one of the first to report on these similarities and differences. Negandhi found that the local firms, both in Asia and Latin America, shared common structural configurations different from those found for the subsidiaries, and different from what one would normally expect in organizations in the United States and Europe. Specifically, the local firms from the developing countries were characterized by: (1) low levels of functional specialization; (2) low levels of formalization; (3) many hierarchical levels; (4) high levels of centralization; (5) rigid stratification; (6) hierarchical form of control; (7) high levels of dysfunctional conflict; (8) paternalistic and authoritarian leadership styles; and (9) low morale and little cooperation among the employees.

Drawing on this research and comparing it with studies from other parts of the world, Lammers and Hickson observed that developing countries were characterized by underdeveloped traditional organizational forms and that these were different from the Anglo-Saxon type of flexible bureaucracy common in North America, or the Latin type of classic bureaucracy particularly common in European Latin countries. Describing the underdeveloped organizational form of the developing country, they observed: "The local firm generally does not utilize specialized staff personnel; decision making takes place at the top and there are relatively few formalized rules and procedures. Leadership practices are described as predominantly paternalistic. Adaptability is not too high while the climate exhibits few positive features" (Lammers and Hickson, 1979:426). Faucheux, Amado, and Laurent (1982) give interesting accounts of the Latin type of bureaucracy both in Europe and Latin America.

Additional researchers have found similar results in organizations in other developing countries. Kim and Utterback's (1983) study of Korean local firms disclosed that these firms had problems of adaptability and that they were mechanistically structured. They also found that operation technology was inefficient because of low wages and low cost pressures, as these firms were enjoying a protected market with little competition. A recent USAID management development study of an agricultural college in Kenya also found evidence of paternalistic leadership and centralized decision making (Nicholson et al., 1985). In a recent debriefing session with Canadian executives returning from a business forum in Kenya, Bernard Z. Dasah and I asked these executives in a telephone interview what they thought about the prospects of doing business in Kenya. The results of these interviews suggest that the Canadian business executives found organizational forms and management styles to be different from what they are used to in their own Canadian organizations. Specifically, they indicated that Kenyan organizations were characterized by: (1) lack of middle management skills and talents; (2) too much paperwork and "red tape"; (3) lack of practical business and industry knowledge; and (4) lack of delegation from the top. Commenting on the centralization of decision making in these organizations, one Canadian executive observed: "Black top level officials have a pathological reluctance to delegate and they tend to cut off winners for fear of exposing their own weaknesses" (Dasah and Kiggundu, 1985:5). The problem, however, has less to do with the managers' race than with the current state of organization and management styles. Peter Blunt (1983), for example, reports on several studies of work alienation in Kenya, Zambia, and South Africa, caused by white managers and supervisors who had little time for their subordinates' problems or personal concerns.

Drawing from these studies, and my own experiences in observing organizations in various developing countries such as Uganda, Kenya, India, and Ghana, I have developed a general profile that describes a "typical" developing country organization. Figure 1.1 gives this profile at the top management, middle management, and operating levels. As anybody who has visited the executive suites of these organizations knows, top management tends to be overworked, putting in long hours and participating in a wide range of extraorganizational activities. These may be civic, political, religious, tribal, or personal family and business activities. The reluctancy to delegate also explains the need to put in long hours, for even the smallest operating decisions are pushed up the hierarchy for executive action. Administrative and technical executive support is weak and quite often the manager ends up doing the support functions like planning, budgeting, background research, and environmental scanning and analysis before attending to the appropriate executive functions. Quite often the organization's mission is not clearly articulated and the organization lacks a clear sense of purpose and direction. Yet, most of the executives in these organizations are often described as highly educated, articulate in their expressions, and widely traveled, especially in Europe and the United States where they might have attended universities and colleges.

Middle management typically provides a different profile. For most of these organizations the middle level is weak, with weak management and organization systems and controls. There is little motivation for independent action either because of top management's authoritarian styles, or because of the middle managers' lack of technical and managerial skills and experience. In return, middle managers exercise close supervision and, like their bosses at the top, allow little or no delegation or participative management. Centralized and personalized management styles are pervasive at both levels of the organization. Motivation is low and, according to a recent Indian study by B.R. Sharma of the Indian Institute of Public Administration in New Delhi, it may have reached crisis proportions, at least in India.

The operating levels are inefficient and costly, putting a lot of financial pressure on the organization's working capital. Productivity is low and, with overstaffing ranging from 18 to 50 percent, the individual employees tend to be underutilized. Pay is poor and reward systems are not contingent on performance or other organizationally relevant criteria. Consequently, morale is poor, although this manifests itself in unexcused absences and worker indolence rather than frequent turnover. The boundaries of the organization are rather porous, leaving the vital technical core of the organization unprotected and susceptible to abuse by outside

Figure 1.1

A GENERAL PROFILE OF A DEVELOPING COUNTRY ORGANIZATION

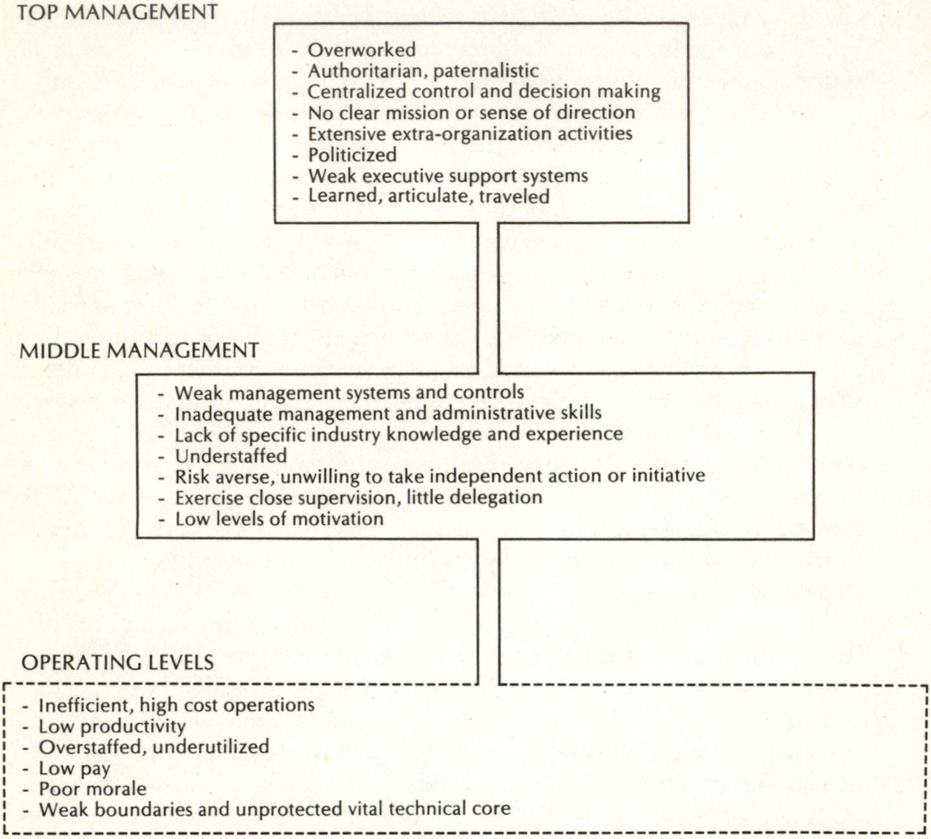

TOP MANAGEMENT

- Overworked
- Authoritarian, paternalistic
- Centralized control and decision making
- No clear mission or sense of direction
- Extensive extra-organization activities
- Politicized
- Weak executive support systems
- Learned, articulate, traveled

MIDDLE MANAGEMENT

- Weak management systems and controls
- Inadequate management and administrative skills
- Lack of specific industry knowledge and experience
- Understaffed
- Risk averse, unwilling to take independent action or initiative
- Exercise close supervision, little delegation
- Low levels of motivation

OPERATING LEVELS

- Inefficient, high cost operations
- Low productivity
- Overstaffed, underutilized
- Low pay
- Poor morale
- Weak boundaries and unprotected vital technical core

societal interests. This state often compromises the integrity and efficient operations of the technical core leading to inefficiency, unfairness, and improper use of organizational resources. The long thin lines between the different parts of the organization suggest inadequate coordination and communication among the three different levels. The broken lines at the operating levels indicate the porous organization boundaries and inadequate protection of the organization's vital technical core.

Of course, this is only a general profile that I believe appropriately describes many organizations in various developing countries. Like any general profile, however, it does not claim to represent each and every organization and manager in every developing country. Part of the motivation for presenting this profile is to challenge the managers of similar organizations in developing countries to show that the profiles of their own organizations are both different and better. This is a descriptive and not a prescriptive profile because there is evidence to suggest that its elements are associated with various organizational dysfunctions and pathologies.

III. Developing Countries: Similarities Versus Differences

When I tell friends and colleagues that I am interested in studying the management of organizations in developing countries, the typical response is one of surprise, accompanied by a barrage of suspicious questions: Which countries? Which regions? Which topics? Which sectors? What type of organizations? The implied assumption is that the study of organizations in developing countries in general is perhaps neither possible nor desirable. In this section I shall discuss, on two different levels, the similarities and differences within developing countries. First, I shall approach the question at the level of the organization. Do organizations in developing countries share common characteristics that make it worthwhile to study them together? Does such an approach have the potential to produce useful knowledge for organization science? Second, I shall address the question at the level of developing countries. Do these countries have enough in common in the area of organization and management to make worthwhile their study as a single unit of analysis?

The World Bank lists about one hundred countries as belonging to the collective commonly identified as the Third World or developing countries. As we all know, these countries are not a homogeneous unit. Rather, they are characterized by diversity, contrasts, and contradictions both within and among themselves. They differ in many aspects including geography, levels of social and economic development, size, population density, technological advances, urbanization, natural resources endowment, political systems, culture, religions, languages, history, racial and ethnic composition, distribution of income, wealth, quality of life, opportunity, and organization and management depth. For example, the difference between Ethiopia, claimed to be one of the poorest countries in the world, and Singapore, another developing country, is perhaps greater than the difference between Singapore and the United States or any other industrialized country. The differences are so compelling that we must always exercise caution in making generalizations about developing countries or treating them as a single concept or unit of analysis.

In spite of all these differences and in spite of the fact that developing countries are increasingly becoming more heterogenous, I strongly believe that, in regard to discussions of organization and management, these countries have so much in common that it makes sense to talk about them as if they were a single homogeneous group. The history of organization and management is short but it is even shorter for the developing countries. In the summer of 1986, the Academy of Management celebrated its 50th anniversary and the centennial (1886–1986) for modern management. However, according to a recent World Bank report authored by Kubr and Wallace (1983), the history of management and organization in developing countries is no older than twenty to thirty years.

Whether it is their common short exposure to modern management and organization science or some other reasons, developing countries share a common set of organization and management problems. I have identified ten organization and management problems that are common to all developing countries. The magnitude and seriousness of each of these problems may vary from country to country and over time, but on the whole, sooner or later, each of the developing countries experiences difficulties associated with the management of every one of the problems listed below. These problems are:

1.   Development and sustenance of high performance systems in order to increase productivity and effective utilization of scarce resources.

2.   Diversification of the economy by introducing new activities within already existing sectors, and by creating new sectorial activities. Examples include introduction of new and better food and cash crops, diversification from agriculture to other sectors like manufacturing and services, and introduction of better production methods.

3.   Development, localization, and utilization of human resources, especially in the managerial, technical, and professional cadres.

4.   Development and maintenance of cost effective and revenue generating infrastructures and social service delivery systems (e.g., education, housing, transportation, communication, health), consistent with the rising expectations and demands of the people.

5.   Development and sustenance of more "democratic" political institutions and practices consistent with local and national security needs and international pressures.

6.   Management of the growth, structure, and composition of each country's diverse population in accordance with its available resources in order to avoid or to minimize the opportunity for conflict among the different ethnic and socioeconomic interest groups.

7.   Localization of the economy so as to place ownership, management, and control of the major economic organizations of the

country in the hands of its citizens.

8. Attainment and maintenance of more equitable distribution and effective utilization of income, wealth, and opportunities.

9. Management of rural-urban development dynamics and inter-dependencies.

10. Management of structural adjustments including public sector reform, divestiture, private sector development, privatization, and internal and external indebtedness.

The nature and the causes of each of these ten problem areas are many and complex, and they vary from country to country. I suggest, however, that an examination of the organization and management systems and practices found in a given developing country will provide a basis for better understanding of the causes and persistence of these problems. It should also aid the development of realistic and sustainable solutions. Because a detailed discussion of all ten problem areas is not feasible, I have chosen to analyze two of the problems and their relevancy for organization and management in developing countries in general.

IV. Management of Inequalities

All developing countries are characterized by gross inequalities in the distribution of income, wealth, and opportunity. In Kenya, for example, according to the Canadian International Development Agency's (CIDA) 1985–90 country briefing review, the richest 10 percent of the Kenyan population receive 45.8 percent of total household income, while the poorest 20 percent receive only 2.6 percent of total household income. In Peru, the lowest 20 percent of the population share only 2 percent of total household income while the highest 10 percent take 43 percent of total household income. The comparable figures for the poorest and richest populations and their share of total household income are: Mexico, 3 percent and 41 percent; Nepal, 5 percent and 47 percent; and Brazil, 2 percent and 51 percent! Attempts to correct these inequalities often have been unsuccessful, have met with serious opposition from the powerful and privileged, and have led to violent changes of government regimes. The situation is not likely to change in these and other developing countries until effective economic, social, and security organizations can be developed and managed in such a way that they are used as instruments of change.

The distribution of opportunities is equally skewed for social services. Although developing countries have made great strides in extending education services in both rural and urban areas, they still have a long way to go before reaching all eligible citizens. According to the World Bank's 1985 World Development Report, in 1982 the numbers enrolled in secondary schools as a percentage of age group were 30 percent for the low-income countries, 42 percent for the middle-income countries, 14 percent for sub-Saharan Africa, and 52 percent for the upper middle-income countries. Likewise, the numbers enrolled in higher education as a percentage of population aged 20–24 are 4 percent for the low-income countries, 1 percent for sub-Saharan Africa, 12 percent for middle-income countries, and 14 percent for upper middle-income ones. These are rather disappointing statistics, especially because education is positively correlated with the propensity to respond positively to development initiatives. These figures indicate that large numbers of people are deprived of education opportunities, as about 60 percent of the population of a typical developing country is 25 years old or younger. The only practical solution to these problems is that these countries develop and sustain effective educational institutions and educational delivery and support systems. The underorganized countries with weak organizations and poor management practices also have the poorest statistics. Health care services are equally unevenly distributed among the populations and require similar organization and management responses. Without the development and maintenance of effective organizations, I predict that all efforts to create wealth, generate income, and distribute opportunities more evenly will always fall short of expectations.

V. Management of Rural-Urban Transitions

Conventional wisdom would have us believe that developing countries do not have urban management problems, as the majority of their population live in rural areas. This view is reinforced by the great emphasis put on rural development, especially in studies of development administration. Moreover, there is a general feeling that urban dwellers are better off than their rural brothers and sisters. Yet recent studies suggest that urban poverty and relative deprivation are as serious in the cities, and in some countries are more serious than in the rural areas. For a detailed discussion of the challenges of metropolitan management in Asia, see Sivaramakrishnan and Green (1986).

Developing countries are becoming increasingly urban. Figures show that urban population is growing at least 2 percentage points faster than the general population. Although the average urban population as a percentage of total population for the low-income countries was 25 percent in 1985, for the middle-income and upper-income countries the figure was 50 percent. Moreover, during the twenty-year period from 1960, the number of cities with one-half million people or more grew very fast. Consequently, by 1985 at least ten developing countries had five or more cities of at least one-half million people in size. The list of countries and their respective number of such large cities include China 78, India 36, Brazil 14, South Korea, Mexico, and South Africa 7, Iran 6, and Argentina 5.

Although productivity is higher in urban areas than it is in rural areas, metropolitan areas of such large magnitude require effective organizations and utilization of modern management concepts and techniques. Formal studies and casual observations indicate that the majority of municipal governments in developing countries experience problems in the following areas: (1) revenue collection and fiscal responsibility; (2) protection of lives and property; (3) garbage collection and related sanitary services; (4) adequate public utilities (e.g., water, electricity, transportation, and housing) at a price people can afford; and (5) physical and urban planning for orderly development and effective utilization of municipal resources. These problems are aggravated by organization and management problems. Every developing country faces increasing urbanization and problems of metropolitan management in addition to the problems of rural development and the movements of people between the two sectors. Therefore, every developing country needs expertise in the effective organization and management of city administrations, rural development, and the interaction and interdependence between the two sectors. In subsequent chapters, we present a conceptual framework for understanding and development of such specific organizations in developing countries.

VI. The Concept of Organization

Like other disciplines, organization science has spent a lot of effort defining the essence of its subject matter—the organization. In particular, the early studies of organization science were caught up in an endless and often fruitless debate over the definition and meaning of organization. Organization scientists from different academic and professional backgrounds have used different terminologies to describe the concept of organization. These include formal organization (Blau and Scott, 1962), informal organization (Roethlisberger and Dickson, 1939), social organization (Bakke, 1959), human organization (Likert, 1967), biological organization (Haire, 1959), complex organization (Galbraith, 1973; Perrow, 1986), bureaucracy (Blau, 1963; Goodsell, 1983), and institution (Williamson, 1985). More definitions have generally led to more confusion and delayed the development of useful knowledge about organizations. The fact that organization scientists came from diverse academic backgrounds including the social, physical, and biological sciences was also not helpful.

Even today, there is no universally accepted definition of organization. This lack should not be either surprising or discouraging. Failure to agree on a single definition of its core concepts does not necessarily stop a discipline from producing useful knowledge and advancing human understanding. To the contrary, diversity may be a source of strength and creativity leading to a more comprehensive and sophisticated discipline. As Penrose (1952) reminded economists more than 35 years ago, and Kimberley, Miles, and their co-workers (1980) more recently reminded organization scientists, even biologists have not yet settled on a single definition of the concept of the organism. Yet this has not stopped scientific advances in the biological sciences, which today form the basic discipline for the life sciences and contribute useful knowledge to many others, including organization science.

It is necessary to provide a working definition of the concept of organization and to show how it compares with others in the literature. More to the point, a working definition serves a specific purpose by setting the stage for subsequent discussions in this book. Following Daft and Steers (1986), I define organization as:

1.   an organic social–technical entity,

2.   which is mission driven and goal directed,

3.   which at any given time has a deliberately structured activity system,

4.   with an identifiable boundary or boundaries,

5.   which has generalized and specific task environment(s), and

6.   which has various internal and external actors and stakeholders (individuals, groups, other organizations) with specific needs and expectations in exchange for contributions to the organization's survival, growth, and development.

Organizations possess some of the characteristics of living organisms: they can grow, decline, decay (Kiggundu, 1985b), and even die (Hall, 1976, 1984; McHenry, 1985). They are mission driven and goal directed in that every organization has a *raison d'être* for its existence which determines the parameters of its vital core or its most important operating tasks. The major activities are deliberately structured so that, ideally, management can exercise *organizational choice* in the selection of methods for designing, structuring, and changing the organization in light of internal and environmental changes. This is the essence of the structural contingency theories of organization (Burns and Stalker, 1961; Hage and Finsterbusch, 1987; Lawrence and Lorsch, 1967; Trist et al., 1963).

Organization boundaries are difficult to visualize because they are not physical or concrete objects but are conceptual maps of the relationship between the organization and its environment, even in developing countries where organizations are often superceded by individual, family, village, tribal, or community considerations. As open systems interacting with the environment, organizations tend to have porous boundaries, especially in the top hierarchies. This organizational porosity causes problems for management particularly in developing countries, where even the technical core is exposed to unfavorable environments (Kiggundu, Jorgensen, and Hafsi, 1983). Finally, organizations face two types of environments: the general environment common to all organizations in the same locale, and specific task environments unique to a specific organization. Each of these environments has actors or stakeholders who play a major role in determining the organization's welfare and destiny.

VII. Organization Science

Organization science (OS) as a discipline has been as difficult and controversial to define as the concept of organization itself. It is clear, however, that organization science is a multidisciplinary study of and about organizations: their internal properties, processes, and dynamics; their relationships with other organizations; the interactions with different elements in the environment; and the individual and collective behavior of their respective actors and stakeholders. Organization science draws not only from the social sciences, but also from a wide range of disciplines. Contributions from the physical sciences include Frederick Taylor's (1911) scientific management from industrial engineering, Deming's (Dewar, 1980) quality control circles (QCCs), and Louis Davis' (1975) sociotechnical systems analysis from chemical engineering. From the biological sciences we get Bertalanffy's (1968) general open systems theory popularized in the 1960s and 1970s by researchers at the University of Michigan's Institute of Social Research including Katz and Khan (1978), McGregor (1967), and Likert (1967). We also get the more pervasive macro and micro contingent theories as exemplified by the works of Aiken and Hage (1968), and Charles Perrow (1986), and Fiedler (1967), House (1971), and Miner (1965), respectively. Medical sciences and psychiatry have contributed diagnostic and intervention theories and methods (Kets deVries and Miller, 1984; Levinson, 1972) and agricultural sciences have provided tools and methods for conducting organizational experiments (Evan, 1971).

Within the social sciences, contributions to organization science have tended to vary by discipline and by level of analysis. Organization sociologists have tended to focus on macro-organization theory, taking the organization as a whole or divisions thereof as the unit of analysis and taking the Weberian theory of bureaucracy as the starting point. British and European scholars have been particularly fond of this approach. Examples include the Aston study group in England (Pugh, Hickson, and

Hinings, 1971; Child, 1972), Woodward's early work (1965), the work of Burns and Stalker (1961), Crozier's study of French bureaucracies (1964), and Hofstede's study of the consequences of culture on organizations (1980). The contributions of psychology and social psychology have been mainly at the more micro individual, interpersonal, and small group levels of analysis. With the major contributions coming mainly from the United States, the main focus of the micro perspective has been that of understanding and changing behavior in organizations. Accordingly, most efforts have been directed at developing, testing, validating, and applying theories and diagnostic and intervention tools and methods for bringing about socially desirable behavioral changes in organizations. It is for this reason that most of the micro-organization theories of motivation (Lawler, 1971), job design (Herzberg, Mausner, and Snyderman, 1959; Hackman and Oldham, 1980), leadership (Fiedler, 1967; Hersey and Blanchard, 1982) decision making (Vroom and Yetton, 1973), group dynamics (Janis, 1972), stress (Albrecht, 1979), and role conflict and role ambiguity (Kahn et al., 1964) have an applied or practical component. American industrial and organization psychologists have done it so well that a history professor from New England accused his colleagues of being "servants of power" (Baritz, 1960).

Political scientists have traditionally been interested in even larger political entities like nation states. They have therefore tended to study organizations as a means to understanding the more macro political systems. Because of their interest in international affairs, political scientists have been among the most active social scientists in contributing to development administration and organization sciences in developing countries. In a relative sense, contributions to development administration from industrial and organizational psychology have been particularly limited. This unintended bias reflects the current stock of organization science knowledge and limits our understanding of organizations in developing countries.

In addition to the basic disciplines, organization science is increasingly found in a wide range of professional schools including business, public administration, international relations, medicine, education, social work, and law. Each of these schools tends to specialize in studying specific types of organizations. For example, business schools tend to study industrial organizations, while those of public administration study civic and public organizations, and those for international relations focus on international organizations. The more specialized professional institutions like the police and military academies, theological colleges, and schools of hotel and hospitality management and of wildlife management, also study organization science, but only within the confines of their particular interests.

VIII. Development Administration

The previous section has demonstrated the multidisciplinary nature and extent of organization science. Although individual researchers and institutions may choose to concentrate on only one or a few aspects of organization science, the discipline must be broadly defined to include all the various perspectives and approaches. Organization science in developing countries is even more demanding because, as I have argued elsewhere (Kiggundu, 1986), in addition to the above disciplines, it must also draw from others, including economic development and international economics, colonial history and administration, international development and technical assistance, technology transfer, rural development, and cross-cultural studies. That it is almost impossible to be knowledgeable in all these areas may explain why very few promising young scholars choose to specialize in development administration. It may be that the scholastic demands far outweigh the potential intrinsic and extrinsic benefits.

Development administration—recently renamed development management by international development agencies (see, e.g., Honadle, 1986) to emphasize the managerial skills requirements as opposed to the routine administrative maintenance functions of development—has other problems as an applied discipline of study. One such problem is that it is highly differentiated. We find subfields of specializations differentiated by region, sector, and topic with each subfield having little or no connection with other subfields or with the general discipline of organization science.

Figure 1.2 illustrates the differentiation of development administration as a discipline. As the diagram shows, individuals tend to specialize within a topic, sector, or region. For example, individuals might specialize in development administration in China, South America, or the Middle East rather than in organization science as a field of study with applications in different parts of the developing world. Moreover, each of these regions can be further subdivided: sub-Saharan Africa can be divided into Anglophone Africa, Francophone Africa, or the nine members of the SADCC (Southern African Development Coordinating Conference) regional grouping. Likewise, each of the sectors can be subdivided into specialist subsectors. Within agriculture, for example, specialists exist in the organization and management of food production, export crops, pastoral farming (dairy, ranching, etc.), fisheries, forestry, or a single generalized function like irrigation. Finally, the topics can also be divided into subfields of study. For example, human resource development can subdivide into human resource planning, education (primary, secondary, university, etc.), industrial and technical training, management develop-

Figure 1.2

**THE DIFFERENTIATION OF DEVELOPMENT ADMINISTRATION
AS A DISCIPLINE OF STUDY**

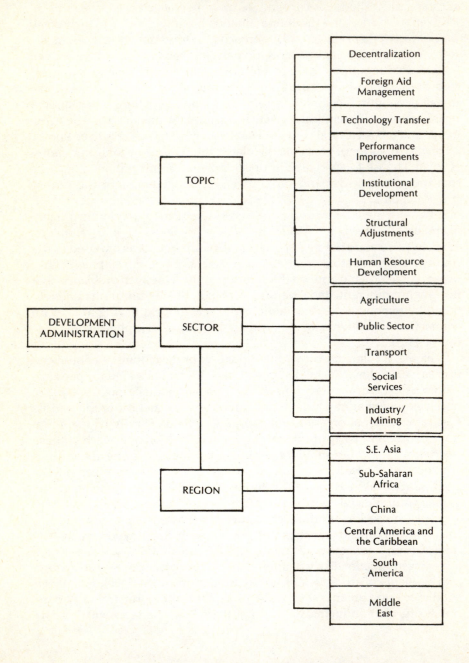

ment, motivation, and population flows.

Several drawbacks are associated with these differentiations. Information and knowledge tend to be scattered and hard to find. Experiences are noncumulative or nonadditive. There is little or no cross-fertilization of knowledge or experience across regions, sectors, and topics. Instead, each study or field experience is treated as a unique subject matter unrelated to others in development administration. Moreover, with so few good researchers and field specialists available on a continuing basis, it becomes almost impossible to cover all the subdivisions. Clearly, there is need for integration. Development administration should be treated as an integral subdiscipline of organization science. Instead of specializing in the management of irrigation schemes in Thailand, one should strive to be a specialist in organization science with special interests in the management of irrigation schemes in developing countries (Plusquellec and Wickham, 1985).

IX. Organization Science and Development Administration: The Need for Integration

In the previous section, I have discussed some of the problems of development administration and suggested that there is a need to integrate the various subfields. In this section, I present evidence of the need to integrate development administration and bring it closer to the rest of organization science. During the early 1980s, while my colleagues Jorgensen and Hafsi and I were at McGill University in Montreal, we started a program of research aimed at investigating the state of the art of development administration in order to advance knowledge and understanding in the field. We began by undertaking a structured survey of the literature to examine how organization science and administrative techniques have been applied in developing countries. A sample of 94 articles was obtained from *Administrative Science Quarterly,* and from a computer search of three data bases: *Management Contents, Economic Abstracts International,* and *Sociological Abstracts.* About two-thirds of the articles chosen were listed in *Management Contents;* the others were distributed equally between the two remaining data bases. These articles covered all of the different geographical regions of the developing world, different methodological approaches (empirical, quantitative, qualitative, and theoretical), and different organization science topics including organization tasks and technology, leadership, organizational goals and effectiveness, motivation, organization structure, decision making, the organization and environment, and attitudes (Kiggundu, Jorgensen, and Hafsi, 1983).

In synthesizing this literature, we found that, although there was a great deal of interest in the utilization of organization science in developing countries as shown by the sheer volume of published materials on the subject, the studies suffered from several weaknesses. First, the methodological approaches and sampling techniques they used were weak or unclear, making it difficult to generalize the results to other organizations. For example, in all the studies reviewed, only seven specified the size of the population from which the samples of firms or persons were drawn. In the majority of cases, the authors were content to provide assurances that the sample was a good cross section or that the organizations were representative of the range of firms.

Second, in many cases, the particular theory or organization science technique used was obsolete. Consequently, studies of development administration were not up-to-date with current thinking and practice in organization science, thus depriving developing countries of the opportunity to use the latest knowledge.

Third, the studies lacked local focus, since most of the authors did not have direct connection with the organization or developing country where the study was conducted. We classified the 94 articles according to the author's name and institutional affiliation. An article was coded as having a direct connection with the developing country that was studied if at least one of the authors had an institutional affiliation in that country or if the author's name appeared to indicate ethnic roots in that country. We were able to code 91 of the articles with a substantial degree of confidence since my colleagues and I have extensive experience in different parts of the developing world. Three-fifths of the coded articles did not have direct connections with the developing countries where the studies were conducted either by institutional affiliations or by virtue of the authors' names. Thus, such studies reflect the potential problems of extractive research.

Extractive research is research undertaken in one organization or country for the sole benefit of individuals or institutions in another country. Elsewhere, I have described extractive research as a process that usually involves a foreign researcher using foreign conceptual models and diagnostic tools, gaining entry into a developing country organization, extracting data from the organization and its members, returning home, and using the data to advance his or her own professional interests or the interests of the sponsoring institution with little or no regard for the needs and interests of the organization or people from whom the data were extracted (Kiggundu, 1985). Our studies have shown that a considerable amount of organization science work carried out in developing countries constitutes extractive research with little or no direct benefits to these countries.

Finally, as there was little evidence to suggest that the results of the large sample of studies had been fed back to the participating organizations or countries, we were led to speculate that most of the work in development administration is extractive research. Unfortunately, the results of such research make little or no contribution to the understanding of organizations and improvements in the performance of their respective critical operating and strategic management tasks.

In a more recent study of the effect of market imperfections on the structuring of organizations in developing countries, we also found a general lack of organization science knowledge in these countries. We observed that ". . . there has been less emphasis on how organizations function in developing countries and how they can be made more effective" (Jorgensen, Hafsi, and Kiggundu, 1986:417). Similar conclusions have been made by other independent researchers. For example, Kim and Utterback (1983), while studying the evolution of organization structure, technology, and local market conditions in 31 Korean consumer and industrial electronic equipment manufacturing firms—both new and established—also complained about the lack of advanced understanding of organizations in developing countries. They blamed this on inadequate systematic organization science research in these countries.

All these studies point to the same inescapable conclusion. There is little systematic organization science research in developing countries and most of what is done is essentially extractive research of little or no benefit to the country or organization in which it is conducted. One way of addressing this problem is to integrate development administration into the mainstream activities of organization science so that both are guided by the same principles, ethics, and methodological requirements.

X. The Current State of Organization Science

Organization science as a discipline is itself not without faults or limitations. There is as yet no definitive or comprehensive theory of organization. Instead, the field is characterized by numerous and sometimes conflicting theoretical frameworks or middle-range theories with limited explanatory or predictive powers. Some of these theoretical frameworks are so general that critical tests are difficult to conduct; thus it is almost impossible to disprove them and replace them with better theories. Secondly, most organization science research has tended to be ethnocentric, that is, most of the theories, research methods, and diagnostic and intervention tools and techniques have been developed, tested, validated, and applied within the industrialized Western technological, economic, political, and cultural contexts. It is therefore not surprising that one of the most popular and at times trifling questions asked in development administration is the extent to which these theories apply in non-Western or nonindustrialized countries, especially in the traditional settings of the developing countries. Moreover, organization science has not always focused on the organization as the subject of study. In the opening remarks of his recent award-winning book in which he quotes from Phil Mirvis, Jeffrey Pfeffer complains that, as organization scientists:

> . . . we have moved away from analyzing organizations as
> what we know them to be, physical entities with relational
> structures characterized by demographic processes such as
> entry and turnover. We have so enjoyed drawing figures on the
> ground speculating and psychologizing about intrapsychic
> processes, and developing complex and convoluted concepts
> and measures that we have at times lost sight of the ground for
> all the figures we have drawn. (Pfeffer, 1982:viii)

In spite of these criticisms, Donaldson (1985) has vehemently defended organization theory and has replied to critics who would like to see either a more micro individual level of analysis, or a more macro societal approach.

Perhaps one of the most serious limitations of organization science from the point of view of making significant contributions to development administration is that it too is highly differentiated. This differentiation and fragmentation of organization science knowledge manifests itself in various ways including the proliferation of specialty journals, the mushrooming of professional associations and interest groups, and the frequent reorganizations of university academic units associated with organization science teaching and research. Perhaps this differentiation should be expected, given the wide range of disciplines from which organization science draws. Diversity can be a source of both strength and weakness. In this case, organization science has not gained strength from its diverse disciplines. It remains a differentiated and fragmented discipline, packaged in a way that makes utilization difficult especially for organizations in developing countries.

The organization of the Academy of Management, a leading academic and professional association for organization science, gives a sense of the differentiation of the discipline. Started over fifty years ago in 1936 by only a handful of university professors, the Academy has grown into an international organization with sixteen professional divisions, three interest groups, and five U.S. regional divisions. It produces three journals, a general newsletter, divisional newsletters, and six conference proceedings for the national meetings and each of the regional meetings. Figure 1.3 shows the professional divisions and interest groups into which organization science is divided by the Academy.

The professional divisions and interest groups give a clear indication of the substantive differentiation of organization science. The regional divisions apply only to internal U.S. geographical areas and repeat the same professional divisions and interest groups. The interest groups are only evolutionary temporary structures because almost invariably, all interest groups eventually achieve full professional division status. A close examination of the professional divisions and interest groups shows no

Figure 1.3

**THE DIFFERENTIATION OF ORGANIZATION SCIENCE
BY THE ACADEMY OF MANAGEMENT**

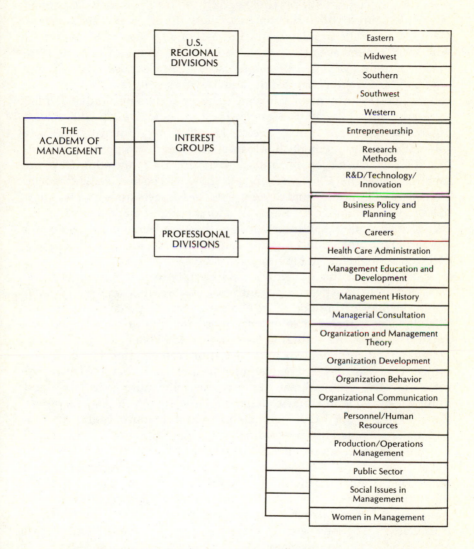

Source: The Academy of Management Handbook, 1983; Academy of Management 1986 Program.

systematic logic or rational basis for dividing up organization science knowledge. Some of the divisions, like Public Sector and Health Care Administration, are sectorial. Others are each associated with one of the basic disciplines of organization science. For example, Organization Behavior is associated with psychology and social psychology, Personnel/Human Resources with industrial psychology, Organization and Management Theory with sociology, and Production/Operations Management with management science, operations research, and management information systems (MIS). The divisions also suggest clear overlaps with one another. Management Education and Development, for example, can concern a publicly owned health care delivery system in a Jordanian ministry of health. However, this categorization would overlap with at least other three divisions: Public Sector, Health Care Administration, and International Management. If attempts are made to improve the health care delivery system organizations, then either Organization Development or Managerial Consultation, or both, would be involved. Moreover, management education and development are usually undertaken as part of a program of human resources development and management. It can therefore be argued that the activities of the Management Education and Development professional division can be subsumed within the domain of the Personnel/Human Resources division.

According to the Academy's 1983 Handbook, its more than 5,000 members come from nearly 40 countries. In spite of this, only one division is responsible for promoting excellence in international management. This division is responsible for accommodating all of the research and applied interests and studies outside the United States. It is the division within which development administration can legitimately be represented. However, development administration has to compete with other more attractive international studies, especially those from Japan and Europe. Consequently, the Academy of Management, through its professional divisions and other channels including its journals and national and regional conference proceedings, provides very limited and insufficient outlets for development administration.

It is clear that the divisions of the Academy of Management do not reflect logical or natural divisions of organization science. Rather, they are the result of half a century of organizational political processes within the Academy and its membership. They represent perhaps an honest but haphazard attempt by the Board of Governors—the executive arm of the Academy—to accommodate as many organization science interests as possible and to prevent a proliferation of competing professional associations.

The Academy's rationale for the professional divisions is that they promote excellence in established management disciplines and that the interest groups are established to recognize management trends. It is also true that the Academy has a number of integration mechanisms for cross-fertilizing knowledge across divisions and bringing divisional members together. The three journals do not recognize the professional divisions in their editorial and publication policies and procedures. The annual meetings and regional conferences contain joint sessions organized by two or more divisions together. Conference proceedings, though organized by divisions, are bound together and distributed to all registrants regardless of divisional membership. Membership is also open for all divisions and most members belong to at least three professional divisions and as many interest groups as they choose. However, the Academy fee structure discourages membership in many divisions and interest groups, because there is an additional charge for both membership to more than two divisions, and membership to the interest groups.

This information should indicate that organization science might be served better by the Academy of Management if it contained fewer professional divisions and interest groups. The integration of organization science subfields not only would advance excellence in the discipline but also would make it easier for development administration to be integrated into a more coherent body of knowledge. I use this discussion as an illustration rather than a criticism of the Academy of Management, because other professional associations face similar problems.

XI. What Needs to Be Integrated

I recommend three levels of integration. First, development administration should be integrated so that the differentiated subfields as shown in Figure 1.2 are merged to enable knowledge and experience gained in one to be generalized for the benefit of others. This is initially a message for those actively involved in advancing knowledge and understanding of development administration. The second level of integration involves organization science as practiced in the United States, particularly by the Academy of Management. The argument advanced above is that organization science is too fragmented and that the discipline would benefit by the amalgamation of the various subfields so that knowledge and experiences can be shared and tested for generalization. This goal is easier to attain with fewer rather than more divisions or interest groups. Organization science is not suffering from a shortage of research but the knowledge gained is not as cumulative and additive as it should be. Finally, I call for integrating the two disciplines of development administration and organization science, a move that would be of benefit to both disciplines.

Development administration would benefit by these suggested changes in several ways. It would be able to draw on better scientific methods of organization research, diagnosis, and intervention. It would avail itself of a wide range of theories and concepts of organization science which would facilitate studies of organizations in developing countries. It could use the theoretical frameworks and research methods available in organization science to codify, analyze, and generalize the results of its studies to other settings in both the developed and the developing countries. It would avoid using dated or obsolete theories, tools, methods, and management techniques. It would avail itself of the same criteria and standards of performance as exist in organization science. Such opportunities would open up many dissemination channels available in organization science but not readily accessible for development administration. As a regular editorial reviewer and contributor to several organization science journals, I know how difficult it is to publish studies of development administration in these journals.

Organization science would also benefit, in different ways, from an integration with development administration. It could develop a more universal body of organization knowledge applicable to all organizations worldwide. Indeed, the call for a universal body of organization science has been made several times before now. James Thompson, one of the founders of modern organization science and the founding editor of *Administrative Science Quarterly (ASQ)*—a leading journal in the field—made this call when he launched the journal. In its very first issue, he challenged other scientists to join hands in developing an applied science applicable to organizations not only in North America but in other parts of the world as well. He was unhappy with a trend he had observed in which concepts, theories, and methods of organization science being developed then were applicable only "to one cultural setting but not to others" (Thompson, 1956:106). As a scientist, he believed that the application of rigorous scientific methods to the study of organizations would enable "the discarding of concepts limited to particular geographical areas" (p. 105).

In a 1974 memorial issue published shortly after his death, Thompson was quoted to advance a theory based on his earlier work on organizational interdependence (Thompson, 1964), in which he speculated about the role of technology in determining the nature and developments of human social organization and the interaction of the family, the local community, and the national and international levels in both developing and industrialized countries. In essence, he was suggesting a multicultural worldwide theory of organization science (Ratiu, 1987).

Others have followed Thompson by making similar calls. C. J. Lammers of the Institute of Sociology, University of Leyden, the Netherlands, working with British and European organization sociologists, has argued that the original European founders of organization science like Max Weber (1947) deliberately avoided a fragmented approach whereby the discipline would be horizontally divided by institutions. He goes on to say that although European organizational sociologists continued to emphasize the "cross-institutional study of characteristics of organizations" (Lammers, 1981:270), later organization scientists have abandoned the vertical approach in favor of the more culture-specific horizontal approach. Empirical studies addressing the need to develop more universal theories and typologies of organizations are reported in a volume edited by Lammers and Hickson (1979).

I believe that organization science will not mature into an internationally recognized full-fledged academic discipline or professional practice unless it has demonstrated that its concepts, theories, tools, methods, and techniques are as applicable in settings outside North America and Western Europe as they are within. It is particularly important that its relevance be demonstrated for non-Western traditional settings in the developing world. An effective strategy of dealing with this credibility gap is that organization science join hands in partnership with development administration. This book makes a contribution toward such integration.

XII. Culture and Organization Science

There is strong empirical evidence to suggest that culture has important consequences for the structuring, management, and behavior of organizations in both developing and industrialized countries. This evidence should not be surprising since organizations as social institutions are expected to take on the cultural attributes of the societies they are designed to serve. Examples of cultural studies include Child's (1981) comparison of British and German firms; Inzerilli and Laurent's (1983) comparison of French and U.S. organizations; and Rieger's (1987) comparative analysis of the influence of national culture on the structure, process, and strategic decision making of the airlines of three industrialized countries—Canada (Air Canada), Italy (Alitalia), and West Germany (Lufthansa)—and five developing countries—Brazil (Varig), Pakistan (PIA), Thailand (Thai International), Singapore (SIA), and Indonesia (Garunda). The results of this extensive field study clearly show the importance of cultural variables in explaining the structure and performance of strategic management tasks by the executives of these organizations. What this and similar cultural studies do not show, however, is the relative importance of cultural (e.g., values, social relations) and noncultural variables (e.g., technology, structure) in explaining management processes and organizational performance at both the operating and the strategic management levels.

One of the best known and influential organization science culturists is Geert Hofstede, an articulate Dutch scholar based at the Institute for Research on Intercultural Cooperation in the Netherlands who does research on organizations in both developing and industrialized countries. In the 1970s, Hofstede collected data from over 1,600 IBM workers and managers in over 60 countries. When he analyzed the questionnaire data, he found that certain countries clustered along specific cultural dimensions and that these dimensions could not be explained by other factors such as job level or the country's level of economic development. Hofstede (1980) came up with four cultural dimensions: (1) *power distance*, the extent to which hierarchical power places people at psychological distances from each other; (2) *uncertainty avoidance*, the extent to which ambiguity is perceived as threatening and risk-taking behavior is avoided; (3) *masculinity/ femininity*, the extent to which masculine traits such as achievement, courage, and competition are valued over feminine values and behavior such as nurturing and sympathy; and (4) *individualism/collectivism*, the extent to which people define themselves individualistically or in terms of the groups to which they belong and the degree to which they see the inner groups (e.g., family, clans, and other social organizations) as the primary source of work and solutions to their problems. More recently, using longitudinal data, Hofstede has shown that individualism is caused by national wealth and income levels.

I believe that Western organization scientists in developing countries are putting too much emphasis on cultural variables and not enough on organization tasks, task performance, and the management process itself. Perhaps cultural variables are more exciting and romantic for a foreign researcher. It may also be that when they go abroad these researchers suffer from cultural shock and develop a bias toward cultural variables. Now that we know that culture has important consequences for organizations, development administration studies should move on to address issues more directly related to the management process both at the strategic and operating levels of the organization. To date, operating level and micro-level analyses such as individual differences, jobs and job design, and small group dynamics have been particularly neglected.

Japan provides an instructive illustration of the relationship between culture and management. Western organization scientists are obsessed with the Japanese management style because of the country's phenomenal economic, industrial, and technological successes. Although the literature on Japanese management is varied and at times contradictory, the more serious studies point to the fact that the Japanese have been quite successful in designing and managing organizations in a manner consistent with their cultural values, beliefs, and practices. When they import technology and know-how from the West, they try to ensure that its applications conform to Japanese culture and core values. Examples of such applications include quality control circles, just in time (JIT) inventory management, and collective responsibility and decision making.

The lesson from the Japanese experience is clear. The challenge for developing countries is not to emulate Japan's or anybody else's management style. Rather, the challenge is to develop organizations and management systems that facilitate the most effective performance of the organization's major tasks by taking into account the society's core cultural values and the challenges and threats of the external environment. In terms of the conceptual framework to be presented in this book, Japanese industrial organizations are structured and managed so as to optimize the efficient performance of their critical operating tasks and the effective performance of their strategic management tasks consistent with the demands of their culture and of local and international environmental constraints and opportunities. Cultural studies complement, not contradict, the basic tenet of this book because they define and clarify the cultural context within which organizational tasks are best understood and performed.

Summary

This chapter discusses the importance of organizations for developing countries and the current state of organization science and development administration. It emphasizes the strategic role organizations play in bringing about and sustaining development and improving human welfare. Differences and similarities among developing countries are discussed to remind the reader that although countries differ widely, they share a common set of problems that can be traced to weaknesses in organization and management of their respective institutions.

The organization is defined as a mission-driven, deliberately structured, sociotechnical open system with identifiable boundaries and stakeholders. Organization science, like development administration, is a multidimensional discipline that draws from various disciplines but that remains fragmented and unintegrated. There is a need to integrate the two subfields in order to develop a universal science of organization applicable to both developing and industrialized countries.

Culture and cultural studies are important because they provide a better understanding of the context within which organizations and the management process take place. However, studies of organizations in developing countries place too much emphasis on cultural variables and not enough on the more direct issues of organization and management. Studies of Japan illustrate that a country can draw from both its own culture and modern management concepts and techniques to build effective organizations. The lesson of the Japanese experience for developing countries is not to emulate Japanese or any other country's management style but to develop effective organizations and management styles consistent with their own respective core cultural values and practices. Although this book does not emphasize cultural variables, the model of organization presented below is not in conflict with that of the culturists.

CHAPTER 2

The Critical Operating Tasks

I. How the Organization Works

In the model presented in Part One, the organization is divided into two task subsystems. Each subsystem has a distinct set of tasks that it must perform for the organization's survival, growth, and development. These subsystems are: (1) the Critical Operating Tasks (COTs) subsystem; and (2) the Strategic Management Tasks (SMATs) subsystem. The *Critical Operating Tasks* are the basic tasks of the organization which it must perform to justify its existence and through which it strives to achieve its mission. They involve acquiring the necessary inputs, organizing the production units to transform the inputs into finished goods or services, distributing them to the intended consumers or clients, providing technical and administrative support to other parts of the organization, disposing of its waste and byproducts, and obtaining information and feedback from the environment concerning its input and output transactions. These tasks are performed within the organization's technical core or production system.

The *Strategic Management Tasks* are managerial and leadership tasks that define the uniqueness of the organization and its dynamic relationships with the outside environment. They involve creating the organization's charter or mission to give it the image of its unique wholeness, legitimizing that image, formulating strategies for the effective achievement of the mission, communicating the organization's mission, management philosophy, and values, managing the external environment to take advantage of emerging opportunities and defend the organization against potential threats, and providing leadership to other members of the organization. These functions are normally performed by the top management of the organization. The critical operating tasks and the strategic management tasks constitute all the important tasks that every organization must perform satisfactorily in order to survive, grow, and develop.

The model that will be discussed fully in this and subsequent chapters has several advantages. First, it is a simple one, dividing the organization into only two subsystems. Second, it is comprehensive in the sense that it captures all the important parts and tasks performed by organizations. Third, it is a useful model for organizations in both industrialized and developing countries. It provides a generic framework for understanding organizations, explaining specific organizational attributes, analyzing the efforts and results of particular interventions, and making suggestions for future strategies for the development of organizations. Finally, it provides a parsimonious framework for diagnosing organizations, discovering operational and strategic strengths and weaknesses of the organization or a set of organizations, and establishing cause-effect relationships.

In the previous chapter, I introduced and defined the concepts of organization, organization science, and development administration and made the case for a more integrated approach to the study of organizations in developing countries. In this chapter, I begin to develop a conceptual framework of the organization, its component parts and how they each function, and the interconnectedness of these parts. Organization scientists are interested in the development of models and conceptual frameworks of how the organization actually works because these help in the identification of important variables for their organizational studies. The results of these studies and the knowledge and experience accumulated over time provide the basis and development of informed strategies for the effective management, control, and development of organizations. Consequently, the future behavior of organization members can be better understood and predicted with a high degree of certainty. The remaining part of this chapter provides a detailed discussion of the critical operating tasks. Chapter Three discusses the strategic management tasks. Chapter Four discusses the various methods used to coordinate these parts to create an integral organization entity.

II. COTs and SMATs in Historical Perspective

The history of the development of management thought and the advancement of management knowledge, skills, and techniques are characterized by an unrelenting search for alternative philosophies and approaches for the performance, structuring, and management of these two task subsystems. Indeed, some theories or models tend to emphasize one rather than the other; a few attempt to deal with both. Table 2.1 summarizes the major theories of management, their respective prescriptive work design parameters, and the extent to which they individually focus on the critical operating tasks (COTs), the strategic management tasks (SMATs), or both. In general, the classical theories of management such as Taylor's scientific management theory (1911), and bureaucratic administrative theories (Gulick and Urwick, 1954; Weber, 1947), being essentially rational theories, have had their greatest impact on the structuring and performance of the critical operating tasks.

Table 2.1

SUMMARY OF SELECTED MANAGEMENT THEORIES: THEIR WORK DESIGN PARAMETERS AND EFFECTS ON COTs AND SMATs

Selected Schools (Authors, Dates)	Work Design Parameters	E F F E C T S O N	
		COTs	SMATs
1. Scientific Management (Taylor, 1911)	• Time and motion studies • Work measurement • Micromotion analysis • Work simplification • Human engineering	• Standardized inputs, outputs, and transformations • Increased productivity • Reduced unit costs • Increased use of performance incentives • Minimal operator control of workload • Better paid operators • Increased operator alienation	• Increased management control of operations • Simplified coordination by RIMs • Freed-up time for management tasks
2. Bureaucratic Administrative Theories (Gulick and Urwick, 1937; Webec, 1947)	• Job analysis • Formal job descriptions • Operator testing, selection, and training • Functional division of labor • Formal hierarchy of authority	• Rationalization of the administrative process • Operator functional specialization • Task fragmentation • Suboptimization • Intergroup conflict	• Improved administrative efficiency • Coordination by RIMs • Separating of power • Conflict resolution and management. • Clearly defined areas of authority and accountability
3. Sociotechnical Systems (Trist et al. 1963; Rice, 1958; Pava, 1983)	• Autonomous work groups • Alternative forms of work/shift design • Group-based rewards/ incentives • Deliberations	• Increased operator workflow control • Increased operator-responsible autonomy • Integration of social and technical requirements • Operator cross-training and multiskilling • Improved task performance • Better operator morale	• Awareness for environmental scanning • Boundary management • No need for close supervision • More developmental management style • Increased awareness of organizational choice • Uses of CIMs for coordination • Participative decision making
4. Contingency Theories: (a) Macro Structural Theories (Burns and Stalker, 1961; Lawrence and Lorsch, 1967; Thompson, 1967; Mintzberg, 1979)	• Task differentiation and integration • Environmental analysis • Increased information processing requirements • Alternative structural forms: divisional, project, matrix, etc.	• Mechanistic operations if technical core is protected • Organic operations if technical core is exposed to environment	• Contingency management approach • Continuing organization design • Increased use of CIMs and MIS • Task ambiguity and stress
(b) Micro Content Theories: (McClelland and Winter, 1969; Hackman and Oldham, 1980)	• Work redesign: enlargement and enrichment • Preference for high achievement/growth operators	• Increased operator autonomy, responsibility and workflow control • Improved operator quality performance • Improved operator morale	• Sharing job feedback with COTs operators • Managing micro-level contingencies

Source: Adapted from M.N. Kiggundu, "Structuring and scheduling of work", Table 9-1, pp. 300-1. In *Human Resource Management: Contemporary Perspectives in Canada*. K.M. Srinivas (ed.), Toronto: McGraw-Ryerson, 1984. © M.N. Kiggundu, 1982.
COTs = Critical Operation Tasks; SMATs = Strategic Management Tasks; RIMs = Routine integrating mechanisms; CIMs = Complex integrating mechanisms; MIS = Management Information Systems.

The principles of scientific management are best suited for improvements in the performance of operating tasks. Scientific management requires the organization and management of work and workers according to strict scientific methods. Tasks are broken down into the smallest possible units and, by the use of methods such as time and motion studies, micromotion analysis, and job analysis, work is organized to maximize efficiency and economy. Standard operating procedures are established for each production unit, and workers are paid according to their individual levels of productivity. The principles of division of labor are strictly observed so that planning and control of work are separated from task execution. While planning and control functions are the exclusive prerogative of the managers, the workers are limited only to operational executions.

Classical theories of management have had profound influence on improving the efficiency and economy of the performance of critical operating tasks, especially in large government agencies and corporate manufacturing organizations. Careful application of these theories results in significant savings of input resources like materials, labor, and machine downtime. It also leads to more efficient transformation processes and distribution of outputs, and rational and efficient administration. Although these are associated with negative worker reactions and low morale often manifested in absenteeism, industrial sabotage, work stoppages, and ill health, they still form the basis for many modern management techniques, including CAD/CAM (computer-aided design and manufacturing) robotics and office automation, as well as a wide range of performance improvement programs. An example of such a program is the guided transmission training developed by ILO and used by the Ethiopian Management Institute to train Africans and to improve the organization and performance of the critical operating tasks (e.g., farm equipment maintenance) of the state farms (Whittaker and Gibson, 1987).

One of the problems facing organizations in developing countries is that they experience difficulties in effectively utilizing the principles of these rational classic theories of management. A careful examination of the structuring and performance of their critical operating tasks reveals weaknesses due in large part to inappropriate applications of the theories and their work design parameters outlined in Table 2.1. For example, both Moris (1981) and Hyden (1983), drawing from research and experiences with Tanzanian organizations, observed that these organizations were performing poorly for the most part because they are found in primarily prescientific societies unable to apply and sustain scientific or rational principles of management and administration. While in industrialized countries complaints against organizations point to excessive applications of bureaucratic principles and scientific management, in developing countries, the problems are different. These principles have not taken hold.

Table 2.1 also shows that the more contemporary theories of management such as sociotechnical systems and contingency theories provide a more balanced focus on both the organization and the performance of COTs and SMATs than do the classical theories. These theories also make prescriptions for the structuring and performance of COTs different from those made by the classical theories. For example, sociotechnical systems theory advocates the increase of control for COTs operators over their respective work flow and their involvement in making decisions that affect their work. This process requires highly trained, experienced, and motivated operators not commonly found in developing country organizations. It is therefore unlikely that the more sophisticated contemporary theories of management can be effectively applied in organizations in developing countries until the more basic principles contained in classical theories have been successfully applied.

The four elements of the critical operating tasks—the inputs, throughputs, outputs, and feedback—are highly interdependent. Commenting on the interdependence among the various coal mining operating tasks, Trist and Bamforth observed: "So close is the interdependence that the system becomes vulnerable from its need for one hundred percent performance at each step . . . Disorganization at the filling shift disorganizes the subsequent shifts, and its own disorganization is often produced by the bad preparation left by these teams." (1951:18)

The interdependence, which may be pooled, sequential, or reciprocal, has structural (Thompson, 1967) and motivational consequences both for the operators and for their supervisors. Specifically, task interdependence is associated with operators' productivity, absenteeism, and health (Kiggundu, 1983). Task interdependence complicates the organization and performance of the critical operating tasks.

III. An Illustration of Critical Operating Tasks

Table 2.2 provides a practical illustration of the critical operating tasks, associated operating problems, and possible solutions of an on-going developing country organization. The illustration, based on a sociotechnical study of the locomotives workshop of the Sudan Railways Corporation at Sennar (Kidwell, El Jack, and Ketchum, 1981), details the component elements of an organization's critical operating tasks. This organization was chosen because it is representative of different forms of organizations typically found in developing countries. It is a service organization with clearly identifiable tasks of repairing, servicing, and testing locomotives for the national railways corporation. In addition, as it is a state-owned enterprise operating in a critical sector of the economy (transport), its efficiency is of great concern to many other organizations in the country.

The table outlines the COTs at four different levels: the inputs, transformation processes, outputs, and feedback. Inputs include tasks such as operator recruitment, selection, placement, training, and motivation; procurement of the right tools; and maintenance of sufficient inventories for spare parts. The transformation processes are the actual tasks associated with repairing, servicing, and load testing the locomotives so that they are once again in good mechanical condition to operate on the trains. The outputs are the finished locomotives, duly repaired, serviced, and tested. Since the workshop is part of a larger corporation, there must exist a continuing flow and dissemination of information and feedback back and forth and within the workshop itself. Such information includes the qual-

Table 2.2
**AN ANALYSIS OF THE CRITICAL OPERATING TASKS OF THE SUDAN
RAILWAYS CORPORATION LOCOMOTIVE WORKSHOPS**

Selected Operating Tasks	Identified Problems	Possible Solutions
1. Staffing the sheds with trained and experienced operators	1. Brain and skill drain without adequate replacement 2. Inadequate staff training and development	1. Improved working conditions 2. Human resource planning 3. Overstaffing 4. Incentives and rewards contingent on staying with company 5. Better designed jobs 6. Hiring from neighboring provinces/regions 7. Implementation of operator training and apprenticeship programs
2. Maintaining sufficient inventories for tools and spare parts	1. Unavailability of spare parts as and when needed 2. Disappearance of tools	1. Introduction of computerized inventory and stores management system 2. Reduction of number or type of locomotives to reduce variety of inventory requirements and streamline ordering of inventory 3. Carry on periodic stores inventory inspections 4. Negotiate long term inventory purchase arrangements with overseas suppliers and central bank
3. Repairing and load testing of locomotives by operators	1. Use of wrong tools and materials 2. Ignorance about proper instructions/procedures 3. Failure to use safety equipment 4. Extended worker absence from work 5. Workers' personal need for overtime pay 6. Lack of standard operating procedures	1. Proper training, supervision, and enforcement of SOPs 2. Improving operator attitudes and morale 3. Improved quality of supervision 4. Better labor and industrial relations 5. Ensure adequate supply of safety equipment
4. Receiving and disseminating information and feedback about operations	1. Unwillingness to share information 2. Lack of proper channels of communications 3. Operator suspicion and mistrust 4. No clear statement of goals, plans, and job expectatons 5. Lack of MIS	1. Development of scientific MIS at the operating level 2. Development of plans, goals, and work expectations for operators 3. Improvement of work attitudes and trust

Note: Based on information provided by Kidwell, J., EL Jack, A., and Ketchum L., Socio-technical Study for Locomotive Maintenance Workshop at Sennar, Sudan," Vol. I, unpublished manuscript, June, 1981.

ity and quantity of performance of the workshop and the individual operators, and the expected demand and available capacity for repair services, tools, and spare parts.

The problems associated with the critical operating tasks shown in Table 2.2 are quite common for organizations in developing countries. There is an insufficient supply of inputs because of lack of spare parts and tools, and enough trained, experienced, and motivated operators. Even when these are available, they are not effectively used to the best advantage of the corporation. Tools disappear from the workshop without being accounted for, and operators and their immediate supervisors spend many hours each work day away from their jobs.

One of the most serious handicaps for the efficient performance of the workshops' COTs was the poor attitude and work behavior of the operators and their supervisors. According to Kidwell, El Jack, and Ketchum (1981), workers had poor attitudes toward their work with little or no sense of responsibility or self-discipline. They stayed away from work for long hours without permission and expected to be paid for the time and be granted overtime privileges. They condoned these dysfunctional behaviors with a belief that, since they worked for a government agency, it did not matter how much the operations cost or how long it took them to get the locomotives repaired and operational. These observations are not limited to the Sudan or to Africa, but are fairly common in organizations in Central and Latin America and parts of Asia (Nath, 1988).

The collection and the dissemination of accurate and timely information are important for the efficient planning and performance of COTs. At Sennar, however, it was found that employees did not want to give information to others and that operators were not told what was expected of them. It was also observed that: ". . . some people might obstruct the flow of information and/or distort the information to serve their personal goals and consequently obtain some personal benefits" (Kidwell, El Jack, and Ketchum, 1981:17–18). For example, the manager of a maintenance unit wanted to carry out a time and motion study to find out how many locomotives can be maintained during a certain period of time. The workers, knowing the purpose of the exercise, automatically changed their operating behaviors and created a situation whereby the results would justify extra time, and thus overtime work for the maintenance crew. This example illustrates the challenges managers of organizations in developing countries face in attempting to apply even the basic principles of (classical) management.

Table 2.2 provides some solutions to these operational problems. Two types of solutions are offered: those that draw from the various management theories outlined in Table 2.1; and those that respond to the demands of the specific environment of the Sennar workshop. The first type includes suggestions for institutionalization of job analysis, standard operating procedures (SOPs), operator training, and supervision. An example of the second type relates to the brain and skill drain, which at Sennar is due to the poor performance of the Sudanese economy and the ready availability of work in the Middle East. This second example also illustrates the relationship between COTs and SMATs. Some of the problems experienced at the COTs level are environmental in origin, and if the COTs are not protected or if the technical core of the workshop is porous, then its operations will be adversely affected by the environmental disturbances. As the next chapter will detail, the responsibility of protecting the organization from environmental disturbances falls not on the operators but on senior management. At Sennar, it was clear that management had not succeeded in buffering the workshop's COTs from the vagaries of its task environment. Indeed, as is often the case with many organizations in developing countries, the Sennar workshop illustrates the fact that the sources and causes of these environmental disturbances and organizational porosity may be so pervasive and complex that even senior management cannot provide sufficient buffers and protection.

IV. The Challenges of Managing COTs in Developing Country Organizations

The model presented above relating to the critical operating tasks and strategic management tasks views the organization as an open system. Previous theorists dividing the organization into task systems (e.g., Bakke, 1959; Trist et al., 1963; Thompson, 1967; Mintzberg, 1979) also draw from the concept of the open systems theory. The critical operating tasks and the open systems model both focus on the organization's transformation processes including inputs and outputs. Thus the open systems model of the organization is an appropriate one to use in a discussion of functions and challenges associated with the performance and management of the various elements of the critical operating tasks.

Figure 2.1 gives a system's view of an organization's critical operating tasks. The input resources obtained from the environment include money, skilled and unskilled labor, raw materials, land, equipment, ideas, information, facilities, and energy. These inputs are so varied that they come from different sources in the environment and each source must be protected by the organization depending on how critical it is for the input supplies in question. Ordinarily, the acquisition and utilization of such inputs are routine critical operating tasks. However, when certain inputs cannot be routinely obtained by the organization, their acquisition becomes a matter of strategic importance to the organization and tasks associated with such supplies become part of its strategic management tasks.

During World War II, many industrial organizations in North America and Europe were unable routinely to obtain basic raw materials because these raw materials had been diverted to the war efforts. Therefore, the functions associated with the acquisition of such materials became part of the organization's strategic management tasks. More recently, following the 1973 oil embargo and the creation of the Organization of Petroleum Exporting Countries (OPEC), oil companies could no longer guarantee secure crude oil supplies. For these organizations as well as for others for whom oil or oil products constitute a significant production input, the functions associated with these supplies were transferred from the critical operating to the strategic management tasks subsystem. Whenever tasks are moved to the strategic management area, the associated transactions become more costly for the organization because resources cost more here than in the critical operating tasks subsystem.

Figure 2.1

A SYSTEMS VIEW OF THE ORGANIZATION'S CRITICAL OPERATING TASKS

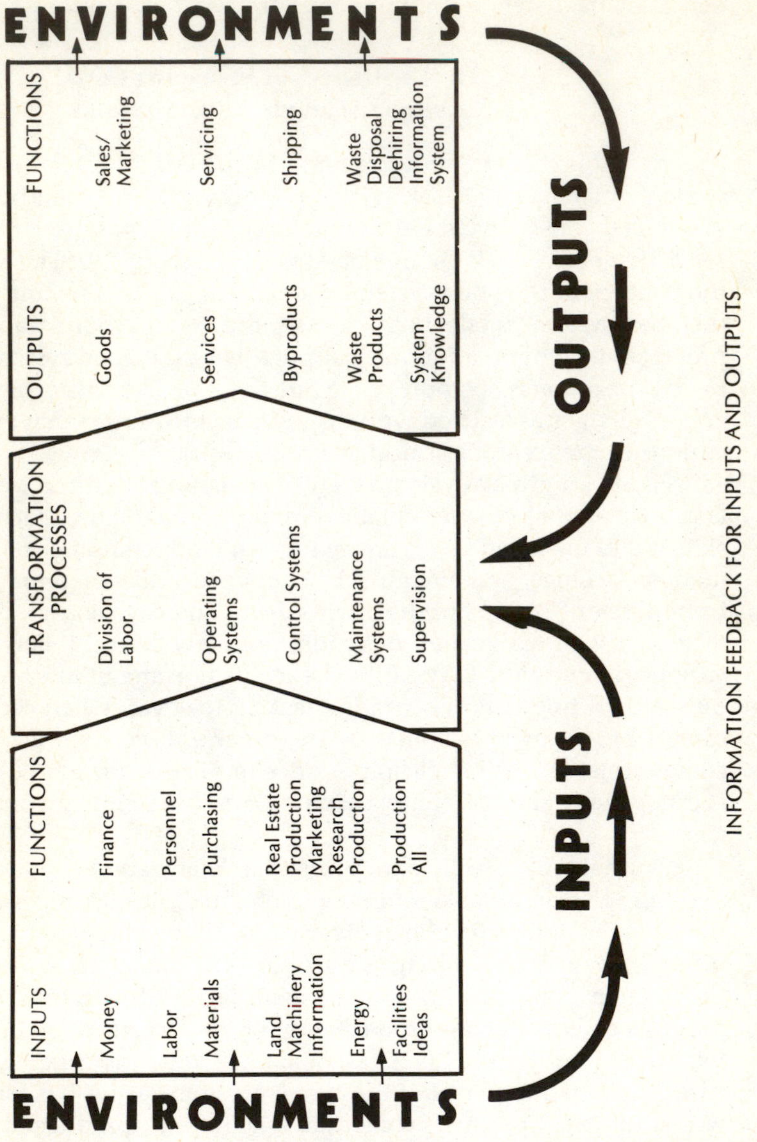

ENVIRONMENTS

INPUTS	FUNCTIONS
Money	Finance
Labor	Personnel
Materials	Purchasing
Land	Real Estate
Machinery	Production
Information	Marketing
	Research
Energy	Production
Facilities	Production
Ideas	All

TRANSFORMATION PROCESSES
Division of Labor
Operating Systems
Control Systems
Maintenance Systems
Supervision

OUTPUTS	FUNCTIONS
Goods	Sales/Marketing
Services	Servicing
Byproducts	Shipping
Waste Products	Waste Disposal
	Dehiring
System Knowledge	Information System

ENVIRONMENTS

INPUTS

OUTPUTS

INFORMATION FEEDBACK FOR INPUTS AND OUTPUTS

Organizations in developing countries are often faced with situations where critical operating tasks associated with input acquisitions are delegated upward to the strategic management tasks. This change may be due to several causes. For example, the supplies of necessary inputs may be interrupted such that routine performance of the critical operating tasks is not sufficient to ensure adequate supplies. Quite often, organizations in developing countries are undercapitalized and, with inadequate credit ratings, may experience difficulty in raising money from banks and other financial institutions. Under these circumstances, raising capital becomes politicized and unsuitable for the lower levels of the organization at the critical operating tasks. Another common cause for shifting tasks upward is that inputs are imported and therefore require state approval for foreign exchange. For many developing countries, foreign exchange is in very short supply and, like any other scarce commodity whose demand far exceeds supply, its distribution is highly contested and depends on extra-organizational considerations. Under these circumstances, top management has no choice but to involve itself actively in obtaining sufficient foreign exchange for the organization's required imported inputs. This was the case for Sudan's Sennar workshop and their problems of obtaining spare parts and other necessary inputs. For organizations with high import content, these strategic tasks may well determine the overall performance or survival of the organization. The skills required to perform the tasks should therefore be considered during the selection, performance evaluations, and promotion of senior managers for these organizations.

It is also possible for critical operating tasks to be taken over by senior management at the strategic management level only because of personal management styles. Senior managers—as a result of style, circumstances, or ignorance—may end up spending more time performing routine critical operating tasks rather than the more difficult and ambiguous strategic management tasks. Senior managers promoted from the critical operating task units who are unable or unwilling to adjust to the different long-term challenges of the strategic management tasks may find comfort in returning to familiar territory where tasks are structured, production cycles and feedback loops are short, clear, and immediate, and there is usually collaboration rather than competition.

Internal weaknesses in the performance of the critical operating tasks may also cause the senior managers to take them over. Small- and medium-sized organizations often experience difficulties attracting and retaining highly skilled and experienced staff. They also experience difficulties in acquiring most up-to-date production systems because these cost more than they can afford. Accordingly, relatively simple critical operating tasks may have to be performed by the chief executive officer because there is nobody else in the organization who can perform them. The sole proprietorship is a good example of an organization where the COTs and SMATs are done by one and the same person. Whatever the cause, the shifting of functions from the critical operating to the strategic management areas increases the cost of doing business for the organization and makes the organization less effective and competitive.

Figure 2.1 shows the major tasks of the transformation processes, including division of labor, organization of the operating units, performance of control functions, regular repairs and maintenance, and general supervision. The organization and performance of these functions depend on the nature of the inputs imported into the organization (e.g., technology), current operating practices and systems within the organization (e.g., hours of work), prevailing management values and philosophy (e.g., status differentiation), and the demands placed upon the organization by the outside environment (e.g., employment legislation).

Operating systems are important because they are directly involved in the production and distribution of the goods or services produced. Control systems are important because they control the quality and quantity of goods produced as well as the use of other resources including money, materials, equipment and personnel allocated for the critical operating tasks. Maintenance systems are important because they ensure continuity so that the transformation processes receive regular repairs and maintenance. Supervision is important because it provides the technical and administrative support for the performance of all the critical operating tasks, and division of labor is important because it facilitates the concept of *organizational choice* (Trist et al., 1963), by enabling the organization to choose among alternative forms of work organization. These tasks constitute the heart or lifeline of the organization. If an organization cannot perform them satisfactorily over a prolonged period of time, or if it has little or no opportunity to do so, it may and perhaps should cease to exist.

Figure 2.1 also shows the outputs characteristic of most organizations. These outputs include goods and services, goodwill or the feeling of support and approval that the organization enjoys in the community, waste products, and system knowledge. Waste products are the by-products or residues from the original inputs which cannot be used or distributed as part of the finished goods or services. Waste products are commonly identified with manufacturing organizations in the form of pollutants, but agricultural and service organizations also have waste byproducts. For service organizations, one of the most common but sometimes neglected byproducts is human obsolescence necessitated by either internal organizational changes (e.g., new technology), or outside environmental pressures (e.g., new markets). When these occur, some employees inevitably become obsolete and have to be retrained or dismissed by the organization. In general, organizations in developing countries have problems dismissing employees who are no longer making a net positive contribution to the performance of the organization's tasks.

Figure 2.1 differs from ordinary open systems models in two important aspects. First, the feedback loop comes from both sides of the critical operating tasks subsystem. The loop from the right-hand side of the figure represents information, data, or rumors about how the various elements in the environment receive and react to the organization's different *outputs*. The loop on the left-hand side, often omitted in open systems models, represents similar information or feedback obtained from those elements in the environment from which the organization obtains the different *inputs*. This distinction is important because studies, especially of organizations in developing countries, show that an organization can use strategies in managing its input-environment feedback different from those it uses for the output-environment feedback. For example, a state-owned enterprise can enjoy support from the government because of its employment practices even if its substantive outputs are of lower quality or high cost. Likewise, organizations importing modern capital-intensive machinery with a view to producing high-quality, low-cost products have been criticized for being insensitive to the employment problems of their countries.

The second difference between Figure 2.1 and the typical open systems model is that its functions and its corresponding inputs and outputs are shown. In addition, the figure also makes clear the relative importance of different functions or departments in an organization. For example, functions associated with inputs that are difficult to secure on a regular basis at affordable prices, outputs difficult to dispose of at favorable prices, or transformation processes difficult to protect from outside environmental disturbances are more important than others. Departments housing these functions are more powerful and have more access to resources than do other departments in the organization. In a typical industrial organization in a developing country, finance and production or manufacturing are more powerful departments than personnel/industrial relations, or sales and marketing. This observation has important managerial implications. For example, in conditions where managerial skills and experiences are in short supply, it is to the organization's advantage to place the few skilled and experienced managers in charge of the departments having the most critical functions.

In a mature effective organization, the critical operating tasks subsystem is protected from outside environmental disturbances and managed as if it were a closed system. This status is gained by standardizing rational methods of organization and management *à la* Weber and Taylor. The inputs can be standardized in several ways: materials and equipment are ordered to exact specifications and checked before being accepted; employees are hired only with specific skills and experience and are given orientation, on-the-job training, and close supervision, and those who do not work out are terminated at the end of an initial probational period; and facilities are built to maximize the flow of work and efficient performance of all critical operating tasks. The transformation processes are standardized by following standard operating procedures (SOPs), adhering to instructions in the machine and equipment operating and maintenance manuals, and rejecting unsuitable inputs by quality control. These practices ensure that the final goods produced or services provided meet at least minimum specified standards. For the distribution of goods, standardization is achieved by using the same packaging and shipping methods, training the sales force to give consistent product information (e.g., price, quality, product performance, and specifications), and providing after-sales service. Market research and intelligence information gathering are conducted to ensure that customer reactions are consistent with the service or products produced.

These actions enable the organization to deal with the twin problems of uncertainty, which, as Thompson (1967) suggests, should be reduced within the critical operating tasks, and rationality, which should be utilized as fully as possible for these tasks. However, as we saw in the previous chapter (Figure 1.1), organizations in developing countries have difficulties protecting the critical operating tasks from environmental disturbances. These increase uncertainty and make standardization hard to achieve. Research has shown that only if the organization's critical operating tasks subsystem is sealed off from the environment can Western management theories and techniques be effectively utilized without necessitating major adjustments. Likewise, when significant environmental interests are involved, modern management techniques can be used only with modifications that suit the needs of the outside interests.

This section has illustrated some of the dilemmas facing organizations in developing countries interested in using modern management methods and techniques. As Faucheux et al. (1982) and others have observed, in developing countries society pervades organizations. Thus, among their many difficulties, these organizations can hardly introduce significant new management techniques without arousing interests in the outside community. The adjustments made to accommodate these outside interests are not necessarily the best ones for the organizations. Rather, they are likely to make it difficult for the organizations to reduce uncertainty and effectively use rational methods in the performance of their critical operating tasks. It is apparent why so many organizations experience difficulties in the performance of these tasks and in preserving and maintaining the integrity of the critical operating tasks subsystem.

The implications for both the organization and the community are clear. The organization should manage its relations with the powerful actors in the environment in ways that allow it a certain degree of freedom to utilize organization and management methods with a minimum of interference. And the outside interests should realize that the organization's continued growth and development may well depend on its ability to adapt new methods of organization and management and that it is therefore in everybody's long-term interests to facilitate this. The organization needs to be given more control, accountability, and responsibility for variables over which it has little or no control. In the final analysis, this is an educational process: changing attitudes and creating awareness and understanding, among the significant stakeholders, of the role, position, and limitations of organizations in society.

V. Critical Operating Tasks and Organization Performance

Although different organizations use different indicators of organization performance, most of these are directly related to the performance of the critical operating tasks. The three most commonly used indicators for organizations in both developing and industrialized countries are efficiency, economy, and effectiveness. Efficiency is a productivity concept that can be expressed as a ratio of outputs to inputs at a given level of quality. It can be measured by comparing the benefit/cost ratios of the relevant transactions. While these are relatively easy to compute for business organizations, the costs, benefits, beneficiaries, and victims of social service and government organizations can be difficult to compute or identify. These therefore relate to the way operations are conducted, the quality of the products or services provided, and the extent to which operational objectives are achieved. As Drucker (1967) rightly points out, efficiency means doing things well. Economy means that operational resources are acquired and used with judicious regard to costs and judicious use of money and expenditures.

An excellent illustration of the concept of economy comes from the auditor-general's report of a Commonwealth country in which a government department paid the equivalent of $163,000 a year for the previous five years to lease a building, when it could have paid $50,000 each year for ten years. Both efficiency and economy are important measures of performance for the critical operating tasks. Although measures of these concepts can be complicated by internal accounting procedures, like overhead allocations or amortization of capital investments, and general problems of cause-effect relationships (Thompson, 1967), they give a fair and accurate assessment of the performance of the organization's operations, especially if they are used comparatively across operating units, over time, and with industry standards. Unfortunately, many business organizations in developing countries are not always up to date with their financial and accounting information. They, therefore, cannot determine the efficiency or economy with which the COTs are being performed.

Effectiveness, like excellence, is a much more difficult term to define. According to Cameron and Whetten (1983), effectiveness is a construct rather than a concept and thus cannot be expressed in quantitative terms without reflecting problems of values and judgments of right or wrong. As Drucker once again says, "effectiveness is doing the right things." It therefore makes sense to define effectiveness in terms of the organization's mission, management philosophy and values, and the extent to which these are being met to the satisfaction of all its members. For a more detailed recent review of discussions of effectiveness in organization science, see Lewin and Minton (1986).

Clearly, efficiency and economy relate more readily to the critical operating tasks, while effectiveness relates to the strategic management tasks. Critical operating tasks are associated with short-term production cycles, and therefore short-term goals and results. Strategic management tasks, on the other hand, are associated with long-term goals and objectives whose achievement can take many years. This distinction has important implications for differences in strategies for managing these two task subsystems. For the critical operating tasks, management systems like incentives, control and feedback should be designed to correspond with the organization and duration of the production cycle. Quite often, organizations fail to use their management information systems to provide the operators of the critical operating tasks with timely and relevant feedback about how well or badly they are doing their jobs. Thus they lose an important and effective potential source of motivation for the operators.

Because critical operating tasks are short term, and because they are directly connected to outside members of the organization through input acquisition and output distribution and disposal, variations in their performance are immediately noticeable outside the organization. When things go wrong in the performance of these tasks, outsiders will know because the organization fails to satisfy community expectations. Likewise, when improvements in the performance of these tasks take place, the community notices them much sooner than they would those for strategic management tasks. The implications for organizations, especially those in developing countries, are clear: not only are critical operating tasks good for business—the bottom line—but they also have an important public relations component.

Discussions of world competitiveness among nations tend to focus on the efficiency with which the critical operating tasks of their respective organizations are performed. For example, Buffa (1983), comparing relative production cost structures in Japan and the United States, observed that the average increase in productivity during recent years has been about 7 percent for Japan, whereas it was 1 to 2 percent for the United

States. He also argues that the productivity/labor cost connection is a major factor in the diminished competitive position of U.S. industry. This message is important, not only for the United States, but also for other trading countries. If a country wants to become or remain competitive in world trade and commerce, its organizations must improve the performance of their respective critical operating tasks. In this context, the practical interpretation of the concept of comparative advantage is that, for certain successful industries or sectors of the economy, the critical operating tasks are performed more efficiently and with greater economy than they are in competing nations. Those developing countries doing economically better than most, especially the newly industrialized countries (NICs) like Singapore, Hong Kong, South Korea, and Brazil, seem to have found practical methods of performing the critical operating tasks of their export-oriented manufacturing firms efficiently and with enough economy to be able to compete in world markets. That other developing countries, especially the least developed countries of Africa and Asia, have not been able to do so is a major factor in explaining the difference in the economic performance of these two groups of developing countries.

Why do some organizations, especially those in industrialized countries but also increasingly those in some select developing countries, perform their critical operating tasks more efficiently and with greater economy than others? The successful organizations seem to have achieved two important related objectives. First, they have internalized the norms and dictates of rational systems of organization and management and they perform their critical operating tasks on the rational principles of Weber's classical bureaucracy, and Taylor's scientific management. Organizations in the industrialized countries have been following these tenets ever since the Industrial Revolution and have so perfected them that they are now in the position to mass-produce goods and services at very low unit-costs so as to satisfy the material needs of almost all their citizens. The developing countries, however, did not start until after World War II, when, through a combination of massive importation of technology and favorable deliberate domestic policy instruments, including market imperfections leading to lower input costs (e.g., labor), they began experiencing some success in the efficient performance of their critical operating tasks. Nevertheless, they have a long way to go before they can catch up or openly compete with the industrialized countries.

Second, successful organizations have adopted these rational systems and altered or modified their applications to suit the changing social and technical internal requirements, and the external changes of the communities in which they operate. As a result they have introduced alternative forms of work organization in the performance of their critical operating tasks.

VI. Critical Operating Tasks: Technology, Jobs, and People

Critical operating tasks have a very high technological component. In this age of advanced technology, it is tempting for managers to think that all that they need to improve the performance of their organizations' COTs is to import leading edge technology. Indeed, talking to senior managers in developing countries, one often hears such sentiments being expressed. If they are in transport, they would wish that their steam train engines were replaced by diesel engines, or that their airlines were able to buy modern larger aircraft such as the AirBus. In manufacturing, they wish that they had more automated fast-moving assembly line plants; and if they are in social services or administration, they seek the most highly qualified specialists. Yet, even if these have been provided, productivity has not always increased. In some cases it has even decreased (Wallender, 1979).

One of the reasons for these disappointing results is that the organization is not only a technological system. It is also a social subsystem with inside and outside stakeholders whose needs, values, sentiments, attitudes, knowledge, and behavior may or may not be consistent with the demands of the new technology. Therefore, the efficient organization and performance of critical operating tasks require that management pays equal attention to and creates an optimal combination of the requirements of technology, jobs, and people. Rice (1958) attempted to attain these very goals in the automated and unautomated Calico Mills textile plants in Ahmedabad, India. Indeed, this is the essential message from sociotechnical systems theory. Organizations that optimize the requirements of technology and the needs of the people perform their COTs more efficiently and with greater economy than those that pay attention either only to technology or only to the people at the expense of the other.

The sociotechnical systems approach to organizing COTs requires a number of conditions. First, there must be the capacity to diagnose the social organization and to analyze the operating technology to identify the different ways by which it can be used. Second, the operators must be trainable, trained, experienced, and highly motivated so as to be able and willing to take on additional responsibility for the performance of their respective COTs. That is, they must be crosstrained and multiskilled to be able to perform more than one single task. Third, the supervisors must be properly trained with attitudes that encourage them to resist close supervision, facilitate boundary management, and allow their operators the freedom and autonomy they need while according them necessary support. Finally, the organization climate and philosophy must be consistent with democratic values allowing lower level participants such as operators and supervisors to participate in making decisions affecting their work. Both individually and collectively, these conditions are very difficult to meet and sustain for most organizations in developing countries. In fact, in spite of over 35 years of experimentation, the sociotechnical systems approach to managing critical operating tasks in developing countries has met with only limited success (Kiggundu, 1986).

Traditionally, the management techniques that provide for the most efficient way of performing the organization's critical operating tasks give rise to poorly designed jobs and unhealthy and unattractive working conditions. For example, the assembly line is known to cause worker alienation, ill health, and morale problems. In the industrialized countries, especially the United States and Western Europe, attempts have been made to alleviate these problems by introducing programs such as work redesign, organization development (OD), sociotechnical systems, and quality of working life (QWL). These programs are legitimized by the human relations movement originating from the work of Mayo (1933), and Roethlisberger and Dickson (1939).

After the results of the Saab-Scandia experiments in which Pehr Gyllenhammar (1977), the then newly hired managing director of Volvo, sought to solve the company's morale problems by redesigning its automobile assembly line and organizing the work in semi-autonomous circular groups, Swedish engineers are now reluctant to build automated fast-paced traditional assembly line plants. In the United States, companies are using automated manufacturing technologies (AMTs) to build plants deliberately designed to remain small, with a maximum limit of only 100 employees (Kolodny and Armstrong, 1985). All these efforts are aimed at alleviating the social problems of industrialization and meeting the challenges of managing postindustrial organizations without sacrificing previous gains achieved in performing the organization's critical operating tasks with efficiency and economy. According to Mintzberg (1979), however, these efforts are not likely to endure because they are inherently in conflict with society's demand for cheap, mass-produced goods and services.

Do these management theories, techniques, or movements have any relevancy for the organization and management of critical operating tasks in developing countries? There are those who believe that developing countries should not be concerned with these humanistic problems until they have become fully industrialized. They point to the widening gap between the two types of countries. For example, while organizations in industrialized countries are grappling with problems of integrating high technology management techniques such as CAD/CAM (computer-aided design and manufacturing), JIT (just-in-time) inventory systems, and MRP (materials requirement planning) in the operations of industrial organizations, and computerized office automation and telecommunications in the service organizations, organizations in developing countries are still having basic operational and management problems. As the

Sudan Railways Corporation study (Kidwell, El Jack, and Ketchum, 1981) shows, they have not even perfected the running and maintenance of the steam engine or rationalized and streamlined the performance of their manufacturing and administrative service organizations.

Others argue that some of the problems of Western industrialization such as worker alienation are quite common in developing country organizations. As late starters, these countries should learn from the mistakes of the West and not ignore or emulate them. Moreover, there is evidence to suggest that workers in developing countries respond positively to modern management programs such as job enrichment, participative decision making, team building, and organization development. In fact, some of the popular management intervention programs such as the management-improvement teams (MITs) (Hage and Finsterbusch, 1987) and the programming and planning for improved enterprise performance developed by the International Labour Office (Abramson and Halset, 1979) and implemented in many developing country organizations (Kubr and Wallace, 1983) draw from some of these management concepts and techniques.

Regardless of which side of the argument we find most convincing, the challenge for development administration and the managers of organizations in developing countries is clear. We must find practical sustainable methods of improving the efficiency and economy in the performance of the critical operating tasks of all types of organizations in developing countries. At the same time, we must pay attention to the individual, social, and community needs of the people who work for or otherwise interact with these organizations. Organization science and development administration theory, methods, and techniques provide a good starting point in the search for the solutions.

VII. Service Organizations in Developing Countries

It is the traditional view that service organizations are different from industrial or manufacturing organizations and they should therefore be organized and managed differently. This view is particularly held for the critical operating tasks of service delivery systems, which, unlike the industrial operations, do not follow systematic linear transformation processes. For example, Calvin Pava (1983) argues that utilization of sociotechnical systems theory and techniques in nonlinear service operations requires significant adjustments and modifications. An alternative view is that the distinction between service and nonservice organizations is both blurred and arbitrary. It is therefore more useful to think of organizations as producing what Earl Sasser and his co-workers call a "bundle of goods and services" because all organizations are invariably involved in the production and delivery of goods and services. Sasser, Olsen, and Wyckoff summarize the argument by saying: ". . . almost all purchases of goods are accompanied by facilitating services, and almost every service purchase is accompanied by a facilitating good" (1978:9).

In spite of this approach, which emphasizes the management of productive or high performance systems as opposed to distinguishing service from nonservice organizations, the literature on management and organization science continues to make a distinction with different "how-to" books for different types of industries. Moreover, the World Bank and development economists continue to analyze world economies in terms of service and nonservice sectors. It is therefore important to discuss the role of the service sector in developing countries and the extent to which the model presented above, especially relating to the concept of critical operating tasks, relates to the organization and management of service

Table 2.3 gives figures on the relative importance of the service sector for different types of developing countries. The table shows that the service sector is quite significant even for the low-income countries (29 percent) and that it becomes more significant as a percentage of the total economy as the economy develops to higher income levels. Even for China and India, which are basically agricultural economies, the service sector contributes 25 percent of the total economic performance (GDP). For the lower middle-income oil importing countries (e.g., Zimbabwe, Thailand, Jamaica), the average contribution of the service sector in 1983 was 52 percent. For individual countries (e.g., Jamaica), however, this figure rises to at least 60 percent. Even in sub-Saharan Africa, the average contribution of the service sector to the overall total output is over 40 percent; moreover, for individual countries like the Sudan, Togo, Senegal, Lesotho, and Zimbabwe, the figure exceeds 50 percent. The table includes figures for the United States and other industrial market economies for comparison.

At least two factors account for the relative importance of the service sector in developing countries. First is the pervasive and growing role of government in most of the developing countries and the fact that most

Table 2.3

THE RELATIVE IMPORTANCE OF SERVICE AND OTHER SECTORS: GROSS DOMESTIC PRODUCT

	Service, %	Agriculture, %	Industry, %	Total, %
Low-Income Economies:	29	37	34	100
China and India	25	37	38	100
Sub-Saharan Africa	42	41	17	100
Middle-Income Economies:	49	15	36	100
Oil Exporters	45	16	39	100
Oil Importers	52	14	34	100
Sub-Saharan Africa	42	26	33	100
Upper-Middle-Income Economies:	52	11	37	100
High-Income Oil Exporters	33	2	65	100
Industrial Market Economies	62	3	35	100
U.S.	66	2	32	100

Source: World Development Report 1985, Table 3, pp. 178-79. The World Bank, Washington, D.C., 1985.

Note: The figures are those for 1983. Readers are advised to consult the original source for sectorial definitions and other technical details.

government transactions fall in the service sector category. This would include, for example, education and health, public administration, and financial services. Second, most of these countries have a sizable and growing agricultural sector. The agricultural sector requires a wide range of service operations for it to be managed effectively. These include, for example, administration, financial services, domestic and export marketing, transportation, research, and the various extension services. Most problems of the agricultural sector for the majority of the developing countries emanate from weaknesses in the performance of the COTs and SMATs of related service organizations. It is clear from the figures above that anyone interested in development administration should become acquainted with the management of service organizations.

VIII. Critical Operating Tasks in Service Organizations

The concept of critical operating tasks applies to service and nonservice organizations. As Elwood Buffa (1983) suggests, it is more meaningful to talk about productive systems rather than to distinguish service from nonservice operations. He defines productive systems as "the means by which we transform resource inputs to create useful goods and services" (1983:9). His quote suggests that the model presented in Figure 2.1 applies equally to all productive systems in service and nonservice organizations. There are, however, a number of differences that need to be discussed, especially as they relate to organizations in developing countries.

In the service production system, the inputs tend to be dominated by labor although, depending on the type of operations, other inputs like vehicles, machines, facilities and buildings (e.g., port facilities), information, and technology may be equally important. Although labor is generally available in large supplies in most developing countries, it is not necessarily inexpensive relative to its productivity. Moreover, certain types of skilled and semi-skilled labor may be in short supply. This may explain why some organizations in developing countries have opted for labor-saving technologies as a way of improving the efficiency and economy of the performance of their critical operating tasks. Stobaugh and Wells (1984), for example, report on a series of studies in various developing countries where labor-saving technologies seem to have been deliberately chosen by management. In addition, the combination and organization of different inputs to create a service-productive delivery system require as much thought and skill as they do for the industrial organization. If the combination of labor with other inputs is not optimal, the service delivery system so created will not be productive or efficient. Likewise, extra supplies of labor cannot accommodate for weaknesses or shortages in other inputs.

The transformation system for service operations also tends to be different. It is usually nonlinear and not highly structured. Instead, the work flow tends to move back and forth among various service operators. Exceptions are common as transactions tend to have unique attributes requiring special attention or interpretation of the standard operating procedures (e.g., rules, policies). This lack of structure requires the operators to be in constant touch with one another or with the supervisor in order to deal with exceptional cases. Exceptional cases are costly and delay the smooth running of the operations. It is therefore administratively more efficient to deal with them differently either by allocating them to other more experienced operators or by allocating different times or places for them. Hospitals are good at tackling exceptional cases as their critical operating tasks are arranged by time, place, and complexity. If you want to find out how costly exceptional transactions can be, go to a fast food restaurant like McDonald's and ask for a combination of items that is not provided on the menu. The results are predictable—not only will you irritate the service person, but you will also hold up the line and inconvenience other hungry customers.

The problem of efficient service has an interesting implication for service operations in many organizations in developing countries where service is slow. A possible explanation is that almost all transactions are processed as if they were exceptional, each unique from the other, and therefore requiring special attention with different rules. Naturally, this approach slows down the transformation process because standardization is impossible if each transaction is considered unique. Various explanations can be advanced for why operators in developing countries have this tendency. Perhaps they are not well trained, and if they were familiar with standard operating procedures (SOPs) they would give uniform and fast treatment to each and every transaction. It may also be that there are no SOPs, or that the SOPs are outdated, incomplete, or not readily accessible to the operator. Exceptional treatment of transactions involving human services may even be intrinsically satisfying for the operators who have a high need for affiliation and social interaction. This approach may be a cultural attribute common to many traditional societies, or it may be a pragmatic way for the operators to redesign their jobs and make them more interesting by enriching the interaction patterns with their clients. This argument seems to be supported by research in developing countries which suggests that social affiliation is intrinsically motivating (Howell, Strauss, and Sorensen, 1975; Kanungo, 1982), and that higher level managers do not delegate downward, implying that the service operators may be starved for sources of intrinsic motivation.

A less generous argument has also been advanced that the reason why each service transaction is treated as a unique case is that it provides an opportunity to offer and receive bribes, kickbacks, and "baqshish." Treating each transaction separately, the argument goes, allows the operators and their supervisors to exercise discretion, return favors, and dispose of cases under considerations of appeasement and affiliation, not of administrative fiat. Conditions of inadequate wages that gave rise to the "baqshish" practices in the Ottoman Empire similarly prevail today in developing countries. In any case, the implications for organization and management are clear. In order to improve the performance of the critical operating tasks of service operations in developing countries, one would have to standardize the transformation processes and reduce the tendency to treat most cases as unique or exceptional.

The distribution system of service organizations also differs from that of nonservice operations in that the clients are part of the service delivery system. The clients provide part of the labor for providing inputs (e.g., information on an application form), throughputs (e.g., in a treatment setting like school or hospital), and outputs (e.g., graduation in a training program). Accordingly, the clients can either facilitate the efficiency of the service delivery system or create serious bottlenecks.

In developing countries, service distribution systems have some interesting features. For example, as anybody who has visited offices of managers or senior administrators may have observed, these offices are usually crowded with clients or potential clients while the offices of lower level officers tend to have fewer "visitors." A friend of mine who is a leading medical specialist practicing in his home developing country often complains that he spends much of his time treating routine or minor cases simply because his patients would not accept treatment from junior medical staff, no matter what the ailment. This situation suggests that the clients, for whatever reasons, prefer to make their inputs into the service delivery system at the highest possible hierarchical or professional levels. This practice overloads the system at the top and makes it difficult for management to spare the time for the more long-term strategic management tasks. Professionals end up being overworked but underutilized. Obviously, there is need to introduce a more balanced distribution of effort and delegate the routine transactions down to operating levels where they belong.

Educating the clients about the system's operating procedures is useful, especially in preparing them for providing the necessary inputs for the transactions. For example, applying for a commercial vehicle road license need not be a complex transaction requiring outside help if the applicant knows the procedures to be followed and his or her rights as a citizen to apply for such a license. This could, however, be difficult if the applicant is unable to read or write or if the application form is in a foreign language as it sometimes is for administrative service delivery systems in newly independent countries. At times, the service delivery system may be overstaffed and cause problems of crowding in the office and inefficient performance of the system's critical operating tasks.

All these constraints can and do cause limitations in the efficient performance of the critical operating tasks of the service organizations in developing countries. There is, however, a need to improve the efficient performance of these tasks drawing on the theory, research, and practice from organization science and management. Efforts to rationalize and standardize the work flow transactions drawing from some of the principles of Weber's theory of bureaucracy and Taylor's scientific management can lead to significant improvements as long as adjustments in the applications of these theories are made to accommodate internal organizational requirements and external environmental demands.

Nonprofit service organizations such as community social service agencies, schools, government, and non-governmental organizations (NGOs) should be as interested in improving the performance of their critical operating tasks as the private business service or manufacturing organizations. What may vary among these different types of organizations are the missions, goals, and values attached to particular outcomes. Once each organization determines its stated goals, the search for efficiency is universal.

Summary

Every organization is made up of two task subsystems, the critical operating tasks (COTs) and the strategic management tasks (SMATs). The critical operating tasks are the basic tasks of the organization which it must perform to justify its existence and through which the organization strives to achieve its mission. The history of management thought is characterized by a continuing search for more efficient and effective theories, methods, and techniques for the performance of these two task subsystems. Some theories such as the classical theories tended to focus on the COTs, while the more recent contingent theories pay more attention to the SMATs. The critical operating tasks, their problems, and possible solutions have been illustrated by a study of the repair and maintenance workshop of the Sudan Railway Corporation.

Various challenges of managing COTs in developing country organizations have been discussed. Limitations of the applications of modern management theories and techniques in basically traditional societies have been emphasized. The problems of protecting the vital technical core of the organization from environmental disturbances and preserving the integrity of the performance of the critical operating core have also been noted. The chapter has also detailed the role and limitation of technology in improving the performance of COTs. Only when technology is used in a way consistent with the needs and attributes of the major stakeholders will it contribute maximally to the efficient performance of the COTs. The difficulties of meeting these conditions for most managers in developing countries have been outlined. The chapter concludes by emphasizing the importance of service organizations in developing countries and by analyzing the performance of critical operating tasks in these organizations. In conclusion, the search for efficiency is universal. The next chapter discusses in more detail the strategic management tasks.

CHAPTER 3

The Strategic Management Tasks

The previous chapter discussed the critical operating tasks and how they help us to understand and improve the performance of operating systems in service and nonservice sector organizations in both industrialized and developing countries. However, the critical operating tasks make up only one subsystem of the organization and therefore describe only one aspect of how the organization works. In order to complete the analysis, we must analyze the strategic management tasks (SMATs). The discussion in this chapter will cover four broad areas. First, we shall define and discuss the concept of strategic management tasks with an emphasis on the development and implementation of an organization's mission statement. Second, we shall briefly describe current practices and difficulties in the performance of strategic management tasks in organizations in developing countries. Third, we shall consider the theory and practice of strategic management in industrialized countries. Finally, we shall discuss the role of the board of directors in strategic management, and conclude the chapter with a presentation of a conceptual organizational framework integrating the critical operating and the strategic management tasks.

I. Definition of the Strategic Management Tasks

The strategic management tasks are those tasks done for the organization to identify, articulate, or develop the organization's: (1) uniqueness and wholeness; (2) environmental opportunities and threats; (3) internal strengths, weaknesses, or resource gaps; and (4) current values and management philosophy. These tasks are performed with medium- and long-term perspectives for the organization and are designed to ensure its future survival, growth, and development. As does its charter (Bakke, 1959), these tasks help define the organization's unique image, provide a frame of reference for people inside and outside the organization to relate to it as an entity, articulate the organization's sense of purpose and direction, and give it a "personality" or character that distinguishes it from other organizations. David defines a mission statement as "an enduring statement of purpose that distinguishes one organization from other similar enterprises" (1986:84). He adds that the purpose of the mission statement is the determination of the organization's reason for being.

The strategic management tasks are normally carried out by top management and their support staff or what Henry Mintzberg calls the strategic apex that is "charged with ensuring that the organization serve its mission in an effective way, and also that it serve the needs of those people who control or otherwise have power over the organization" (1979:25). In some cases, however, the strategic management tasks may not be performed by top management or anybody inside the organization. An intriguing investigative exercise is to locate where, if at all, the strategic management tasks of state-owned enterprises are performed over a period of years. Strategic management tasks of state-owned enterprises may be performed by the chief executive officer and the board of directors of the holding company, by the ministry to which the enterprises report, by the national cabinet, or—in the case of developing countries— outside the country by, for example, an international funding agency like the World Bank.

As the emphasis in the performance of the strategic management tasks is one on organization-environment relationships, the orientation is therefore external and political in nature. David Leonard, though talking about projects rather than organizations, recognized the external political orientation when he observed: "The largest part of a leader's efforts are probably directed at factors external to his or her organization—securing funds and authorization, negotiating the cooperation of other agencies and the support of clients, and trying to avert political threat to a project's image or mission" (1986:58). This focus, however, should not be confused with the extraorganizational activities that senior managers, especially those from developing countries, engage in and that may not be directly relevant to the organization's mission. A distinction must be made between organization-environment and extraorganizational tasks. The former are strategic management tasks designed to benefit the organization as a whole, while the latter seek to satisfy individual or collective interests outside the organization.

II. The Need for Strategic Management Tasks

Strategic management tasks are managerial tasks that the organization must perform on a continuing basis. They are not intermittent tasks performed only every five to ten years. As we shall see in this and the next chapters, they are an integral part of the management process of the organization. These tasks can be useful to the organization in achieving the following objectives:

1. Developing, articulating, and sustaining the organization and its mission—giving it a sense of purpose, direction, and focus so that its

internal systems (e.g., incentive or control systems) and processes (e.g., individual behavior) are consistent with the organization's overall mission and objectives. Because the organization's environment is likely to be changing, as will also its internal properties, the strategic management tasks can ensure that these are integrated.

2. Enabling the organization to adapt under conditions of externally imposed stress or crisis, and avoiding or getting itself out of "the doldrums." All organizations must grapple with the challenges of the changing realities of the environment within which they operate. For some organizations, however, an otherwise benign environment can become hostile almost overnight. Robert Miles and Kim Cameron (1982) gave a moving description of how the senior executives of the leading "Big Six" corporations of the U.S. tobacco industry, through the performance of their respective strategic management tasks, have been able to deal effectively with the antismoking, antitobacco sentiments in the United States. Through various forms of strategic management tasks—strategic choice, domain defense, diversification, cooperation, lobbying, product innovation, etc.—these corporations have been able to adapt and weather the storm. Although these strategic management moves have bought the industry time to adapt, in the end it is likely to lose because tobacco products are fundamentally wrong and harmful to the public.

This longitudinal case study of the adaptation of the American tobacco corporations facing a hostile environment is instructive for organizations in developing countries, not only because for a number of these countries tobacco-growing and consumption is a major economic activity, but also, and more importantly, because many of these countries have organizations in need of adaptation as their respective environments change and, as is often the case, become hostile or negative. For example, organizations dependent on natural resources based on extractive industries like tin, rubber, copper, iron ore, aluminum, and even oil, are facing less benign environments and must therefore adapt in order to ensure long-term survival and development. The effective performance of the strategic management tasks provides these organizations with the basis for readiness to adapt. We should note, however, that organizations not only can adapt to their environment, they can and often do actively create it.

3. Strategic management tasks can also help the organization to undertake major internal management changes. These changes may be made either to improve the efficiency and economy of the performance of the critical operating tasks, or to realign the internal operations with the new mission and direction of the organization. These internal changes can take different forms including changes in management philosophy and values, in managerial succession, or in structure and technology. As such changes require management to make strategic choices of long-term importance to the organization, it is more effective to undertake them

with an overall picture of the organization and its mission in mind rather than a piecemeal, short-term one. Strategic management tasks provide a framework for the organization-wide, long-term perspective and therefore facilitate introduction of important internal operational changes.

4. Strategic management tasks are also important for the management of the organization-environment boundaries or interface. These tasks involve scanning and monitoring the environment and relating the information to the relevant internal operations of the organization consistent with the stated mission and prevailing management philosophy. Employees whose jobs require them to interact with both inside and outside stakeholders of the organization are called boundary spanners, and the positions they occupy are boundary roles.

While top management performs most of the important symbolic or politically sensitive boundary-spanning functions, some lower level employees also occupy boundary-spanning roles in the performance of the critical operating tasks. They include, for example, purchasing agents, contract administrators, sales and marketing personnel, recruitment officers, public and government relations staff, and the more specialized boundary spanners like credit managers, research and development managers, lawyers, and accountants. Some of the most important but often neglected lower level boundary spanners include receptionists, telephone operators, order clerks, cashiers, messengers, and doormen. These jobs require the employees to be in contact with various members of the public on a continuing basis and their behavior can have a lasting impact on the public's image of the organization. Effective performance of the strategic management tasks associated with the organization-environment boundary is important because it helps to develop and sustain the legitimacy of the organization and enhance the quality of its relationship with the outside environment.

III. Strategic Management in Developing Countries

Unlike that in industrialized countries, the theory and practice of strategic management in organizations in developing countries is very limited indeed, particularly for the indigenous organizations in both the public and the private sectors. The only two areas in which aspects of strategic management have been discussed and applied are in the management of development programs and national policy reform programs. Both of these are areas of keen interest and active involvement by international development and funding agencies. This section summarizes evidence of the use of strategic management in these two areas. It also speculates on some of the reasons why there is only limited interest in the use of strategic management in organizations in developing countries. Although subsidiaries of multinational corporations (MNCs) operating in developing countries enjoy a high level of utilization of strategic management, they will not be discussed here because the strategic management tasks and associated techniques are performed at the headquarters away from the subsidiaries' locations.

Two of the studies on planning and strategic management for development programs—those by Samuel Paul (1983a) and Tom Kent and Ian McAllister (1985)—were funded by international development agencies, the International Labour Office and the Canadian International Development Agency, respectively. Kent and McAllister's work discusses the effective performance and supervision of the critical operating tasks (COTs) associated with specific development projects in Ghana and Zimbabwe. It emphasizes the use of elementary techniques for the performance of project cycle tasks (e.g., planning, implementation, appraisal), and human resource development (e.g., training) to ensure adequate performance. There is no explicit discussion of the Ghanaian or Zimbabwean implementing agencies as free-standing organizations or the management of the organization-environment interdependencies. They treat public management in these countries as a unitary concept or single organization.

Paul's discussion focuses on the use of strategic management in developing countries but is also limited to projects and programs. Accordingly, within this short- to medium-term perspective, he defines strategic management as "the interrelated set of top management interventions which create the framework within which operational decisions and actions are taken to accomplish the goals of a development programme" (Paul, 1983:2).

Although Paul does not concern himself with long-term organizational problems, he identifies the following four dimensions of strategic management: (1) the environment of the program; (2) the program's strategy; (3) the program's organization structure; and (4) the organizational process of the program. In the rest of the book, Paul gives practical techniques and "guidelines for action" for the use of each of these four dimensions for the management of development programs.

Paul's overall observation is that even in the management of development programs there is little or no utilization of strategic management knowledge and techniques. He believes that this is an important cause of failure of many development programs in developing countries. As expected, Paul calls for more utilization of strategic management techniques and it is likely that his guidelines would apply, with minimal adjustments, as well to organizations as they do to projects and programs.

The second area in which the use of strategic management has been discussed is that for national policy reform programs. Although the discussions are at national rather than organizational levels, the concepts and techniques are relevant for strategic management. As with development projects, the interest comes mainly from international development organizations. For example, in its 1986 World Development Report, the World Bank outlines a number of strategic management initiatives undertaken by several developing countries that have resulted in significant improvements in the performance of their respective agricultural sectors. The strategic management (policy reform) initiatives detailed in the report include: improvements of rural financial markets in Indonesia by reorganization of the Bank Rakyat Indonesia (BRI), the country's rural bank; introduction of rubber replanting programs in Thailand; cotton sector reforms in the Sudan; and various agricultural policy reforms and improvements in Bangladesh and China.

These case histories do not provide details or analysis of the organizations within which these reforms were implemented or indicate the nature of the specific task environments to which they were responding or adapting. It is clear, however, that these government policy initiatives were in answer to crises both from within the organization and from the outside environment. For example, in Bangladesh, "the government responded . . . by expanding public investment in agriculture, concentrating on small irrigation projects with low costs and quick returns, increasing the role of the private sector, and improving the effectiveness of public agencies" (World Bank, 1986:106).

The reports' conclusions point to the fact that effective organization and management (e.g., extension services, marketing, distribution, and incentive systems) are among the most serious bottlenecks for the successful implementation of many of these agricultural policy reforms. Therefore, the concepts and techniques used, and the lessons learned in the introduction of policy reforms in developing countries, can be helpful in advancing the utilization of strategic management in these countries' organizations.

More recently, David Hunt and Peter Gufwoli (1986) have produced a casebook on strategic management focusing on specific Kenyan organizations. The book contains a representative sample of twelve case studies of Kenyan business organizations including General Motors (Kenya) Limited, the National Bank of Kenya, and the East African Breweries Limited. However, as the authors are quick to point out, these cases are intended for classroom instruction to enable students to learn about strategic management rather than to provide a comprehensive critical analysis of business or organizational strategic management in Kenya.

We now return to the important question of why the use of strategic management in organizations in developing countries is very limited indeed. I suggest the following five reasons: (1) limited basic research; (2) highly volatile environment; (3) weaknesses in the performance of the critical operating tasks; (4) lack of strategic management skills and motivation; and (5) institutional weaknesses.

There is very limited strategic management research on organizations in developing countries. The lack of basic research limits the possibility of informed decisions about utilization because the potential users would have no useful knowledge upon which to base such decisions. Unlike in developing countries, however, there is an active research enterprise in the area of strategic management in industrialized countries which provides further impetus for utilization. There is an obvious need for both basic and applied strategic management research on organizations in developing countries.

Organizations in developing countries often face a highly volatile environment with too many unknowns. Unexpected political changes, debt problems, hyperinflation, staff turnover, and international competition create so much environmental uncertainty and complexity that managers consider almost any planning or strategic management responses impossible. In Latin America, top management is preoccupied with "increasing the certainty of outcomes to protect the business from unforeseen and potentially threatening situations" (Quezada and Boyce, 1988:263). Consequently, decision making is highly centralized and teamwork is often sacrificed in favor of individuals and individual areas of responsibility. This focus causes a real dilemma because organizations are expected to respond to high environmental uncertainty by utilizing strategic management. When an environment is especially volatile and organizations do not use strategic management to adapt or respond to its changes, they become even more vulnerable to future environmental threats. Thus they find themselves mired in a debilitating "Catch 22" situation.

Weaknesses in the effective performance of critical operating tasks may also make it difficult for senior management to attend to strategic management tasks. Critical operating tasks have short production cycles lasting one working day, a shift, or an even shorter period of time. When serious production problems arise, the feedback should be immediate; if they are not corrected, they turn into a crisis. Crisis management often involves redirecting organizational resources away from planned activities or programs to the most critical areas of the moment. Under these circumstances, the tendency would be to redirect resources normally planned for strategic management to the critical areas of the operating tasks. Paul seems to have made the same observation when he complained that managers in developing countries had so much pressure from the day-to-day problems that they hardly had time to attend to the long-term problems. He asserts: "In practice, however, many senior administrators and managers are totally absorbed by the course of operations. They claim that they have little time for strategic management. In reality, their problem is that they spend too much time on operational problems" (1983:121). His statement again implies that utilization of strategic management may be dependent on the organization's ability to perform its critical operating tasks with efficiency and economy.

Lack of skills and motivation on the part of senior managers and administrators has also been blamed for their disinterest in the performance of strategic management tasks. It has long been known that developing countries have inadequate supplies of skilled and experienced specialists. In recent years perhaps the most critical shortages are in the areas of management and administration. The skills and experience required for effective strategic management are particularly rare in developing countries because one needs to draw from a wide range of management and non-management disciplines and experiences; as formal management education is a recent undertaking in most of these countries, it is unlikely that they would have adequate numbers of managers with the required background. Problems also exist regarding the selection, placement, and utilization of senior managers. It is not unusual for appointments to be made on the basis of extraorganizational considerations. Even when proper criteria for selection and placement have been followed, the appointees may not be effectively utilized as senior managers. For example, they may not be accorded authority commensurate with their responsibility and therefore may be unable to make any significant strategic management choices. This limitation would obviously affect their motivation as well.

Finally, the existence of weak institutions and weak social and physical infrastructures may make it difficult for organizations to utilize strategic management. Kenneth Murrell and Robert Duffield (1985) attribute the problem to an undeveloped management infrastructure that needs strengthening. Many reasons can explain institutional weaknesses in developing countries. These include preference for strong personalized—as opposed to institutionalized—leadership; cultural and religious values and practices that emphasize the influence of the past on the present rather than the independent planning of the future; lack of positive reinforcement to planning and strategic management activities for the senior managers and their specialists; lack of adequate technical and administrative support systems for effective performance of strategic tasks; and strong personal self-interests that are best advanced without rather than with a clear organization mission. Lack of reliable data or information about strategic aspects of the environment or about critical internal operations is not conducive to effective strategic management of organizations.

The pervasive nature of government and government controls and regulatory agencies, and a small ineffective private sector can cause institutional weaknesses and limit the effective utilization of strategic management. When government influence is extreme, managers learn to believe that government is the only element in the environment that matters. They also tend to believe that government action (or inaction) can protect them from environmental threats. They therefore have little incentive to

pay attention to strategic management. They respond to environmental
threats or challenges by going to the government for protection. If the government were not so readily available, these managers would find other
methods of protecting their organizations against environmental threats,
including utilization of strategic management.

The existence of only a small private sector also constitutes a form of
institutional weakness. Organizational size is important for the effective
utilization of strategic management. Small organizations do not have the
resources for the effective performance of strategic management tasks.
Moreover, they tend to be vulnerable to environmental changes and have
little or no mastery over the environment. They would not have the internal organizational culture, structures, incentives, and systems that promote planning and strategic management. As these internal dynamics develop slowly over a period of time, many organizations in developing
countries might not have had sufficient time to build the necessary institutional framework for effective utilization of strategic management.

IV. Basic Steps in Strategic Management Tasks

The performance of strategic management tasks involves three broad
steps: (1) strategic formulation; (2) strategic implementation; and (3)
strategic monitoring and evaluation. *Strategic formulation* is the process of
developing or confirming the organization's mission, purpose, strategy,
and tactics. It involves determination of the business the organization performs or should perform; its goals, plans, and objectives; the management philosophy and values that guide its judgments of right or wrong;
and its strategies for achieving its goals, plans, and objectives. It requires
a clear understanding of the organization's relevant environment and, by
means of environmental scanning, identification of potential opportunities for the organization. It also requires an accurate assessment of the
internal capacity of the organization to perform with efficiency and economy the critical operating tasks resulting from the organization's new mission. Capacity building must be related to the organization's mission.

Strategic formulation is performed by top management often with
the help of outside consultants who, in addition to objectivity, are skilled
in organizational science and have knowledge and expertise about the industry or industries to which the organization belongs. It usually takes
place off-site to provide uninterrupted concentration and to provide opportunities for team building among the senior managers or officials of
the organization. The process lasts anywhere from a couple of days to several weeks.

Strategic implementation is the most difficult step, especially for organizations in developing countries. It is the process of acquiring, organizing or reorganizing, and utilizing the organization's resources for the effective achievement of the goals and objectives resulting from the stated mission, consistent with the espoused management philosophy and values. It also involves the communication of the mission, goals, plans, and objectives and the rationale behind them to the organization's inside and outside stakeholders. This is the essence of the management process because it requires that the performance of the critical operating tasks and the strategic management tasks be in concert with each other and that these in turn be consistent with the organization's mission and objectives. As Lawrence Hrebiniak and William Joyce (1984) indicate, these may be implemented either sequentially or concurrently.

Strategic monitoring and evaluation is the third basic step in the performance of the strategic management tasks. It involves the collection and analysis of information from within and outside the organization to assess the extent to which the implementing strategies and performance results of both the critical operating tasks and the strategic management tasks are in conformity with the organization's mission statement, management philosophy, and operating goals and objectives. The information obtained from monitoring and evaluation enables management to assess the extent to which past strategic decisions have been realized, the ability of the internal operating capacity to perform the required critical operating tasks with due efficiency and economy, and any significant change in environmental conditions that would necessitate making adjustments in the strategic choices. These tasks are so important for determining the direction and internal structure of the organization that they, too, are often performed with the help of outsiders who bring in objectivity and added professional expertise. These may be members of the board of directors, private or public shareholders, bankers or other creditors, accountants, management consultants, or other stakeholders.

Even in North America, mission statements are not common among public and private organizations. In a recent survey of 218 *Fortune* 500 firms, only 28 percent (61 firms) provided complete information about their mission statements. Over 40.4 percent (88 firms) responded that they have no mission statements, and the chief executive officers of 10 percent of the respondents requested information and assistance on how to develop mission statements. Yet the executives of 5 percent (11 firms) replied that their mission statements were confidential documents not available to the general public because they constitute part of their comparative advantage over the competition (Pearce and David, 1987). There has been no such study done for organizations in developing countries, but it can be reasonably assumed that the level of awareness and actual practice of developing mission statements are significantly much lower.

V. Development of a Mission Statement

A mission statement is a brief, written statement of the organization's image, its purpose for being, and its plans to achieve and sustain that image. Usually expressed in a paragraph or two, it gives the underlying purpose or actual identity of the organization. An increasing number of organizations, especially in the industrialized countries, are spending time and money to develop their own mission statements, articulate them to the employees, and make them freely available to their clients and members of the general public.

I am in the habit of collecting organization mission statements. I find them interesting reading because of their diversity, which—if you have some knowledge about the organizations—can be remarkable. The president of a fast-growing local high technology firm proudly and immodestly gives as his company's mission statement: "to be the number one application development software firm in the world." He also explains the purpose of the statement to be that "it motivates; it provides a common purpose; and it is a guide to action and decision making throughout the company" (Potter, 1986:5). My local schoolboard's mission statement is "to develop and provide to each student, regardless of age, an education of the highest quality in a positive environment, with caring and dedicated staff members." It goes on to say that in "pursuit of excellence in the school system, the Board is committed" to equity, open communications, fiscal responsibility, and a corporate philosophy for the "governance of the system" (Carleton Board of Education, 1986).

The Manufacturers Life Insurance Company, a large financial institution operating both in industrialized and developing countries and one that I have studied in the past (Kiggundu, 1978; 1984), has developed one of the most interesting and comprehensive corporate mission statements and declaration of company aims and purpose. The mission statement declares that the company ". . . in representing its participating policyholders, dedicates itself to the effective use of its organizational resources to design, market and administer those products and services for financial planning and protection that will meet the needs, expectations and aspirations of its customers at the lowest possible cost consistent with high quality standards" (The Manufacturers Life Insurance Company, 1985). The statement also gives six company aims, each associated with the performance of its critical operating tasks (e.g., product design, marketing, and investment) and promises that the company is dedicated to provide for its inside and outside stakeholders by ensuring, for example, maximum returns on invested funds, a responsive organization, and opportunities for personal growth.

In explaining the rationale for developing and articulating its mission, the company states:

This Charter is a statement of purpose and direction for our company. It is a formal and realistic definition of our long-range, fundamental aims; it expresses the "why," and "where," and the "how" of our existence. It is a foundation on which we will build our entire future corporate structure, a nucleus from which we will be able to grow. It is a guide-post against which this growth can be measured. . . . This Charter establishes the criteria against which all objectives and planning of Manufacturers Life will be formulated and tested. (The Manufacturers Life Insurance Company, 1985)

This statement is useful because, as management of the company rightly points out, it provides a framework in the determination of the role the company plays in society, its criteria for deciding upon its business plans, and the means and organizational resources by which those plans and ideals are to be realized. It is also a planning instrument for formulating company goals and objectives, and for determining programs, policies, and procedures consistent with the company's overall mission. Additionally, it is an action-implementing document that provides for the realization of company plans and the growth and development of the company. Finally, it can be used as an instrument for environmental scanning, monitoring, and evaluation to find out whether or not changes have taken place either in the outside environment or inside the organization (or both) to necessitate significant adjustments. Emphasizing the importance of environmental adaptation, the company documents state, "This Charter is a check-point to which we return in order to measure and assess this growth as well as the instrument of its own change, as the fundamental aims of our company adapt to the opportunities and demands of a changing world" (The Manufacturers Life Insurance Company, 1985).

According to information provided by its Corporate Relations Unit in Kuala Lumpur, Malaysia's Council of Trust for the Indigenous People (MARA), which in 1966 replaced the Rural and Industrial Development Authority (RIDA), states as its corporate mission "to encourage, guide, train and assist bumiputera [native Malays] to enable them to participate actively and progressively in small and medium scale commercial and industrial enterprises towards creating a strong and viable bumiputera business community." Based on this mission statement MARA's (Mojlis Amanah Rakyat) management developed four strategies aimed at: (1) creating and increasing the number of native Malay entrepreneurs; (2) actively participating in specific commercial and industrial enterprises; (3) increasing the number of trained native Malays at all levels; and (4) providing transport and other facilities and services to local communities for their economic and social development. This plan gave rise to four corresponding programs for entrepreneurial development, investment, education, and rural transport. As of 1985, MARA owned thirty-two subsidiary companies in the fields of commerce, industry, and transport and these and all its other activities correspond to its four strategies and programs aimed at fulfilling its stated mission.

The International Rice Research Institute (IRRI) in Manila is charged with the mission of conducting "research on the rice plant, and on all phases of rice production, management, distribution, and utilization with the objective of improving the nutritional and economic rice-growing areas of the world through improvement in quality and quantity of rice" (IRRI, 1985:10). Its basic organization structure of research, training, and international collaboration reflects the nature and scope of this mission, which is focused on small-scale rice farming.

The development of mission statements is a relatively new strategic management task, and experience to date shows that different organizations do it differently with varying degrees of quality and comprehensiveness. It is therefore necessary to develop a framework for assessing how comprehensive a mission statement is. Table 3.1 gives the dimensions, elements, the respective definitions for these elements, and a rating scale for assessing a specific mission statement for each of the elements and dimensions. A mission statement should have three dimensions: a statement of vision (Charter) and management philosophy, planning systems, and motivational and control systems. The Charter is similar to the mission statement described above for the Manufacturers Life Insurance Company. The management philosophy outlines the dominant values, belief systems, ideology, and common understanding among the members of the organization. It is important for organizations to have a dominant management philosophy that the members understand, respect and are committed to. Large organizations, organizations in varied lines of business (e.g., conglomerates such as Marubeni of Japan), and widely dispersed organizations (e.g., the Roman Catholic Church) experience difficulties in developing and sustaining a unitary management philosophy, making it hard for them to predict and control behavior, especially during an unexpected crisis. Accordingly, organizations spend a lot of effort to articulate and inculcate to their employees the dominant management philosophy so that they can use it as a frame of reference or a guidepost for deciding between wrong and right even in novel situations.

The planning systems translate the ideals contained in the mission statement and in the management philosophy into operational goals, objectives, plans, strategies, and tactics for implementation. The translation provides the basis for determining the quantity and quality of organizational resources required for achieving the goals and objectives without violating the organization's fundamental values and belief systems. Planning systems are widely used, especially in organizations in industrialized countries where rational-logical thinking dominates manage-

Table 3.1

FRAMEWORK FOR THE DEVELOPMENT OF ORGANIZATIONAL MISSION STATEMENTS

DIMENSION	ELEMENT	DEFINITION	RATINGS
1. Charter and Management Philosophy	1. Values	Shared understanding of what is important to the organization both internally (e.g., people, systems, technology), and externally (e.g., clients, technology, owners, competition, suppliers, community groups).	H M L ?
	2. Beliefs	Common understanding and perceptions of how and why things work or don't work in that organization and what needs to be done (norms) to keep them to work in concert with the new mission. Cause-effect relationships.	
	3. Inspiration	The continuing excitement, commitment, and strength of fellowship generated by the mission statement.	
	4. Vision	The extent to which there is a clear image of the organization and how different (or similar) it will be at various times in the future (e.g., internally: task environments, niches).	
2. Planning Systems	5. Goals	Broad statements of the future direction of the organization.	
	6. Strategies	Broad, often long-term plans and methods for achieving the goals of the organization and sustaining the desired management philosophy.	
	7. Objectives	Specific statements of expected achievements for the organization and its component parts down to the level of the individual employee.	
	8. Tactics	Operational methods for achieving the desired objectives at the various levels of the organization.	
3. Motivational and Control Systems	9. Performance Measurements	Timely, accurate, and mission-relevant performance indicators for different levels of the organization and its constituencies.	
	10. Communication and Feedback	The effectiveness with which the ideology and meaning of the mission statement is communicated to all internal and external significant actors (e.g., managers, employees, clients, public) and feedback obtained from them so as to generate excitement and enthusiasm about the "new" organization.	
	11. Incentives	The extent to which reward systems reinforce the espoused management philosophy and the practices or behavior associated with the mission's planning systems.	
	12. Resources	The qualitative and quantitative adequacy of the resources (e.g., money, management, leadership, human resources, technology) required to implement and sustain the mission statement: its management philosophy, and planning, control, and motivational systems.	

Note: The rating scale can be modified to suit specific requirements.
H = high; M = medium; L = low; ? = cannot be assessed.

ment practices. They include business plans, budgets, resource acquisition, allocation and utilization, division of labor, and organization of the critical operating tasks. They draw from a wide range of disciplines in both the physical and the social sciences, and the tools for planning systems are well advanced and readily available. In the 1960s and 1970s organizations, particularly in the industrialized countries, were very much attracted to the development and use of planning systems in support of the performance of their strategic management tasks. Many of them created high profile departments of corporate planning that gave impetus to the creation and development of a new management profession of corporate planners. There are indications, however, that corporate planning as a function is losing its steam in management owing to problems of analysis rather than of implementation (Mintzberg, 1980).

The motivational and control systems provide the energy that drives the organization. They can also be a source of frustration, as it is sometimes difficult for the organization to live up to its stated image. Thus top management must articulate and communicate the organization's mission with a missionary zeal and excitement so as to energize the lower level participants. They must put in place proper incentives to provide a source of intrinsic and extrinsic motivation, and allocate resources to facilitate the achievements of desired goals and discourage undesired or counterproductive behavior. Timely and accurate performance measurements help provide information and feedback on how well or badly individuals and groups are performing relative to their set goals. Both feedback and goal setting are potentially powerful sources of motivation. Goals are an effective source of motivation, especially if: (1) they are specific with explicit measurable targets or deadlines; (2) they can be understood and internalized by the employees; (3) they are set participatively with the employees to enhance understanding and commitment; (4) they are moderately challenging or difficult, but not impossible to achieve; and (5) they are tied to the relevant unit's reward systems. Feedback is motivational to the extent that: (1) it is timely, accurate, relevant, direct, and valid; (2) it is specific and understandable to the receiver; and (3) it is behavioral and within the receiver's control to act on it.

The control systems should be designed and enforced consistent with the organization's mission, philosophy, and objectives. Rules, policies, and procedures should be periodically reviewed to ensure consistency with the overall direction and management style of the organization. Supervisory styles and functions should be used judiciously to promote motivation and exercise controls to ease the achievement of individual, unit, and corporate goals. Likewise, organizational choices relating, for example, to choices of technology, structure, organization of work, and overall reward systems should be related to the organization's motivational and control systems, and ultimately to its goals, philosophy, and mission.

VI. From Mission Statement to Individual Behavior

What is the relationship between the organization's mission statement and what people actually do? A mission statement is an expression of official goals of what the organization wishes to be known for and may or may not have any resemblance with actual behavior inside the organization. In organization science, a distinction is made between official goals and operating goals. Operating goals are behavioral representations of what people actually do, as opposed to what the mission statement says they do, how they perform their tasks, and why they do what they do (cause-effect relationships). If the mission statement has not been clearly articulated or if it has not been internalized by the majority of the members of the organization, a discrepancy is bound to arise between the official goals (mission statement) and the operating goals. One of the important strategic management tasks is to develop and maintain understanding and commitment to the mission statement for all the members of the organization. This step helps to ensure consistency between official and operating goals.

In organizations in developing countries, the discrepancy between official goals and operating goals can be particularly large. Most of these countries have three- to five-year development plans that identify national goals, priorities, targets, resources, and strategies, and that are similar to mission statements or official goals for individual organizations. These plans are often broken down by sector, ministry, or government agency or corporation. They, therefore, constitute the official goals at each of these levels. Reading the national development plan, and watching public servants at work in these organizations, it is not always clear how the two complement each other.

Figure 3.1 gives a conceptual framework for linking the mission statement with what members of the organization actually do. The boxes to the left (A1–A4) show the translation of the mission statement into objectives, strategies, and tactics at the corporate level. The center boxes (B1–B3) indicate the translation of the corporate strategy into functional objectives like marketing, human resource management, or management information system. This is the area where the strategic perspectives of the individual functions is particularly important because they have to be realigned with the strategic choices at the corporate (organizational) level. The C boxes (C1–C4) show how, through internal functional (or divisional) differentiation, unit objectives can be identified for each function and broken down into unit strategies, tactics, and unit operations—input, throughput, output, and feedback transactions. Box D is the most concrete observation of what the individual member of the organization may be doing at any point in time.

In Figure 3.1, the mission statement may emphasize the idea of "business with a heart," i.e., running a successful business while at the same

Figure 3.1   **RELATIONSHIP BETWEEN THE ORGANIZATION'S MISSION STATEMENT AND INDIVIDUAL BEHAVIOR**

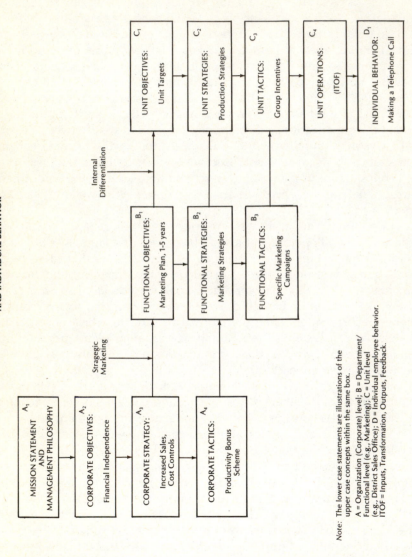

Note: The lower case statements are illustrations of the upper case concepts within the same box.

A = Organization (Corporate) level; B = Department/Functional level (e.g., Marketing); C = Unit level (e.g., District Sales Office); D = Individual employee behavior.
ITOF = Inputs, Transformation, Outputs, Feedback.

time being a socially responsible corporate citizen. This philosophy may translate into the corporate objective of maintaining financial independence and integrity so that the organization does not depend on others for its financial input requirements. The strategy adopted by the organization to achieve financial independence may be increased sales and cost controls, and management may introduce a productivity bonus to motivate people to increase productivity (sales) or reduce costs.

Each function must then develop its objectives in line with the corporate objective of financial independence, but it may develop its own specific strategies and tactics. For example, in Figure 3.1 the marketing function would develop its own sales and marketing plans for the next one to five years and its strategies may include introducing new products, opening up new territories, closing unprofitable sales offices, or improving the quality of service to its important clients. The important concern in making all these functional strategic choices is that they are consistent with the corporate objectives. Likewise, each individual unit must go through the same logic and steps.

Finally, when an employee engages in a specific activity like making a telephone call (Box D1), it is possible to assess the extent to which it contributes or detracts from the organization's mission, objectives, or strategies, at the different levels of the organization. In the example given above (Figure 3.1), if the telephone call (D1) is not a business call (A1), if it does not contribute to the organization's financial independence (A2), if it does not contribute to increased sales or cost control, or if it does not facilitate the achievement of the functional and unit objectives, then ultimately, it does not contribute to the organization's mission. Therefore, it should not be made on company or government time.

In addition to providing a conceptual link between the organization's mission and the critical operating work activities in different parts of the organization, Figure 3.1 can be used as a general diagnostic tool for determining the relative importance and impact of different activities both inside and outside the organization. It can therefore be particularly helpful to anybody engaged in the performance, monitoring, or evaluation of the organization's strategic management tasks.

VII. Dimensions of Strategic Management Tasks

The strategic management tasks are comprised of six dimensions. These are: (1) the development of the mission statement and management philosophy; (2) strategy formulation; (3) communication and legitimization of mission, philosophy, and objectives; (4) internal coordination and management; (5) nichemanship; and (6) the management of contextual interdependencies.

The first four dimensions have been discussed above in sufficient detail. In this section, the last two—nichemanship and managing contextual interdependencies—are each briefly described.

Nichemanship is a strategic management task that involves the process of finding opportunities or potential opportunities in the environment that are not being exploited, and redirecting the organization to take advantage of these opportunities. These opportunities may be found in the organization's input acquisitions, throughput transformation processes, output distribution, or waste/byproduct disposal. For example, an organization might find a new source of raw materials, or use alternative and less expensive inputs for its production. During the oil boom, some organizations in Saudi Arabia, faced with domestic shortages of high-level professional personnel, found that they could recruit many developing countries' professionals much more cheaply than professionals from Europe or the United States.

Nichemanship requires a constant search for alternatives to existing systems and practices and continuing intimate knowledge and contacts with both the internal operations (critical operating tasks) of the organization and the external environment. Successful niche finders do not take anything for granted; they thrive on constant reinterpretation of and enactment with the world around them. For example, in India, Larsen and Toubra Limited, a private sector equipment manufacturer started from scratch by two European engineers, continually seeks opportunities from the environment and turns them into commercially successful businesses by a strategy of technical innovations, sound financial management, and utilization (Pereira, 1987).

Some organizations find it difficult to find niches in the environment either because they define their mandate and operations too narrowly, or because they think of niches only in the context of the marketing function. State-owned enterprises tend to define their mandates narrowly because these are often prescribed by legislation that may specifically forbid them from dealing with certain markets or aspects of the environment. For example, the Kenya Railways Corporation is not allowed to compete with the private trucking operators on the profitable Mombasa/Uganda route either by establishing its own trucking fleet, or by providing potential clients with nonrail transport services. Under those restrictions, the corporation's ability to find new niches is quite limited. Thus we can see at least in part why the concept of nichemanship is traditionally more appealing to private sector organizations, especially those in diversified markets or operations. Public sector organizations, however, can also take advantage of nichemanship. For example, the Eastern and Southern African Management Institute (ESAMI) found a niche in providing senior and middle level management training and development because national institutes of public administration and private consulting firms cannot compete on a regional basis.

VIII. Managing Contextual Interdependencies

One of the most difficult sets of strategic management tasks is managing contextual interdependencies. As indicated above, the organization operates within an environment with which it is constantly in a state of mutual influence and adjustment. The environment, however, is not a unitary concept. It can be divided between the *general environment*, and the *specific task environment*. The general environment refers to any general conditions outside the organization whose effects on the organization are only indirect or infrequent. The general environment affects all organizations operating in the same region or industry and is not unique to a single organization. The general environment includes the following areas: (1) the political climate; (2) economic conditions; (3) cultural attributes; (4) technological advancements; (5) the legal/administrative framework; (6) social conditions; and (7) the state and functioning of the social and physical infrastructure.

All organizations are affected by and do affect each of these environmental considerations in a general and indirect way. When these considerations are experiencing extreme conditions, they can be very instrumental either in facilitating or in hindering the operations and development of organizations. For example, organizations in developing countries are aware of the limitations imposed by a weak or ineffective infrastructure where transport services, communication facilities, power and water supplies, and general administration can cause serious operational bottlenecks. In India foreign firms have been forced to close or to scale down their operations because of inadequate external telecommunication services, while in Lagos, traffic jams and irregular supplies of utilities significantly increase the cost of doing business. It is for this reason that members of the ASEAN (Association of South East Asian Nations) are spending large sums of money investing in their respective physical infrastructures in order to remain competitive in attracting foreign and domestic investment.

The specific task environment refers to those elements in the environment—individuals, interest groups, other organizations—that have an immediate relevancy for the focal organization. These are the outside elements that the organization must deal with on a regular basis in order to perform its tasks and achieve its mission, goals, and objectives. As Richard Daft and Richard Steers explain, "Task environment refers to those parts of an organization's external environment that are directly relevant to goal-setting and attainment" (1986:287). They also observe that the organization must respond to or interact with these environmental elements in order to survive. Environmental elements include, for example: (1) suppliers; (2) customers; (3) the labor force; (4) shareholders; (5) local population and its leadership; (6) competitors; (7) banks and other funding agencies; and (8) government regulatory agencies. In addition to the usual business task environment requirements, organizations in developing countries generally spend an incredible amount of time and resources managing their relationships with a wide range of regulatory agencies including the central bank for foreign exchange controls, licensing agencies, marketing boards, and foreign investment review agencies.

Organizations must deal with three types of interdependencies in the performance of their strategic management tasks. These are: (1) internal interdependencies; (2) transactional interdependencies; and (3) environmental interdependencies. Internal interdependencies refer to the interactions and linkages between different parts of the *same* organization. For example, the coordination and relationships between extension and research within an agricultural development agency involve internal interdependencies within the agency. Transactional interdependencies are direct interactions between the focal organization and specific elements in the environment involving the acquisition of inputs, or distribution of outputs. For example, the purchasing department of a business organization deals with many organizations looking for suitable raw materials such as equipment and supplies for its internal use. The city police department also deals with other city departments, organizations, and community groups in the performance of its tasks. These interdependencies are similar to what Eaton (1972) terms functional interdependencies, but, as Fred Emery and Eric Trist (1965) clearly show, it is necessary to distinguish between input and output transactions. Environmental interdependencies are relationships or linkages between two or more elements in the external environment whose conduct has significant implications for the focal organization. For example, if farmers and transporters of a major export crop link up together, their joint actions might have significant implications for the crop export marketing board.

These interdependencies are presented in increasing order of complexity; that is, internal interdependencies are relatively easy to manage while the environmental interdependencies, also called "causal texture" by Emery and Trist (1965), are the most complex and difficult to manage. As Robert Miles explains, these "causal texture" relationships are potentially dangerous because "they represent the area of interdependencies that belong to the environment itself that can potentially determine the ultimate survival of the focal organization" (1980:203). The danger is particularly pronounced in situations where, as often happens for organizations in developing countries, these "causal texture" relationships involve powerful international players outside the country where the focal organization is located.

Figure 3.2 gives a diagrammatic presentation of the different types of interdependencies—for a hypothetical developing country organization called the Rural Development Agency (RDA). The RDA is government

Figure 3.2 **CRITICAL CONTEXTUAL INTERDEPENDENCIES OF A RURAL DEVELOPMENT AGENCY**

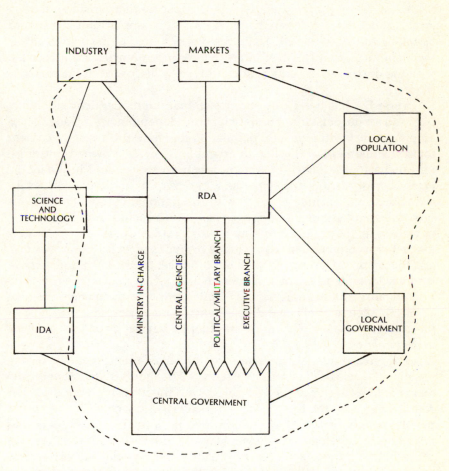

Note: RDA= Rural Development Agency; IDA= International Development Agency
Zigzag lines show the many facets of the government.

--------- National boundaries

owned and has both commercial and development responsibilities. It is expected to be a viable commercial entity while at the same time playing a leading role in the integrated rural development of that particular rural region of the country. Internal interdependencies within the RDA are easy to identify. They include, for example, linkages between one department such as the personnel and welfare department, and another such as the finance and accounting, over internal matters like accountability and cost control of the employee welfare budget. Most conflicts arising out of internal interdependencies are handled by routine application of standard operating procedures (SOPs), and the power vested in the organization's hierarchy of authority. Most internal interdependencies are associated with the organization's critical operating tasks discussed in the previous chapter.

The RDA has two types of transactional interdependencies—for inputs and for outputs. Input transaction interdependencies include, for example, contacts with the local population for labor, the local government for land and other local facilities, perhaps another state-owned enterprise for purchase of fertilizers, Toyota of Japan for trucks, and International Harvester for tractors and harvesters. The output interdependencies for the RDA would include linkages with the national marketing board for processing and selling its crops overseas, local agricultural firms engaged in various food and agricultural processing and packaging, local farmers interested in buying disposable items or byproducts for their own use, and international buyers of the RDA's produce. As these examples show, the interdependencies can be numerous and, while some of them are simple and fairly routine, others may be quite complex and demand of a lot of adroit management skills and experience. The performance of most of the tasks associated with these interdependencies is part of strategic management.

The environmental (causal texture) interdependencies and their complexities can also be illustrated by Figure 3.2. It shows that most of the domain relating to science and technology and the industry lies outside the country in which the RDA is located. Science and technology represent new knowledge relevant for the effective performance of RDA's critical operating and strategic management tasks. Industry includes all those elements in the environment operating in the same or similar line of business as the RDA and therefore constituting the competition for the Agency's final products. Again, most of these are located outside RDA's country. If a large industry competitor approached one of the firms manufacturing machinery used for the RDA's major operations and together they developed a more efficient and cheaper piece of machinery that would not be immediately available to the RDA, then the interaction between the competitor and the manufacturer could drive the RDA out of the international market for its products by making its technology obsolete and its cost structure noncompetitive. If the two elements in the external environment operate from outside the RDA's home country, they can threaten the Agency's survival with impunity.

Strategic management tasks associated with environmental interdependencies are supposed to ensure that the RDA is protected from hostile linkages from the environment. They involve frequent environmental scanning, monitoring, and intelligence gathering to be able to predict the behaviors of the environmental elements both domestic and foreign. They also involve preparing the organization either to adapt quickly and efficiently if faced with a major environmental change, or to respond proactively by changing the nature or direction of the environmental shift. These are difficult and expensive tasks for which very few organizations have the resources to perform effectively, yet they must be done. Research has shown that organizations that manage the external environmental interdependencies are, overall, more successful than those that do not. Miles (1980), for example, has used a model similar to Figure 3.2 to explain how a police department can work with the community.

With information provided by Samuel Paul (1982), I have used the model to provide an alternative explanation for the success of the Kenya Tea Development Authority (KTDA) and Mexico's Council for the Promotion of Education (CONAFE) rural education project. My conclusion was that one of the determinants of success for both organizations was their ability to protect themselves from undue outside interferences, both domestic and foreign (Kiggundu, 1985a). More recently, Mumbi Kiereini (1985) has used the same model for a comparative study of the success of KTDA on the one hand, and the Million-Acre Settlement Scheme and the Special Rural Development Program of Kenya on the other. Drawing from Eaton's (1972) concept of institution building, and Esman and Uphoff's (1984) approach to rural development that, among other things, emphasizes the development of strong local institutions, she found that, by managing its environmental interdependencies, the KTDA is a much more effective organization than the others in Kenya. She concludes: "Where strong and efficient institutions were created, namely KTDA, there was a clear grasp of the objectives and goals of the organization. There was also a high incentive level amongst staff and growers" (Kiereini, 1985:108).

Institutional building and development require the effective performance of the organization's critical operating tasks and, perhaps more important, its strategic management tasks. Linkages between the organization and higher, more macro levels such as government and international markets, lower, more micro levels such as small communities, and laterally to other similar organizations or groups is a very important strategic management task. It enables the organization to develop and sustain constituencies with significant stakeholders.

IX. Strategic Management Tasks in Organization Science

The study of strategic management in organizations in industrialized countries is one of the most active subfields of organization science. It deals with both the theory and the practice of strategic management tasks in private, public, and international sector organizations. In fact, some of the leading management classics like Chandler's (1962) historical analysis of the strategy-structure relationships, Barnard's (1938) account of the functions of the effective executive, Sloan's (1963) analysis of General Motor's divisionalized structural form, and Mintzberg's (1973) empirical analysis of the "nature of managerial work" all focus on better understanding of strategic management and improvements in the effective performance of strategic management tasks.

Today, strategic management studies are highly sophisticated and grounded in theory, examining a wide range of issues which include: conceptual and operational problems (Andrews, 1971); implementation strategies (Hrebiniak and Joyce, 1984); mutuality of influence and adaptation between the organization and its task environment (Pfeffer, 1982); the changing top-level strategic management priorities in different stages of the organization's life cycle in the private sector firms (Smith, Mitchell, and Summer, 1985); and state-owned enterprises (Hafsi, Kiggundu, and Jorgensen, 1987).

The McGill University group on strategic management led by Henry Mintzberg has worked on various aspects of business and public sector management. These studies cover areas such as conceptual and definitional clarification of strategic management, strategic tracking and formulation in business (Mintzberg and Waters, 1982), and public sector organizations such as a national film board (Mintzberg and McHugh, 1985), a national airline (Mintzberg, Brunet, and Waters, 1987), and a university setting (Hardy et al., 1983). In general, these studies distinguish between deliberate and emergent strategies and contradict the traditional view that strategy management is a logical, carefully planned, rational process. Instead, Mintzberg and Waters (1985) and their coworkers see strategy as an emergent and not necessarily deliberate process. These studies also suggest that strategy formulation need not necessarily precede implementation and that it can exist without the efforts of a central planning agency. Brunsson (1985) has extended these views by arguing for irrationality as a basis for action and change in organizations. For those who claim that organizations in developing countries are unable to utilize modern management thought because it is grounded in rationality, which is inherently in conflict with traditional societies, Brunsson offers an interesting conceptual rejoinder.

These studies may have interesting implications for strategic management in developing countries where the approach toward public policy management (strategy formulation and implementation) is almost exclusively rational, logical, formalized, planned, and highly centralized at the highest level of government. They seem to suggest that more attention should be paid to the informal, participative processes of strategic formation and implementation in the management of organizations in developing countries. For example, a comparative analysis of emergent and deliberate strategies for state-owned enterprises might reveal interesting differences that could then be related to the operational and strategic effectiveness of these organizations.

All business schools require their undergraduate and graduate students to take at least one course in strategic management (often called Business Policy or Strategic Management) before they can graduate. Among periodicals in the specialty, the *Strategic Management Journal* is published bimonthly by John Wiley in order to provide "the leading forum for advancing strategic management theory and practice." In addition, Robert B. Lamb of New York University edits an on-going series called *Advances in Strategic Management*, which reports on current advances in the theory and practice in strategic management (Lamb, 1985). There are no equivalent publications or formal courses that focus attention on the operating tasks.

Within organizations, current efforts are increasingly being directed toward the integration of strategic management with the traditional line functions. Consequently, the literature is now replete with intervention theories and methods relating to strategic human resource management (Fombrun, Tichy, and Devanna, 1984), strategic marketing management (Aaker, 1984; Cady and Buzzell, 1986), strategic international management (Doz, 1986), strategic organization development (OD) (Tichy, 1983), and strategic decision support systems (SDSS) (David, 1986: chap. 10). All these studies demonstrate how pervasive strategic management has become in the running of organizations. They also clearly show that it is not enough for line managers to be technically competent within their own functional areas; they must, in addition, be able to relate the function to the effective performance of the organization's relevant strategic management tasks. In the United States, industrial organizations are turning to effective applications of strategic management as a response to international competition, especially from Japan.

In Europe, strategic management research and practice are quite active fields. For example, in a recent ten-year study based at the Bradford Management Centre and the Netherlands Institute for Advanced Study in Humanities and Social Sciences, my colleagues David Cray and Geoffrey Mallory and their co-workers (Hickson et al., 1986) have tracked down 150 case histories of top-level strategic decision making in public and private organizations. Although they found variations across organization types in the making of decisions associated with the performance of various strategic management tasks, the study results show wide acceptance of strategic management in these organizations. It also confirms the importance of extraorganizational considerations in the performance of strategic management tasks.

A recent World Bank report also confirms the wide acceptance of strategic management in European organizations. In a review of strategic planning and management experiences of 90 organizations equally distributed between the United States and Europe, the report found that strategic management is common among all organizations surveyed and that these organizations increasingly use more sophisticated strategic management models and techniques like cross-impact analysis and scenario-building. The report also found that strategic management is more effectively implemented by progressive organizations who are responding to accelerating rates of change and increasing competition from the environment, especially since 1980. Emphasizing how critical strategic management tasks are for the survival of organizations, the report observed that "strategic management has come to be seen as an essential goal for organizations to learn and develop, to maintain their excellence, to remain responsive, even to survive" (Hanna, 1985:80). Regrettably, this review did not include organizations from developing countries.

X. Role of the Board of Directors in the Performance of COTs and SMATs

The structure, composition, and role of the board of directors remains one of the most controversial issues in the management of organizations in both industrialized and developing countries. Four of the most controversial facets relate to representation, function, composition, and effectiveness of the board. In assessing these facets, we must always remember that the board of directors, trustees, or governors, as the case may be, is part of the organization's structure and that, as a management tool, its ultimate objective is to make the most effective contribution possible to the performance of the organization's strategic management and critical operating tasks.

Representation refers to the question of whose interests the board represents. A capitalist institution in origin, the board serves as an instrument for the protection of shareholders' interests. Williamson, using the contractual approach, observes that ". . . the principal function of the board remains that of providing governance structure protection for the shareholders" (1985:317). Others, however, see the board as representing a wider audience and becoming an instrument of representative democracy. Evidence also suggests that if a board limits its focus only to shareholders' interests, it may lose its vitality. For example, in Venezuela, "If the board primarily represents capital . . . without experience of the particular industry involved . . . the board is inefficient as a method of influencing the policy or administration of the Company" (Bacon and Brown, 1977:317). Following the German example of *Mitbestimmung* (workers' participation), a number of developing countries including Tanzania, Cuba, Algeria, and Venezuela have provisions for workers' representatives on company boards. Experience from these as well as European countries shows, however, that workers from the shop floor often lack the training, experience, background, and confidence to make a genuine contribution to boardroom deliberations and decision making, and to the effective performance of the organization's strategic management tasks. Although the role and functions of the board vary across organizations, a study of 17 Venezuelan companies found that the director's role was:

> . . . policy determination and planning; oversight—of the interests of the shareholders, of management performance, of major decisions such as mergers and acquisitions, important borrowing, and sale of assets, of the execution of policy and plans; and the election, appraisal and, as needed, dismissal of senior management, particularly the chief executive officer. (Bacon and Brown, 1977:134)

The study clearly indicates that the board can and should contribute to the performance of the organization's strategic management tasks as well as to the monitoring and evaluation of those tasks. Often less appreciated is the potential for the board also to make an important contribution to the planning, monitoring, and evaluation of the performance of the organization's critical operating tasks.

The determination of the appropriate role, structure, and composition of the board should begin with a clear statement of the organization's mission, goals, and objectives. Figure 3.3 shows the relationships between the contributions of inside board members and those of outside board members to the organization's COTs and SMATs resulting from its mission statement. As members of senior management, inside board members have more intimate knowledge and experience about the internal operations of the organization—its operating technology, markets, social relations, and industry knowledge. Therefore, they can better contribute to the performance of the organization's COTs. Outside directors, who have many outside contacts and are in tune with the sentiments, rumors, gossip, and general changes in the outside environment, are more strategically placed to make contributions to the SMATs. Such strengths do not imply that inside directors do not contribute to strategic management tasks or that outside directors do not contribute to the critical operating tasks. Indeed, inside directors often formulate the initial strategic plans and initiate board deliberations, and outside directors, depending on their technical background, can take initiatives to assist the

Figure 3.3

**THE BOARD OF DIRECTORS AND ITS CONTRIBUTIONS TO THE
ORGANIZATION'S MISSION, COTs AND SMATs**

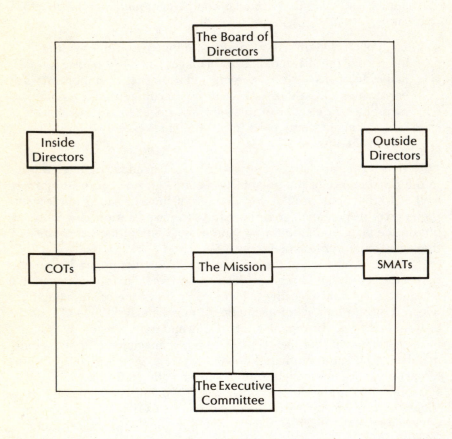

COTs = Critical Operating Tasks SMATs = Strategic Management Tasks

organization to improve the performance of its critical operating tasks. The executive committee, if one exists, undertakes the internal strategic management tasks, supervises the performance of the critical operating tasks, and provides the link between the board and the rest of the organization.

Questions are often raised about the effectiveness with which boards perform their statutory and management functions. It is generally believed that boards both in industrialized and developing countries are not as effective and accountable as they need to be. Board ineffectiveness is often caused by the following problems: (1) lack of information about the management, operations, limitations, and capabilities of the organization; (2) lack of up-to-date industry knowledge and information; (3) lack of competency and confidence to pass judgment on executive decisions; (4) inability or unwillingness to confront management; and (5) lack of time, motivation, and technical or administrative support to attend to the organization's business.

Evidence also suggests that the effectiveness of boards differs from function to function such that they are more effective in providing information from the environment relevant for strategic management tasks, but less effective in contributing to the organization's critical operating tasks. Bacon and Brown, quoting a Venezuelan director who evaluated the performance of that country's board of directors, observed the board to be: ". . . 35 per cent effective for establishing policies and approval of major matters such as sales of assets, major credits, and mergers and acquisitions; 60 per cent effective for electing and dismissing the chief executive; and 80 per cent effective for providing environmental information to the executives and representing the company" (1977:134).

These problems can be overcome and board effectiveness can be enhanced as an organization's resource, if the board is properly managed. Like any other resource, the board needs to be effectively managed and utilized, by, for example, the careful selection, briefing, training, directing, and, if necessary, supervision of its members for the performance of its respective tasks. Board members should be chosen only on the basis of their potential contribution to the organization's current demands for its strategic management and critical operating tasks, by means of careful analysis of the organization's mission, the resources available inside the organization for implementing the mission, and the management gaps that need to be filled. Training, briefing, and orientation can provide new board members with the knowledge, confidence, and frame of mind necessary for effective board deliberations and decision making. European countries including West Germany and Sweden which require boards to include workers' representatives have held regular training programs with considerable success. Such programs should be mandatory for organizations in developing countries whose directors have no previous relevant experiences.

Board membership should be protected so as to provide continuity, especially when, as often happens in developing countries, executive turnover is high. Unfortunately, available evidence suggests that board membership is equally unstable. For example, the Venezuelan survey showed that the average median term of office for the directors was only two years. Overlapping directorships should be kept to a minimum, especially in state-owned enterprises, because, in addition to overburdening the board members and therefore preventing them from contributing effectively to the performance of the organization's tasks, they create more opportunities for bribery and personal gains. In state-owned enterprises, civil servant directors should be kept to a minimum so as to create a more balanced combination of specialists, generalists, and ideologists. Finally, the personal and professional attributes of the chief executive officer and the chairman of the board, their leadership qualities, and the manner in which they work together and with other board members and senior managers, are all important considerations for making the board an effective management institution.

XI. COTs and SMATs: The Integrated Model

The critical operating tasks (COTs) and the strategic management tasks (SMATs) subsystems have thus far been presented separately. In this section, the two subsystems are integrated into a complete organization model. The model can be used to improve understanding of how organizations work, to do basic organization science research, and to provide a guide for organizational diagnosis and intervention.

Figure 3.4 shows the strategic management and critical operating task dimensions of the organization. The four quadrants represent extreme positions of how well (high) or badly (low) an organization may be performing its critical operating tasks and strategic management tasks at any given time. Quadrant 1 reflects an extreme situation in which the organization's performance of its COTs and SMATs is inefficient and ineffective, respectively. It implies an unclear strategic mission or plan and ineffective operations suggesting organizational failure, decline, and possible demise. In this quadrant, the organization would face pressures from within as well as from the outside environment as those associated with it became unable to meet their expectations. Employee morale would be poor and outside stakeholders would be equally dissatisfied and asking for reform. The organization's continued survival would be threatened.

Rosalie Tung, in a study of China's more than 400,000 industrial enterprises, describes the problems associated with both their strategic man-

Figure 3.4

STRATEGIC MANAGEMENT AND OPERATING TASK DIMENSIONS OF THE ORGANIZATION

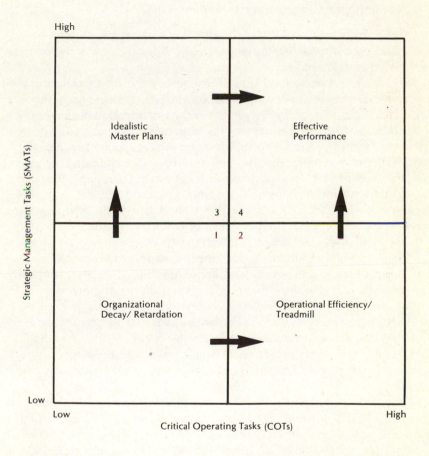

agement and their critical operating tasks:

> . . . bottlenecks in operations; the production of certain com-
> modities that had no immediate market; the production of de-
> sirable production in insufficient quantities; excessive delays in
> decision making; and a spirit of unhealthy complacency
> among certain managers and workers in the industrial enter-
> prises because state-owned enterprises were not treated as in-
> dependent accounting units and hence not responsible for
> their own profit and loss . . . the concept of marketing was
> foreign to the Chinese industrial scene. (1987:141)

These problems would tend to push these enterprises toward quadrant 1 and would most likely precipitate a call for reform by the owners
and powerful stakeholders.

Quadrant 2 represents a situation whereby the organization is efficiently performing its operating tasks but not its strategic management
tasks. This is a common difficulty for many an organization because, since
its operations are doing well, it gives the impression of a successful organization. Since the organization's mission and strategic plans are at best unclear, with no systematic allocation of resources, determination of priorities, or guidelines for strategic decisions or choices, the organization faces
an uncertain future. Although the internal operating systems may be efficient, the organization has become merely a treadmill, with no clear
vision of its future: what it will be doing, what it will look like, what resources it will need, and how it is to achieve them.

Management consultants report finding many organizations in quadrant 2. Senior managers have a false sense of security, because it usually
takes a significant change, either internally within the organization or, as
is often the case, from the outside environment in the form of a potential
threat or missed opportunity, for the organization to become aware of its
strategic management limitations. In the long run, if the organization
does not address its strategic management tasks, and thus moves out of
quadrant 2, the performance of its critical operating tasks could also begin
to suffer.

Quadrant 3 represents a situation in which the organization's internal
operations (COTs) are inefficient but it has a clear sense of mission, plans,
and objectives. Management has a clear vision for the organization but
does not have the capacity to attain it. That is, the organization has an
idealistic master plan but lacks the internal technical core to turn these
ideals into action. Examples of organizations in this quadrant include
small start-up business firms where the entrepreneur may have a clear
vision of the infant business but lacks organizational resources for the required operations. Unsuccessful newly created state-owned enterprises
can also be found in this quadrant with clear official statements of the cor-

poration's mission and direction, but without the ability to develop the technical core commensurate with the stated mission. This is the infant state-owned enterprise (Hafsi et al., 1987) that is unable to perform its critical operating tasks and measures its performance only in symbolic terms. National development plans for developing countries also create situations for organizations similar to those reflected by quadrant 3. The documents provide articulate statements of where the country wants to be three to five years down the road and goals the individual sectors, industries, or organizations will be expected to achieve in that period of time. However, most of these ambitious plans are rarely achieved mainly because the individual organizations within these countries do not have the capacity to perform the necessary critical operating tasks. Like quadrant 1, quadrant 3 is very risky for independent private sector organizations, whose survival depends only on their ability to produce and exchange goods and services with the environment. If they cannot produce, they cannot survive. In practice, very few organizations would survive in quadrant 3.

Quadrant 4 represents an ideal situation in which the organization excels in its performance of both its critical operating and strategic management tasks. Although it is only an ideal in the Weberian sense as it cannot be achieved in its absolute, organizations strive toward reaching it. Moreover, it is not a static frozen position but a dynamic process reflecting changes both within the organization and in the external general and specific task environments. Management responds to these constant changes by striving to establish an optimal balance between the performance of the critical operating and strategic management tasks. We can now understand the phenomenon, often observed by both researchers and experienced managers, that organizations seek to protect their critical operating task subsystem (technical core) from outside environmental disturbances. Leaving both operating and strategic management task subsystems exposed to the environment would introduce too much uncertainty and complexity. Because management cannot have any reasonable control over changes in the outside environment, the most realistic option is to build buffers behind the critical operating task subsystem. These buffers reduce or eliminate organizational porosity. As William Dyer (1983) observed, if you have a clear strategic mission and plan of action, and if your operations are efficiently performed, you have a high possibility of organizational success.

The model depicted in Figure 3.4 can be used for several organizational purposes: (1) it provides a structure for understanding how the organization works and is structured; (2) it can also be a conceptual framework for doing basic organization science research; (3) it can be a framework for preliminary organization diagnosis, for example, by assessing the extent to which the dimensions of the COTs and SMATs are adequately performed and whether or not they contribute to the achievement of the organization's mission, goals, and objectives; (4) the model can be a guide for the selection of interventional tools and methods for organizational improvements; and (5) it can be the basis for evaluation and impact assessment of organization change and development initiatives. If the intervention has no significant impact on the performance of either the COTs or SMATs, perhaps it is of no consequence for the organization.

The model provides a framework for adding meaning to many current discussions in development administration and organization science. Public management reforms in developing countries can be analyzed for each organization by examining the performance and integration of their COTs and SMATs, as outlined by the model. Organizational innovation can also be discussed using this model. For example, it is often stated that organizations with a record of successful innovations are more likely to succeed in introducing new innovations than those with little or no history of innovations. We can now be more specific and state that, if an organization has had previous experience in introducing innovations in the performance of the COTs or SMATs, new innovations will be more successful in the same innovative subsystem. If the innovations have been limited to one task subsystem and not the other, the risk of failure in the noninnovating subsystems will be significantly higher and perhaps as high as in the noninnovating organizations. Innovations in organizations in developing countries do not have high success rates because their COTs and SMATs subsystems do not have a history of frequent innovations. One needs to establish a pattern, an organizational learning and knowledge base, a critical mass of innovators in each of the task subsystems, and an internal innovative culture or climate within the organization.

Mariann Jelinek developed a corporate-wide system for innovation based on the OST (objectives, strategies, tactics) model. She then tested it with data collected from Texas Instruments, an elite American electronics firm known for its leadership in technological and management innovations. Emphasizing the need for innovative learning and behavior in both subsystems of the organization, she wrote: "Because lower-level managers are necessarily involved in generating strategic plans no less than implementing them, typically while also carrying on operational activities, they quickly begin to see management as both strategic and operational" (Jelinek, 1981:564).

The COTs/SMATs model presented here is powerful because it provides an explanation for some of the commonly observed phenomena in organizations in developing countries. On the positive side, national and local institutions succeed when they have strong institutional linkages with similar institutions abroad (e.g., the International Rice Research Institute). International joint ventures succeed when the overseas partner has the capacity and motivation to assist the local firm to enhance its own and the partnership's critical operating and strategic management tasks, and export-based firms such as international airlines and tourist organizations succeed because the international marketing conditions necessitate the development of effective task performance systems to enable these firms to remain internationally competitive. Development projects "succeed" during the period in which they are run like "sheltered experiments" with their critical operating tasks effectively performed by a system totally dependent on technical assistance. Finally, in sectors such as urban transport, small, private, independent operators have been reported to outperform large public companies because the former pay special attention to reducing the costs of operations (COTs), and because they are so small that they do not need to be concerned with complex strategic management tasks. Instead, if the industry becomes unprofitable, highly regulated, or too complex, they just exit into other sectors, a move the bigger companies cannot make.

On the negative side, the model can explain a number of typical organizational pathologies. Nationalized subsidiaries of international companies fail because nationalization deprives them of both the critical operating and strategic management tasks support that they used to enjoy from their overseas headquarters. Newly created state-owned enterprises fail because they lack the capacity to develop and sustain an effective critical operating task subsystem. Development projects lack long-term sustainability because they depend on superficial, temporary critical operating systems created by foreign development agencies and because they are not properly integrated with the implementing agency's strategic management tasks. Indigenous private sector organizations fail to grow into commercially viable enterprises because they lack the necessary resources for developing and sustaining effective COTs and SMATs performance systems. Finally, social and community service organizations fail from a lack of concern for operational efficiency and strategic management.

Figure 3.5 shows the relative positions of the COTs/SMATs performance of about twenty different types of organizations commonly found in developing countries. The figure indicates that international interdependence, properly designed and implemented, can be of advantage to these organizations by enhancing the performance of their task systems. For example, the multinational-indigenous private sector firms (MNC-IPS), the international joint ventures, export-based firms, international development projects (in progress), and subsidiaries of MNCs are shown to perform relatively better than other organizations with little or no international linkages. Traditional peasant farmers lack the capacity and motivation to improve their farming practices (COTs) and to manage and plan for the future (SMATs).

The figure also shows an inverse relationship between government

Figure 3.5

**RELATIVE POSITIONS OF DIFFERENT TYPES OF ORGANIZATIONS ON
THE COTs/SMATs PERFORMANCE GRID**

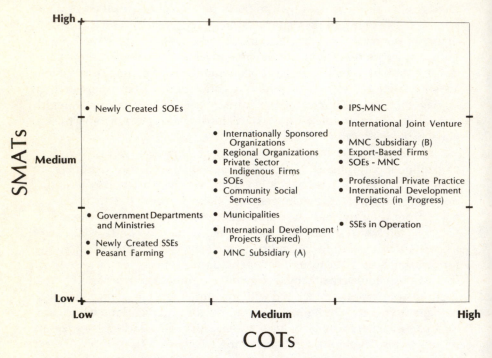

Note: COTs = Critical Operating Tasks; SMATs = Strategic Management Tasks;
        IPS-MNC = Indigenous Private Sector-Multinational Corporation;
        SOEs = State-Owned Enterprises; MNC Subsidiary A (after), B (Before) nationalization;
        SSEs = Small-Scale Enterprises.

involvement and the propensity for the organization to locate toward the top right-hand side of the grid. Of course, the grid is only illustrative. It does not imply, for example, that all international joint ventures will outperform nationalized industries or municipal utilities. It does suggest, however, these types of organizations have the potential to perform better. The figure can also be a diagnostic tool for a set of organizations either belonging to a single policy sector such as agriculture, or owned by a large state-owned holding enterprise (see Chapter Eight). It also provides as a conceptual framework for the comparative analysis of organizations in developing countries.

   In the final section of this chapter, I present illustrations of two different international organizations, operating in both industrialized and developing countries, whose *modus operandi* is similar to that of the COTs/SMATs model presented above. These firms are Decision Processes International Limited, headquartered in Montreal, Canada, with offices in 13 other countries spanning all continents, and Bell Canada International, a telecommunications consulting firm with operations in all regions of the developing world.

Decision Processes International (DPI) is a management consulting firm with offices in several developing countries including Brazil, Hong Kong, the Philippines, Singapore, and South Africa. It was established with the idea that a combination of strategic management, Schein's (1969) process consulting, and management training and development, properly packaged, would be helpful to client organizations. Its basic approach, called strategic thinking, is to assist the organization in formulating and implementing its strategic management tasks. As Michel M. Robert, the founder of the firm, explains, "Our approach to this subject, which we have chosen to call *Strategic Thinking*, has been to identify the *key factors* that dictate the *direction* of an organization together with the *process* that the management of that organization uses to set direction" (1985:1, emphasis is in original).

The company's focus on strategic management helps the client organization to define its mission, while its use of process consulting skills and training provides the organization with the management process, structures, and systems for the articulation and implementation of the mission. Although Robert and his coworkers recognize the importance of the operating tasks for the efficient management of organizations, they deliberately chose to concentrate exclusively on strategic management tasks, partly because ". . . most of the time management spends in meetings is spent discussing operational issues and not strategic ones" (Robert, 1985:18–19).

Drawing from the COTs/SMATs model and Figure 3.4 above, we can determine the organizational conditions under which DPI is likely to be successful or not. If the client organization is in quadrant 1, DPI's approach would be necessary but not sufficient for improving the effective performance of that organization. If the organization is in quadrant 3 or 4, DPI's approach would be almost redundant. Only in quadrant 2 would this approach have the best chance of successfully helping the organization to move toward quadrant 4. As pointed out above, however, quadrant 2 is probably the most densely populated and therefore provides an adequate niche for a small consulting company.

Bell Canada International (BCI) is a telecommunications and management consulting company based in Ottawa, Canada, with operations in Africa, the Middle East, the Indian Subcontinent, South East Asia, South and Central America, and the Caribbean. Its main function is to assist individual countries in the development and management of successful telecommunications organizations. In doing this, it is guided by five distinct areas that combine both critical operating and strategic management tasks. These functional areas are:[1]

1. Managing customer service (COTs) in order to ensure that business and residential customer needs are met in a timely manner and that customers receive high quality service.

2. Managing the network (COTs), which requires the development of procedures for creating and sustaining a viable telecommunications network, infrastructure, and services and for operating and maintaining them effectively.

3. Managing support services (COTs) to ensure that specialized skills and expertise are brought together in support of key operating tasks of the organization. These support services include vehicle fleet operations, building maintenance, cost effective procurement and supply procedures, finance and accounting, data processing, and general administration and supervision. Technical and administrative support functions cause serious limitations in the performance of both critical operating and strategic management tasks in organizations in developing countries. Unfortunately, these areas including clerical and secretarial services, office administration, technical support services (e.g., draftsmen, lab technicians, computer programmers and analysts, insurance adjusters) tend to be neglected in the formulation of development programs for organizations in developing countries.

4. Achieving internal management coordination (SMATs) to enable the organization to direct its efforts and resources to the attainment of its mission and to enable managers to understand how their individual jobs fit into the overall goals of the organization.

5. Managing the environment (SMATs) by which the organization communicates with its many stakeholders including employees, shareholders, customers, governments, or any other groups that have a vital interest in the organization's activities.

These five areas cover task dimensions for both the COTs and the SMATs. It would therefore appear that Bell Canada International's approach would have a high probability of success in developing effective

---

[1]This section is based on *A World Experience*, Bell Canada International, Ottawa, Canada (undated).

organizations with systems capable of sustaining the effective performance of the organizations' critical operating and strategic management tasks. Drawing its technological leadership and management expertise from Bell Canada, its parent company, BCI has been particularly successful in attracting long-term contracts not only from oil rich countries like Saudi Arabia and Indonesia, but also from the medium- and low-income developing countries of Africa and the Caribbean.

Summary

This chapter has discussed the theory and practice of strategic management tasks in developing and industrialized countries. Strategic management tasks help define the organization's uniqueness; provide a frame of reference for people inside and outside the organization to relate to it as an entity; articulate the organization's sense of purpose and direction, and give it a personality or character that distinguishes it from other organizations. The chapter discusses the need for and the current state of theory and practice of strategic management in developing and industrialized countries. Limitations to the effective performance of strategic management tasks in organizations in developing countries are also described.

The chapter outlines a framework and step-by-step process for the development and implementation of a mission statement down to the level of individual behavior. A mission statement is a brief but enduring statement of purpose which distinguishes the organization from other organizations and articulates the organization's philosophy, values, and belief systems. This framework can be used for organizational analysis and diagnosis, evaluation, and basic and action research. Six dimensions of strategic management tasks are identified and discussed.

Also discussed in the chapter is the role of the board of directors, particularly its potential contributions to the effective performance of the organization's strategic management and critical operating tasks. It has been emphasized that the ultimate purpose of the board, regardless of its composition or representation, is to assist management in the performance of the organization's important tasks. To achieve this, the board, like any other organizational resource, needs to be properly managed by, for example, careful selection, training, motivation and support of its members.

The chapter concludes by presenting an integrated organizational framework combining the critical operating tasks and the strategic management tasks. The next chapter provides a more detailed analysis of how these two task subsystems can be integrated.

CHAPTER 4

Integration of Operating
and Strategic Tasks

The previous two chapters presented the critical operating tasks and the strategic management tasks as if they were independent subsystems of the organization. They did so for analytical purposes only; in real life, these two subsystems are highly interrelated. Toward the end of Chapter Three, Figure 3.4 introduced a discussion of how the two task subsystems are integrated. This chapter gives a more detailed view of the specific integrating mechanisms used for each of the critical operating and strategic management tasks.

The first section of the chapter discusses the three types of *routine integrating mechanisms* (RIMs): (1) the hierarchy of authority; (2) standard operating procedures, and (3) alternative forms of work organization. These mechanisms, derived from the principles of classical theories of management and organization, are simple, routine, and generally available to most mature organizations. They constitute the basic elements of organization and are commonly, though not exclusively, used for integrating the critical operating tasks. The chapter will also introduce alternative forms of work organization used to alleviate some of the dysfunctional consequences of hierarchical or mechanistic structures.

The second section deals with a wide range of *complex integrating mechanisms* (CIMs), used when the internal operating and strategic management tasks are complex and when environmental uncertainty makes routine integrating mechanisms inadequate or inappropriate. Interorganizational coordinating mechanisms (IOCs) are also discussed. Both of these mechanisms are used in response to task complexity characteristic of strategic management tasks. The section ends with the presentation of the criteria used by managers in selecting integrating mechanisms for designing organizations.

The third and final section of this chapter introduces and discusses the concept of *collaborative institutional arrangements* (CIAs), which are integrating mechanisms across organizations designed to coordinate and strengthen the operating and strategic management tasks of participating organizations. Throughout the chapter, illustrations from organizations in developing countries are presented. The chapter concludes with a discussion of the criteria used in selecting appropriate integrating mechanisms for each of the task subsystems, and for the organization as a whole.

I. Routine Integrating Mechanisms

The routine integrating mechanisms (RIMs) are programmed methods of coordinating various parts of the organization. They are designed to deal with simple, repetitive, predictable task requirements between two or more workers. They are simple to administer and are relatively inexpensive. The three types of RIMS—the hierarchy of authority, standard operating procedures, and alternative forms of work organization—are each described below.

1. The Hierarchy of Authority

Every organization has a hierarchy of authority that differentiates among the various levels of the organization and provides a formal link integrating the critical operating tasks and the strategic management tasks. The hierarchical lines represent channels of communication and interdependence through which coordination can be achieved both within and between the two task subsystems. The hierarchy is also vested with power, expertise, authority, and responsibility such that higher officers, by virtue of their positions, can send directives to lower officers and expect compliance and obedience.

Figure 4.1 shows that the hierarchical responsibility is cumulative from the lowest operator to the chief executive officer and the board of directors. The temporal dimensions indicating the time span of responsibility for different hierarchical positions are also cumulative. For example, while the shift supervisor is responsible only for the shift's production cycle, the general manager is ultimately responsible for all temporal dimensions encompassed by that position, including the annual production cycles (e.g., budgets), seasonal production cycles, quarterly returns, even the moment-by-moment operations at the individual work station. The figure shows that the responsibility for the spatial dimensions depicting the work environment for different hierarchical levels is also cumulative. For example, while the lead hand is responsible for only the work station and the immediate surrounding area, the chief operating officer is responsible for all organizational facilities as well as different aspects of the environment outside the organization. It is for this reason that the chief executive officer of every organization is ultimately accountable for the day-to-day events taking place at individual work stations as well as the events likely to take place ten years or more in the future in the general or specific task environment that will have an effect on the organization.

Figure 4.1

The Organization Hierarchy of Authority:
CUMULATIVE RESPONSIBILITY AS A FUNCTION OF SPATIAL AND TEMPORAL DIMENSIONS

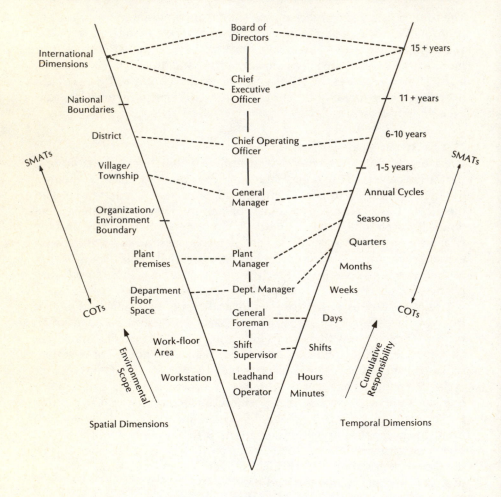

COTs = Critical Operating Tasks; SMATs = Strategic Management Tasks.

In practical terms, for example, the chief executive officer of a rice-growing organization in the Philippines is responsible for the day-to-day field operations as well as for reacting appropriately to those events that happen in the world today and in the future that affect the international production, processing, marketing, and consumption of rice. The chief executive officer is ultimately responsible for integrating all the operating and strategic management tasks of the organization. The hierarchy is one of the organization's resources designed to assist the chief executive officer to fulfill all these multidimensional responsibilities.

Organizations use a variety of methods to make the hierarchy more effective. These include: (1) creating staff positions; (2) varying the span of control; (3) varying the number of hierarchical levels from top to bottom; and (4) training and providing socialization of all members of the organization who deal with the organization through its hierarchy (e.g., employees, clients, the public).

Large organizations in developing countries tend to have tall structures with many hierarchical levels, and they tend to depend on the hierarchy as the single most important integrating mechanism. In these organizations, the hierarchy is often weak, partly because of shortage of administrative and management skills and expertise, and partly because of the extraorganizational disturbances that affect the smooth running of the hierarchy. For the small scale enterprises that are of increasing importance in most regions of the developing world, the hierarchy is both weak and underdeveloped. As a recent World Bank report by John Page and William Steel (1984) indicates, small-scale entrepreneurs operate with little or no hierarchical structures as a way of conserving scarce managerial expertise. For these and similarly underorganized organizations, the hierarchy is not an important integrating mechanism and, because they are small in size, their needs for integration or coordination are very limited indeed.

Close Supervision. Close supervision is a system common in many production enterprises in which the supervisor takes direct responsibility for the work of subordinates. While the subordinates do the actual work, the supervisor does the coordination with other parts of the organization. The subordinates have no responsibility for coordination of their work, even among themselves. Close supervision is labor intensive and highly personalized. It relies on the formal hierarchy to communicate information to and from different parts of the organization with the supervisor as the most critical element in receiving, encoding, sending, and acting on messages as they come in from or go out to different parts of the organization. Under the principle of close supervision, the supervisor is constantly and physically the person in charge. Bowen describes this kind of supervision: "The operational side of his work deals with administration, the getting things done. Men and machines have to be kept at work, materials obtained at the right time and the finished product kept flowing through" (1971:14).

For close supervision to be effective, both in getting the work done and in coordinating the various parts of the organization, it must adhere to a number of conditions. Some of these conditions are:

1. The supervisor must be technically competent in all the jobs being closely supervised.

2. The supervisor must have effective administrative skills for activities such as planning, organizing, staffing, directing, coordinating, reporting, and budgeting (POSDCORB). These functions are particularly important for performance and fulfillment of the integration and coordination roles required of the close supervisor. These functions originate from the work of classical management writers such as Henry Fayol (1949) and Gulick and Urwick (1954) but still remain with us in both theory and practice.

3. The supervisor must be effective in human relations skills, including coaching, interviewing, communicating, counseling, motivating, and giving and receiving feedback both in interpersonal one-to-one relationships and in small groups. These are crucial because supervision often contributes to conditions for poorly designed or very routine jobs lacking in motivation for the subordinates and therefore human relations skills are necessary in order for the close supervisor to deal with the consequent morale problems. The supervisor should have the capacity to protect the work unit's vital core from undue environmental interference while at the same time seeking opportunities in the environment and within the organization for beneficial collaborative institutional arrangements.

4. The supervisor should have leadership qualities and skills. Such a person should at least be able to command the respect of the subordinates and other members of the organization. He or she should have the skills to diagnose situations and take decisive action.

5. The subordinates themselves should be able and willing to work under close supervision. Close supervision can induce stressful working conditions for the subordinates, particularly because the supervisor is constantly watching to make sure that the work gets done and is moved to the next department or work station. This surveillance causes animosity, hostility, and conflict between the supervisor and the subordinates. Mechanisms for re-

solving conflict and alleviating work stress should be in place if the organization wants to use close supervision as an effective integrating mechanism.

6. Finally, certain conditions in the organization either facilitate or impinge on the effective use of close supervision. Both the supervisor and the subordinates must be in the same physical space in order to facilitate close supervision. Where this is not possible, either because of plant/office layout, or because of geographically dispersed work stations, close supervision would be highly restricted, as remote and isolated work stations are not conducive to close supervision. Span of control—the number of people directly reporting to the same supervisor—can also be a limiting factor for close supervision. As the supervisor is expected to watch the subordinates constantly, there is a natural limit to how many subordinates he or she can supervise. The narrower the span of control—the number of subordinates per supervisor— the more effective close supervision is likely to be. Jobs requiring individual initiative and creativity are not suitable for close supervision.

In summary, close supervision is limited to routine jobs for which progress can be monitored externally by the supervisor, the jobs can be clustered together in one or a few physical places, the close supervisor is highly skilled and motivated, and subordinates' attributes are suited to the characteristics of the particular types of jobs.

For organizations in developing countries, close supervision should appeal to management because it is consistent with a management philosophy that makes a clear distinction and separation of tasks between management and the worker. This philosophy is prevalent in many organizations in the developing world. Research has shown (e.g., Negandhi, 1979) that close supervision is indeed practiced in many situations in these organizations. Although the reasons for this choice are not exactly clear, I suspect that close supervision is used as a way of putting pressure on the workers to get the job done and not necessarily as an integrative or coordinating mechanism.

Whatever the motivation, there are limitations to utilizing close supervision in organizations in developing countries. The acute shortage of supervisors with the requisite knowledge, skills, and motivation for close supervision is a serious limiting factor. In addition, the demands for close supervision are much more stringent than those for the generalized supervisory positions. Before close supervision can become a realistic option for most of these organizations, enough people must be carefully selected, trained in both technical and supervisory skills, socialized, and given proper indoctrination consistent with the organization's management philosophy. Likewise, the subordinates must be selected and trained so that they are capable of working effectively under close supervision. This strategy of organizational human resource development is slow and needs patience and perseverance.

Obviously, close supervision has problems and limitations; even if enough close supervisors and subordinates were available to these organizations, there would still be difficulties. Problems associated with job design, morale, remote locations, and span of control have already been discussed. Close supervision also inhibits employee creativity and the organization's capacity for innovation. In fact, it is in response to some of these problems that organizations in industrialized countries have attempted to abandon close supervision in favor of more humanistic participative approaches to supervision and management. Under the acronym of QWL (quality of working life), these approaches have attempted to enrich the subordinates' jobs, often at the expense of the supervisor (Kiggundu, 1984). Although attempts have been made to introduce QWL into organizations in developing countries (Kiggundu, 1986; Trist, 1975), there are those (i.e., Mintzberg, 1979) who are quite skeptical about the efficacy of QWL in dealing with the negative practical effects of traditional management at the workplace.

2. Standard Operating Procedures

The second type of routine integrating mechanism (RIM) is standard operating procedures (SOPs). The term standard operating procedures is used here broadly to include rules, policies and procedures, plans, budgets, goals, and standardization. Like the hierarchy of authority, SOPs are particularly suited for the more predictable, repetitive, or less complex tasks. These tend to be particularly, but not exclusively the critical operating tasks, although some strategic management tasks like corporate planning can be coordinated by use of the SOPs.

Rules, Policies, and Regulations   Rules, policies, and regulations provide common codified and publicly known methods of dealing with specific organizational decisions or problems. They are designed to reduce the work pressure from the hierarchy by allowing lower level officers to make decisions that would otherwise be pushed high up in the hierarchy. This practice serves the dual purpose of freeing up the more senior officers and their channels of communication to process information and attend to nonroutine, novel, and more complex problems of the organization. It also facilitates decentralization and delegation of authority so that lower level officers can make important decisions within the framework provided by the rules, policies, and procedures.

If the rules are not observed, or if they are inconsistent or irrelevant to most important organizational events, then the hierarchy becomes over-loaded with work as junior officers constantly consult their superiors for advice and decisions. This state creates serious performance bottlenecks leading to inefficiency and ineffectiveness in the performance and integra-tion of both types of organizational tasks (COTs and SMATs). Rules can be abused during their interpretation or application and, although junior of-ficers are expected to exercise judgment in utilizing organizational rules, senior officers should monitor these applications to minimize incidents of intended or unintended abuses.

Organizations in developing countries face problems of dated or in-appropriate rules, policies, and procedures. Even if the rules are current and relevant, they are sometimes not fairly and consistently interpreted or applied. A management resource audit of a national financial institu-tion that I recently conducted in Africa showed almost total breakdown of institutional rules and business procedures and practices. Accordingly, management was unable to ensure satisfactory performance of the organi-zation's various critical operating tasks. However, when rules are clear, fair, relevant, and properly applied, they reduce role conflict and role am-biguity, clarify expectations, and control and coordinate individual and group behavior at different levels of the organization.

Plans, Budgets, and Goals.   Plans, budgets, and goals specify, in measurable terms, the performance requirements for the whole organiza-tion and its various subunits right down to the level of the individual operator. They regulate the work interdependencies among the different units within and between the operating and strategic management tasks by providing specific input and output performance requirements. For example, a detailed sales budget can indicate quite precisely the required level of production for the manufacturing department, the quality and quantity of materials needed for the purchasing agents, the required working capital for the accounting department, and the skill levels and numbers of employees required for the personnel department. The budget would therefore integrate the work of all these departments and their respective critical operating tasks while management would under-take internal management and supervision to ensure effective overall or-ganization performance in accordance with the budget. Management would also use the budget to monitor internal organizational perfor-mance and assess changes in the environment to determine whether or not they need to make adjustments to the budget and therefore to the internal interdependencies.

Plans and budgets should be realistic and achievable. They must be perceived by the employees to constitute realistic expectations of levels of performance. Unrealistic plans lose their integrative capacity because in-dividual organizational units disregard them in the performance of their respective tasks. That the plans are perceived to be unrealistic by some of the units in the organization can be a source of conflict, as it creates work flow imbalances, especially between the interdependent organization units that meet their planned targets and those that do not.

As research has shown (Wildavsky, 1972), organizations in developing countries do not use budgets and plans as integrating mechanisms as effectively as in industrialized countries. Several explanations can be offered. First, plans and budgets in these organizations are usually not taken seriously. The perception among employees is that such plans are either unrealistic or irrelevant given the organization's internal resources and the external environmental constraints it faces. These perceptions are particularly reinforced if in its past, as is often the case, the organization has consistently been unable to meet its planned targets and live within its budget. Second, plans and budgets may be deliberately ignored by management, which believes that the organization's environment is changing so much that plans and budgets would be out of date before they are published. This attitude is particularly prevalent for organizations in developing countries facing high levels of inflation or political instability where working capital budgets and annual business plans would become obsolete only months after they have been developed.

Third, the organization may lack internal management resources and discipline to make and live up to the requirements of the plans and budgets. Plans require effective monitoring, control, and management information systems to enable management to enforce plan compliance for the different units of the organization. Most organizations in developing countries would not have the resources to develop and maintain these systems. Consequently, management would be unable to obtain the necessary information to coordinate the activities of the various task subunits in accordance with the requirements of the plan and budget targets. Most small- and medium-sized organizations do not have the capital or management expertise to develop and effectively utilize these plans as integrative management tools.

Another limiting factor that is common for organizations in both developing and industrialized countries is the ineffective communication of the plans and budgets down to the operating levels in a language that all understand and identify with. Organizations generally experience difficulties in communicating plans, budgets, the rationale behind them, and their implementation. These difficulties become more serious for the lower levels of the hierarchy, particularly in organizations in which these plans are developed only by top management with little or no participation or involvement from their lower levels. In response to these problems, some organizations adopt participative forms of management like management by objectives (MBO) whereby plans and budgets are developed jointly between the individual employee and his or her immediate supervisor. This bottom-up approach to planning increases understanding, involvement, and acceptance of the plans by employees and managers. When plans and budgets are understood and accepted by the employees at different levels of the organization, they become more effective management integrating mechanisms both within and between the operating and strategic management tasks.

Organization plans can, however, be an effective source of employee motivation, especially if they clarify task requirements, provide challenging but attainable goals and timely and relevant performance feedback, and relate to the organization's reward and incentive systems.

Standardization.   In addition to applying plans and rules, an organization can standardize its operating procedures. Standardization is the extent to which the requirements and processes for the performance of the organization's tasks are specified in advance and performed in such a way that there is uniformity and comparability across jobs and different parts of the organization. Standardization reduces variability and increases predictability. Organizations pay a lot of attention to standardization because it improves efficiency and predictability, and reduces costs and the need for coordination. Like other routine integrating mechanisms (RIMs), standardization is particularly suitable for routine, repetitive, or predictable events characteristic of operating tasks (COTs). Organizations strive to standardize within four different areas: (1) inputs; (2) transformation processes; (3) outputs; and (4) knowledge, skills, values, beliefs, and attitudes.

When an organization states its mission, it automatically implies the nature of inputs that it must obtain from the environment to meet its mission. These inputs are usually of a rather narrow specified range as the organization determines the specifications and attributes of acceptable inputs. Although organizations differ in regard to how much variability of inputs they should accept, most find it advantageous to limit the range so that they can accurately predict and effectively control the behavior of the inputs at different stages of the production process. Inputs that are normally highly standardized include raw materials, clients, equipment, machinery and tools, land, especially in the case of agricultural organizations, human resources, and capital.

The purchasing department of a manufacturing organization, or the admission offices of human services organizations spend a lot of effort checking and testing to make sure that the raw materials conform to the organization's standard specifications. Likewise, these departments order machinery, equipment, and tools according to specifications designed to fit with the internal production requirements of the organization. The organization's recruitment and selection efforts are designed to assure that only people with certain attributes or traits join the organization as employees. Once these inputs are standardized, it becomes relatively easy to coordinate the activities of other units that process the inputs into outputs. Input standardization can be so important for an organization that it may decide to integrate vertically and make its own inputs, or it may otherwise control those who supply its inputs so as to ensure conformity with its specifications for standardization. In performing and integrating its critical operating tasks, an organization must make a tradeoff between investing in operating systems for restricting the range of inputs allowed in the vital core, and developing the internal capacity to deal with input variability while at the same time achieving acceptable output standards.

The transformation process turns inputs into outputs. It involves organizing, combining, and processing various inputs to produce outputs, and it is one of the most standardized parts of the organization. In a manufacturing organization, the core of the transformation process is the manufacturing plant and its facilities. In a government department, the transformation processes involve the implementation and administration of plans and programs, provision of services to the public, enforcement of rules and regulations, and maintenance and protection of public assets and interests. These tasks require practical knowledge of government procedures and regulations. They are highly mechanical and routine, and all transactions are regulated according to preprogrammed standard treatment. The transformation process is buffered from outside environmental disturbances to ensure standardization of treatments and outputs. The three challenges involved in the management of the transformation process are to ensure that only inputs of a given standard specification are allowed in, that treatments on transformation materials are administered according to preprogrammed specifications, and that only outputs that meet certain specifications are allowed out. This method of standardization provides effective and inexpensive coordination among the various production stages of the organization.

Output standardization is achieved by standardization of the inputs and the transformation processes and by effective quality control. Quality control ensures that outputs that do not meet the organization's standards, in spite of the standardization of inputs and transformation processes, are not allowed to leave the organization. The sales force can also be trained to detect defective outputs and to provide customers with replacements in case their original purchases were defective. In this way, standardization can provide the necessary coordination among the various parts of the organization including purchasing (inputs), production (transformation processes), and quality control and sales and distribution (outputs).

The fourth area is standardization of knowledge, skills, beliefs, attitudes, and values among the various members of the organization. Unlike other forms of standardization, this one is equally applicable to the critical operating and to strategic management tasks. Standardization based on the establishment of common knowledge and attitudes is not necessarily limited only to employees, except in the closed or partially closed task systems sometimes found in the operating tasks or technical core. It includes various interest groups (e.g., customers, suppliers, farmers, politicians), especially in those aspects of the organization like the strategic management tasks which necessitate contact and interaction with the outside environment. The purpose of this type of standardization is to reduce human behavioral variability, to increase control and predictability, and to provide relatively inexpensive and reliable coordinating mechanisms across different parts of the organization over a relatively long period of time.

The methods of achieving standardization of knowledge, beliefs, and attitudes are quite specific. They include formal and informal training, briefing, indoctrination, socialization, culturalization, articulation of a management philosophy, and maintenance of incentive systems that reinforce the learning, acquiring, and utilization of the desired knowledge, skills, and attitudes. These methods are effective in bringing about the desired changes in knowledge, skills, and attitudes. They are difficult to maintain, however, because of changes within the organization that may lead to different knowledge requirements, changes in the outside environment, and changes in the employees themselves.

For most mature organizations and established bureaucracies, standardization of knowledge, skills, and attitudes for the performance and coordination of operating tasks requires relatively little formal training but a lot of on-the-job training and indoctrination. In combination with the hierarchy of authority, rules, plans, and other forms of standardization, they can achieve effective and relatively inexpensive coordination of the critical operating tasks by using routine integrating mechanisms (RIMs).

Standardization of knowledge and attitudes for strategic management tasks requires relatively long periods of training, socialization, and "grooming." Socialization is particularly important in order to ensure internalization of the values and attitudes associated with the knowledge and skills being developed. While employees can be trained and retrained to maintain the required levels of knowledge and skills, outside members of the organization—such as customers, suppliers, and outside board members—over whom the organization has little or no control are hard to train and keep up-to-date. Yet, it is becoming increasingly important to keep outside members of the organization trained and supportive of appropriate attitudes and beliefs, especially in the service organizations where outsiders are part of the service delivery system.

Standardized knowledge and skills are designed to ensure that the members of the organization have the expertise to diagnose the organization and respond accordingly, while standardized attitudes and values are designed to ensure that individual interpretations of novel or complex organizational problems will not vary widely, and will be done in the best interests of the different parts of the organization. Standardized values are a necessary alternative where standardized knowledge is neither possible nor desirable. In this way the organization achieves coordination and unity of purpose. Conversely, an organization lacking a common knowledge base, values, or orientation is likely to be highly differentiated and hard to integrate. For example, studies show that organizations whose members have widely different formal training, values, and attitudes tend to be highly differentiated (Lawrence and Lorsch, 1967). Extension service organizations, for example, are highly differentiated partly because the agricultural scientists, the extension officers, and the farmers all have different knowledge and skills, and values and attitudes, and partly because they are dispersed in different locations. It therefore becomes difficult for such organizations to achieve coordination and unity of purpose among the various interest groups.

Standardization of knowledge, skills, beliefs, and attitudes in organizations in industrialized countries is highly developed. It is facilitated by a combination of factors within both the organization and the outside environment, including: (1) a generally high and rising standard of education where the average worker has had at least eight years of formal education; (2) highly competitive and well-developed educational and training institutions that provide general and specialized training and influence attitudes and beliefs through long periods of socialization and indoctrination; (3) active and powerful industry, trade, and professional associations that certify qualified members with demonstrated levels of knowledge, skills, and professional attitudes, and keep them up-to-date with current developments in their respective trades and professions; (4) continuing in-house training and indoctrination programs within each organization designed to develop specific organization-relevant skills, management philosophy, attitudes, and norms; (5) specialized training opportunities and facilities offered by the manufacturers and suppliers of advanced technologies used in the operating and strategic management tasks; and (6) availability of management consultants to advise individual organizations on the development and implementation of strategies for enhancing the knowledge, skills, and appropriate attitudes and norms of the various members of the organization.

The combination and relative importance of any of these approaches depend on the type of organization in question. For example, as Mintzberg indicates, professional organizations like teaching hospitals and law and accounting firms depend more on training and indoctrination provided by outside institutions and professional associations, while "in-house indoctrination programs are particularly important where jobs are sensitive or remote" (Mintzberg, 1979:98). Many organizations in developing countries are involved in critical operating tasks that are considered to be sensitive, secretive, or remote. For such tasks, indoctrination must be combined with cognitive training for the operators.

Once the members of the organization have acquired the necessary knowledge and skills and internalized the organization's belief systems and norms, the integration and coordination of the various parts of the organization both within and between the operating and strategic management tasks are facilitated, as role requirements and expectations are understood and accepted. Everyone should know what to do and how to do it even when internal and outside environmental conditions change.

In organizations in developing countries, the situation is very different. Nonstandardization of knowledge, skills, and organizational norms is one of their most serious problems. Virtually none of the facilitating factors for knowledge and skills acquisition, socialization, and indoctrination discussed above for organizations in industrialized countries exists, and if they do, they are usually not as well developed or equipped. Opportunities and facilities for formal training are very limited indeed, and the result is a bi-modal distribution with a few highly educated members of the organization in the strategic management and professional operating tasks, and a majority of people with little or no education. There are still significant numbers of organization members both inside and outside the organization who cannot read or write. Industry, trade, and professional associations as well as local training institutions, where opportunities do exist, are weak and lack the necessary infrastructure including training materials, equipment, and personnel. Some of these problems and limitations as they relate to management training in developing countries have been investigated by John Kerrigan and Jeff Luke (1987). Although some in-house training is done by organizations in developing countries, such efforts are well below the effective need for training and indoctrination, and they tend to be limited in focus only to specific job skills. Opportunities for upgrading one's job skills and knowledge are limited as well. Under such conditions, coordination of the various parts of the organization by standardization of knowledge and skills is very difficult for organizations in developing countries.

As has been pointed out above, studies show that in-house indoctrination programs are very important, particularly if jobs are remote. Organizations in developing countries have their fair share of remote jobs. Scattered population distributions necessitate that a number of government services in the areas of education, health, public works, social and community services, and local government have to be provided by people working in remote areas. The problem of providing education to isolated remote villages was discussed by Samuel Paul (1982) in the Mexican CONAFE program for the development of rural education. The resource management sector requires a number of technical and professional postings in remote and isolated areas. For example, the management of water resources, fisheries, forestry, minerals, wildlife, and forest resources all require people to work in remote isolated areas. In Indonesia, the size of the country and the fact that it is made up of over 3,000 islands mean that most of the jobs away from the major urban centers are remote, not only for agriculture, but for other sectors as well. Yet, as we have seen, in-house training and indoctrination in organizations including those with technical and professional remote jobs are very limited indeed. Thus, coordination and integration of the various parts of these organizations are particularly difficult. Other developing countries such as Brazil, Zaire, Iran, the Sudan, and the Philippines face similar problems of remoteness and dispersion.

In remote job situations, input variability tends to be high, the transformation processes are easily exposed to outside environmental disturbances, and quality control is hard to enforce. Accordingly, coordination by standardization of the production processes can be difficult. Moreover, close supervision is not possible because of the physical distances between head office and the remote posts. Under these and similar circumstances, greatly increased investments in training and indoctrination are highly appropriate. As Kaufman (1960) illustrated in his study of the American forest ranger, indoctrination and standardization by knowledge are the most effective integrating mechanisms for remote and isolated organizations.

The nature and composition of the various groups that make up the membership of the organization in developing countries cause special problems for indoctrination and socialization. These groupings are normally formed on the basis of extraorganizational considerations including race, religion, ethnic background, education, or gender. While the individual work groups are internally homogeneous and highly cohesive, the membership as a whole is heterogeneous and fractious. These conditions make it difficult to develop and instill a common management philosophy and organization norms internalized and practiced by all. As a result, we would find different "management philosophies" and norms for individual groups in different parts of the organization. Loyalty for the group comes before loyalty for the organization. Under these conditions, it becomes difficult to achieve coordination by means of indoctrination, socialization, and norm formation. Rice (1958) had to use clinical group processes in India in order to develop effective teamwork between the Hindu and Moslem employees at the textile mills.

3. Alternative Forms of Work Organization

When the negative consequences of poor employee morale resulting from hierarchical divisions of labor and specialization outweigh the positive aspects of large economies of scale and lower unit costs, management may seek alternative forms of structuring and integrating the critical operating tasks. These alternative forms affect the organization and work flow of the operating tasks, the utilization and morale of the operators, and the integration of the operating tasks among themselves and with the strategic management tasks.

Alternative forms of work organization are based on the principles of sociotechnical systems theory that were discussed above in Chapter One. Two of these principles are: (1) that jobs, organizational units, and work groups need to be designed and coordinated according to task requirements; and (2) that jobs need to fulfill certain employee psychological and social needs beyond safety, security, and wages as specified in the employment contract. It is therefore necessary to give operators more meaningful jobs, opportunities to learn and use new skills, freedom to exercise control over their own work, challenge to plan and schedule their work and participate in decisions relevant to their jobs, and a climate of mutual trust and social support.

Figure 4.2 shows the organization of work according to the traditional functional grouping, and the alternative form based on product lines. In the functional groupings, work is organized according to functions such that each of the functions (e.g., painting, assembling) is under a different supervisory group. The products move from one group to the next in a typical assembly-line work flow. None of the individual groups gets a chance to do a complete task. Sequential interdependence is high as functional groups depend on others to get their own work done. Under these conditions, the potential for conflict and suboptimization is high.

The alternative form is organized quite differently. Each supervisory group is responsible for the performance of all five functions including inspection of their own work. Specialization exists here but through cross-training the operators become skilled in performing more than one function. For example, in Figure 4.2., the painter can also do inspection and the sheet-metal worker can also do assembling. In this way, the work group builds additional organizational resources with flexibility in staffing, scheduling, and job design. The product groups are relatively independent of each other and have little need for coordination. There is less need to balance the line or work flow across the groups. The added responsibilities increase the necessity for coordination *within* each work group but reduce it for *between-group* coordination. Work integration is achieved at higher levels of the organization.

When work is organized according to the product lines, as shown by Figure 4.2, and when certain conditions are fulfilled, the groups are called self-managing or semi-autonomous work groups. The following conditions are necessary for the creation of self-managing work groups:

1. The operators must be cross-trained and multiskilled so that they can change work roles within the group. That is, the operator

Figure 4.2 **ALTERNATIVE FORMS OF WORK ORGANIZATION FOR COTs**

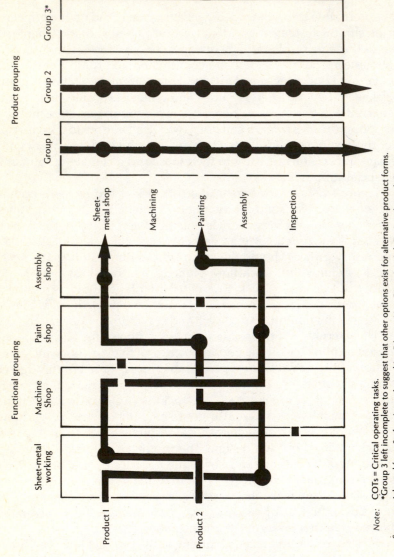

Note: COTs = Critical operating tasks.
       *Group 3 left incomplete to suggest that other options exist for alternative product forms.
Source: Adapted from Stefan Augurén and Jan Edgren, *New Factories: Job Design through Factory Planning in Sweden.* Stockholm: Swedish Employers' Confederation 1980, p. 52. Used by permission.

must have the knowledge and skills to perform as many different jobs in the work group as possible.

2. Operators must be given more responsibility to control their work flow. They must be allowed to do the planning, scheduling and inspection of their work. When a self-managing work group is fully developed, it takes on most of the responsibilities traditionally performed by the supervisor.

3. The group must be able to control or have ready access to support services like repair, maintenance, administration, and information systems.

4. The supervisors have to be trained and encouraged to operate effectively under the new structural arrangements. They must be able and willing to give up close supervision, to learn to supervise and coordinate group and not individual efforts, and to develop those problem-solving and decision-making skills needed at higher middle management levels.

5. These structural and behavioral changes must be institutionalized and given legitimacy by top management. This is one of the hardest conditions to fulfill because it often requires changes in management philosophy and organizational norms at the very top.

6. The management, control, reward, and incentive systems must be changed in regard to their effect on the work group in order that the desired behaviors of the new structures are reinforced. For example, these systems and practices must support and reward group and not just individual effort, collaboration, willingness to learn and to use new skills, and individual and group flexibility.

7. There must be periodic review and evaluation of group performance and the new form of work organization to make any necessary adjustments. Reorganization under these conditions is an on-going process.

8. Finally, a self-managing group must have clearly defined boundary conditions with stable inputs, outputs, and territory.

Alternative forms of work organization have both economic and social benefits for the organization and its employees. Lindholm and Flykt summarize these benefits by stating that the structure:

. . . cuts down on materials handling and in-process materials inventories, shortens throughput times and therefore reduces the cost of working capital tied up in products moving through the manufacturing process. In addition, . . . it means that work organization can be simpler and better. Supervisors and workers span a portion of the production process that contains many different tasks and makes possible varied and enriched jobs. This means that workers have the opportunity to sharpen their skills and learn additional jobs. Moreover, it is easier to define, keep track of and arrange feedback of meaningful results and to create a unified responsibility for work results in a supervisor and his coworkers. This can induce more involvement of the workers in their jobs. (1981:47–48)

Alternative forms of work organization can be designed at different levels of the organization in both production and service organizations. They have been applied in organizations in both industrialized and developing countries including India, Tanzania, and the Sudan. In a recent review of these initiatives in developing countries (Kiggundu, 1986), I found that results were mixed. While some of the initial results were positive and encouraging, subsequent problems of inadequate preparation, lack of training for the workers and their supervisors, and the inability to diffuse and institutionalize the new structural changes often led to loss of support. Yet, as Kanawaty et al. (1981), and Trist (1981), among others, have found, when enough attention is paid to background preparation, training, and institutional support, these forms of work organization can be effective integrating mechanisms for organizations in developing countries.

Table 4.1 summarizes the organizational effects of the five routine integrating mechanisms (RIMs) discussed above. It shows that most of these RIMs are mainly applicable for the organization and integration of critical operating tasks (COTs) only. Other RIMs such as plans, budgets and goals, knowledge, skills and values, and alternative forms of work organization are relevant for both the COTs and the strategic management tasks (SMATs). These mechanisms provide the link and integration between the organization's operating and strategic management tasks. For example, the plans and budgets of the organization should flow directly from its mission statement and be translated directly into operations down to the lowest operating level. The hierarchy provides the authority, communication channels, and supervision for the performance and integration of the COTs and SMATs.

Table 4.1 also outlines some of the advantages and disadvantages of using each of the routine integrating mechanisms. For most RIMs, the advantages are associated with operational efficiency and the desire to re-

Table 4.1

SUMMARY OF THE ORGANIZATIONAL EFFECTS OF ROUTINE INTEGRATING MECHANISMS

RIMs Integrating Mechanism	Main Effects on COTs or SMATs?	Reasons for Applications	Disadvantages or Limitations
1. Hierarchy of Authority	COTs/SMATs	Establishes clear lines of authority and communication	Alienates lower level operators and other members
2. Close Supervision	COTs	Ensures operator complience with SOPs	Stifles creativity, innovation, and initiative. Creates morale problems among operators. Not practical in certain (e.g., remote, complex, dispersed) job situations
3. Standard Operating Procedures (SOPs): a. Rules, Policies, Procedures	COTs	Clarifies role expectations and work procedures. Uniform performance across jobs and work units	Cannot cover unprogrammed work events. Must be kept up to date, communicated, understood, and accepted or respected by all. Not appropriate for complex tasks
b. Plans, Budgets, and Goals	COTs/SMATs	Provides basis for establishing performance standards and systematic appraisals	Causes suboptimization within work units
4. Standardization: a. Inputs	COTs	Increases predictability and control of input behavior	Limits capacity to handle input variability
b. Transformations	COTs	Increases operational efficiency	Keeps operating core closed. Inability to process "exceptional" cases
c. Outputs	COTs	Reduces incidents of rejects	Requires investments in stringent quality control
d. Knowledge, skills, beliefs, and attitudes	COTs/SMATs	Increases predictability and eliminates need for close supervision	Requires heavy investments over long periods of time
5. Alternative forms of work organization	COTs/SMATs	Improves operator morale, commitment, responsible action, and initiative. Eliminates need for close supervision	Requires highly trained, experienced, and motivated operators and supervisors Compromises on operational efficiency

Note: COTs = Critical Operating Tasks; SMATs = Strategic Management Tasks.

duce organizational porosity and to achieve at least partial closure of the operating core. The disadvantages, however, are associated with operator morale problems resulting from poorly designed jobs, the requirement of long and expensive investments in human resource development, suboptimization resulting from excessive division of labor and specialization, and the inability of most of the RIMs to deal with complex tasks. The next section deals with the integration of the more complex strategic management tasks.

II. Complex Integrating Mechanisms

Complex integrating mechanisms (CIMs) are structural arrangements designed to integrate and coordinate the more complex tasks of the organization. Unlike the routine integrating mechanisms, the complex integrating mechanisms are used for unstructured tasks characteristic of the strategic management tasks performed under conditions of internal and environmental uncertainty. Complex unstructured tasks require complex mechanisms for integration and coordination. The more complex the organization is in terms of its tasks and the internal and environmental context within which it operates, the greater its need for complex integrating mechanisms. CIMs are labor intensive, take a longer time, and are generally more expensive to utilize effectively.

1. Internal Integrating Mechanisms

Complex internal integrating mechanisms are structural arrangements developed to bring about coordination and unity of purpose between two or more parts of the organization performing unstructured, complex tasks that cannot be adequately coordinated by any of the routine integrating mechanisms. There are various ways of conceptualizing task complexity and organizational responses to achieve appropriate integration. For example, Galbraith (1977) thinks of task complexity in terms of the organization's needs for information processing. Accordingly, the internal integrating mechanisms should be designed in order to increase the organization's capacity to process information, or to reduce the need for information processing.

Two types of internal integrating mechanisms—the creation of lateral relations, and the facilitation of informal communications—are discussed below. Alternative forms of work organization, described in the previous section, can also be used to bring about integration across complex operating units.

Creation of Lateral Relations.   When the internal tasks of an organization become too complex, it must develop lateral relations to complement the hierarchy of authority and other routine integrating mechanisms. Lateral relations increase in importance, scope, and complexity as the internal tasks and requirements for integration become more demanding and complex. These lateral relations, which cut across hierarchical lines of authority, can range from simple direct contacts between supervisors or managers of interdependent work units, to more complex structural arrangements like the matrix design. Four types of lateral relations are discussed below: (1) direct contacts; (2) task forces; (3) teams; and (4) the matrix design.

Direct Contacts.   Contacts can be made between two or more managers who share a common problem. These can take place on the phone, in meetings, or by exchanging personnel across departments. The exchange of personnel is particularly effective as a solution to recurring interdepartmental problems because it facilitates empathy and understanding of the problems from the other department's point of view. In this way, the departments can engage in cooperative problem solving, seeking solutions beneficial to all the affected departments. In most organizations, conflicts occur between the purchasing, production, and distribution departments because of the high level of interdependence among them. By facilitating direct contacts or transferring personnel on a regular basis, these conflicts can be effectively managed with little or no dysfunctional consequences.

If the regular meetings or exchange of personnel is not adequate to deal with the common problems between interdependent departments, the organization can create a special part-time or full-time position charged with the responsibility of bringing about better coordination and problem solving between the departments. This position could alleviate difficulties, for example, between a government central agency such as the treasury, and a big-spending line ministry such as national defense. The person assigned to the position should have knowledge and practical experience from the interdependent departments. In addition, this liaison role should be assigned to someone who can bring objectivity to it so as to be able to deal with the departments without fear or favor. The location and reporting relationships of this role must be acceptable to the departments involved. If the liaison office is located within and reports to one of the departments, it may be subjected to undue influence and may lose its credibility, which is so important for the effective performance of its unbiased role. Liaison roles are quite demanding because they require the incumbent to have at least a basic knowledge of the work and problems of each of the departments or agencies and because they often deal with conflict situations. They therefore tend to be assigned to experienced senior employees. They operate on influence rather than formal authority.

Task Forces.   Direct contacts and liaison positions are used for problems affecting two or only a few departments. These structural arrangements, however, are inadequate for problems involving many departments or the whole organization. In this section I use the term task force to indicate a temporary structural arrangement whereby representatives from different parts of the organization or set of organizations sharing a common problem come together to find a mutually acceptable solution to the problem. Task forces, in this sense, are similar to ad hoc committees; they have no permanent legitimacy and must be disbanded as soon as the problem for their existence has been solved.

Task forces may be established formally by high officials like the chief executive officer so as to give them formal recognition, authority, and resources, or they can arise informally through direct lateral contacts. They may be appointed directly by and be responsible to the board of directors. Formal task forces have the advantage of official legitimacy and therefore easy access to organizational resources, while informal ones enjoy more grassroots support from the rank and file. In any case, it is important—for several reasons—that the membership of the task force is representative of all the affected interdependent departments. First, relevant information about the problem, as well as that department's perspective or understanding of the problem, must be obtained from each of the departments. Second, participation enables the departments to gain a broader appreciation and understanding of the problem from the perspective of departments other than their own. Third, participation, and thus improved understanding of the problem, increases the chances of a common acceptance of problem definition and solution, which in turn facilitates solution implementation by the departments.

Teams.   Teams or standing committees resemble task forces except that they are permanent and are formed to deal with frequently occurring problems. Like task forces, teams may cut across hierarchical levels and draw their membership from different parts of the organization. They are used to facilitate internal coordination by dealing with and resolving organizational problems that cannot be routinely addressed by simpler integrating mechanisms.

Teams can be used to achieve internal integration at different hierarchical levels of the organization. For example, quality control committees usually operate at the lower levels of the organization unless quality problems are so severe that they require the attention of senior management. Finance committees, on the other hand, tend to be made up of senior management or board members. As a team moves up the organization from lower levels to top management, its role as an integrating mechanism increases. This is one explanation of why senior managers spend more time in meetings than do junior managers. Most organizations have functional teams or committees dealing with matters like finance, audit, personnel, compensation, investments, or government relations. Such committees are often created at a board level so that membership includes both senior officers and managers of the organization as well as members of the board. Such a structure provides effective coordination between the board and the organization and creates a more open organization since neither the chief executive officer nor the chairman of the board can sit on all these committees.

Teams are expensive and they can be unproductive. Senior managers often complain that they spend long hours in unproductive meetings. Highly bureaucratic hierarchical organizations with formal approaches to problem solving are not particularly good at using teams effectively. As well, organizations with a highly competitive climate, where individual managers work to maximize their own performance with little or no regard for the effectiveness of the whole organization, are not conducive to good teamwork. When an organization's internal tasks necessitate utilization of teamwork to achieve coordination, it should change its management, control, and incentive systems, and train its members on how to conduct effective meetings. This is quite difficult and requires introduction of major organizational change and development.

Matrix Design.   A matrix organization is defined "as any organization that employs a *multiple command system* that includes not only a multiple command structure but also related support mechanisms and an associated organizational culture and behavior pattern" (Davis and Lawrence, 1977:3). Matrix organizations originally evolved from the U.S. aerospace industry as a way of bringing together highly specialized professionals and operators to work on leading edge scientific and technical projects that required complex, close coordination and mutual adjustments. Since then, the matrix design has been widely used in industrialized countries in sectors such as manufacturing, service organizations such as banking and construction, professional organizations, nonprofit organizations such as municipalities, government agencies, hospitals, universities, and international organizations. One of the advantages of the matrix design is that it can bring about effective coordination and integration between two or more critical operating tasks in different departments or parts of the organization, as well as integration of the critical operating and the strategic management tasks.

Figure 4.3 illustrates the possible application of the matrix design in the implementation of a structural adjustment program (SAP) in a developing country. The SAP, imposed on countries by the International Monetary Fund (IMF), is essentially a series of national strategic management tasks that require active participation of a wide range of national organizations. Experience has shown that most developing countries run into problems of implementation and coordination resulting from the SAP; that is, the individual organizations' critical operating tasks are not integrated with the SAP-imposed changes in regard to their respective strategic management tasks. Only by synchronizing these organizations' COTs and SMATs, and building the necessary capacity for their continued performance and integration, can these countries be able to implement the structural adjustment program (see Chapter Eight).

Figure 4.3 shows how a matrix design can be used to bring about better coordination between central agencies and line ministries. The central bank and the ministry of agriculture both play an important role in the implementation of a structural adjustment program. Their respective operating and strategic management tasks are coordinated and integrated by the creation of the matrix position of a manager of crop financing who reports to both the central bank and the ministry of agriculture. A major limitation of the matrix design, however, is that it requires fairly complex management systems not commonly found in developing countries and it takes a long time to develop.

If the matrix design is not adequate or practical, it may be necessary

Figure 4.3

APPLICATION OF THE MATRIX DESIGN FOR A STRUCTURAL ADJUSTMENT PROGRAM

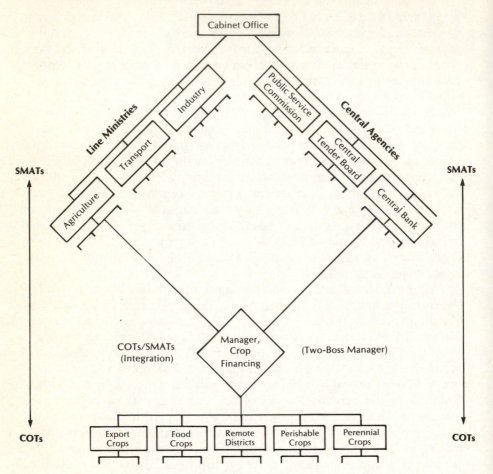

Note: COTs = Critical Operating Tasks; SMATs = Strategic Management Tasks.

to use a collateral organization. This is a parallel structure that co-exists with the formal organization but draws its membership from different ministries and agencies. Unlike the task force, the collateral organization is more permanent and is better suited for solving and coordinating complex and apparently intractable problems characteristic of the structural adjustment program. The collateral organization has the advantage of integrating complex operating and strategic management tasks from different parts of the organization without interfering with its day-to-day operations (Huse and Cummings, 1985; Rubinstein and Woodman, 1984).

Collateral organizations have been used by organizations such as General Motors' central foundry division and Compu Corp of the United States. According to Huse and Cummings (1985), Compu Corp, a high-technology firm, used the collateral organization form to address operation and management problems resulting from rapid growth and growing competition. The company established a steering committee made up of managers drawn from different departments. Reporting to the steering committee were several action groups made up of employees from different operating units. The action groups, under the general supervision of the steering committee, initiated a number of programs that resulted in improvements in productivity and morale and enabled the employees to acquire new and valuable skills.

Facilitation of Informal Communications. As tasks become complex, formal internal integrating mechanisms become inadequate. Under these conditions, informal communications become necessary to enable managers and employees from different interdependent parts of the organization regularly to exchange information, perceptions, expectations, and so forth, on an informal basis. Informal communications must not be seen as a residual or last resort of integrating mechanisms but as a purposeful facilitation to achieve higher levels of integration. Some aspects of work cannot be integrated by other than informal communications. For example, Mintzberg indicates that mutual adjustment (informal communication) "is the only one that works under extremely difficult circumstances" (1979:3). Because many organizations in developing countries operate under "extremely difficult circumstances," it is perhaps imperative that they use informal communications for integration and coordination.

Informal communications are particularly effective for unstructured complex tasks or tasks performed under conditions of uncertainty. Thus, they are also particularly suited for strategic management tasks. An effective, well-integrated organization should show a complicated network of both formal and informal communications in which the informal network crisscrosses the organization and is more concentrated at the management levels of the organization and at its boundaries. Informal communications are effective integrating mechanisms because they are organic, face to face, spontaneous, and live, use multiple media, and provide instant feedback.

Organizations spend a lot of effort encouraging and facilitating informal communications. Methods include:

1. Developing a common belief system, management philosophy, language, and knowledge base for easy and efficient communication.

2. Providing common work areas and pooled or shared resources or open office space to facilitate informal contacts during the course of employee job performance.

3. Creating facilities for social interactions including common rest rooms, cafeterias, lounges, and recreation facilities; transportation to and from work; housing; libraries; coordinated or synchronized elevators (e.g., by floors); and other amenities that encourage employees from different parts of the organization and different parts of the environment to meet for both business and social reasons.

4. Encouraging managers and supervisors to spend more time with other managers and employees. In the military tradition this would be called "keeping in touch with the troops." Peters and Waterman (1984), in describing America's best run companies, called it "keeping close to the customers," though this should be extended to keeping close to all important members of the organization. Timm and Peterson (1986) have described a management style whereby the manager spends so much time walking around on the floor that eventually he or she earns a management by walking around (MBWA) degree! The integrative aspects of this management style are described by these authors as follows: "Just walking around with your eyes and ears open, asking questions like crazy and trying to understand what the guys working for you are doing. A good place to start is to see if they understand what they are doing" (1986:148).

Perhaps organizations in developing countries should recruit more managers with MBWA rather than MBA degrees. Management by walking around enables the managers to acquaint themselves with the requirements and challenges of the organization's critical operating tasks.

Trust is one of the most important facilitators of informal communication. There must exist a climate of mutual trust and respect in the organization for effective informal communication. In his popular book on how American business can meet the Japanese challenge, William Ouchi observed that "the first lesson of theory Z is trust," and that "productivity and trust go hand in hand" (1981:5). Human relations theorists like Chris Argyris (1968) and Peterson and Pace (1978) regard trust to be one of the most important dimensions of organization climate. Trust within the organization is fostered by treating employees like adults and by improving accessibility, predictability, and loyalty among members of the organization. These conditions are hard to maintain in hierarchical organizations with distinctive social class structures and factious groupings that are sometimes found in organizations in developing countries. If trust is low and animosity high, an organization can attain operational success only if its routine integrating mechanisms are one hundred percent foolproof.

I am not aware of any research that has been done to determine the frequency and effectiveness of informal communications as integrating mechanisms in organizations in developing countries. I suspect, however, that a lot of informal communications go on in these organizations, especially where other integrating mechanisms are particularly weak or ineffective. I also suspect that most of these communications may not necessarily be job related or organization relevant. The natural groupings in these organizations within which most informal communications go on, do not necessarily correspond with the organization's task groups; thus, information shared with these groups, while relevant for individual employees, may be of little integrative value from the organization's point of view. Secondly, the existence of rigid class structures may inhibit informal communications across social/economic classes. Linguistic and cultural differences also inhibit informal communications. Thirdly, chief executive officers and other senior managers tend to spend most of the time on extraorganizational activities and therefore have limited time "to manage by walking around," or otherwise facilitate informal communications.

In observing how senior managers in organizations in developing countries spend their time at work, I found that they spend a greater proportion of the time with outside interactions than they do with inside members. Such a pattern suggests that these managers believe there is a greater need to coordinate and integrate organizational tasks with outside stakeholders than with inside stakeholders. The next section discusses interorganizational coordination and its relevancy for these organizations.

2. Interorganizational Coordination

Interorganizational coordination (IOC) has attracted a lot of interest in organization science. Various theories have been developed and empirically tested; however, I make no attempt here to review or synthesize these theories because Pfeffer (1982), and Rogers and Whetten (1982), among others, have already done so. The purpose of this section is limited to a discussion of the basic elements of IOC and their relevancy for organizations in developing countries.

According to Charles Mulford and David Rogers, interorganizational coordination can be defined as the "process whereby two or more organizations create and/or use existing decisions that have been established to deal collaboratively with their shared task environment" (1982:12). This definition has a number of attractive features: (1) it conceptualizes IOC in terms of the specific task environment and not the organization's generalized environment, and assumes that the task environment is shared; (2) it emphasizes that decisions affecting IOC are made jointly by the organizations involved or by a third party; (3) it focuses on the organization set—the organizations in the interdependent relationship—and not the individual organizations. IOC implies both structural arrangements and behavioral processes for the entire organization set.

The motivation for individual organizations to participate in IOC is to deal with environmental complexity and uncertainty. As the environment becomes more complex and uncertain, organizations become more specialized and thus increase their need for interorganizational coordination. Increased internal differentiation and environmental interdependencies create greater needs for internal and interorganizational coordination. Specific reasons for participating in IOC include the necessity of dealing with system inefficiencies, of reducing fragmentation of services and overlap, of regulating and directing programs and activities, and of maintaining a reasonable degree of autonomy for the individual participating organizations.

Organizations choose various strategies for participation in IOC. In order of preference, these strategies, and their attributes, are:

1. Proprietary strategies that enable individual organizations to retain possession and control over critical resources, and protect boundaries and technical core;

2. Cooperative strategies requiring dyadic negotiation on a one-to-one basis with another organization; and

3. Multiorganizational, multilevel strategies that require the participation and involvement of many organizations at many different levels.

In choosing among these strategies, the primary objective for the individual organization is to maintain its autonomy in the performance of its critical operating and strategic management tasks. It is with this goal in mind that Einar Thorsrud observed "it is more appropriate to define objectives in terms of the relative dependence of an organization upon the various parts of its environment" (1981:15).

This dependence is often conceptualized in terms of resources (Aldrich, 1979; Pfeffer, 1982; Pfeffer and Salancik, 1978) that the organization requires for the performance of its critical operating and strategic management tasks. Because organizations can not be self-sufficient, they must go out into the environment to get needed resources. This dependence creates an asymmetrical relationship that imposes external controls on the organization and on the way it performs its operating and strategic management tasks. This relationship can be particularly problematic when, as often happens with international joint ventures, the powerful organizations reside outside the focal organization's country of residence. As part of performing their strategic management tasks, organizations respond to the dependence by adapting various cooperative and competitive strategies that enable them to strike a balance between maintaining access to needed resources and retaining a level of autonomy and freedom from external control. These strategies include long-term supply contracts, joint ventures, mergers, acquisitions, contract farming, management contracts, exchange of personnel, programs, money and other resources, and sharing of interlocking directorships.

This dependence can affect the performance of the organization's critical operating tasks, strategic management tasks, or both. When control is over critical operating tasks, its effects are immediate and they directly affect the operations and survival of the organization. When an organization loses a major supplier or buyers of inputs and outputs—for example, when a multinational corporation terminates or adversely changes its terms with contract farmers of a developing country for whom it provides the only access to the world market for their produce—the organization loses its capacity to perform its critical operating tasks with economy and efficiency.

When an organization is dependent on another for the performance of its strategic management tasks, the effects of such dependence are slow and take long before they can be noticed, as these tasks are oriented toward the future with only incremental effects on the immediate or short term operations of the organization. The effects of the external control on the organization over the performance of its strategic management tasks are less dramatic and rather subtle for COTs. They are, however, equally debilitating for the organization over the long run. Examples of organizations in developing countries whose strategic management tasks suffer from external control by other organizations are the state-owned enterprises, and the international joint ventures. Evidence shows that state-owned enterprises owe at least some of their poor performance to inappropriate external control of their strategic management by powerful parent ministries, holding companies, or central agencies. Likewise, international joint ventures with asymmetrical power relationships suffer from similar dependencies because the more powerful international partners usurp all the important strategic management tasks (Gomes-Casseres, 1985). When the external control is total—that is, it involves both the critical operating and strategic management tasks—the organization loses its identity as a separate, unique entity.

Compared to cooperation, coordination is much more formal, affects both horizontal and vertical linkages, involves more serious commitment of resources from either party, affects the structure and behavior of the parties, and constitutes a greater threat to individual organization's autonomy in the performance of their respective operating and strategic management tasks. Organizations are therefore reluctant to adopt IOC unless they must, and even then they do so advisedly.

Interorganizational coordination can have both intended and unintended consequences. Intended consequences include a development of a more stable and predictable task environment that ensures continuity of resource supplies, more efficient operation of both operating and strategic management tasks, internal and environmental conflict resolution, and more effective utilization of resources. Unintended consequences include reduced competition among the IOC participating organizations, uneven distribution of costs or benefits, a zero-sum game or win/lose situations, and biased evaluation of the benefits intended for only specific interest groups. These unintended consequences, and the frequent failure of some IOC strategies like mergers and acquisitions, suggest the need for careful consideration and effective management of interorganizational coordination by the participating organizations or a neutral third party.

Contingencies of Interorganizational Coordination.   There are at least two schools of thought on interorganizational coordination and its effects on organizations in developing countries. The first and most popular school in the literature is the one advanced by writers like Faucheux and Laurent (1982), who believe that in developing countries "society pervades organizations." This philosophy would suggest that the individual organization has little or no control over the environment and must therefore adjust to environmental dictates in order to survive. Accordingly, the organization is subject to external control and the external environment exercises power over the performance of its critical operating and strategic management tasks.

The second school of thought argues that organizations in developing countries are not different from those in industrialized countries in regard to their relationship with the environment. They face complex and uncertain environments upon which they must depend for needed resources. But they also have the potential to manage their respective task environments to reduce dependency and increase their individual and collective autonomy. The argument is also made that, even in industrialized countries, the difference between effective and ineffective organizations is not that one set of organizations operates under a complex and potentially pervasive environment while the other set does not. Rather, the difference is that the effective organizations, regardless of the nature of the environment in which they operate, have developed and implemented effective strategies for performing and managing their respective tasks. These strategies enable the organizations: (1) to continue to get access to the resources they need; (2) to avoid being totally dependent or externally controlled by the environment; and (3) to enjoy a reasonable degree of autonomy and freedom from the environment in the performance of their tasks.

This school of thought is more proactive than arguing environmental domination. Its emphasis is not so much on the pervasive and debilitating nature of the external environment but on two developmental aspects. First, it points out the need for managers of organizations in developing countries to attain environmental strategic management skills. These would, among other things, enable them to manage more effectively regardless of the nature of the environment in which they happen to operate. Second, it also points out the need for basic and applied research to produce useful organizational knowledge for understanding and identifying appropriate IOC strategies and mechanisms, and the organizational contingencies under which they are most suitable for organizations in developing countries.

Two important contingencies are organizational size and industry concentration or market imperfections. By far, the majority of organizations in developing countries are small in size (Page and Steel, 1984). Only large organizations have the capacity and expertise proactively to manage their environments to the benefit of their task performance. The only way that small organizations such as small-scale enterprises or small-scale farmers can have an effective impact on the environment is by banding together into associations and cooperatives. This strategy has been used effectively in the United States by small farmers and retailers. (Pfeffer, 1982)

There is empirical support for the U-shaped hypothesis relating the amount of interorganizational linkages to industry concentration (Pfeffer and Salancik, 1978). That is, when concentration is high or low, the amount of interorganizational linkages is small. When, however, industry concentration is moderate, interorganizational linkages are high. In research with Jorgensen and Hafsi (1986) I have documented evidence of market imperfections and the existence of industry concentration in most of the industrial sectors of developing country economies. Industries like mining, manufacturing, plantation farming, and forest products are typically characterized by high levels of concentration with one firm or a few large firms in each sector. On the other extreme, I found very low levels of concentration in peasant farming and small-scale enterprises where the market is much more competitive and entry into and exit out of the industry relatively easy. Under these conditions, we can conclude that the typical profile of industrial organization, concentration, and market imperfections in most developing economies is not conducive to large amounts of interorganizational linkages as a strategy for IOC and environment management, and thus that organizations in developing countries do not readily engage in cooperative strategies with other organizations in the performance of their operating and strategic management tasks.

COTs and SMATs Across Interdependent Organizations.   There exist several situations in which a set of organizations is so interdependent that the performance or nonperformance of the tasks of one affects the performance of the tasks of the others—for example, when organizations are so operationally interdependent that one's outputs become another's inputs. In the educational sector the quality of performance of COTs by secondary schools for such facets as programs, subject coverage, and teaching methods has a direct impact on the structuring and performance of COTs by the post-secondary institutions. Similarly, the performance of COTs by the secondary schools is affected by the quality of performance by the primary schools with whom they are operationally interdependent. Thus, any changes or improvements in the performance of the tasks of the receiving organization must be made in cognizance of the nature and performance of the tasks of the other interdependent organizations.

It is also possible that the critical operating tasks of one organization are taken on as the strategic management tasks of another. For example, in many developing countries, routine acquisition, use, and distribution of raw materials and finished goods to and from abroad may be not only an operational matter for the producing organization but also a major strategic decision of how to allocate and utilize scarce national resources such as foreign exchange. In this way, an operational task by the producing organization becomes a strategic management task for the government regulatory agency. For a private importer of agricultural implements, the purchase of such stock abroad is a routine operating task. It may, however, have strategic importance for the country's central bank in the allocation of foreign exchange resources, for the agricultural development corporation in the implementation of the country's regional diversification agricultural policy, and for the ministry of international trade in the development of international markets for the country. Under these conditions, it is unlikely that the private importer will be left alone to make the purchasing decision as a purely commercial critical operating task.

In situations in which the state-owned enterprise (SOE) has little autonomy because its internal management is weak, its performance levels are well below major stakeholders' expectations, the history of the SOE government relations is short and turbulent, public institutions are weak, or the country's political situation is unstable or changing, government interference tends to be pervasive, affecting both critical operating tasks and strategic management tasks. Such circumstances are illustrated by Ben Turok, who, writing about control in the private sector in Zambia, observed that:

> Government intervention in state corporations is substantial
> and on the whole corrosive. It went beyond prescribing policy

objectives and cut across operational freedom. Government prescribed projects and programmes, insisted on selecting locations, appointed and dismissed personnel, laid down conditions of service and set pricing policies and levels. (1984:233)

Whenever the critical operating tasks of one organization are performed as strategic management tasks by another organization, the cost of doing business goes up and the advantages of market forces are lost because transactions are then subject to a wide range of market imperfections and extraorganizational considerations. State-owned enterprises are particularly susceptible to these problems (Hafsi, Kiggundu, and Jorgensen, 1987).

It also happens that the interdependence between organizations is such that the strategic management decisions of one affect the structuring and performance of the critical operating tasks of another. For example, when a firm decides to expand its production facilities, or to make significant changes in its technology or markets, these strategic decisions will have significant effects on the critical operating tasks of its major suppliers or customers. Likewise, when a government introduces a new policy initiative (SMATs), individual government ministries and agencies must make corresponding changes in the organization and performance of their critical operating tasks. Failure to do so would result in difficulties in policy implementation and coordination.

Finally, situations exist whereby the strategic management decisions of one organization form the basis for the SMATs of another organization. Examples include subsidiary-parent relationships, industry leaders *vis-à-vis* industry followers, and dominance of power or influence, for whatever reasons, by one organization over one or more organizations. In developing countries, we can find many cases of a single firm or a few industry leader firms with many small ones taking on the role of followers— or, all following the lead of an international organization. For example, when the international airlines introduced wide body aircraft on their international routes, the smaller national airlines of the developing countries had no choice but to follow suit. This step set up a chain reaction that has affected the small airlines' COTs such as aircraft maintenance and service, training, and marketing as well as the COTs of other organizations that do business with these airlines.

The analysis of COTs and SMATs across interdependent organizations can be applied to the analysis of a set of organizations constituting a policy sector. A policy sector can be defined as a "cluster or complex of organizations connected to each other by resource dependencies and distinguished from other clusters or complexes by breaks in the structure of resource dependencies" (Benson, 1982:148). Policy sectors provide organizations with a useful framework within which to manage and coordinate their task interdependencies using the overall sector mission instead of the missions of the individual organizations. When the sector mission corresponds with government policy for that sector, these clusters can be instrumental in the effective implementation of such a policy. Policy sectors, however, are much bigger with more complex interdependencies than single organizations have. They pose a bigger management challenge for developing countries than do individual organizations.

III. Collaborative Institutional Arrangements

In addition to the integrating mechanisms discussed above (RIMs, CIMs, IOC), there are special mechanisms for institutional collaboration that are particularly suited for organizations in developing countries. Collaborative institutional arrangements (CIAs), structural and behavioral arrangements between two or more organizations, are designed to enhance the operational and/or management capacity of all or some of the organizations participating in the collaborative exchange. Here, the focus is not limited to managing resource dependencies, but also concerns building and sustaining the internal capacity of the participating organizations. The ultimate objective of these arrangements is to bring about sustained improvements in the performance of the critical operating and strategic management tasks of the participating organizations. This is the practical meaning of concepts such as institutional building and organization development (Hage and Finsterbusch, 1987).

The common methods of collaborative institutional arrangements include: (1) management contracts; (2) turnkey operations; (3) service contracts; (4) subcontracting; (5) licensing; (6) contract farming; (7) industrial incubation; (8) franchising; (9) joint ventures; (10) buy-make decisions; and (11) technical assistance. Each of these, however, is not a unitary concept but represents variations of organization forms. A management contract involves the invitation of an organization usually from an industrialized country to take over responsibility for the operations and management of another organization, usually in a developing country, for a fixed period of time for fixed or contingent fees. Management contracts are common in organizations in developing countries if new or large complex systems require advanced management expertise not easily available locally. They have been used in managing sugar estates in Kenya and the Caribbean, rubber plantations in Asia, and airports and modern hospitals in Africa and the Middle East. Management contracts are developmental and can be modified or withdrawn as the local organization develops its own management systems. Whereas certain collaborative institutional arrangements such as turnkey operations usually concentrate on installations for improvements in critical operating tasks, management contracts include both operating and strategic management tasks and contingent fees can be determined on the basis of the extent to which these tasks are performed with efficiency, economy, and effectiveness.

Service contracts and subcontracting are similar to one another in terms of collaborative arrangements. In both cases, an organization contracts another organization to provide specified services or products needed for the operations of the former organization. In the management literature, subcontracting was made popular by Toyota of Japan, which maintains a permanent collaborative arrangement with many smaller Japanese companies for the supply of auto parts. As Williamson (1985) and others point out, these arrangements are important for institution building and their success depends on a relatively long history and experience in collaborative arrangements, commonality of interests or destiny among the collaborating organizations, effective safeguards against opportunism, and mutually acceptable mechanisms for resolving conflicts among the collaborating organizations. Collaborative institutional arrangements can be asymmetrical, as is the case with Toyota and its subcontractors or KTDA and the Kenya tea growers, but they must be mutually beneficial. Arrangements such as subcontracting and service contracts can be a prelude to privatization if they are undertaken systematically by state-owned enterprises.

The advantages of certain aspects of CIAs can be illustrated by a recent study of the regional aircraft maintenance centers of the PTA (Preferential Trade Area) member states of Eastern and Southern Africa. Currently, each member state organizes its own aircraft maintenance involving some domestic maintenance and a European service contract. For example, Zambian aircraft are maintained with an Alitalia service contract while Kenya aircraft are serviced in Nairobi, Addis Ababa, and England. The study found that these arrangements cost the region at least $35 million per year more than if they had a collaborative institutional arrangement for the whole PTA region. The study therefore suggested the establishment of PTA regional aircraft maintenance centers that would reduce dependence on European service contracts. It recommended that ". . . the development of implementation strategies based upon sound economic analysis and increasing collaboration and cooperation in aircraft maintenance among PTA member states be considered a high priority, especially in view of large foreign exchange savings to the region and the availability of infrastructure capacity at little or no immediate additional cost" (Kaunda and Pendakur, 1986:75).

This study illustrates several points. Collaborative institutional arrangements can be local, national, regional, or international. They can have economic, social, and political benefits (and costs). They can also translate into a buy-make decision. If subcontracting to Europe can be regarded as a buying decision and establishment of regional maintenance centers as a decision to make, buy-make decisions can be analyzed in the context of vertical integration (Harrigan, 1985), involving collaborative institutional arrangements and strategic environmental management decisions of an international policy sector. In this case, the regional aircraft service centers as a form of collaborative institutional arrangement would enhance the operational and strategic management capacity of the individual national service centers and provide a framework for the development of other CIAs in the relevant policy sector (e.g., air travel, importation of common services) at an international (PTA) level. By 1987, efforts were underway to develop collaborative institutional arrangements for the purchase of wide body aircraft for the regional airlines' international routes.

Collaborative institutional arrangements are widely used by organizations in developing countries. They are regarded as an effective mechanism of importation of technology, management know-how, and other organizational resources not otherwise available locally. They have been particularly attractive to the newly industrialized countries (NICs) of Southeast Asia and Brazil where various forms of collaborative arrangements exist with American, European, and Japanese organizations. According to Sarathy (1985), the Brazilian commuter aircraft industry benefited from collaborative arrangements with U.S. organizations. Organizations in the People's Republic of China are seeking collaborative institutional arrangements with their more internationally sophisticated sister organizations in Hong Kong and ultimately with the multinational corporations of Japan, Europe, and the United States.

In Singapore, the Minister of Communications and Information Yeo Ning Hong, addressing the International Telecommunications Union in May 1985, suggested that organizations in that country should play an intermediary role in the transfer of telecommunications technology between organizations in other developing countries who have not yet learned the difficult art of technology assimilation or made modifications suitable to their local needs and circumstances, and the more sophisticated suppliers and manufacturers of this technology in the industrialized countries. In this way, Singapore organizations would serve as the link pin in the international collaborative institutional arrangements by facilitating effective transfer of technology. This is an important notion because, as a recent World Bank report by Bell, Ross-Larson, and Westphal (1984) seems to suggest, the problems of infant industries in developing countries may be related to their failure to develop and utilize appropriate collaborative institutional arrangements with other relevant organizations either locally or internationally. Consequently, they are unable to reach international competitiveness or develop the capability to manage continuous technological change.

Various studies strongly support the view that complex organizations in developing countries are more likely to sustain higher levels of performance with, rather than without, on-going collaborative institutional arrangements with similar organizations, preferably from one or more industrialized countries. The early work on institutional building by Hill et al. (1973), which provided the conceptual and normative framework for international collaborative arrangements between MIT's Sloan School of Management and the Harvard Business School on the one hand, and the Indian Institute of Management, Ahmedabad, the Indian Institute of Management, Calcutta, and the Administrative Staff College of India, Hyderabad, on the other, illustrates the importance of these arrangements. The Indian Institute of Management, Ahmedabad, one of the leading management institutes in the developing world, owes its prestige and consistent good work to its continued efforts to foster international collaborative arrangements with similar institutions.

Available evidence suggests that regional organizations such as the International Rice Research Institute (IRRI) in Manila, and the Eastern and Southern African Management Institute in Arusha, are more effective than their national or local counterparts tied down to their respective governments. In the case of the IRRI, "Progress in science and technology is moving so rapidly that no single institution can initiate research in every frontier of science. Collaborative programs allow IRRI to tap *upstream* technology—the scientific expertise and equipment available in advanced institutions in developed countries—to solve the *downstream* problems of small-scale rice farming" (IRRI, 1986:87).

Canada's International Development Research Centre (IDRC) supports research in developing countries by initiating and developing complex networks of collaborative institutional arrangements (CIAs) and interorganizational coordination (IOC) which benefit the participating organizations in various developing countries. In one of its publications, the agency explains its strategy:

> The funding granted to the Tropical Agricultural Research and Training Centre (CATIE) in Costa Rica will be used to test multiple cropping systems that link plantains and root crops. The work at the Centre, which is regional in scope, will be done in collaboration with the staff of the Panamanian and Nicaraguan national programs. Specialists from the University of West Indies in Trinidad and Tobago and from the branch office of the Institut national de la recherche agronomique (France), in Guadeloupe, will also contribute. (IDRC, 1986:24)

The airline industry provides additional evidence in support of the advantages of international collaborative institutional arrangements. Air Afrique, started in the early 1960s by a group of Francophone states, became nonoperational when member states pulled out to form independent national airlines. It is now able to operate scheduled flights because of collaborative institutional arrangements with Air France. Ethiopian Airlines, in spite of the country's domestic political, economic, and security problems, is one of Africa's best airlines, largely because of a long-standing collaborative institutional arrangement with Trans World Airlines. Zambia Airways and Air Zaire have also developed similar linkages with Alitalia and Pan American, respectively, for the same reasons. Conversely, inability to develop and sustain domestic or international collaborative institutional arrangements can lead to institutional decay (Kiggundu, 1985b), or organizational demise, as was the case with Nigeria's Cross River State Agricultural Corporation (McHenry, 1985) and the East African Community (Jorgensen, 1985). To be effective, however, such arrangements must be directly relevant to the organization's mission and critical operating and strategic management tasks.

The Mondragon Co-operative Federation in the Basque Province in Spain owes its remarkable success partly because it is managed as a total system whose individual enterprises are linked together by complex collaborative institutional arrangements. As Clayre (1980) rightly points out, the Mondragon is run as a federation in which more than 70 individual enterprises draw on one another in the performance of their respective operating and strategic management tasks. They coordinate any major structural or technological changes in response to market or environmental changes. Moreover, the federation maintains strong CIAs with the Caja Laboral Popular, a cooperative bank that provides financial discipline and expert management advice to the federation and its constituent enterprises. These collaborative institutional arrangements, both within the federation and with outside organizations, provide the framework for the effective management and profitability of the federation and the individual enterprises.

Multinational corporations use various forms of CIAs to advance their business and commercial interests. Varity Corp. (formerly Massey-Ferguson) is revitalizing its international business by using alternative forms of collaborative institutional arrangements with organizations in developing countries including peasant farmers. According to Valpy (1986), the company created two subsidiaries, PanAgric Trading Corp. and AgriWorld, through which it assists developing countries to export their agricultural produce by buying it from them and reselling it to the international market if these countries in turn buy Varity's agricultural implements. In the Philippines, the company has formed a partnership with several hundred peasant family farms by promoting commercial farming and assisting these farmers to develop a sustained capacity to utilize modern farming methods. In this way, Varity is changing the nature and requirements for the performance of the critical operating tasks (e.g., crop production, pest control, irrigation, storage) associated with peasant farming and, in so doing, it is creating a market for its own products.

Organizations must also be integrated with their immediate domestic environment. Therefore, management's challenge is to develop and sustain a dynamic balance between the domestic and international environmental demands. The relative importance of each of these environments depends on several factors, including the nature and requirements of the organization's task subsystems and the industry or policy sector it belongs to. For example, KTDA, as an agricultural enterprise whose operating tasks are intimately related to its immediate environment including its growers, requires a balance different from, say, that needed by Tanzania's Friendship Textile Mills, whose operating technology was imported as a gift from China.

In choosing among the various collaborative institutional arrangements, an organization should give consideration to the following dimensions in which they differ:

1. The degree of formal commitment required of the participating organizations. Franchises and joint ventures impose strict formal requirements, while service contracts do not.

2. The degree of autonomy. Fights among partners in international joint ventures often involve decision-making autonomy over matters like dividend policy, management control, export privileges, and choice of partners in other collaborative arrangements (e.g., suppliers).

3. The duration and degree of involvement by the participating organizations. Management contracts last for a specified number of years and often contain provisions for modifications or withdraw. Franchises and joint ventures are like marriages; they are supposed to last forever and can only be dissolved with pain and difficulties.

4. The extent to which the CIA focuses on improving the performance of the critical operating or strategic management tasks or both. Turnkey operations, service contracts, and licensing are generally designed for critical operating tasks. Franchises, joint ventures, and management contracts address both operational and strategic tasks. Technical assistance and development projects have traditionally concentrated on operating and not strategic tasks.

Choice of CIAs can be made according to the particular needs of the organization in terms of improvements in its operational or strategic management tasks (see Chapter Three). Underorganized systems—organizations and policy sectors whose operations and strategic management tasks require improvements—should select those collaborative institutional arrangements that include both types of organizational tasks. The organizational and management principles of franchising appear to be particularly relevant for emerging or underorganized systems requiring overall rehabilitation because they provide the rigor and discipline that such weak organizations, left to themselves, are unable to enforce. Specifically, franchising principles can facilitate: (1) standardization; (2) strong hierarchy of authority; (3) close supervision; (4) quality control; and (5) effective strategic management of the environment.

The conditions imposed by the IMF can be viewed as a form of collaborative institutional arrangements designed to assist member states to improve the management of their respective economies. IMF imposes conditions that individual member states, left on their own, would be unable or unwilling to impose or enforce but that are necessary for their economies to turn around. In so doing, the IMF provides CIAs to public management organizations, especially in developing countries, for improved performance of a wide range of tasks including managing the budgetary process, managing and utilizing foreign exchange earnings, and managing the implementation of the necessary structural and behavioral adjustments of the economy. These CIAs are modified or withdrawn as the economy improves.

Collaborative institutional arrangements, like other integrating mechanisms, are not without costs or drawbacks. In a recent review paper on the vices and virtues of collective strategies for participating organizations, Rudi Bresser and Johannes E. Harl (1986) conclude that, necessary as these strategies may be, they can reduce strategic flexibility, increase the impact of external disturbances, lower organizational adaptability, and increase competition by attracting new entrants. Moreover, international joint ventures are notoriously unstable forms of organization and can cause dissatisfaction among the partners (Gomes-Casseres, 1985; Lasserre, 1983). IMF conditionalities can cause internal dissent and political violence as recently happened in Egypt, the Sudan, Tanzania, Nigeria, and Zambia. Clearly, collaborative institutional arrangements should be used judiciously.

IV. Summing Up All the Integrating Mechanisms

Figure 4.4 provides a summary illustration of the different types of integrating mechanisms discussed in this chapter and the hierarchical levels at which they are most commonly applied. The routine integrating mechanisms (RIMs) are mainly used for the routine tasks at the lower levels of the organization where the operating tasks (COTs) are found. The complex integrating mechanisms (CIMs) are used for the more complex strategic management tasks (SMATs) commonly found at the top levels of the organization. In the middle levels of the hierarchy, we find a combination of routine and complex integrating mechanisms. As both RIMs and CIMs are associated with costs and benefits for the organization and its members, it is important that management keeps a proper balance in their application of both types of mechanisms.

If two or more organizations are involved, integration is brought about by interorganizational coordination (IOC) or collaborative institu-

Figure 4.4

COTs, SMATs, AND THE INTEGRATING MECHANISMS

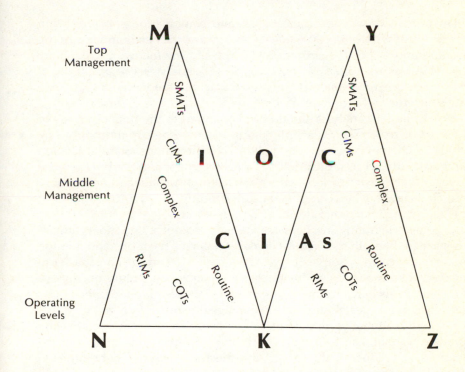

Note: MNK; KYZ represent hierarchies of two separate organizations;
        SMATs = Strategic Management Tasks; COTs = Critical Operating Tasks;
        CIMs = Complex integrating mechanisms; RIMs = Routine integrating mechanisms;
        IOC = Interorganizational coordination; CIAs = Collaborative institutional arrangements.

tional arrangements (CIAs). IOC, although usually conceptualized at the top levels of the organization as part of the strategic management tasks, translates readily into critical operating tasks, especially for professional organizations. Likewise, collaborative institutional arrangements are conceptually part of the SMATs, but their most practical value for the participating organizations is at the level of the critical operating tasks.

Table 4.2 summarizes the various complex integrating mechanisms and their relative effects on COTs, SMATs, or both. Mechanisms that are mainly focused on COTs but also affect the SMATs, such as franchising, are shown as COTs/SMATs. Those that mainly affect the SMATs but may also have an effect on COTs, such as management consultancy, are shown as SMATs/COTs.

V. Criteria of Choice of Integrating Mechanisms

Management must choose individual and combinations of integrating mechanisms with care, taking into consideration the needs and prevailing circumstances of the organization(s) involved. The following criteria are useful in making such choices: (1) cost benefit analysis; (2) complexity of the integrating mechanism; (3) organizational requirements; and (4) operative rewards and incentive systems.

Cost benefit analysis should not be limited to the financial costs or benefits of using particular integrating mechanisms. It should also include psychological, social, and political considerations. Standardization and close supervision contribute to more efficient operations but they also create poorly designed jobs, which cause employee alienation and poor morale. Some IOC mechanisms ensure continuous resource supplies at the cost of organizational autonomy and freedom.

Some integrating mechanisms are more complex and more difficult to manage than others. In this chapter, they have been presented in the order of increasing complexity so that the RIMs are simpler and easier to manage than the CIMs or the CIAs. An organization should not choose integrating mechanisms more complex than its needs for integration or its resources and expertise available to manage the integration.

Organizational requirements can be complex and may require comprehensive diagnosis before the exact nature of those requirements is determined. In general, the integrating mechanisms should be directed either to the operating or strategic management tasks or both according to the needs of the organization. They should be consistent with the characteristics of the general and task environments of the organization, and they should not unduly tax the internal resources of the organization. Organizations in developing countries wishing to conserve scarce management skills and expertise may not choose the more complex integrating mechanisms unless they are absolutely required by the task conditions.

Table 4.2

SUMMARY OF THE COMPLEX INTEGRATING MECHANISMS AND THEIR EFFECTS ON COTs AND SMATs

Integrating Mechanism	Design Elements	Main Effects on COTs or SMATs?
I. Internal Integrating Mechanisms	• Creation of lateral relations	COTs/SMATS
	• Direct contacts	COTs/SMATS
	• Task forces	COTs/SMATS
	• Teams	SMATS/COTs
	• Matrix	COTs
	• Informal Communications	SMATS/COTs
II. Interorganizational Coordination (IOC)	• Joint decision making	SMATS
	• Resource dependency/sharing	COTs
III. Collaborative Institutional Arrangements (CIAs)	• Service contracts	COTs
	• Industrial incubation	COTs
	• Turnkey operations	COTs
	• Subcontracting	COTs
	• Licencing	COTs
	• Technical Assistance	COTs
	• Franchising	COTs/SMATS
	• Joint ventures	COTs/SMATS
	• Buy-make decisions	SMATS/COTs
	• Management contracts	COTs/SMATS
	• Management consultancy	SMATS/COTs

Note: COTs = Critical operating tasks; SMATs = Strategic management tasks.

In the early stages of creation, organizations are mostly concerned with establishing organizational systems for perfecting their critical operating tasks. Accordingly, the emphasis for coordination should be on routine integrating mechanisms (RIMs). As organizations grow bigger and more complex, management of the environment becomes more important and complex integrating mechanisms are necessary. If an organization wishes to be a world-class organization, almost invariably it must develop international collaborative institutional arrangements.

Finally, perhaps one of the most important criteria is consistency between the integrating mechanism and the operative reward and incentive systems. While the integrating mechanisms create the necessary structural arrangements, it is the incentive systems that motivate the appropriate behavior within those structural arrangements. Incentives can make or break the organization's integration. If the organization uses individually based rewards and incentives, integrating mechanisms based on group effort like alternative forms of work organization are not likely to be effective. Likewise, if the incentives reward obedience and loyalty, integrative mechanisms requiring risk-taking and innovation will not work. Developing countries go through phases when they seek out or withdraw from international contacts. If a country happens to be in a withdrawal phase, it would be inappropriate for its organizations to seek out international collaborative institutional arrangements, no matter how attractive and beneficial these would be for the individual organization or policy sector. In choosing the appropriate integrating mechanisms, management must examine the internal characteristics and resources of the organization, and the nature of both its general and specific task environment within which it must perform its tasks.

Summary

The critical operating and the strategic management tasks must be integrated to form a fully functioning organizational entity. This chapter discusses the uses and limitations of routine integrating mechanisms (RIMs), complex integrating mechanisms (CIMs), interorganizational coordination (IOC), and collaborative institutional arrangements (CIAs) with a section on the criteria for choosing any of these integrating mechanisms.

Three different types of routine integrating mechanisms, the hierarchy of authority, standard operating procedures (SOPs), and alternative forms of work organization are discussed. RIMs are particularly suitable for the integration of critical operating tasks. The hierarchy of authority is discussed in terms of its spatial and temporal cumulative responsibilities up the hierarchy, and the advantages and limitations of close supervision. SOPs are discussed as a part of rules, policies, and procedures; plans and budgets; and standardization. Standardization can be applied to inputs; transformation processes; outputs; knowledge, skills, and beliefs; and values, attitudes, and behavior.

In the discussion of CIMs, a distinction is made between the internal integrating mechanisms used for integrating the operating and strategic management tasks within the organization, and the interorganizational coordinating mechanisms for two or more organizations. Internal integrating mechanisms include direct contacts, task forces, teams, matrix design, and informal communications. The matrix design is illustrated by the problems of management and coordination of national structural adjustment programs, which are commonly found in many developing countries. In the discussion of interorganizational coordination, special attention is paid to the performance and coordination of operating (COTs) and management (SMATs) tasks across two or more interdependent organizations. CIMs are particularly suitable for the more complex strategic management tasks.

Collaborative institutional arrangements (CIAs) are structural and behavioral mechanisms between two or more organizations designed to benefit the participating organizations by enhancing their sustained capacity to perform their respective COTs, SMATs, or both. It is observed in this chapter that most organizations in developing countries stand to gain from selected domestic and international CIAs.

The choice of which of these integrating mechanisms or combinations thereof to use is a management responsibility that must be exercised after careful thought and analysis. The criteria for the selection of the appropriate integrating mechanisms include costs and benefits, complexity, organizational requirements, and operative rewards and incentives.

PART TWO

Selected Applications of the Model

The first four chapters of this book provide a framework for understanding the manner in which an organization works, its two task subsystems, and their internal integration and environmental coordination with other organizations. Chapter One has introduced development administration and organization science and set the stage for the rest of the book. Chapter Two has discussed the critical operating tasks (COTs) and their significance for the day to day operations of the organization. Chapter Three has described the strategic management tasks (SMATs) and their importance in shaping the direction of the organization and managing its relationships with other elements in its general and task environments. Chapter Four has provided an elaborate discussion of the various forms and structures by which the organization is internally integrated and externally coordinated. The topics in these chapters are illustrated with examples from organizations in developing countries.

In Part Two of the book, discussion focuses on the applications of the model presented in the previous four chapters. In substantiating the applicability of this model, I have selected some of the most important current issues in development administration, as well as the management of organizations in developing countries. Obviously, it is not possible to discuss all the relevant issues, interventions, or management techniques found in these organizations. Nevertheless, the model provides a framework for understanding and analyzing the probable effects of any intervention or management techniques on the performance of the organization's task subsystems, or the welfare of its members. Likewise, the measurement, evaluation, and impact assessment of development initiatives can be related to these three aspects for the target organization or organizations.

Whether they are called empowerment (Brinkerhoff, 1979), capacity building, institutional rehabilitation, and development (Kiggundu, 1986), technology transfer (Stobaugh and Wells, 1984), bureaucratic reorientation (Korten and Uphoff, 1981), leadership (Hage and Finsterbusch, 1987), or organization development and change (White, 1987), development management (Rondinelli, 1987), or structural adjustments, these interventions should be directly related to a specific organization and its target task subsystems for which the change is intended. For example, empowerment of the organization and its members should specify whether it is for improvements in the performance of the organization's critical operating tasks, strategic management tasks, or integrative and coordinative mechanisms, or just for the improvement of the welfare of its members. Moreover, in order to build the organization's capacity and management infrastructure, analyses and interventions are required for the performance of the critical operating tasks that are different from those for the strategic management tasks or for coordination. Even within each task subsystem, there may be conceptual and practical differences. For example, the internal strategic management tasks require the development of management capacities associated with internal management systems like supervision, management information systems, planning, and reward and control systems, whereas contextual strategic management tasks require complex interorganizational coordinating mechanisms. Yet, in developmental administration, in discussions of important issues like decentralization, technology transfer, human resource development, and their associated intervention methods, these distinctions are rarely made and therefore the organization, and its management, can never be sure of the nature of the cause-effect relationships.

In the following chapters the issues and interventions are presented in terms of their differential effects on the various task subsystems. Chapter 5 discusses human resource development and utilization for the performance of both critical operating and strategic management tasks. Chapter 6 defines technology and knowledge transfer and emphasizes the need to build an effective local technological capacity that is sustainable. Chapter 7 describes decentralization, while Chapter 8 discusses the management of structural adjustment including the role of the state in the organization and management of the economy, state-owned enterprises, divestiture, privatization, and the development of the indigenous private sector. The last chapter provides a synthesis and a final note regarding the future challenges of managing strategic organizations in developing countries.

CHAPTER 5

Human Resource Development and Utilization

Developing countries have three great assets: the land, the gods, and the people. Reference to land includes the vast size, diversity, and richness of natural resources. Reference to the gods relates to the existence of conditions whereby the "higher" and "lower" gods coexist in apparent harmony and give the people the strength, faith, and resilience to live and persevere in some of the most impoverished of human conditions. This chapter discusses the challenges and prospects of developing and utilizing one of the greatest assets—the people. Drawing from the COTs/SMATs model developed in the previous four chapters, this chapter shows that the future prospects for social, economic, and political developments for most developing countries are intimately related to their ability to develop and effectively utilize their human resources. To date, however, human resources remain among the least developed and used, and often the most abused resources in these countries.

This chapter contains four sections. The first section sets the stage by presenting a general model describing the internal organizational factors and environmental context within which human resource management (HRM) operates. The second section distinguishes between human resource development (HRD) and human resource utilization (HRU) and suggests that more emphasis should be put on the latter. The third section, drawing on concepts developed in earlier chapters, discusses the various aspects of the human resource management function and how it relates to the performance of the organization's critical operating and strategic management tasks. The chapter ends with a discussion of five current issues regarding human resource management. These are: (1) training; (2) utilization; (3) motivation; (4) the brain drain; and (5) effective utilization of expatriate staff. It also provides a framework for thinking about HRM research and development for organizations in these countries.

145

I. A General Model of Human Resource Management

Human resource management (HRM) is the development and utilization of personnel for the effective achievement of individual, organizational, community, national, and international goals and objectives. HRM does not operate in a vacuum but is best conceptualized as an open system made up of component subsystems interacting with one another and with the outside environment. The system must be internally consistent such that the component subsystems are not contradictory or in conflict with one another. It must also be in harmony with the external environment or context within which it operates. Internal contradictions or external discordance leads to ineffective or counterproductive human resource development and utilization. Several models can be used to analyze or diagnose an HRM system of an organization, policy sector, or country. Examples include those developed by Dunlop (1958), Glueck (1982), and Fombrun (1984). Dunlop's model operates at a macro national or international level, and Glueck's at the level of the organization, while Fombrun's model applies to strategic human resource management. In Glueck's model, the external environment is made up of government requirements, society's expectations, economic conditions, labor market conditions, and union expectations. In developing countries, government dominates all discussions of human resource development and management.

In order to understand and diagnose a country's or organization's HRM system, it is necessary that we consider the internal organization and management structures, processes, activities, and outcomes, and the demand characteristics of the context or external environment within which the system operates. Within the organization, we must assess the nature, scope, complexity, and coordination of the critical operating and the strategic management tasks. If the organization's HRM system does not contribute to the organization's efficient and effective performance of the operating and strategic management tasks, its existence can hardly be justified. We must also consider the organization's mission, management philosophy and practice, objectives, strategies, operational tactics, structure, and resource endowment. Within the organizational context, we should analyze specific and general environmental factors such as economic and market conditions, the local technological capacity, labor and industrial relations, the political environment, international relations, social and physical security, sociocultural values and practices, and population dynamics. All these factors combine to determine the appropriate composition, design, organization, and level of sophistication of the activities of an organization's HRM system. Likewise, effective development and utilization of human resources requires an understanding of these factors and their individual and interactive effects on the performance of the HRM system.

Drawing from the above criteria, Figure 5.1 presents a model for understanding the interrelationships between human resource management and the internal and external factors. These relationships must be understood in terms of the organization's requirements for the performance of its critical operating and strategic tasks and how the human resources are developed, and used to perform those tasks with economy and effectiveness. In addition, these relationships are dynamic and change with time as both the external and internal factors and the nature of their relationships also change. For example, changes in economic or political forces can result in new ownership of an organization; this

Figure 5.1

THE INTERNAL AND EXTERNAL CONTEXT OF HUMAN RESOURCE MANAGEMENT

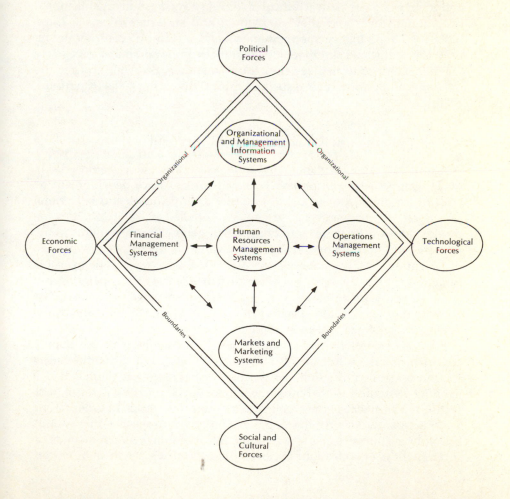

change in turn brings about a different internal management philosophy and direction, necessitating changes in human resources. The model shows that focusing on a single human resource activity like training without systematic analysis of its relationships with other internal or external dimensions of the organization can be unproductive or even counterproductive.

The results of a management resource audit of an African central bank which I recently conducted show the possible effects of contextual and internal factors on the organization's state of its human resources. The country's history of political instability and violence had led to "organizational hemorrhage" (e.g., brain drain), economic deterioration had eroded employee wages and precipitated serious motivational problems, and the weakening local technological capacity made it almost impossible for the bank to fulfill its regulatory and supervisory critical operating tasks as well as its advisory strategic management tasks. The prevailing cultural and social practices made it difficult to develop and sustain organizational commitment over and above individual and sectarian interests. Internally, the bank's management, financial, and accounting controls and incentive systems had almost totally broken down. It was almost impossible for management to manage (i.e., carry out their SMATs), and for the operators to perform their respective critical operating tasks (Kiggundu, 1988c).

II. Development and Utilization

A distinction must be made between *human resource development* (HRD), and *human resource utilization* (HRU). Human resource development relates to the development of institutional arrangements and behavioral processes for the acquisition of general knowledge, skills, abilities, attitudes, and values in order to bring about general improvements in the human condition. Human resource utilization is the extent to which an organization has the capacity for sustained deployment of available human resources for the effective performance of its critical operating and strategic management tasks. It is organization specific, and it relates directly to the organization-specific tasks required by its mission and by the strategies that it has chosen to fulfill its mandate.

Most discussions of human resource management in developing countries focus on human resource development but virtually neglect human resource utilization. Yet, without human resource utilization, it cannot be guaranteed that human resource development will result in effective performance of the organization's important tasks. In order for the various human resource development initiatives undertaken by various developing countries and international development agencies to be of direct benefit to organizations in developing countries, we must be as concerned with problems of human resource utilization as we are with issues of development. Organizing for effective utilization, however, is much more challenging than organizing for development. It requires comprehensive analysis and understanding of the organization's task requirements, its management control and incentive practices, current and potential capabilities of available human resources, resource endowment, incentives, and the external context within which the organization operates.

1. Development

It is now generally recognized that the human condition and human resources constitute one of the most serious bottlenecks for development. This is particularly critical in Africa where, as a recent World Bank report observed, ". . . the lack of human resources constitutes the major constraint on the development of the region . . . The lack of skills and experience to man the modern public and private sectors has always been regarded as the major constraint on economic development in Africa, and hence, the most serious human resource problem" (Davies, 1980:55, 60).

The problem, however, is not limited to Africa but is widespread across organizations in other developing countries. For example, a recent high-level discussion on financial and human resources management issues held in Istanbul by the North South Round-Table (NSRT) and the Development Study Programme of the UNDP observed that: ". . . it is the quality, sophistication and level of skills in the public and private sectors that determine the development, productivity and economic growth of developing countries and their capacity to respond to changing requirements" (North South Round-Table, 1983:34).

The report went on to recommend that: "Particular attention should be paid in developing countries to the establishment of a creative educational system, structured to meet prospective needs of a country's economy, avoiding both overqualification and structural skill deficiencies in the available human resources. It is essential that an appropriate balance between different levels of education be struck, in order to allow the emergence of as wide a talent base as possible" (North South Round-Table, 1983:35). These strategies, if implemented, would address questions of human resource development but not necessarily human resource utilization.

In most developing countries, human resource development is no longer seen only as a means of supplying trained personnel for employers in the formal sector. Rather, it is increasingly being regarded as a basic human need, as a means for meeting other basic needs, and as an activity that sustains and accelerates overall development. It helps to relieve poverty, ignorance, and disease by improving income, health, and nutritional practices; by reducing fertility; by transmitting cultural, religious, political, and technological values; and by preserving national identity and cohesiveness. Human resource development through education is one of the most effective means of fighting underdevelopment at the individual, organizational, community, and national levels.

Because economic growth has not eliminated absolute poverty in the developing countries, other strategies for improving the human condition, such as human resource development, should be encouraged (Bussink et al., 1980). More efforts should be made to provide poor people with the living and social skills they need to look after themselves, especially in the areas of health, nutrition, family planning, education, self-employment, and, in politically disturbed countries, security and protection. This perspective gives education and HRD institutions the greatest possible mandate, bringing their work closer to the totality of the human condition, and posing a greater challenge for all types of organizations in developing countries.

Human resource development efforts have yielded some positive results. More people are being educated than ever before. Enrollment ratios at all levels have risen. For example, in a relatively short period of time, Zimbabwe has had to more than double its enrollments at all levels of the education system bringing the average primary school enrollment as a percentage of the age group to 130 percent (134 boys, 125 girls). Percentages higher than 100 are possible because in a country with a universal educational system, repeats and re-entry into the educational system could lead to enrollments exceeding that country's standard primary school age, usually 6 to 12 years. More relevant curricula are being developed, tested, and revised. For example, Tanzania and Colombia have been experimenting with diversified schools in which a number of pre-vocational subjects such as agriculture and industrial arts are taught in addition to the regular academic program. Public spending on education by developing countries, except China and other centrally planned economies, rose in real dollars from about $9 billion in 1960 to $38 billion in 1977. This growth represents an increase from 2.3 percent to 4.1 percent of GNP, and from an average of 11.7 percent to 16.3 percent of annual national budgets (Baum and Tolbert, 1985). Education, especially for women, has led to more effective family planning, better health and nutrition, and reduced fertility rates. These have multiplier effects since educated parents are likely to bring up fewer, healthier, and better educated children. Yet these remarkable achievements have not been translated into effective human resource utilization for the direct benefit of developing country organizations in terms of performing their respective critical operating and strategic management tasks.

In spite of all these efforts and results, serious problems still abound. Demand far exceeds available supply for education and human resource development. An estimated 250 million children and 600 million adults have had little or no access to education. Illiteracy is growing in some of the low-income countries, especially in Africa. The distribution of educational opportunities remains highly inequitable. According to a recent World Bank report by Hinchliffe (1985), the enrollment ratio for higher education in sub-Saharan Africa ranges from a high of only 7 percent for Guinea, to a low of 0.03 percent for Burkina Faso. The overall quality of education still needs improvements especially in rural areas where many of the teachers are unqualified and facilities are inadequate. Wastage, dropout, and repeat rates are high. School leavers have little or no portable skills to offer prospective employers. Diversified schools have not succeeded in enhancing student learning or employment. In spite of increased government expenditures, schools, colleges, universities, and other educational and training institutions continue to experience inadequate capital and operational resource shortages. Governments are finding it more and more difficult to meet local and foreign exchange recurrent cost requirements, especially in a climate of economic and financial restraint characteristic of the 1980s. The less developed a country is, the higher its unit costs for education are likely to be. For example, Hinchliffe (1985) found that the average unit costs for higher education in sub-Saharan Africa were two times those of Latin America, and ten times those of Asia. In many developing countries, human resource development organizations experience varying degrees of institutional decay (Kiggundu, 1985). These limitations are important because there can be no effective utilization of human resources without effective sustainable indigenous human resource development.

2. Utilization

Utilization relates to the extent to which human resources are acquired, developed, organized, managed, and deployed for the maximum achievement of individual, collective, organizational, or national goals and objectives. It is the appropriate organizational criterion for assessing the effectiveness of human resource development initiatives. From an organizational point of view, human resource utilization must be understood in the context of its impact on the effective performance and coordination of the organization's critical operating and strategic management tasks.

In most organizations, human capital tends to be underutilized in comparison with other forms of capital resources. This trend is particularly detrimental to organizations in developing countries where labor constitutes one of the factors of comparative advantage. Organizations can overcome some of these problems by taking a strategic approach to human resource development and utilization. This approach requires that the organization focus on the development and utilization of its human resources in combination with other resources (e.g., financial, technological, political): (1) to prepare for and respond effectively to the changing threats and opportunities of its general and specific environment; and (2) to organize itself internally for the efficient and effective performance of its critical operating and strategic management tasks. If an organization fails to utilize its human resources strategically, it may not be able to achieve the strategic goals and objectives arising out of its mission statement (Fombrun, 1984).

Organizations vary by the extent to which they effectively utilize their human resources. In order for an organization to utilize its human resources effectively, it must have:

1. clearly stated, understood, and widely accepted organizational mission, goals, and objectives;

2. a critical mass of human resources with the requisite skills, knowledge, abilities, experience, attitudes, and values for the effective performance of the organization's operating and strategic management tasks;

3. appropriate supervisory and managerial styles and practices;

4. opportunities for human resource training, upgrading, development, and advancement in preparation for the performance of the organization's future critical operating and strategic management tasks;

5. management, control, reward, and incentive systems supportive of efforts for human resource utilization;

6. current valid individual job information, performance standards, measurements, and feedback; and

7. a benign or supportive external environment.

Figure 5.2 shows the relationship between human resource development and human resource utilization as well as some of the determinants of human resource utilization. Human resource development is influenced by environmental factors such as government policy or demographic facts, individual and organizational attributes such as willingness and incentives to learn and to transfer the learning to the work situation, and job information such as job analysis and labor markets. Individual and organizational attributes lead to individual behavior, which translates into task performance, which in turn leads to human resource utilization. C_1, C_2, and C_3 represent contingencies or moderator variables between organization attributes and behavior; between behavior and performance (desired outcomes); and between performance and effective utilization of human resources. That is, for example, all behavior does not translate into

Figure 5.2

**THE RELATIONSHIP BETWEEN ORGANIZATIONAL HUMAN
RESOURCE DEVELOPMENT AND UTILIZATION**

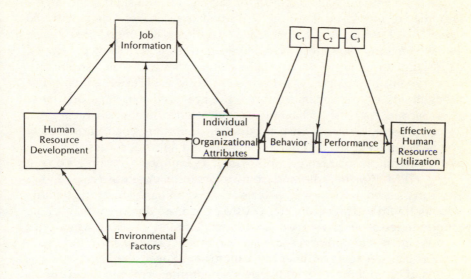

Note: C_1, C_2, C_3 = Contingencies or moderator variables between individual attributes and behavior; organizational behavior and performance; and performance and effective utilization of human resources, respectively.

task performance and task performance does not necessarily mean effective utilization of the organization's human resources. The extent to which an individual employee's performance translates into effective human resource utilization (C_3) may depend on the extent to which such an employee understands and internalizes the organization's task goals and objectives.

III. The Human Resource Management Function

Human resource management is one of the weakest functions in organizations in developing countries. Most of the organizations either do not have it, overload it with other, often extraorganizational functions, use it as a dumping ground for employees who cannot succeed elsewhere in the organization, deprive it of organizational resources and political support, provide personnel specialists discouragingly low compensation, or accord them low status and recognition in the overall management of the enterprise. In most cases, HRM positions are the first to be localized partly because they are considered inconsequential, and partly because they tend to be politicized rather than professional.

Several reasons account for the general lack of attention to the HRM function in most organizations in developing countries. Most of them have to do with the nature and size of the organizations. First, the largest number of employers are those in small organizations employing 50 people or less. Even in industrialized countries like the United States, small companies with less than 250 employees do not have developed HRM functions, largely because of lack of economies of scale. An effective way for small employers to get access to HRM expertise is either to use consultants, or to collaborate through their respective trade associations.

Second, for most developing countries, agriculture is still the biggest sector by employment. Most production units are small, individually owned farms employing family members and a few outsiders. Even the large agricultural plantations employing large numbers of workers do not have HRM functions beyond routine maintenance functions. Other resource-based industries such as mining, wood harvesting, and fishing, do not traditionally use advanced HRM expertise. Moreover, many of the modern sector or private sector organizations are foreign-owned ones whose interest in human resource management is rather circumscribed.

Third, where government is a major employer, the HRM function tends to be underdeveloped. In government ministries and departments and, to a lesser extent, in state-owned enterprises in developing countries, the HRM function is quite undeveloped and limited only to routine administrative functions. The difficulties of demonstrating the relationships between efforts, performance, incentives, and rewards in the public service is one of the reasons for the lack of emphasis on the development of the HRM function.

Finally, employers in both the private and the public sectors avoid the necessity of developing advanced human resource management by finding alternatives to using indigenous human resources. Production organizations in developing countries have a high propensity to use capital-intensive or labor-saving technology. Organizations using this strategy would have less need for developing human resources. Organizations operating in developing countries, with less developed and skilled human resources, make extensive use of expatriate personnel and outside consultants. Although these guest workers include some highly experienced international specialists, by far the largest number are low-level employees working in places such as South Africa's resource-based industries, the Middle East, and Europe. To the extent that the organization relies on outside supplies for its human resource requirements, it has little or no incentive to develop its own human resources. This is particularly true in the performance of its operating tasks where most of the people are employed but where technology, close supervision, and other routine integrating mechanisms (RIMs) are used as substitutes for advanced operator skills and knowledge.

Management strategies designed to undermine the HRM function of an organization are short-sighted and detrimental to the long-term interests of the organization or country in which it operates. Studies in both developing and industrialized countries have shown that organizations with a progressive HRM function are more effective and competitive than those without. For example, Tung (1982) has argued that a key element in the development of China's industrial society after Mao is the more effective development and utilization of the country's human resources using both material and intrinsic incentive systems. Comparing U.S. and Japanese multinational corporations, Tung (1983) has also shown that Japanese companies are more successful and competitive abroad because they pay more attention to critical HRM functions such as selection, training, and briefing of their employees for overseas assignments.

1. Dimensions of Human Resource Management

HRM functions can be characterized as: (1) maintenance or developmental; (2) operational or strategic; and (3) personal growth or organization development oriented. Each of these categories has implications for human resource development and utilization and the performance of organizational operating and strategic management tasks.

Maintenance and Developmental Functions. Maintenance HRM activities are routine administrative functions designed to maintain the status quo, or to provide employees with services mandated by law or employment contract. They include functions such as payroll and benefits administration, employee records keeping, and administration of welfare programs such as food supplies, housing, transport, loans, and sick and holiday benefits. Developmental HRM functions, on the other hand, are designed to improve individual ability, motivation, and commitment to the organization, and to enhance the organization's capacity to utilize its employees more effectively in performing their present and future job requirements. Developmental functions include training and development; organization design; job design aimed at achieving an optimum person-job match; career planning and development; reward and compensation contingent upon effective contribution to organizational goals; meritorious employee recruitment, testing, assessment, selection, and placement; comprehensive and up-to-date job analysis and evaluation; performance appraisal designed to reward exceptional performance and provide employees with the opportunity for self-improvement; team building for effective collaborative work groups and constructive conflict management; and personnel research for the development of more effective HRM programs. They also include management development and leadership training for future managers and leaders of the organization. Only the developmental HRM functions have direct effects on the organization's capacity to perform its tasks.

Developing country organizations tend to limit themselves only to maintenance functions with little or no attention paid to developmental functions. As a recent World Bank report observed, within the public service "the activities of most personnel offices go little beyond record keeping and drafting personnel procedures" (Ozgediz, 1983:47). Moreover, human resource management is not regarded as a specialized area of study. Out of 45 developing countries surveyed by the World Bank, only 40 percent had special cadres for HRM specialists. Even in the private sector, the personnel department is often assigned maintenance or extra-organizational functions. In Kenya, such functions include renewal of expatriate work permits and public relations. In Zambia, Crosby (1976) found that the departments were extensively involved in community welfare and political activities.

Developmental HRM functions are more difficult and expensive to undertake than maintenance functions because their design requires specialized HRM expertise, and their implementation requires sustained technical and political support from all levels of the organization. Both of these requirements are hard to fulfill in most organizations in developing countries. Yet, in order for organizations to become and remain effective and competitive, they must design and implement developmental HRM programs for the benefit of all their employees. The individual functions must also be consistent with one another such that training, for example, is supportive of the required level of performance, which in turn is linked to the trainees' rewards and incentives. When the individual functions are in conflict with one another, as when training is undertaken for extra-organizational considerations, or when promotions are not based on job performance or skills acquisition, they are of no benefit to the organization or its employees in terms of enhancing its capacity to perform its COTs and SMATs.

Utilizing development aspects of human resource management, however, does not necessitate overhauling the whole organization, its management philosophy, values, or practices. Even in an organization driven by patronage or nepotism, some of these functions can be used to advantage. Even in situations where entry into the organization is limited to a select group of people predetermined by race, ethnicity, religion, or political affiliation, it helps to undertake systematic testing and assessment of the candidates so as to determine their vocational interests and areas of strength and weaknesses. This information can be useful in making informed staffing, training, and career development personnel decisions that would benefit both the individuals and the organization.

Moreover, size is not an important consideration as small organizations can utilize HRM functions equally as well as large ones. For example, an entrepreneur choosing among his children to succeed him as head of the family business can use assessment center methods (Thornton and Byham, 1982) to determine the child with the greatest leadership and managerial potential. Placing the right people in the right jobs is the first step in the development of an effective task-performing organization that also effectively utilizes available human resources.

Operational and Strategic Human Resource Management.   Operational HRM activities are short-term efforts designed to meet current or immediate needs of the organization. Functions such as employee selection, staffing, performance appraisal, assessment, training, and compensation are carried out in response to the organization's current requirements without regard to its requirements for long-term or strategic management tasks. An example is an organization that continues to hire from its traditional sources in order to meet current human resource requirements even though changes in its strategic plans necessitate a different skills mix. This practice would have negative consequences on its capacity to develop and maintain high performance systems for its changing COTs and SMATs.

Organizations in developing countries with an active HRM function tend to focus on operational HRM functions. The reasons for this are easy to understand. First, operational tasks are simpler and easier to justify, as they tend to be initiated in response to a crisis or urgent need from the line departments. Second, if the people involved in human resource management do not participate in the development and implementation of the organization's strategic plans, they will not know what is required from a strategic HRM standpoint. Without the necessary expertise and other organizational resources, the best they can do is to react to the immediate needs as they come from line management. Organizations whose HRM activities are limited to maintenance and operational functions do not provide the necessary job challenge and development opportunities for attracting and retaining progressive HRM professionals or achievement-oriented operators looking for challenge and rewarding work.

In strategic human resource management, all programs, projects, and activities relating to the HRM function such as selection, staffing, assessment and performance appraisal, reward and control systems, and training and development must be designed, implemented, and evaluated in the context of the organization's mission, business strategy, goals, and objectives. In this regard, human resource management becomes an important consideration in the process of overall formulation and implementation of strategic plans. The overall organizational or corporate strategic management tasks provide the basis for human resource strategic management tasks, which in turn give rise to the resulting human resource critical operating functions.

In organizations in developing countries, HRM functions are rarely linked to the organization's overall strategic plans. Consequently, human resource shortages—both qualitative and quantitative—create serious bottlenecks in the implementation of otherwise sound development initiatives. A recent report based on a workshop of CIDA country program managers, professional development specialists, and representatives from various executing agencies revealed that shortages of skilled and experienced personnel constitute one of the most serious limitations to the implementation and sustainability of development programs (Dasah and Kiggundu, 1986). Workshop participants recommended that a comprehensive HRM audit be undertaken before the proposed development initiatives are implemented. The audit would provide a realistic assessment of the availability of the necessary human resources for the successful implementation of the project. If the implementing organization lacks the necessary human resources for the continued performance of its COTs and SMATs arising out of the project, the project should either be postponed, or be redesigned to reflect the human resource realities.

It is not uncommon for organizations in developing countries to have no explicit corporate mission or strategic plan. If an organization has no articulate operational strategic plan, it cannot have a strategic HRM function. It would therefore have no basis for preparing its employees for the future. As organizations in developing countries become more complex, and as they begin to operate in a less protected and increasingly uncertain, competitive, and often hostile environment characterized by economic restraint and resource scarcity, political and international pressures, sociocultural changes, and technological advances, they are going to need, more than ever before, carefully crafted missions and strategic business plans. For such plans to be implemented meaningfully and to contribute to the development process, they must be backed up by professionally designed strategic human resource management functions that in turn must be translated into practical applications for the organization's COTs and SMATs. In this way, the HRM function will have a significant and sustainable impact on the development and utilization of an organization's competence in the performance of its tasks.

Individual Growth and Organizational Development.   Some HRM functions contribute more directly to individual growth while others are focused on the development of the work group or organization. For example, career planning, training, and development may enhance the growth and self-actualization of the individual employees without contributing to organizational development if the employees' newly acquired skills and expertise are not needed by the organization. HRM functions designed to enhance organizational capacity do not always take into account individual needs for growth and development. For example, most of the technical training provided to operators for the performance of the organization's critical operating tasks does not normally consider the social and intrinsic needs of the individuals. Likewise, humanistic interventions designed to enhance individual self-awareness and growth such as T-groups (Training) and sensitivity training do not directly contribute to organizational development or effectiveness. Many overseas training and study tours can be difficult to justify from the point of view of an organization's human resource utilization.

It is also common to find inconsistencies between individual and group activities and incentives. For example, in most organizations, while work is organized and performed in groups, training, performance appraisal, rewards, and incentives are individually administered. These reduce the effectiveness of HRM functions as employees attempt to reconcile the conflicting cues from management. If employees perform their jobs and receive performance feedback in groups, their performance appraisal and compensation should be group-based as well.

The HRM challenge for an organization is that it develop management systems and practices that integrate the operational and strategic management demands of the organization and the immediate and long-term needs of the employees individually and collectively as a team. It can do this by: (1) specifying the strategic plans of the organization and translating them into operational goals and objectives down to the level of the individual employees; (2) assessing individual employee's current and future abilities, interests, motivation, and needs; (3) providing employees with the resources and opportunities needed to meet their job requirements; and (4) compensating employees and assisting them to meet their legitimate needs contingent upon effective job performance and organizational goal attainment. Drawing from human relations, Argyris (1964) challenges managers to integrate the needs of the individual and the task demands of the organization by appealing to the workers' higher needs and intrinsic motives, and by treating them like mature responsible adults.

These conditions are difficult to meet, particularly for organizations in developing countries. Strategic planning operationalized to the level of individual employees requires information and expertise that may not be readily available. Assessing employee current performance and future potential requires testing, job analysis, and performance appraisal tools and methods that so far have not been adapted to most organizations in developing countries. Accurate, reliable, and valid performance measurements do not exist, especially in the public service organizations. These are some of the limitations to the effective utilization of progressive HRM programs.

Current Issues in Human Resource Management.   This section discusses some of the current HRM issues facing organizations in developing countries. These issues are: (1) training; (2) human resource utilization; (3) motivational crisis; (4) the brain drain and skill shortages; and (5) utilization of expatriate staff.

Training.   Training is by far the most popular prescription for curing organizational pathologies. Most organizations in developing countries have considered training the most practical solution to their chronic human resource inadequacies and organizational weaknesses (Kerrigan and Luke, 1987). At the time of independence, faced with acute shortages of skilled and experienced personnel in all fields at all levels, most developing countries undertook ambitious programs to train their own nationals and reduce dependency on expatriates. They were assisted by the international community, which provided money and facilities for training both at home and abroad. Existing training institutes were expanded, and new ones were built. According to a recent World Bank report, by 1980 developing countries had 276 government institutions, university departments, and independent institutions providing training in public administration and management. Although this figure may seem small, it is four times the number of institutions in existence in 1960. Most of the early training was of a general nature but increasing attention is being given to applied fields like engineering, management, and agriculture. Over the years, training has become so pervasive that for a number of international aid agencies it is equivalent to human resource development.

In spite of all these efforts, however, training —especially but not exclusively in the public service organizations—remains both inadequate and ineffective. It is inadequate because existing opportunities are too few to meet the growing demand for training. Ozgediz (1983) estimates that in 1978, only 4 percent of Malaysia's federal and state government workers received some form of training. In India, only one-fifth of all civil servants are likely to receive some in-service training during their entire career. In Turkey, only one-seventh of public servants receive training in public administration. The Indian central government is estimated to spend about 0.5 percent of its payroll on training. In comparison, large multinational corporations like IBM and Unilever spend 5 percent of payroll on training and the Japanese and U.S. governments offer training to about 25 percent of their employees every year (Paul, 1983a).

In most cases, training is not only inadequate, it is also ineffective. Several reasons account for the ineffectiveness. First, there is no systematic approach to training: no needs analysis, no impact assessment, and no follow-up. Second, training is performed as a discrete activity unrelated and almost irrelevant to other functions and activities in the organization. Third, the training function and the institutions themselves lack competent motivated trainers and managers and the necessary organizational resources, facilities, and political support to do an effective job. The danger is that, as the efficacy of training becomes more questionable, and as resource restraints become tighter, training in particular, and the developmental HRM function in general, is likely to receive less, not more, attention as a development priority. Fourth, most of the training is off-site and often outside the country. Thus, any of these newly learned skills or behaviors are hard to transfer to the workplace. Although off-site training may be attractive for personal reasons, such as travel abroad and time off from work, its usefulness can be limited because of problems of relevancy and transfer. It also biases the selection process such that those who end up traveling abroad are not necessarily the ones who need to be trained.

A fifth reason for ineffective training in organizations in developing countries is inadequate or inappropriate organization and management systems and practices. For example, for training to be effective, it is necessary for the trainee to have a clear understanding of his or her job expectations including the methods by which performance is to be measured and appraised. Very few organizations in developing countries undertake systematic job analysis and produce for each employee an up-to-date job description based on accurate and comprehensive job information. Yet, without an accurate statement of the knowledge, skills, and abilities (KSAs) required for the job, it is very difficult to design training programs that will improve the performance of the trainees.

Management and supervisory styles, incentives, and control systems in the trainees' organization should be supportive and should reinforce learning and the use of the new knowledge and behavior for solving problems at work. During training sessions, it is not unusual that trainees complain and respond with a "don't train me, train my boss" attitude. Too much emphasis is placed on formal academic education and possession of certificates and not enough on the relevancy or actual utilization of the qualifications for the performance of the organization's tasks. Until recently, technical and vocational training at best received benign neglect. It is also necessary to change the incentive systems so that employees are rewarded for learning and bringing new approaches to problem solving at work rather than to use seniority or extraorganizational criteria for rewarding, punishing, or controlling employees.

Learning is a continuous process and, moreover, most learning takes place not in formal classroom settings but in informal settings and contacts with others of similar professional interests. It is therefore necessary for organizations to develop internal and external coordination and collaborative institutional arrangements (CIAs) to facilitate learning and continuing flow and exchange of ideas and experiences with others. Because trade and professional associations are underdeveloped in most technical and professional fields, the organization wishing to promote professionalism and continued learning for its employees must assume some of these responsibilities.

In summary, the causes of ineffective training go beyond the training function and training institutions. They include problems of ineffective organization and management of the HRM function, and the quality of the overall management and coordination of the trainees' organization and its environment. Addressing these problems requires a systematic diagnosis of the organization, the tasks (COTs and SMATs) it needs done, the skills inventory of its employees, the management system in place, and the training and nontraining interventions that must be undertaken to create and sustain an effective learning and responsive organization. Training then becomes one among many (optional) interventions.

Figure 5.3 shows a systematic step-by-step approach to effective training. It starts with an organizational diagnosis or management audit to identify the organization's capacity to perform its COTs and SMATs. Out of this comes an identification of a wide range of training and nontraining interventions that are necessary for improving the organization's performance and effectiveness. The distinction between training and nontraining interventions is important because all organizational problems need not be solved through training. It is also important because it underscores the importance of integrating training with consulting and research. Nontraining interventions are best implemented through consulting and, sometimes, research. If a training institute has no competency in these areas, it tends to approach all organization problems by prescribing training.

A distinction must be made between training designed to enhance the organization's capacity to perform its COTs and that designed for its SMATs. The various steps for systematic training shown in Figure 5.3 (e.g., program design, delivery, impact assessment) should be separate ones for training for COTs and SMATs. Training for COTs is much more specific and concrete, it is easier to test for knowledge and transfer, and it often yields more immediate results. It is best done on the job, in-house, or in close simulation to the operators' jobs. Training of pilots, air traffic controllers, and heavy vehicle drivers provides examples of jobs where simulation provides an effective and inexpensive operator training method for the COTs.

Training for strategic management tasks, however, is broader in scope, is more intellectually demanding, and emphasizes analytical and social behavioral skills. It is best carried out away from the managers' place of work. It does not provide specific solutions to specific organizational problems but articulates guidelines and provides frameworks for appropriate managerial problem solving and decision making. Its impact is difficult to assess as it tends to be long term. Line supervisors and middle managers often get both COTs- and SMATs-oriented training be-

Figure 5.3

A SYSTEMATIC APPROACH TO EFFECTIVE TRAINING

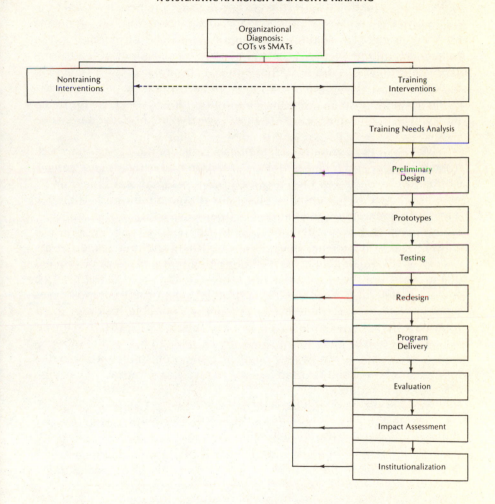

Note: COTs = Critical Operating Tasks; SMATs = Strategic Management Tasks.

cause of the nature and mixed composition of their jobs. Senior managers who are not promoted from the same organization should receive some COTs training to gain first-hand knowledge of the organization's internal operating tasks.

Training needs analysis requires information about the trainees' jobs, their skills and experience, and their job performance. Job analysis provides the information for the trainees' job description, which outlines the duties and requirements of the job, and job specification, which details the minimum required education, training, and experience for a particular job. Both these pieces of information are independent of job incumbents. Information about job performance is obtained through personnel records showing how well or badly job incumbents have performed the different dimensions of their jobs. This information then allows the determination of those aspects of the trainees' jobs that are not adequately performed and for which training is needed.

During the preliminary design phase, consideration is given to both methodological and practical aspects of training. Methodological considerations include choice of training methods, presentation of the training materials, appropriate combinations of on-site and off-site and on-the-job and off-the-job training, methods of competency testing, if any, and built-in incentives and motivation to complete the training program. Practical considerations include location, choice of trainers and trainees, duration, and other administrative matters. Prototyping refers to the development of a training module or modules that sample or simulate the trainees' job content and context in which it is performed. The prototype must be as representative of the trainees' job situation as possible, in order to increase the trainees' motivation to learn and to facilitate transfer to the actual place of work. The prototype should be tested on a small but representative sample of employees doing the same or similar work as the trainees, and the results should be used to revise and improve the design of the training program.

Program delivery should be carried out in accordance with the final program design, by competent and motivated trainers. Some of these steps can be performed with computer-assisted instruction (CAI) whereby the trainee interacts directly with the computer, learns new materials, and applies them in solving problems similar to those found at work. It is important, however, that every effort be made during program design and delivery to draw upon the trainees' indigenous knowledge systems (IKS). This practice facilitates learning and yields generative themes and imagery to which the trainees are familiar.

Figure 5.3 makes a distinction between evaluation and impact assessment. Evaluation is aimed at assessing the effectiveness of the training program as an administrative activity and learning exercise. It is usually done immediately after the training program is completed and focuses on the trainees' cognitive learning, and the quality of the training delivery system (e.g., instructor evaluation) and related administrative matters. Impact assessment, on the other hand, assesses the extent to which the training program has had an impact in changing the trainees' work-related attitudes, values, skills, behavior, or job performance. This is the actual measure of transfer and it is done several weeks or months after the trainees have returned to their jobs and have had the opportunity to try out some of the new behaviors they have learned during training. Impact assessment should be related to the training goals and objectives that were identified and agreed upon during the needs analysis stage.

Impact assessment is very important because the ultimate objective of all training is the successful transfer of the attitudes, values, orientation, knowledge, skills, and behaviors from the training site to the work place in order to improve job performance and organizational effectiveness. According to Goldstein (1986), transfer of training is facilitated if: (1) there are identical elements in the training and work situations; (2) the general principles covered in the training are applicable to the performance of the trainees' jobs; (3) the individual trainees have the ability and motivation to learn course materials and adapt them to the requirements of the job with little or no behavioral relapse; (4) the organizational climate is supportive; (5) obstacles to transfer are identified before, during, and after training and practical and realistic solutions are proposed; (6) managers and supervisors of the trainees are given technical and administrative support to foster learning and transfer by, for example, involving them in the various phases of the training cycle; and (7) a comprehensive task analysis is performed to ensure content validity of the training program.

It is difficult to obtain conclusive evidence about the effects of the training program on work behavior and job performance. It is therefore desirable to use field experimental and control groups to minimize internal and external threats to validity (Goldstein, 1986). In this way, any observed improvements in job performance would be attributed to the training program and not to other contaminating factors.

Figure 5.3 can also be used as a framework for diagnosing the operational capacity of a training department or institution. It outlines the major training tasks and areas of expertise that are required for providing clients with effective training organizations. If a training organization does not have the expertise to perform any one of these functions, it can either develop it in-house or subcontract it out to other organizations or individual consultants.

Human Resource Utilization. The concept of human resource utilization, and its relevancy for organizations in developing countries, has been discussed above. It relates to the employment of people in productive and meaningful occupations using their valued knowledge, skills, and abilities (KSAs) for the effective performance of the organization's critical operating (COTs) and strategic management (SMATs) tasks, and for the fulfillment of their personal and career aspirations. Research on human resource utilization, in comparison to human resource development, has not received adequate attention in developing countries. A recent comprehensive overview of human resource development in Kenya, however, warns that training more civil servants would not have much impact on organization performance unless the utilization systems are improved.

Organizational underutilization of human resources can be caused by a variety of factors including: (1) underemployment; (2) job-person mismatch; (3) poor employee motivation; (4) unclear job requirements; (5) ambiguous organizational mission and management philosophy; (6) inadequate or inappropriate organizational resources; (7) poor supervision; (8) political interference; and (9) lack of an effective HRM function. Underutilization may also be a function of the poor quality of jobs generated by the economy and the patterns of growth and urbanization (DeFranco, 1979). Effective utilization is a dynamic concept because over time, people change and grow and organizational goals and task requirements change in response to changes in the environment.

Government departments, especially in low-income developing countries, seem to be experiencing serious problems utilizing technical and professional staff. A recent Canadian International Development Agency report found that, in the Zambian planning division of the Ministry of Agriculture and Water Development, young Zambian professionals complained that "their talents are not being adequately utilized, and that they are essentially providing support services to foreign advisors" (Canadian International Development Agency, 1985:26). A more comprehensive study of the utilization of professional planners and economists in Kenya also concluded that ". . . evidence shows that the government has not succeeded in utilizing fully the skills and knowledge which the students acquired in their programmes of study" (Haddow, 1982:65). One of the limitations to human resource utilization is lack of good management in these organizations. Recognizing this limitation, Haddow recommended that ". . . to the extent that a trade-off exists between training more analysts and technical professionals and training government managers, the government should give priority to the training of managers" (1982:133).

In a number of cases, low levels of human resource utilization are caused by lack of attention paid to the development of technical and support staff, budget imbalances, and high levels of turnover in certain critical skill areas. In designing human resource development programs, there has been a tendency to focus almost exclusively on the high level professional cadres while neglecting the lower level technical, administrative, and clerical support staff. Consequently, the professional staff end up being underutilized because the organization's technical and administrative support system is weak. This trend was illustrated by a study of water development projects in Kenya which found acute shortages of plumbers, attendants, engineering assistants, assistant hydrologists, bailiffs, surveyors, and draftsmen. The report also noted that maintenance workers were not being trained in sufficient numbers to ensure that this and other projects constructed at great government expense, such as dams, will be regularly maintained and kept operational.

Budget imbalances can also cause poor utilization of staff. They usually occur because of the inability to provide recurrent financing for capital investments. For example, the same Kenya report, discussing human resource utilization in the country's extension service, noted that lack of adequate operational funds for fuel and travel allowances prevented the extension officers from visiting the farmers. The report observed that "the existing staff is therefore 80 percent underutilized because of the lack of operational budget" (Loubser, 1982:81).

Turnover in certain technical, professional, and managerial jobs causes disruption and underutilization of the remaining staff. In some areas, turnover is so high that for every position up to seven people must be trained in the hope that at least one will stay. The problem is not only that staff turnover is so high, but also—and more serious—that in most cases those who leave are the good ones, the self-starters and the "change masters." Thus, the organization is left with the less capable or mediocre staff. Their departure has a direct adverse effect on the organization's capacity to perform its COTs and SMATs. In situations in which the jobs are highly interdependent, frequent turnovers can negatively affect employee morale and organization performance. A common response is to bring in expatriate staff and overseas consultants. But an emerging question is, how effective are these as a long-term HRM strategy?

Questions of effective utilization of human resources are likely to become more important as hard economic conditions create pressures for macroeconomic adjustments, rationalization of production, and privatization of public agencies leading to possible layoffs. Available evidence suggests that many organizations in developing countries are overstaffed. For example, a 1982 ILO report estimated that overstaffing in Egypt's civil service in 1976 comprised 42 percent of the total public service. Ozgediz (1983) quotes a consultant's report on West Africa which found that at the headquarters of two ministries, 6,000 out of 6,800 employees (88 percent) were redundant. Recently, an East African national airline had to lay off 40 percent of its employees because they were redundant. Under pressure from the IMF, Bolivian mining companies are laying off thousands of miners. These problems, coupled with political interference and lack of an effective strategic HRM function, create conditions for serious underutilization of human resources.

At a more macro national or regional level, problems of human resource utilization are likely to become more serious as early as the year 2000. Countries such as Bangladesh, Iran, Vietnam, China, Nigeria, Ethiopia, and Pakistan are characterized by a young, fast-growing population, high unemployment and underemployment rates, and political instability. It is not hard to imagine that within the next twenty-five years, these countries will have tens of millions of young, energetic but unemployed, unemployable, underemployed, uneducated, undereducated, and terribly underutilized citizens. Nobody knows, and few are seriously asking the question of what kind of organizations, leadership and management styles, incentive and control systems, will be required for the management and governance of overpopulated countries with the majority of its citizens so young, so underutilized, so frustrated, and so alienated!

Motivational Crises in Developing Countries. A small but increasing body of literature suggests that organizations in developing countries are experiencing employee motivational problems reaching crisis proportions. If this is true, the technological, structural, and financial interventions being carried out in various developing countries are not likely to contribute significantly to development until the nature and causes of these motivational problems are identified and systematically addressed. Motivational problems manifest themselves in various attitudes and behaviors including low productivity, inefficiency, corruption, industrial sabotage, lack of will, inertia, indecision and risk-avoidance, and lack of loyalty and commitment to the organization. The evidence of these motivational problems comes from the civil service and the parastatal and private sectors. In Latin America, workers tend to strive to please, conform, and look good in the eyes of managers but avoid making decisions, taking risks, or accepting responsibility. In a study of 67 Indian middle-level public officers in Delhi Administration, Sharma found evidence of serious motivational problems. Drawing from his and previous studies, he observed that "In various work studies carried on in different government departments, one consistent conclusion is that a significant proportion of work hours is lost simply for the reason that the people working at different levels were not appropriately motivated to work. If these people are not properly motivated, it is hardly possible for them to execute national development programmes" (Sharma, 1986:13).

He attributed the cause of these motivational problems to employee: (1) lack of professional commitment; (2) preoccupation with lower level needs such as food, shelter, clothing, transport, housing, and working conditions; and (3) competing and conflicting demands between individual and family needs on the one hand, and organizational demands and expectations on the others. Sharma's study is particularly interesting because these officers were highly educated with at least a university degree, and they were well paid (pay range Rs 900 to 2,900), at least by Indian standards.

Kanungo, following his earlier cross-cultural studies on work alienation, also discusses the pervasiveness of motivational problems among Indian organizations. He (Kanungo and Misra, 1985) explains these motivational problems in terms of poor work ethic and early socialization of the Indian people characterized by *chalta hai* (tolerance for substandard and mediocrity) and *aram* (leisure) culture. He also believes that Indian workers at all levels of the organization have developed a personal sense of helplessness. Drawing from India's sociocultural ethos, he explains these motivational problems in terms of: (1) a deep sense of insecurity and dependence on others; (2) a personalized rather than contractual work relationship; (3) personalized leadership; (4) preoccupation with seeking and maintaining personal status at the expense of organizational goals; and (5) a highly developed family-centered work ethic. These cultural values are reinforced by: (1) authoritarian practices; (2) reward systems that promote helplessness; (3) time perspectives that emphasize the past rather than the present or future; and (4) restrictive family systems of obligations.

In Africa, motivational problems have been researched and discussed by several researchers including Blunt (1983), Machungwa and Schmitt (1983), and Kiggundu (1987). Using the Herzbergian theory of job design and collecting critical incidents from 341 Zambian employees from government, parastatal, and private sectors, Machungwa and Schmitt found evidence of motivational problems. The major sources of low motivation reported by these Zambian workers are: (1) personal problems such as domestic quarrels, hangover resulting from alcohol consumption, hunger due to inadequate food intake, and death or sickness in the family; (2) unfair organizational practices; (3) poor relations with superiors, co-workers, or subordinates; (4) lack of fit between the job and the worker including work overload or underload, and role conflict and role ambiguity; (5) inadequate intrinsic and extrinsic sources of motivation, such as pay, recognition, and physical working conditions; and (6) lack of opportunities for growth and advancement.

The Zambian study provides strong empirical evidence of the negative effects of employee perceptions of unfair treatment by others in the organization. Employees believing to have been victims of such practices showed strong negative reactions by promising: (1) to look for another job; (2) to engage in voluntary absenteeism and tardiness; (3) and to restrict effort and output deliberately.

Blunt (1983) has done an extensive review of the empirical studies of alienation and motivation in African private sector organizations. In a study of Kenyan organizations, he found that the urban African workers suffered from alienation, low self-esteem, isolation, normlessness, and powerlessness. He gave several reasons for these results. First, many workers found the discipline and structures of a modern working environment not only imposing but also unduly restrictive. Second, he found communication problems across organizational levels, especially where the workers and management belong to different racial or ethnic backgrounds. Many of the employees indicated their displeasure at not being listened to or not being allowed the opportunity to explain their problems fully. Older workers were more affected by this mistreatment and felt more alienated.

Motivational problems manifesting themselves as resistance to change have been found among rural farmers and agricultural workers. In rural areas, farmers are not given enough incentives to boost production or to abandon traditional agricultural practices. In a recent study of six agricultural projects in six African countries, White (1986) found inadequate and inappropriate incentive practices. She also found that, although incentives and monitoring are related, these countries did not have good performance-monitoring mechanisms. Corruption and unfair treatment of workers can also cause poor motivation (Gould and Amaro-Reyes, 1983).

Table 5.1 provides separate qualitative evaluations of the most common motivational problems associated with operators of the critical operating tasks and managers of the strategic management tasks. For the operators, the most serious motivational problems are associated with coming to work and staying at their work stations, keeping professionally current and upgrading their skills, accepting responsibility, and internalizing the employing organization's mission, philosophy, goals, and objectives. For the managers responsible for the organization's SMATs, Table 5.1 shows that the most serious motivational problems are associated with making decisions and accepting responsibility, protecting the interests of the organization, developing and utilizing new management tools and techniques, motivating and utilizing subordinates, implementing organizational plans, and building effective collaborative institutional arrangements (CIAs) of benefit to the organization.

In summary, available evidence suggests that motivational problems are pervasive across organizations in developing countries. Even under the best of times, these organizations are hard to manage or work for. They have heterogeneous membership, limited resources, diffused goals, weak management systems, and inadequate incentives and are highly politicized. These factors may contribute to the problems of low motivation among employees. Motivation is not caused by a single factor but is the result of complex psychological, sociocultural, economic, political, and organizational processes. Research is needed to study the complex

Table 5.1

EVALUATION OF MOTIVATIONAL PROBLEMS RELATING TO COTs AND SMATs

COTs	Extent of Problem	SMATs	Extent of Problem
Motivation to:		**Motivation to:**	
1. Learn new skills	L	1. Make decisions and accept responsibility	H
2. Come and stay at work (absenteeism)	H	2. Protect organization against outside threats	H
3. Stay on the job (turnover)	M	3. Acquire industry experience	M-H
4. Perform adequately	M-H	4. Develop and utilize management KSAs	H
5. Work overtime	L	5. Develop, motivate, and utilize employees	H
6. Utilize new skills	M	6. Formulate strategic or business plans	M
7. Keep professionally current	H	7. Implement organizational plans	H
8. Upgrade KSAs	H	8. Perform routine critical operating tasks	M-H
9. Accept responsibility	H	9. Build collaborative institutional arrangements of benefit to the organization	H
10. Internalize organizational mission and goals	H	10. Seek promotion	L
11. Seek promotion	L		

Note: COTs = Critical operating tasks; SMATs = Strategic management tasks.
H means the motivational problem is very serious; M it is moderately serious; L it is not serious.
KSAs = Knowledge, Skills, and Abilities.

causes of these motivational problems and to find effective practical solutions that would increase effective utilization of human resources.

The Brain Drain and Human Resource Management.   The brain drain constitutes one of the most serious problems for the development and utilization of human resources for organizations in developing countries. For example, Niland's (1970) study of the Post War Movement of professional engineers from India, China, Korea, Thailand, and Japan into the United States illustrates the detrimental effects of the brain drain on these countries and their respective organizations. In discussing the causes, consequences, and solutions to the brain drain, this section emphasizes its detrimental effects on the organizations' sustained capacity to perform their critical operating and strategic management tasks with efficiency and effectiveness.

According to Adams and Dirlam (1968), some of the reasons for the brain drain from developing to industrialized countries include: (1) salary and benefits differentials; (2) inadequate professional and career opportunities; (3) large technological gaps and inadequate or weak local technological capacity; (4) lack of willingness to change by the home country; (5) the relevance or applicability of foreign education, training, and attitudes; (6) discrimination; (7) political balkanization or instability; (8) lack of realistic and accurate human resources policies and plans; and (9) restrictive trade practices in the West causing artificial shortages of skilled professionals. Nearly all developing countries suffer a net loss due to brain drain but those most affected include India, the Philippines, Korea, the Sudan, Ghana, Lebanon, Iran, Bangladesh, Pakistan, Uganda, and the small Caribbean islands. For example, an estimated two-thirds of Sudanese professionals, technicians, and workers are employed outside the country. More Iranian doctors live in New York City than live in all of Iran.

There are three types of brain drain experienced by developing countries. Most widely discussed is the *international* brain drain, in which case nationals of developing countries seek permanent employment in industrialized countries such as the United States, Britain, Canada, and Australia. It involves mostly highly trained and experienced professionals or academics whose skills are in high demand internationally. The motives for seeking employment outside their home countries are primarily intrinsic professional achievement and opportunities for career advancement. These are usually the best brains and their loss, especially to small low-income countries like Togo, Chad, Ghana, Uganda, and Sri Lanka can significantly delay the development process. Reversing the brain drain among this group is difficult because of the material and qualitative differences in the terms and working conditions between the industrialized and developing countries. The brain drain can also be self inflicted, as when Uganda expelled members of its Asian community, thus depriving itself of entrepreneurial, managerial, professional, and technical expertise.

The second type of brain drain is *regional*, whereby workers, usually young men, seek employment outside their country but within the same geographical region. Examples include Southern African countries like Malawi, Swaziland, Lesotho, and Mozambique, whose workers leave for employment in South Africa; the Caribbean region, where the smaller islands including members of the Organization of Eastern Caribbean States (OECS) lose personnel to larger and more prosperous islands like Trinidad and Tobago; and the Middle East, where thousands of workers from countries such as Egypt, Somalia, Jordan, Pakistan, Lebanon, and Sri Lanka seek employment in oil-rich countries such as Saudi Arabia and Kuwait. This brain drain is not limited to professionals but includes technicians, kindred, semiskilled, and even unskilled workers. These workers are motivated by economic considerations and often return to their home countries after their work contracts expire. In addition to the sociological effects of their absence resulting from lengthy family separations, the effects of this type of brain drain are largely limited to the critical operating tasks. Most immigrants, even those who might have been involved in strategic management jobs in their own countries of origin, tend to be concentrated in operational jobs. In some countries, like Jordan, Egypt, and Swaziland, the remittances these workers make back home constitute one of the most important sources of foreign exchange. Both regional and international brain drain can be caused by political instability and violence as happens in Africa where, with 10 percent of the world population, the continent contains almost 50 percent of the world's total number of refugees.

The third type is the *internal* brain drain whereby human resource movements take place across sectors or regions within the same country. Examples include movements from rural to urban organizations, and from the public sector to the parastatal and then the foreign or indigenous private sector. This type of brain drain involves professionals, technicians, and kindred (PTK) as well as unskilled workers. It is quite pervasive among all developing countries and has a direct negative effect on the development process, although it has not received as much attention as the international brain drain.

Economic and professional terms and conditions of service play an important role in the determination of the nature and direction of the internal brain drain. For example, in the CIDA Zambian study cited earlier, it was observed that "there is a continuous drain of trained and experienced staff from the public sector to the private sector and parastatals, which are able to offer higher salaries, a foreseeable career development plan and a better benefits package" (Canadian International Development Agency, 1985:5). A recent World Bank report blames salary differentials between the private and public service sectors for the sizable flow of experienced staff in Jordan to the private sector and to oil-producing countries. Specifically, it disclosed that the salaries of government managers at the undersecretary/director level were about one-third of their equivalents in the private sector, and slightly more than one-half the level in public corporations.

There is evidence to suggest that public service organizations are less attractive to young professionals in developing countries than they used to be. In the Middle East and the Mediterranean countries, college graduates join the public service only as a last resort. In a survey reported in the same World Bank report, it was found that in Turkey, more than 40 percent of those who had recently joined the public service, indicated that they did so because they could not find work elsewhere. Thirty-two percent had made up their minds to leave the public service, and another 50 percent were actively looking for work elsewhere. Work dissatisfaction was widespread (Ozgediz, 1983). By contrast, in Latin America, where the terms and conditions of service between the two sectors are comparable, there are no significant flows from one to the other. Although the internal brain drain does not constitute a net brain drain loss for the country as a whole, it can cause serious dislocations and management problems leading to delays in development, especially in those countries where the government plays a leading role in the management of the economy.

In discussing solutions by developing countries to the brain drain problem, Adams and Dirlam (1968) suggest that these countries should: (1) raise and revise salary structures; (2) increase professional opportunities; (3) increase the receptivity to change; (4) reform the educational system and rationalize manpower policies; (5) promote regional economic integration and resist political balkanization; (6) eliminate discrimination and bigotry; and (7) remove trade restrictions of professional associations in the "pull" (receiving) countries which create artificial human resources shortages. The causes of the brain drain are so complex that different countries must seek their own unique solutions based on a clear understanding of its causes and consequences. The international brain drain is the most difficult to resolve. Yet, some countries like Korea and Sri Lanka have in the past tried to lure their nationals back home by offering more attractive terms. In 1979, Sri Lanka developed a program in which returning professional nationals joined the public service pension plan, obtained foreign exchange to pay for their children's education abroad, and could compete for senior civil service jobs previously restricted only to internal competition. Although the program's initial responses were positive, subsequent sociopolitical and economic difficulties in the country prevented its long-term success.

An important aspect of the brain drain in most developing countries is the low level of participation and utilization of women both in the management of organizations, and in the general development process. Women work long hours performing a variety of unpaid domestic jobs such as toiling on the family farm, raising children, preparing meals, fetching water and firewood, washing clothes, and looking after the general welfare of the family. However, their participation rate in paid employment, especially in management, professional, and technical jobs, remains very low indeed. In many of these countries, women have traditionally had limited access to income, wealth, and opportunities to participate in development activities such as education, credit, and senior political and administrative appointments. Even in matters where women have more knowledge and experience than men, they are often excluded from the making or implementation of important decisions.

The causes of the underutilization of women are not only economic; they are also deeply rooted in the social, cultural, and political ethos of society. They are often based on long-standing traditional religious, ethnic, racial, and tribal values, belief systems, and practices. Accordingly, solutions to the underutilization of women must be systemic and long term, and must deal with society's inherent gender biases. Practical programs must be directed especially at the men and women in these countries who are already in positions of power and influence and whose decisions directly affect present and future utilization of women in the development process.

Another solution is the development of more creative HRM programs. For example, a national carefully designed program of public/private sector personnel exchanges, whereby the participants are selected and paid on the basis of superior performance, can minimize the negative effects of the internal brain drain to the private sector. The small island states of the Organization of Eastern Caribbean States (OECS) are experimenting with a program of borrowing staff from regional and international organizations to which many of them lost some of their best brains. Through the program a small country like St. Lucia would approach the United Nations Development Programme (UNDP) and ask to borrow one of its senior employees originally from that country. The UNDP would agree to release its employee over a specific period of time but would also supplement his or her salary and benefits. According to Pompey (personal interview, January 5, 1987), an OECS ambassador, the program seems to be working well and meeting its initial objectives. Clearly, carefully planned collaborative institutional arrangements (CIAs) involving personnel exchanges and other HRM functions can assist organizations in developing countries to alleviate some of the serious problems of chronic skill shortages caused by the brain drain. From an organizational point of view, the brain drain is a symptom of an ineffective HRM function and its solution therefore requires systematic management of the variables identified in Figure 5.1 as they apply to a specific country or organization at a particular point in time. For employees who are professionally mobile, the decision to live and work in a given place is a subjective cost-benefit estimate of available alternatives. Organizations wishing to attract and retain them must understand the process and context of making these subjective trade-offs.

Recently, the UNDP, working with individual governments of several developing countries, has developed the Transfer of Know-how Through Expatriate Nationals (TOKTEN) program. The purpose of the program is to recapture some of the experience of highly skilled expatriate professionals residing outside their countries of origin. The program seeks out those nationals whose outstanding level of expertise in their fields of specialization renders them qualified to serve their countries of origin. The program builds on the cultural and linguistic affinity of the expatriate nationals as well as their strong motivation to serve their country of origin. Consultancies usually last between two weeks and three months and can be repeated in subsequent years.

According to a recent UNDP program newsletter published in Ankara, Turkey, by January 1988, twenty-five developing countries had implemented TOKTEN projects involving about 1,850 consultant assignments. Among the participating countries are: Argentina, Benin, China, Dominica, Egypt, Greece, Haiti, India, North Korea, Sri Lanka, Turkey, and Uganda. Although the UNDP seems to suggest that the program is gaining in popularity, it is too early to tell whether it will produce more sustainable results than have similar previous programs.

Blanket programs that seek to attract back all expatriate nationals have not been effective. A country facing serious brain drain problems must, instead, identify the critical skills requirements for the performance of the operating and strategic management tasks of its most strategic organizations—and thus those persons whose functions are critical for the effective implementation of the country's development plan—and develop a custom-made program to go after only those nationals with requisite skills, knowledge, and experience.

Effective Utilization of Expatriate Staff.   Expatriates are used extensively in organizations in developing countries in order to alleviate local skills shortages, especially in professional, technical, and managerial positions. The term expatriate is broadly used to refer to all nonnationals working in a developing country organization on a temporary basis with the stipulation that, at the end of the contract, one or more host national counterparts will have been trained to take over the job (Silverman, 1984). Ozgediz (1983) found that more than half the technical assistance to developing countries is spent on expatriates. In Botswana, although the number of expatriates as a percentage of total public service employment has declined from 8.5 percent one decade ago to 6 percent in 1982, they still occupy 51 percent of the professional and 29 percent of the technical positions. Moreover, here, as elsewhere in Africa and other low-income regions, they exert greater influence in managing and shaping the direction of these organizations, much more than their numbers would suggest.

This section discusses the question of the effective utilization of expatriate human resources working with host national counterparts as part of the organization's overall human resources development strategy. The focus here is on the development and exchange of knowledge, skills, abilities (KSA), and expertise required for the effective performance of the organization's critical operating and strategic management tasks. The two most important variables in this process are ability and motivation, without which neither the expatriates nor the counterparts can perform their respective tasks.

In a discussion of the effective utilization of expatriates, it is necessary to explain two important aspects of these assignments. First, the expatriate is normally expected to work with at least one counterpart. An important aspect of the former's effective utilization is that the two are able to work together with enough success that, at the end of the contract, there will be enough counterparts able and willing (motivation) to continue the work. Counterparts are host country nationals charged with the responsibility of learning and taking over the expatriate's job as soon as possible with little or no disruption of the organization's performance. The counterpart may be a single individual, a work group, or, in the case of new programs, the staff of an entire organization. Second, the jobs of both the expatriates and counterparts are made up of the three important dimensions of performing, learning, and exchanging, which must be used in evaluating the performance of these assignments, and the effective utilization of both the expatriates and counterparts.

Performing refers to the achievement of the organization's on-going tasks as specified in the expatriate's or counterparts' terms of reference or job description. This is the part of the assignment most emphasized by aid missions, executing agencies, and implementing organizations. *Learning* refers to the requirements to acquire new knowledge, skills, abilities, attitudes, behaviors, and values required for the technical performance of the job and understanding of the context within which the job must be performed. This aspect is often emphasized for counterparts but neglected for expatriates whose image as "experts" perpetuates a "know-it-all" attitude. *Exchanging* refers to the need for both the expatriates and counterparts to share information, ideas, knowledge, skills, professionalism, and feelings pertinent to effective learning and task performance. This aspect is often neglected by both the expatriate and counterpart, causing conflict and misunderstanding. The expatriates and their counterparts must be able and willing to perform all three aspects of their jobs. They must be properly trained, briefed, and motivated with appropriate organizational incentives for performing and maintaining an effective balance among the three job dimensions.

Figure 5.4 shows the three job dimensions of the counterpart-expatriate system and the ways in which they may be combined to achieve some kind of balance. The relative sizes of the boxes reflect the importance or attention paid to each of the dimensions by the counterpart or the expatriate. Figure 5.4a shows a hypothetical expatriate balance with more emphasis on task performance than on learning or exchanging information. Similarly, Figure 5.4b shows more emphasis on learning and less on performance by the counterpart rather than the expatriate. Differences in the relative emphasis given to the three tasks can cause misunderstanding and conflict, with the expatriate accusing the counterpart of inefficiency and ineffectiveness, and the counterpart complaining of not receiving enough training or opportunities for career advancement.

Figure 5.4c gives a hypothetical project-specific "ideal" balance whereby the relative weights assigned to the three dimensions are identi-

Figure 5.4

BALANCING THE JOB OF THE COUNTERPART-EXPATRIATE SYSTEM

Performance	Exchange	Learning

a)   The Expatriate Balance

Performance	Learning	Exchange

b)   The Counterpart Balance

Expatriate	Performing	Learning	Exchanging
Counterpart	Performing	Exchanging	Learning

c)   A Project-Specific "Ideal" Balance

cal for both the expatriate and counterpart and also happen to fulfill the
nature and requirements of the project or assignment. The "ideal" balance
is not a chance occurrence but is the result of deliberate effort and mutual
adjustment by both the expatriate and counterpart. It is also a dynamic
concept; as the nature or complexity of the assignment changes, and as
the two actors become more skillful in performing their COTs and SMATs
and in working together as a team, the relative weights are likely to
change.

The matching of expatriates and counterparts is an important determinant of their effective utilization and development. They should both
have the same emphasis and definition of job performance. The counterpart's needs and motivation for learning should correspond with the expatriate's ability and motivation to provide the necessary information and
training. They should both have the capacity for the necessary social and
interpersonal skills to facilitate cross-cultural communication and exchange. Yet, in practice, the expatriates and counterparts are hired independently and are assigned to each other almost at random.

2. What Is Exchange of Skills?

Exchange of skills is the process where: (1) an individual acquires knowledge, skills, and expertise; (2) he or she is called upon to pass them on to
some other person or persons by teaching, coaching, training, persuad-
ing, cajoling, or any other means of social and interpersonal influence;
and (3) the other person(s) is able and willing to learn, internalize, and
utilize, on a continuing basis, the knowledge, skills, and expertise that
have been acquired in the performance of the organization's tasks. This
process is called exchange rather than transfer to emphasize the two-way
interaction and communication between the expatriate and the counterpart to enable them to perform the three dimensions of their jobs
effectively.

Exchange of skills can occur in a monocultural environment, as happens between children and parents, or between training and educational
institutions and employers. The counterpart-expatriate system is a more
complex process because it requires cross-cultural communication and
transfer of know-how across national, political, ideological, social, cultural, economic, technological, and geographical boundaries involving
participants from significantly different backgrounds and value systems.
Unless their respective perceptual blinders are synchronized, they are not
likely to see eye to eye.

Exchange of skills is a very important aspect of international human
resource utilization as well as organizational and national development.
First, it facilitates development and sustains projects beyond official sponsorship by outside aid agencies. Second, it reduces dependence and fos-
ters individual and collective political, economic, cultural, psychological,

technological, and managerial independence. For countries just emerging out of long periods of colonial domination, this is an important aspect of rebuilding individual self-confidence, collective empowerment, an effective organizational local technological capacity, and a national capacity for self-governance and self-determination. Third, it helps spread expertise among host nationals and creates the critical mass necessary for promoting genuine professional conduct. Fourth, it is cost effective. In Canada, the average cost of maintaining a family in a developing country is about $100,000 per year. For that sum, an organization could hire more than ten Tanzanian engineers. Finally, exchange of skills boosts morale for all involved. The principles underlying exchange of skills and the counterpart-expatriate system can be used within the same country across regional, racial, ethnic, or sectorial groupings. Organizations in developing countries such as Malaysia, Zimbabwe, the Sudan, Brazil, and Guyana and in industrialized ones such as the United States, Canada, and Australia with multicultural societies at different levels of human resource development can use these concepts and methods.

3. Determinants of Expatriate Effectiveness

Several studies have investigated various determinants of expatriate effectiveness in private multinational corporations and public sector projects funded by international donor agencies (Spitzberg, 1978). Hawes and Kealy (1981) identified several factors including the expatriates' expectations, open-mindedness, respect for others' values and belief systems, trust, tolerance of ambiguity, personal control, flexibility, patience, adaptability, self-confidence, sense of humor, interpersonal interest, interpersonal harmony, and spousal-family communication. Other studies have concentrated on the selection (Conway, 1984; Willis, 1984), training (Casse, 1982), and briefing (Dasah and Kiggundu, 1986) of expatriates before and during their overseas assignments, with the Culture Assimilator (Triandis, 1972) being one of the best researched and most used instruments. Short-term expatriate assignments are not suitable for strategic management tasks and do not promote exchange of skills.

For more than five years, Bernard Dasah and I have been involved in the briefing of Canadian expatriates going for overseas development assignments. Drawing on these experiences, which include predeparture (Dasah and Kiggundu, 1986), in-country (Dasah, 1986), and end-of-assignment debriefings, we have found that the determinants of expatriate effectiveness are complex and operate at different macro and micro levels of analysis. Table 5.2 summarizes the nine major categories of factors that determine expatriate effectiveness. The table also provides a diagnostic framework for assessing the effects of each of the factors on the performance of each of the three task dimensions of performance, learning, and exchanging. The first three factors, operating at the more micro

Table 5.2

A DIAGNOSTIC FRAMEWORK FOR THE EFFECTIVE UTILIZATION OF EXPATRIATE STAFF

Dimensions of Performance: COTs and SMATs

Assessment Factors:	Task Performance			Learning			Exchanging		
	H	M	L	H	M	L	H	M	L
1. Expatriate Attributes:									
- Biodata and personality traits									
- Knowledge, skills, abilities (KSAs)									
- Vocational interests and motivation									
- Cross-cultural sensitivity									
- Health, family circumstances									
2. Counterpart Attributes:									
- Biodata and personality traits									
- Knowledge, skills, abilities									
- Vocational interests and motivation									
- International exposure									
3. Counterpart Expatriate Relations:									
- Perceived mutuality of interests									
- Interaction patterns									
4. Task conditions:									
- Working/living conditions									
5. Project Design and Management:									
- Clarity of goals and objectives									
- Resource availability									
- Importance to stakeholders									
- Quality of management and supervision									
6. Executing Agency:									
- Project management capabilities									
- Relevant foreign experiences									
- Long-term interests in the country									
7. Implementing Agency:									
- Project management capabilities									
- History of technological change									
- Relations with parent/holding organization									
- Resource availability									
8. Local Technological Capacity (LTC):									
- HRM systems									
- Institutional infrastructure									
- Indigenous knowledge systems									
9. Country Specific Factors:									
- Macroeconomic conditions									
- Cultural/linguistic									
- Political climate									
- International relations									

Note: H = High; M = Medium; L = Low in terms of the extent to which each factor facilitates the effective performance of each of the three performance dimensions for the implementing organization's COTs and SMATs.

levels of analysis, focus on the expatriate and counterpart attributes and the personal and working relationships between them. Technical competency alone is not sufficient, for the best engineer does not necessarily make the best expatriate. Likewise, counterpart interest and motivation are often more important than education or training.

It is necessary to understand the different types of counterparts often assigned to projects to understudy expatriates. First, there are the *professional* counterparts whose professional background and interests are directly related to the project's technical task requirements. Such counterparts are likely to be technically competent and interested in learning and exchanging ideas because they see the assignment as a natural extension of their career and their personal growth and development. Second, there are the *administrative* counterparts who are assigned to the project to provide only administrative support such as budgeting and financial control or management of employee (expatriate) welfare programs. These counterparts have limited interests in the project because their career aspirations are not linked with the success or failure of a particular project. Third, there are the *political* counterparts who are appointed to look after the country's political interests as they relate to a particular or a set of projects. These counterparts have no technical or administrative interests in the project and any attempts by the expatriates to draw them into project operations can cause only frustration, conflict, and misunderstanding. A careful examination of the counterpart's resume and work history can provide clues as to what category he or she falls in.

Counterpart-expatriate relationships are an important determinant of expatriate effectiveness. Factors such as time, language, perceived mutuality of interests, and professional equivalence can enhance or frustrate the working relationships between the two. Compared to Americans or other Westerners, nationals of developing countries have a much more elastic sense of time and do not react favorably to undue pressures for deadlines. In East Africa expatriates are often nicknamed "Mr. Haraka" (Speed) because of their obsession with punctuality and deadlines. Lack of professional equivalence can also cause bad relationships. Drawing from World Bank experiences, Baum and Tolbert (1985) found that when the educational levels of the expatriate and counterpart are significantly different, it is almost impossible to develop an effective working, learning, or training relationship between the two. Yet, the majority of expatriates have one or more university degrees.

The task and working conditions can make a difference. For example, on rural projects such as road construction and maintenance where the expatriates have the opportunity to spend long hours working, traveling, and even living with their counterparts, they are more likely to develop a more effective working and interpersonal relationship than in urban office situations where the expatriates and counterparts often live in different "ghettos" and have little or no opportunity to interact outside the circumscribed office environment.

In preparing expatriates for overseas assignments a lot of emphasis is placed on language training. Knowledge of local language(s) enhances perceived similarity, facilitates communication, and improves interpersonal relationships with the counterparts or beneficiaries. Yet the ability to speak the language without cultural sensitivity can be counterproductive. Moreover, evidence seems to suggest that, other things being equal, the expatriate and counterparts will overcome linguistic barriers and find alternative creative ways of relating to one another.

It is important for the expatriates' terms of reference and job description to be clear, relevant, and realistic. The expatriates are often faced with the problem of having to make a tradeoff between training and "getting the job done." Moreover, the requirements for training or exchange of skills may not be part of the formal job description. Yet the implementing organization's capacity to sustain the project may well depend on the expatriates' effectiveness in preparing the counterparts. Effective exchange of skills requires clear terms of reference and proper incentives for both expatriates and counterparts. A recent study of the problems of exchange of skills between Canadian and Indonesian engineering firms observed that: "It is the ambiguity of roles and task-related responsibilities that accounts for much of the variability to be found within individuals and between the relationships of expatriate consultants and their indigenous counterparts" (Scott-Stevens, 1985:5).

In Botswana, the government's Department of Personnel has found effective practical country-specific ways of hiring, placing, utilizing, and phasing out expatriates. For example, Raphaeli, Roumani, and MacKellar (1984) found that the recruitment of expatriates as individuals rather than through firms with individualized employment contracts, and the use of a uniform compensation of expatriates based on standard salary "topping" and a carefully controlled use of expatriates contributed to their effective utilization as well as to the localization of their positions. In Indonesia, Hofstede (1982) warned that Dutch expatriates would be effective only if they understood the limitations of utilizing Dutch management methods in Indonesia. These limitations included: (1) personnel decisions based on family and ethnicity; (2) Indonesians' discontent with performance appraisals, payments by results, employee dismissal, problem-solving and conflict resolution by direct confrontation, participative management, egalitarianism, and sympathy for the weak; and (3) time and patience required for Indonesians to internalize the virtues of punctuality and technical precision. He recommended that expatriates should consider using go-betweens or third-party intervention methods in resolving problems with counterparts, and that from time to time *gotong royong* (the tradition of community tasks) should be taken advantage of.

The international community is becoming increasingly aware of the limitations of human resource management in international development. For example, in 1985, the four Nordic countries' development agencies—Swedish International Development Agency (SIDA), Norwegian Agency for Development (NORAD), Danish International Development Agency (DANIDA), and Finnish International Development Agency (FINNIDA)—jointly undertook an evaluation of the effectiveness of the human resource component of fifty-five of their development projects in Kenya, Tanzania, and Zambia. According to Oborn (1988), the purpose of the evaluation was to assess the extent to which current human resource practices of these agencies are consistent with their overall development objectives as well as the needs of the recipient countries' local implementing agencies and counterpart staff.

The study's main findings were that: (1) there are too many foreign experts in these African countries, that they cost too much, and that many of them are not necessarily better qualified than indigenous personnel or personnel from other developing countries; (2) foreign experts are not effective in training indigenous personnel or developing local institutions; (3) the counterpart system has not been successful because to be a counterpart is not very attractive for indigenous personnel who prefer jobs with responsibility of their own; and (4) Nordic projects, especially those with foreign executing agencies, are not sustainable because they are implemented through parallel institutions and systems instead of through existing local institutions.

The study made a wide range of recommendations including: (1) using consultants and local institutions as executing agencies; (2) borrowing personnel from other local institutions; (3) using local volunteers; (4) increasing use of local and foreign short-term consultants; (5) fostering institutional collaboration within and among donor and recipient countries; and (6) putting more emphasis on training and development of indigenous personnel and institutions.

In general, effective exchange of skills is possible only if it is specifically provided for during project design and not as an afterthought during the later parts of project implementation. General statements about the need for training or human resource development are not sufficient but must be backed up by specific on-going programs, incentives, and support. Members of the executing, implementing, and funding agencies should be convinced of its merits as an integral part of technical assistance, not as something "nice" to do.

4. Skills Gap Analysis

How does the manager find out what the newly hired expatriates or counterparts know or need to know to perform their jobs satisfactorily? Resumés are not sufficient because, for the expatriates, formal education and previous domestic work experience are not good predictors of performance on overseas assignments. For the counterparts, formal paper qualifications do not necessarily translate into desired work behavior. Skills gap analysis is one useful way of obtaining this information.

Skills gap analysis is a procedure for identifying specific knowledge, skills, and abilities (KSAs) required for the project or assignment, and comparing with the current level of KSAs for each of the expatriates and counterparts. This information is of immediate application for assigning specific tasks to both types of employees and for identifying specific KSAs training needs. The information can also be used for the application of incentives tied not only to performance but also to learning, training, exchanging, and other developmental activities.

Table 5.3 provides a framework for undertaking a KSAs gap analysis for expatriates and counterparts. It lists more than ten different skill areas that are common for most projects. The KSAs include technical, managerial, and environmental areas for the performance of operating and strategic management tasks. The information must be as specific as possible in order to allow assessment of whether or not the employees possess the required levels for each of the KSAs. By comparing project requirements with the current level of KSAs, it is possible to identify what each of the counterparts or expatriates needs to know in order to perform the more advanced tasks. The KSAs that both the expatriates and counterparts need to know constitute the area of learning and exchange from each other. Although expatriates are usually competent in technical and administrative areas, they often lack knowledge and understanding of the local language(s) and the local environment. Identifying these KSAs gaps can provide a basis for negotiating the process of exchange of skills between the expatriate and the counterpart.

The information obtained from the skills gap analysis can be used for other purposes including designing training programs, clarifying project objectives and requirements, making personnel decisions such as screening, placements and transfers, selecting expatriates, breaking the ice and initiating dialogue between the expatriates and the counterparts, purchasing equipment, and performing other human resources development activities.

In summary, expatriate effectiveness is determined by a wide range of factors, some of which are beyond his or her control. Although there has been no empirical research investigating the relative importance of all

Table 5.3

KSAs GAP ANALYSIS FOR EXPATRIATES AND COUNTERPARTS

Knowledge, Skills and Abilities (KSAs)	Project/ Assignment Requirement (KSAs)	Expatriate		Counterpart	
		Current Level of (KSAs)	Needs to Know	Needs to Know	Current Level of (KSAs)
		Performance	Learning and Exchange		Performance
1. Technical					
2. Administrative					
3. Project Management					
4. General Supervision and Management					
5. Social and Interpersonal					
6. Cross-cultural Communication					
7. Consulting and Problem Solving					
8. Cross-cultural Communication					
9. Leadership					
10. Language					
11. Knowledge of Local Environment					
12. International Contacts					
13. Others					

NOTE: KSAs = Knowledge, Skills, and Abilities.

these factors, experience shows that expatriate technical competency may not be the most important factor, especially if exchange of skills is important. The rationale for the counterpart system is to facilitate exchange of skills and to ensure the sustainability of technical assistance and the development of stronger organizations. Although intuitively appealing, the process is in practice difficult and frustrating. A Canadian manager of a government executing agency with projects in various developing countries expressed such frustration on a recent visit to Zambia: "Things at the project are not much different [from] last year. The progress is slow especially with exchange of skills. There is much talk but little action. I hope things will improve soon, before 1990, when the program ends" (Singhal, personal communication, November 2, 1986). Many expatriates, counterparts, managers of executing and implementing organizations, and development specialists would share these sentiments.

Summary

This chapter has discussed the problems and prospects for human resource development and utilization in developing countries and their effects on the organizations' sustained capacity to perform their respective critical operating and strategic management tasks. It is organized in four sections. First, it has presented a general HRM model that takes into account internal organizational and contextual factors affecting human resource development and utilization. Second, it has made a distinction between human resource development and human resource utilization. Although a lot of attention is paid to human resource development for organizations in developing countries, very little attention has so far been paid to the effective utilization of nationals or expatriate staff in the performance of the organizations' COTs or SMATs. Some of the determinants of effective utilization are discussed.

The third section has dealt with the human resource management function and how it is currently organized and performed in organizations in developing countries. It is observed that the function remains largely underdeveloped in most of these organizations. Three dimensions of the HRM function—maintenance vis-à-vis developmental, operational vis-à-vis strategic, and individual growth vis-à-vis organizational development—are also discussed. Organizations wishing to improve the development and utilization of their human resources should emphasize the developmental and strategic aspects of human resource management, which also integrate individual needs with organizational task (COTs, SMATs) requirements.

The chapter has ended with a discussion of five current HRM issues that have significant implications for the effective development and utilization of human resources in developing countries: training, utilization of human resources, the motivational crisis, the brain drain and skills shortages, and the utilization of expatriate staff.

CHAPTER 6

Transfer of Technology, Knowledge, and Expertise

There are few topics as controversial in the development literature as the transfer of technology. Fewer still that are so important and crucial for the development and management of organizations in developing countries. Accordingly, much has been written on the subject. Most of it is descriptive and prescriptive and comes from a wide range of disciplines including science and technology, engineering, international relations, economics, political science, sociology, and international business. The literature, particularly from the social sciences, tends to be atheoretical with a heavy dose of political ideology and public policy debates.

In this chapter I shall make no attempt to synthesize such disparate approaches. Instead, the chapter focuses on four aspects of technology transfer. First, it presents a process model of international transfer of technology, knowledge, and expertise that provides a framework for analysis at different levels of the transfer process. Second, it describes the need and mechanisms for the effective utilization of technology by building local technological capacities. Third, drawing from the model of the organization developed in Part One, the chapter outlines the effective management of the transfer process. The chapter concludes with a discussion of special considerations, including transfer of technology for small-scale enterprises and extension services, and for small and island states.

This chapter is based on a number of tenets that are briefly outlined here. First, the ultimate purpose of technology is to bring about development by solving predetermined socially important problems, improving peoples' standards of living, and promoting more equitable distribution of income, opportunity, and wealth. Second, the organization is considered to be the most effective agency for the acquisition, development, utilization, transfer, and diffusion of technology within and across industrial sectors or countries. Third, technology is not a one-time purchase of a simple product to be bought or sold. Nor is it just the hardware machinery or equipment that transforms inputs into outputs and the specifications of those inputs into outputs. Rather, it is a complex, dynamic process of organizational interactions which, as a recent World Bank report rightly points out, includes the "procedural and organizational arrangements for carrying out the transformations" (Dahlman, Rose-Larson, and Westphal, 1985:9).

Fourth, effective transfer of technology, knowledge and skills necessitates building local technological capacities. These can be developed and sustained only through strong and effective indigenous organizations in collaboration with outside organizations from which the technology is imported. Therefore, this chapter describes the organizational arrangements and management processes for the effective transfer and utilization of technology through the development of local technological capacity (LTC) with outside assistance. It recognizes the importance of public policy and environmental factors in facilitating or preventing effective transfer and utilization of technology.

Evidence of ineffective and costly acquisition and utilization of technology has been documented in all parts of the world including Africa (Mytelka, 1986), the Andean countries (Stewart, 1979), Asia (Cooper, 1980), and various specific developing countries (Stobaugh and Wells, 1984; Wallender, 1979). The evidence from these case studies shows that these problems occurred where no LTC for effective transfer and utilization was developed and sustained. It also demonstrates that the latest or most modern technology is not necessarily the best technology for every organization, industry, or country. Therefore, the fifth tenet is that the appropriateness of any form of technology and the methods used for its acquisition and utilization are very situation specific.

Stewart defines appropriate technology as consisting of technology "more in line with developing country needs and resources, it consists of more labour intensive processes in the modern sector, and the development of new and improved techniques and products for the traditional sector" (1979:xvi). In this book, appropriate technology is defined as innovation that enhances the technological capacity of one or more organizations, and enables it to perform its critical operating and strategic management tasks with greater efficiency, economy, and effectiveness on a sustained basis, and to satisfy the salient and legitimate needs of its internal and external stakeholders.

This definition contains a number of important elements that are discussed in different parts of the chapter. It emphasizes the need for the development of an LTC and uses the organization as the focal unit of analysis. It emphasizes the importance of improved task performance as one of the most critical tests of the efficacy of new technology. It recognizes that technology transfer is not a quick fix or short-term organizational intervention, but a long and protracted process whose success depends on perseverance and conscious effort. It is the long-term effective utilization of new technology that has defied many organizations in developing countries.

The definition also requires the identification of the major actors or stakeholders with whom the organization must contend in order to acquire and utilize the technology under the most optimal conditions. For organizations in industrialized countries, the most important stakeholders are usually those within the organization such as employees; but, for organizations in developing countries, outside stakeholders and environmental factors are absolutely critical for the introduction and effective utilization of technology. Finally, the definition recognizes that technology is not value-free. Value judgments must be confronted and made concerning a wide range of issues such as the criterion of organizational effectiveness, delineation of significant stakeholders and their legitimate demands, and choice of strategies for building and sustaining the local technological capacities.

In summary, for any organization in a developing or industrialized country, appropriate technology is a function of the hardware—machinery, equipment, and tools; the software—programs and manuals for operating and maintaining the hardware; and the organware—the organizational arrangements, management processes, environmental factors, and human resources and sentiments required to work the hardware and software. Focusing on only one of these at the expense of others would seriously compromise the ability to develop and sustain the necessary LTC and the effective acquisition and utilization of technology.

The state of technology and the processes or methods of technology transfer provide two of the most graphic illustrations of the contrasts and contradictions within and among developing countries. For example, while India, Brazil, and South Korea are bracing themselves for the development of industrial complexes in competition with the industrialized countries, and Singapore and Hong Kong are working hard to excel as world class technology intermediaries, African countries like Tanzania are still grappling with problems of operating and maintaining steam engine trains. In spite of this diversity and contrast, the discussions in this chapter are relevant for countries at different levels of economic, social, and technological development and political ideology.

I. A Process Model of the International Transfer of Technology, Knowledge, and Expertise

According to a recent World Bank report (Stewart, 1979), the world's stock of innovations and technology is concentrated in a few industrialized countries such as the United States (60 percent), the United Kingdom (14 percent), and West Germany (11 percent), with the developing countries accounting for only 3 percent. Faced with this oligopolistic situation, organizations in developing countries seeking new forms of technology have almost no choice but to go to these few countries. Most of this technology is in the hands of private firms whose primary objective in the technology transfer transaction is to turn a profit. Because these firms negotiate from a very powerful asymmetrical position, it is not surprising that the literature on technology transfer to developing countries is full of accounts of dissatisfied clients.

This section describes a model of the processes and organizational structural arrangements by which technology, knowledge, and expertise are transferred from the place the technology is made to the place where it is imported and utilized. Figure 6.1 is a flow diagram of the processes and structural arrangements involved in the transfer. The figure covers two distinct time periods: the period immediately after World War II, and the period following independence for most of the developing countries. It also shows that technology transfer is transactional and it identifies the major actors for each time period and their respective roles as either recipients or providers of technology. The arrows indicate the direction of the major flow of technology.

Nine different levels of technology transfer (I to IX) are identified and shown in the model. Level I relates to technology transfer among industrialized countries. The best known example of this type of transaction is the Marshall Plan (Organization for Economic Co-operation and Development, 1978) by which the United States exported massive forms of technology, such as capital goods and financial assistance, to European countries whose economies and industrial physical infrastructure had been destroyed by the war. Even today there is a great deal of on-going technology transfer among the industrialized countries, particularly Japan, the United States, France, West Germany, and the United Kingdom. Small technology producers like Canada actively promote the importation of technology from the major producers in order to remain competitive in international trade. Japan's Ministry of International Trade and Industry (MITI) and Canada's Technology Inflow Program (TIP) are specifically designed to facilitate the flow of foreign technology into these countries.

In the discussion below of this and other levels of technology transfer, it is not implied that the actor or actors receiving the technology play only a passive role. For example, speaking of the Marshall Plan, Gordon pointed out that, ". . . while the initiative came from the United States, its development into operational form and its subsequent implementation were joint products of trans-Atlantic political, intellectual, and administrative collaboration" (Organization for Economic Co-operation and Development, 1978:16–17). The Marshall Plan is important because it was expected to provide a frame of reference and delivery mechanisms for future forms of technology transfer. It is widely accepted that the success of the Plan depended to a considerable degree on the existence of highly sophisticated LTC of the European countries even though their infrastructure and hardware had been destroyed. The situation in developing countries

Figure 6.1

A PROCESS MODEL OF INTERNATIONAL TRANSFER OF TECHNOLOGY

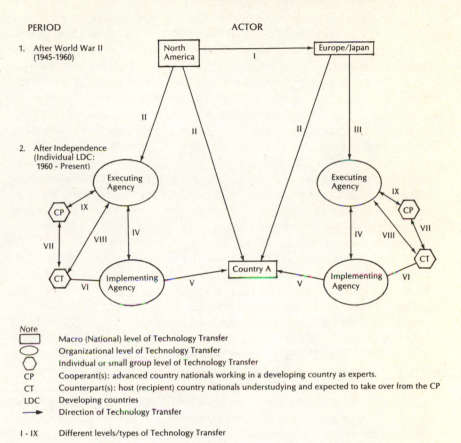

Note

☐ Macro (National) level of Technology Transfer
⬭ Organizational level of Technology Transfer
⬡ Individual or small group level of Technology Transfer
CP Cooperant(s): advanced country nationals working in a developing country as experts.
CT Counterpart(s): host (recipient) country nationals understudying and expected to take over from the CP
LDC Developing countries
⟶ Direction of Technology Transfer

I - IX   Different levels/types of Technology Transfer

is different in that most of them lack both the technology and the local technological capacities for its effective utilization.

Problems of costly and ineffective acquisition and utilization of technology sometimes discussed in the context of developing countries can also occur at level I between industrialized countries if the transfer is not accompanied by conscious effort and careful planning. Figure 6.1 does not show the transfer of technology, knowledge, and expertise within individual industrialized countries, but the structural arrangements and transfer processes described below for levels II to IX contain applicable concepts.

Level II technology transfer directly involves both the industrialized and developing countries as provider (donor) and recipient, respectively.

This is the level most commonly discussed in international relations and development, aid, technical assistance, and North-South dialogue. It is often bilateral in nature and highly politicized by both countries. It frequently starts on a large scale only after the developing country has achieved political independence and is therefore free to seek development assistance from a variety of countries. The most recent example is Zimbabwe, which gained independence in 1980 after a period of destructive internal strife and economic sanctions imposed on the illegal (Rhodesian) regime. Another example is the People's Republic of China, which, coming out of the Cultural Revolution, is now much more interested in the importation of technology from the United States, Japan, and Western Europe. Today, most industrialized countries are involved in a competitive "mini-Marshall Plan" providing technology, knowledge, and expertise to each of these two countries. Level II technology transfer can also involve countries that have been independent for a long time, such as Egypt, Brazil, and the Philippines, each of which has at one time or another received massive assistance from the United States and other industrialized nations.

Technology transfer at both levels I and II occurs at a macro country-to-country level of transaction and analysis. Discussions at these levels, which tend to be concerned with matters of international relations, are global, political, and ideological, and are often lacking in operational details of implementation. The subsequent levels of technology transfer (III to IX), shown in Figure 6.1 and discussed below, deal primarily with more micro levels of the transfer process, focusing on the organizational levels of analyses but including individual actors from the participating organizations.

Level III identifies the actors as the technology-exporting country and the agency or organization it uses to undertake the actual transfer. The executing agency is an organization used to transfer technology, knowledge, and expertise from the exporting country to the importing country or organization where the technology is utilized. The executing agency can be a private, public, or voluntary organization. It can be local, national, or international. As a private firm, it can be either a subsidiary of a multinational corporation, an international joint venture, a consortium, or a state-owned enterprise. For example, Great Britain used British Petroleum (BP) to transfer technology associated with oil exploration, mining, refinery, and marketing to countries such as Nigeria, Syria, Egypt, and Trinidad. The executing agency can be an international organization like the ILO or USAID, transferring management know-how to organizations in developing countries (Wallace, 1985; Rondinelli, 1987), a United Nations agency, a non-governmental organization (NGO) such as a trade union or church-based organization, a municipal organization or association, a university, a private corporation, or an individual citizen. Multinational corporations play an important role in transferring technology to the developing countries (Shelp et al., 1984).

A distinction must be made between the country from which the technology is imported and the executing agency used for its importation. Emphasis is put on careful analysis of the executing agency because it acts as an agent of change, and its conduct in searching, selecting, packaging, and installing, and its interaction with the implementing agency influence the effectiveness with which such technology is acquired and utilized. Yet most discussions of technology transfer from industrialized to developing countries tend to focus almost exclusively on country of origin and the restrictive terms (costs) under which the technology is acquired. Although these are important considerations, they do not deal with the substantive and practical problem of the role that the executing agency plays in facilitating or frustrating the development of the LTC for effective utilization of the acquired technology. No matter whether it comes from a "friendly" or "unfriendly" country, and no matter how much or how little it costs, if it cannot be effectively used to develop an LTC, such technology is of little practical value. The executing agency can play a key role in this regard.

The nature and the ownership of the executing agency are important considerations. For example, the more independent the executing agency is from the suppliers or manufacturers of technology, the more it is likely to provide technology that is appropriate for the needs of the importing country or implementing organization. The more the executing agency is closely associated with the manufacturers or suppliers of technology either through ownership or licensing, the more it is likely to make decisions reflecting the interests of the suppliers rather than the technology importer. Nayar's (1981) description of the operational and management problems of Kirloskar Cummins Limited, an international joint venture between the Kirloskar group of India and Cummins Engineers of Ohio, illustrates the inherent conflicts between the interests of a foreign technology supplier and those of a developing country technology importer.

On the other hand, the more practical experience the executing agency has with the acquisition, operation, and maintenance of the technology, the more effective it is likely to be in assisting the importing country or implementing organization to build a sustainable LTC—particularly if the implementing organization's technological capacity is rather low. In this case, organizations in the same business using technology similar to that used by the implementing organization would make better executing agencies. Airlines that have used other airlines from the industrialized countries as their executing agencies—for example, Ethiopian Airlines— have been more successful in building the necessary LTC for their effective operation and management. On the other hand, when Bombardier, a Montreal consulting engineering firm, acted as the executing agency for the supply of locomotives, it was not successful in assisting the Tanzanian Railway Corporation (TRC) to develop the necessary local capacity to operate and maintain the locomotives. TRC would have been better off to use, as its executing agency, another railroad company having the same or similar technology and facing similar tasks (COTs and SMATs) and task conditions.

The wider the gap in business orientation, motivation, and incentives as well as technological sophistication of the respective technologies of the executing and implementing agencies, the more difficult it is for them to work together to mutual advantage. An important aspect of building the LTC is the development of the expertise to identify and select the executing agency with the competency and motivation to source, package, install, and maintain the technology and negotiate the terms of transfer and acquisition all in the best interests of the implementing organization.

In Figure 6.1, level IV shows the relationship between the executing and implementing agencies. The implementing agency is the organization that receives and uses the technology in the performance of its tasks. Distinction must be made between the importing agency and the implementing agency. In developing countries, it is common for government departments, agencies, or state-owned holding enterprises to import technology and pass it on to other organizations to use. The discussion here focuses on the implementing agency because it is the one that must build its LTC for the effective utilization of the technology.

Like the executing agency, the implementing organization may be a government department, a state-owned enterprise, a local or international joint venture, a social services agency, a nongovernmental organization, or a privately owned firm. The effective transfer of technology, knowledge, and expertise very much depends on the quality of the working relationship, effective communication, mutual understanding, trust, and respect, and the mechanisms for problem solving, decision making, and conflict resolution between the two organizations. Yet, in the majority of cases, little or no effort is spent for the development of this relationship.

In a study of 27 Indian organizations with over 100 agreements, Davies (1977) found that many of the agreements were not the result of policy but the outcome of casual encounters with the executives of the executing agencies (MNCs). There was no serious planning or careful consideration of the impact of the agreements on the Indian conditions. Yet, as Spielman points out, the imported technology must become a part of the implementing agency's normal system of operations. He acknowledges, however, that the "process of integrating the technology into an organization is the most difficult step of all" (1983:35). Both organizations must involve themselves right from the beginning in diagnosis of the implementing organization's existing technology, its level of technological capacity, its current mission and future goals and objectives, and its alternative technological options for performing its COTs and SMATs. The implementing organization provides the sociopolitical context within which the technology is to be utilized, while the executing agency provides the technical alternatives for solving task performance problems and accommodating local task conditions.

Organizations in newly industrializing countries and other developing countries with a more successful record of the transfer of technology, knowledge, and expertise, pay a lot of attention to the management of the transfer process and the development of the LTC for the effective utilization of the technology. For example, in a study of the ASEAN, de Bettignies (1978) found that the executives of the implementing organizations were intent on acquiring the skills necessary for managing the complex process of transfer of technology. Specifically, they were interested in improving their organization's capacity to bargain for the most overall advantageous transfer conditions with the executing organizations at the different levels of the transfer process. Using the seven cumulative criteria of planning, generating, searching, negotiating, supporting, training, and using new technology, Baranson (1981) found that a number of Brazilian corporations, especially those with foreign affiliations, had made significant progress in building the necessary internal technological capacity.

Level V of Figure 6.1 shows the interdependence between the implementing organization and the country within which it operates. It includes direct dealings with various government agencies, current and potential users of the imported technology, the competition, local technical, business, and professional organizations, labor, educational institutions, external stakeholders, and society in general. The implementing organization must be able to draw from its own country's resources in developing and sustaining the technical and managerial capacity it needs to utilize the technology efficiently and effectively. It must also be able and willing to reciprocate by sharing its acquired expertise and benefits with others in the country.

Most discussions at Level V concentrate on the role of the government in facilitating or frustrating the inflow of technology, particularly in developing countries where government is pervasive in matters affecting international relations. Indeed, many governments have elaborate systems of monitoring, controlling, and financing the inflow of technology. For example, India, Mexico, and Brazil each have a foreign investment board that ensures that contracts with foreign executing agencies meet legal requirements covering a range of issues such as royalty payments, maximum level of foreign equity holding, and restrictions on the use or sale of technology. However, these boards tend to concentrate on regulating the terms of technology transfer rather than on facilitating the effective domestic utilization of the technology.

In addition to consideration of the role of government, the two organizations participating in technology transfer—the executing and the implementing agencies—should examine other aspects of the country which might be relevant for the importation and utilization of the technology. For example, they should survey local organizations and identify those with current or potential capacity to participate in the utilization or adaptation of the technology for domestic applications. They should also identify the available and relevant national or local training resources. In addition, they should undertake a study of the local market conditions for alternative technological options for the inputs, outputs, and byproducts of the adapted technology.

Levels VI to IX of Figure 6.1 deal with key players in the transfer process as they interact either among themselves (level VII), or with the executing (levels VIII, IX) and implementing (level VI) agencies. These key individuals represent two types of employees: those working for the implementing organization (CT) and those representing the executing agency but working for the implementing agency. Other key players—such as the financiers, government officials, clients, and community groups—are not shown in Figure 6.1. They too are important and must be included in the organizational diagnosis and environmental analysis before making decisions about the technology and its transfer processes. Faucheux et al. (1982) and Kiggundu et al. (1983) found that, in developing countries where society pervades organizations, importation of technology affecting significant interests of powerful outside stakeholders requires major adjustments. The necessary adjustments to the imported technology should be made collaboratively by the executing agency and implementing organization in consultation with the affected stakeholders.

The two types of key individuals in Figure 6.1 (CT and CP) were selected for special attention for several reasons. First, they are directly involved in the actual process of the transfer of technology, knowledge, and skills. They are the actual operators and managers of the implementing and executing agencies' critical operating and strategic management tasks. Second, they operate within the two implementing organizations and serve as the link pins between these organizations as well as with other organizations or groups connected with the technology transfer process. Finally, they complete the multilevel analysis of the transfer process illustrated by Figure 6.1. The three levels are: (1) country-to-country; (2) organization-to-organization; and (3) individual- (or workgroup-) to-individual right down to the operating levels of the implementing organization. A complete analysis and understanding of the technology transfer process must include all three levels and their impact on the effective acquisition and utilization of technology.

Levels VI to IX are mainly concerned with human resource development and utilization, which was discussed in the previous chapter. Suffice it to say here that in the long run the employees of the implementing agency hold the key to the development of a sustainable capacity for the effective utilization of technology. As Young (1983) has shown, by drawing from a detailed analysis of Canadian development assistance to Tanzania, the most underdeveloped countries experience difficulties in utilizing new technology because they lack an adequate supply of people (CT) with the necessary expertise and motivation to operate and maintain the new facilities. The representatives of the executing agencies (CP) often fail to develop the necessary LTC because they stay for short periods of time and because they find themselves operating in a technologically impoverished environment with an alien and confusing cultural, social, economic, political, and bureaucratic climate.

The managers and operators (CP, CT) of the implementing and executing agencies are the most important actors in determining the effectiveness with which the technology is utilized for the performance of the implementing organization's critical operating and strategic management tasks. Together, they should undertake a complete organizational diagnosis of the implementing organization, its local technological capacity, and its human and organizational resources, and develop a joint strategy and detailed but flexible plan of action for the integration and utilization of the new technology on a sustained basis for the best advantage of the performance of current and future operating and strategic management tasks. Although most of the technology is introduced into the organization at the operating levels, its effects are often realized at the SMATs. It is therefore important that the plan of action should prepare both operators and managers for the changes in the performance of their respective task systems. The introduction of computers and office automation (Ingle and Smith, 1984) illustrates the pervasive nature of new technology across COTs and SMATs subsystems. The expatriates (CP) are more effective for the performance of the organization's COTs and not SMATs because of their short stay and their lack of intimate appreciation of the local environment.

Figure 6.1 and its different levels of analyses clearly show the complexity of the technology transfer process. The whole process is so complicated that it is best understood as a series of tradeoffs among competing demands, benefits, and costs for different stakeholders. The only way to optimize these competing pressures is to analyze carefully the costs and benefits of the available options before making final decisions about the technology and the processes by which it is to be imported and effectively utilized. The technology transfer process is inherently complex, frustrating, and potentially adversarial. It must be carefully planned and managed. The greater the effort that is put into the front-end before major decisions are made, the more the technology is likely to pay off in the broader context of the participating organizations and the national interests of the importing country.

II. Effective Utilization by Building Local Technological Capacity

In the previous section, a process model of the international transfer of technology, knowledge, and expertise was presented and discussed. It was emphasized that the purpose of technology is to enhance the local technological capacity and the effectiveness with which organizational tasks are performed by using local resources. In this section, discussion is focused on the process of building an LTC for the implementing organization as well as for the entire country. Building an LTC is a long-term systematic, practical, learning-by-doing process that requires careful planning and the mobilization of local resources at the organizational, sectorial, and national levels with selected and focused assistance from outside.

There are several ways of conceptualizing the development of the LTC. For example, Dahlman, Rose-Larson, and Westphal (1985) see it as being made up of three stages: building the production, investment, and innovation capacities. Production capacity includes the ability to oversee and improve operations, production engineering, quality control, trouble-shooting to overcome problems, cut costs, and increase productivity, repair and maintenance, and respond to changing circumstances such as finding new markets or uses for the organization's outputs. Investment capacity involves management and engineering work required to improve or expand available facilities and resources including human resource development.

Innovation capacity concerns the invention of new products or processes or improvements of existing technology to the point of making such discoveries commercially viable. However, as Dahlman and his coworkers are quick to point out, the central focus of building an LTC, especially in the initial stages, is not to acquire the capacity to invent products or processes. Rather, it is to enhance the capacity to use existing technology with greater efficiency and economy, to establish better production facilities, and to apply local experience to adapt and improve the technology in use and thus to improve the performance of the implementing organizations' COTs and SMATs.

Stewart (1979) sees the process of building the LTC as being made up of the capacities for: (1) independent search and choice; (2) minor technical changes; and (3) development of new indigenous technology. Different types of organizational capacity and expertise are required for both the executing and implementing agencies. For example, the development of the capacity for independent search and choice of technology requires a thorough understanding of local tasks and task conditions and the alternative technologies available on the world market to meet those conditions. The first two stages require entrepreneurial and engineering skills and only the last stage requires formal research and development. This structure has at least two implications. First, establishing formal R and D facilities for an organization or country still grappling with the initial stages of building the LTC may be unproductive. Second, countries whose public policies discourage the development of entrepreneurship may inadvertently discourage the development of a local technological capacity.

1. What Is the Local Technological Capacity?

The term local technological capacity means the entrepreneurial, techni-cal, managerial, intellectual, institutional, sociopolitical, cultural, and physical resources and infrastructure that exist in an organization (sector or country) and its immediate environment. It relates to the extent to which an organization or a group of organizations is able to utilize effec-tively its existing or new technology by progressively moving up the tasks progression depicted in Figure 6.2.

In order to build an LTC for an organization, it is necessary to begin with a comprehensive diagnosis or management audit of the organization and the environment within which it operates. Such a diagnosis would provide information about the organization's future direction, corporate mission, management philosophy, organizational climate, and specific goals and objectives. It would also assess the organization's existing ca-pacity and the extent to which it currently performs its operating and strategic management tasks with efficiency, economy, and effectiveness. Finally, it must assess the possible effects of the opportunities and con-straints imposed by the environment in which it expects to operate in pur-suit of its stated goals and objectives. It must also evaluate, in the context of the information obtained from the organizational diagnosis, additional resources brought into the organization including new technology or im-provements of existing technology. The guided transmission training (GTT) methods used by the ILO for African enterprises (Whittaker and Gibson, 1987) provide an example of an intervention designed to improve the organization's LTC.

Figure 6.2 gives a progression of technology transfer tasks that, when performed efficiently and effectively, constitute the building blocks of an LTC. This capacity can occur at the level of an organization, a group of organizations within a policy sector, a country, or a group of countries linked together by some institutional arrangements (e.g., OECD, ASEAN, SADCC). The eleven technology transfer tasks from technology acquisi-tion to export are listed in increasing order of complexity and the extent to which they contribute to the development of a local technological capac-ity. The listing, however, is not strictly linear. It is possible for an organiza-tion, for example, to acquire and export technology before it has been dif-

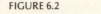

FIGURE 6.2

BUILDING THE LOCAL TECHNOLOGICAL CAPACITY FOR EFFECTIVE UTILIZATION OF TECHNOLOGY

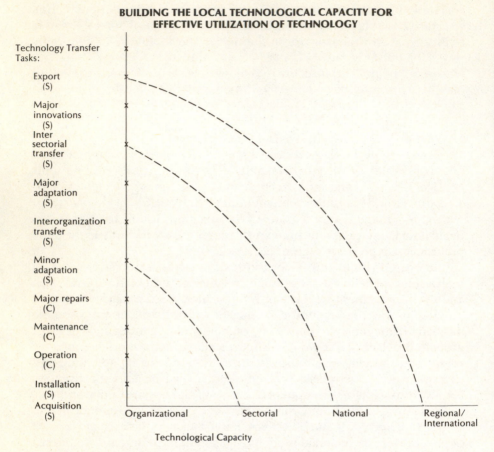

Note: C = Critical Operating Tasks.   S = Strategic Management Tasks.

fused to other organizations in the country. Dahlman et al. (1985) relate the story of VITRO, a Mexican firm that imported technology from the United States, made adaptations that increased its productivity, and sold it to a Brazilian firm, which in turn introduced further modifications that made the technology more energy efficient.

The first six technology transfer tasks, from acquisition to making minor adaptations, specifically relate to the development of the LTC for the implementing organization. Technology acquisition is by far the most critical task in the development of an LTC. The performance of subsequent technology transfer depends on the decisions and trade-offs made at the acquisition stage. Once the technology has been acquired, the organization loses flexibility and, if mistakes have been made, they can be difficult and costly to correct.

Proper acquisition of technology requires matching available technologies in the price range the organization can afford with its task requirements and conditions, and choosing the technology package that offers the most optimal comparative advantage for the organization. It is important to analyze the immediate, intermediate, and long-term effects of local constraints such as the availability of skilled labor, foreign exchange restrictions affecting recurrent expenditures, energy and transport costs, and the existence of technical, managerial, and community support and infrastructure for the new technology. In making the cost-benefit analyses of the alternative technology packages, it is important to include social costs and benefits and to project them over the duration of the productive life of the technology. The final acquisition decision should be made in favor of the technology that contributes most to the development of the LTC and its effects on the organization's COTs and SMATs.

Many organizations in developing countries lack the capacity for informed acquisition of technology. Consequently, the literature is full of examples of inappropriate technology both in terms of its contribution to organizational performance and social responsibility. In a study of textile and pulp and paper manufacturing firms in Brazil, Colombia, Indonesia, and the Philippines, Amsalem (1984) found that, in a significant number of cases, the acquired technology was less than optimum in terms of both its contribution to the firms' productivity and reduced costs, and employment creation. Mytelka (1986) found similar evidence in some of the textile firms she studied in Kenya and the Côte d'Ivoire. Because of these problems, governments of a number of newly industrializing countries such as Brazil, Singapore, and Mexico provide assistance to their organizations interested in acquiring new or foreign technology. This assistance takes many different forms ranging from setting up of technology information centers, subsidized feasibility and engineering studies for projects, technical training, and subsidized travel abroad.

Technology acquisition through international development and bilateral technical assistance is often unsatisfactory to the implementing organization. Frequently, the implementing organization, which may be either a government department, institution, or state-owned enterprise, lacks the capacity for independent search and acquisition. It therefore accepts the donor's technology package as a "gift" without the diagnosis, careful planning, and preparation required for it to develop the necessary LTC and utilize the acquired technology effectively. In addition to being tied to the donor's brand of technology and its inherent biases, the implementing organization has little or no choice over the selection of the executing agency, and the manner in which the technology is packaged, installed, and operated. Under these conditions, it is hardly surprising that such technology would at best make minimum contributions to the development of the LTC, improvements in organizational task performance, and utilization of local resources. Perhaps the most useful technical assistance should be the enhancement of the implementing organization's capacity for independent search and technology acquisition.

Should an organization in a developing country buy the most modern technology on the market? Although this question requires consideration of many substantive and symbolic variables, Figure 6.2 gives a framework within which it can be analyzed. The important concern is whether or not the latest technology makes the best contribution to the performance of the organization's critical operation and strategic management tasks and whether the implementing organization(s) has the necessary LTC for its effective continued utilization. The latest technology from industrialized countries is likely to represent a wider gap between the technological capacity it needs for its effective utilization and the capacity that is locally available to the implementing organization. Technologically underdeveloped countries are particularly susceptible to this LTC gap.

2. Building the Organization's Local Technological Capacity
The first six tasks of technology acquisition, installation, operation, maintenance, major repairs, and minor adaptations shown on Figure 6.2 are contained within an organization and constitute the building blocks of the development of the organization's local (internal) technological capacity. The implementing agency should, at a minimum, think through these six tasks and, with the assistance of the executing agency, develop a plan of action for their effective continued performance before accepting any technology package. Operations, maintenance, service, and repair constitute the minimum critical requirements of the LTC for any technology package. Yet many organizations in developing countries, especially those that are technologically underdeveloped, face serious problems in meeting these minimum requirements. Consequently, there is considerable amount of underutilization of technology because these organizations lack the LTC required to operate, maintain, repair, and service the new facilities. Experience from many of these organizations has led to the conclusion that, if an organization or a country does not have the capacity to operate, maintain, and service a new technology package, it should not acquire it no matter how attractive it may otherwise be. After learning how to operate and service the equipment, the implementing organization should base additional technology purchases, modifications, or adaptations on its own experience and needs and not on the recommendations of foreign experts. It is therefore necessary for the organization to document its experiences and lessons from the introduction of new technology. Technology transfer is a continuous learning process.

The twelve technology transfer tasks outlined in Figure 6.2 have been classified as critical operating (C) or strategic management (S) tasks, with the implementing organization as the point of reference. Most technology transfer tasks of the internal organization are operational; exceptions are acquisition, which is a strategic management task, and aspects of installation of technology, which might be strategic in terms of the organization's long-term considerations. Moving up the progression, the tasks become more strategic. Export of internally generated technology is a strategic management decision because it requires consideration of the organization's relationships with its environment including its competition, clients, and markets. Of course the classification of these tasks as operational or strategic is not absolute, as some operational tasks can take on strategic importance, especially in times of crisis.

Figure 6.2 divides the technology transfer tasks into four phases: (1) organizational; (2) sectorial; (3) national; and (4) regional/international. In the sectorial phase, the focus is to build the LTC for a group of organizations constituting a clearly defined policy sector. The policy sector may be broadly defined, such as manufacturing, or, better still, it may be narrowly focused, such as cotton textiles. The concepts and strategies of interorganizational coordination (IOC) and collaborative institutional arrangements (CIAs) discussed in Chapter Four are also applicable to the building of the sectorial LTC. The goal is to develop a network of mutually supporting organizations whose combined LTC is greater than the sum of their individual capacities.

At the national level, the technological capacity can be conceptualized differently, as this is likely to vary across policy sectors. Strategies aimed at building the national technological capacity should reflect public policy priority sectors. For example, if a country is committed to using agriculture as its engine of growth, it should mobilize its national resources for the development of a national technological capacity appropriate for the effective utilization of agricultural technology. This development plan should be reflected in its science and technology policy and its allocation of resources.

It is important to realize that technology, which promises to maximize social benefits such as employment creation, is not necessarily the best choice in all situations; other objectives need to be optimized at different phases and times of the transfer process. Nayar (1983), for example, provides a detailed longitudinal study of this complex balancing act for India in its quest for technological independence.

3. Institutional Considerations

A number of important institutional considerations influence the development of local technological capacity. Briefly discussed below are four of these considerations: (1) the role of government; (2) informal networks; (3) organizational incentives; and (4) organizational ownership.

Most governments in developing countries are actively involved in the technology transfer process. They tend, however, to concentrate on custodial rather than facilitative aspects of the transfer process. Specifically, governments have been mainly concerned with control over the terms of technology imports. Although this emphasis may have yielded some benefits—especially in India where local technological capacities have been developed in industries such as fertilizers, iron and steel, and large-scale mechanical engineering, and in Mexico and Algeria, where similar results have been experienced in the oil and petrochemical industries—elsewhere, government intervention has not been facilitative. A proper strategy would be to combine control and innovation. For example, Japan's Ministry of International Trade and Industry performs a dual function of controlling the terms of access to foreign technology and assisting in the development of innovation for the local industry.

The development of local technological capacity and the effective utilization of technology both require the existence of a critical mass of a network of individuals and organizations. Such an informal network provides the opportunity for individual organizations to exchange information and to provide mutual support so as to take full advantage of their combined experiences and knowledge. This enables the various actors to learn from one another's experience and to keep abreast of new developments. Professional associations, manufacturers associations, engineering firms, intermediate goods producers, machinery producers, research and educational institutions, and government scientists are some of those who would benefit from such a network. Yet, these networks are either weak or nonexistent in most developing countries and the potential for using them in the development of local technological capacities has not been fully exploited.

It is important to assess the nature of the incentive systems operating at the different levels and stages of the technology transfer process and the extent to which they facilitate or prohibit the development of local technological capacities and effective utilization of technology. For example, in the process of technology acquisition, a lot of important decisions are made by the senior executives of both the implementing and executing agencies. The personal and organizational motives behind these decisions are important considerations. At the lower levels of these organizations, the motivation and incentive systems operating on cooperants and counterparts (see Figure 6.1) are important determinants of their willingness to promote the development of technological capacities and the utilization of the new technology as an integral part of the organization. Government financial, political, and administrative incentives can also promote effective transfer or development of technology, as was the case with the development of gasahol in Brazil.

Organizational ownership is also important. For example, Williams (1984) and Chambua (1985) found that state-owned enterprises have a tendency to choose capital-intensive technology, and Mytelka (1986) found that small family-owned firms, drawing from their own experience rather than depending on foreign advisors, are more effective in utilizing available technology. These results seem to suggest that the indigenous private sector may have a more important role to play in promoting effective transfer of technology and developing the LTC than has been realized by most developing countries. In international joint ventures, the outside partner is expected to contribute to the performance of the venture's critical operating tasks, while the local partners, by virtue of their intimate knowledge of the local situation, can contribute most effectively to the performance of the strategic management tasks. In this way, the joint venture can develop an effective LTC.

III. Local Technological Capacity for Critical Operating and Strategic Management Tasks

Building an effective local technological capacity (LTC) through technology transfer depends on how well the implementing organization performs its strategic management tasks (SMATs). Quite often, however, these organizations seek technologies to solve specific problems with critical operating tasks (COTs), such as quality control, while their actual need is to strengthen strategic management skills. Yet, because quite often operational problems are caused by weaknesses in strategic management, most of these organizations should develop their strategic management skills in order to utilize the new technology effectively for the performance of their COTs.

In a study of the Korean Food Products Ltd., a food canning and packaging company with six plants in Seoul and four other cities, Wallender found that operational quality control (COTs) problems were caused by strategic management problems at the top level. He specifically observed that the company's "ability to improve packaging depended to a large extent on the ability to plan ahead. Only through long-range planning could the company make the necessary changes in existing facilities, which were poorly laid out and severely limited in space, to permit economical mechanization and improvements in production methods" (1979:71–72).

General management skills are necessary for developing an effective LTC through technology transfer because they enable management to define and identify the actual needs for new technology and the appropriate procedures by which such technology is to be acquired and utilized effectively; to plan appropriate modifications and additions to the organization's resources; and to seek more systematic and longer term solutions. Emphasizing the importance of a more strategic management approach, Wallender once again observed, ". . . those technology transfers that combine organization structure changes, personnel motivation, and value changes are much more useful than those that deal only with the specific modifications of systems such as production" (1979:100). As Wasow (1984) clearly shows for the American insurance subsidiaries in the Philippines, Nigeria, and Kenya, however, the strategic management tasks are often reserved for the head office.

Drawing from the results of sixty-seven consulting projects from specific organizations in Brazil, Kenya, Korea, Peru, and Tanzania, Wallender (1979) found that a firm's ability to acquire, utilize technology, and build an effective LTC depends on its internal characteristics, and its external task and general environment. Internal factors include the firm's history of technology acquisition; present state of task technology and organization structure; organizational climate including the existence of charismatic leadership, a positive organizational myth, labor-management relations, and management's knowledge and attitudes toward technology; and the availability of resources such as general management skills, technical personnel, and financial resources.

External factors affecting the firm's ability to utilize new technology depend on the availability of markets for inputs and outputs, external competition, environmental turbulence, government action or inaction, local technological infrastructure, and the cost and appropriateness of technology.

All these are basically strategic management tasks. The market and the demand it creates for new products or services and the existence of external competition provide management with the impetus to seek out methods to remain competitive. In general, when the organization is faced with potential threats from the environment, it increases its managerial search behavior. For example, in a study of the Kilimanjaro Textiles (KILTEX) of Tanzania, Mytelka (1986) found that external threats, in the form of scarcity of foreign exchange to buy necessary imported inputs such as technology and management know-how, forced the firm to undertake major technological adjustments and transfer the technology to other firms in the country.

Accordingly, the organization's capacity to acquire and utilize new technology and to build an effective LTC is intimately related to the effectiveness with which it performs its strategic management tasks (SMATs). The implications are quite clear. Any technology transfer package designed to improve the organization's COTs must include programs for enhancing the organization's SMATs. Executing agencies should be selected not on the basis of their ability to supply the hardware, but on their ability and motivation to enhance the implementing organization's strategic management skills. In short, an effective LTC is a function of the organization's capacity to perform its SMATs, and then its COTs.

1. Technology Transfer as a Negotiated Transaction
Technology transfer requires numerous domestic and international

negotiations with a wide range of powerful stakeholders both inside and outside the implementing organization. These are particularly necessary for large or highly interdependent organizations whose behavior affects many other organizations, communities, and individuals. Research shows that negotiation and conflict management are among the strategic management skills lacking or underdeveloped in organizations in developing countries (National Association of Schools of Public Affairs and Administration, 1985). Serious problems arise because powerful or influential actors are not involved in the technology transfer process. In agriculture, farmers and their community leaders are ignored (Moris, 1981); in factories, operators are not consulted; in education, teachers, parents, and prospective employers are left out of the decision-making process; and in service organizations, the needs of the prospective clients are not considered. These problems are particularly prevalent with international development projects for which consultations are very circumscribed.

What are needed are a framework and a method for negotiating technology transfer with as many stakeholders as possible. Pava describes the concept of deliberations as "determining the full range of pertinent topics, analysing their components and ensuring their examination through a series of forums (structured, semistructured, or unstructured) in which all the relevant parties present their various perspectives so that optimum trade-offs can be achieved" (1983:166). Deliberations can be useful for organizations before the technology transfer process begins because they are suited for complex decisions, like technology transfer, which involve many interested parties, and many different trade-offs. They provide the process and structures for facilitating the participation of all interested and affected parties. They can widen the consultation process to bring about greater understanding and support for the new technology. It is obviously important that negotiation and conflict management skills be part of the overall strategic management skills provided to the implementing organizations before the technology transfer process begins.

2. Operational and Strategic Variances for COTs and SMATs
The effectiveness of the local technological capacity can be determined by its contribution to the management of the organization's operational and strategic variances. Variances, derived from sociotechnical systems theory, are defined as any deviation in the work flow or production process from some standard or norm that affects the organization's performance in terms of quality or quantity of outputs. Key variances, sometimes called "super variances" (Davis and Cherns, 1975:278), are those with a significant impact on the whole production process or work flow effectiveness. Key variances can be operational or strategic. Operational key variances are those associated with the performance of the organization's critical operating tasks, and strategic variances are those that occur

as a result of inadequate or unsatisfactory performance of its strategic management tasks.

Figure 6.3 shows the relationships between operational and strategic key variances, and the effective performance of operating and strategic management tasks. Effective performance of critical operating tasks requires the effective management of operational key variances. This is typically accomplished by manipulation of one or more of the organization variables listed in Quadrant 2; for example, acquiring new or improving existing machinery and equipment, improving operational skills and technical know-how through activities such as on-the-job training, enforcing standard operating procedures, upgrading quality control, streamlining the organization's work flow, performing regular and preventative maintenance, repair, and service, and improving shop-floor supervision are means by which operating variances and critical operating tasks can be effectively performed. These types of interventions, if successful, either keep the organization in Quadrant 2, or move it from Quadrant 1. They do not by themselves, however, contribute directly to the effective performance of strategic management tasks or elimination of strategic key variances.

Figure 6.3

**ORGANIZATIONAL TASKS, OPERATIONAL AND STRATEGIC VARIANCES,
AND THE MANAGEMENT OF TECHNOLOGY TRANSFER**

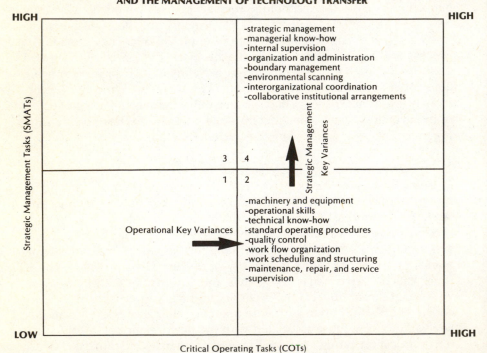

The organizational variables through which strategic management variances can be controlled are listed in Quadrant 4 of Figure 6.3. They include improvements in general and strategic management skills, boundary management, environmental scanning, interorganizational coordination, and development of collaborative institutional arrangements.

In order for the implementing organization to remain in Quadrant 4, it must develop its LTC for the effective management of *both* the operational and strategic key variances by maintaining high levels of performance of the tasks associated with the variables listed in Quadrants 2 and 4. The appropriateness of the choice of technology, the processes by which it is transferred, the choice and utilization of the executing agency, and the requirements for internal local technological capacity and external interorganizational coordination and collaborative institutional arrangements all depend on the quadrant in which the organization is located.

Like the Sudan Railway Corporation discussed in Chapter Two, the Tanzania Railway Corporation and the Egypt Railway Corporation suffer from problems of shortage of spare parts, material, store management, and maintenance (Quadrant 1). In order to alleviate these problems, the Canadian International Development Agency provides technical assistance designed to improve these corporations' performance of those critical operating tasks. Both projects have been extended at least once but, unless attention is paid to the overall management of these corporations (SMATs), it is expected that chronic shortages of spare parts will persist after the technical assistance agreements expire.

Organizations in developing countries can use the concepts of international interorganizational coordination (IOC) and collaborative institutional arrangements (CIAs) to improve the management of the technology transfer process, and to expedite the development of their own local technological capacity. Dahlman, Rose-Larson, and Westphal (1985) give several examples of successful applications of these concepts. For example, during construction of their first large shipyard, the Koreans sent 50 workers to a shipyard in Scotland. Thirty months later they were able to produce their first world-class tanker. Brazil sent many technical personnel for training at a petrochemical plant in France; this enabled the local plant to produce up to capacity much faster than would otherwise have been the case. According to Dahlman and his colleagues, a Mexican firm producing steel cable, discovering a market for its products in the oil wells, entered into a collaborative institutional arrangement with Krupp of West Germany. Krupp agreed to do the preliminary fabricating work for the Mexican firm's logging steel cable. The Mexican firm then perfected the production process and set up subsidiaries in the United States and Canada to compete with the only two world producers. Without the collaborative institutional arrangement with the German firm, the Mexican firm would have taken much longer to develop the necessary local technological capacity for technology export (see Figure 6.2). In transferring mass merchandizing in Peru and Mexico, Sears, Roebuck and Company of the United States facilitated international collaborative arrangements with the local appliance manufacturers in order to enhance their LTC up to Sears' product standards (Truitt, 1984).

Use of international interorganizational coordination and collaborative institutional arrangements is not limited to developing countries only. Members of NATO and the OECD have well-developed formal and informal arrangements for technology transfer. Canada, one of the smallest members of these organizations, spends millions of dollars facilitating technology exchange. Its technology inflow program (TIP) alone costs more than $12 million over four years. It is designed to assist businesses interested in importing new technology into Canada. Japan is known for using similar structural arrangements to facilitate technology transfer and the development of a local technological capacity. In his book about multi-divisional forms of organization, Ouchi (1984) describes how, in the 1970s, the big six Japanese electronic firms and the government of Japan through MITI used collaborative institutional arrangements and created a joint laboratory facility to do research on VLSI (Very Large Systems Integration) in order to be able to compete with IBM and other American companies. Developing countries can use the concepts of interorganizational coordination and collaborative institutional arrangements locally, nationally, regionally, or internationally to improve the management of the technology transfer process and to expedite the development of the local technological capacity.

IV. Special Considerations in Technology Transfer

Developing countries are characterized by diversity, dualism, contradictions, and contrasts. These differences give rise to special considerations that must be examined for a more comprehensive understanding of the technology transfer process and the challenges and prospects of building an effective LTC. These special considerations arise as a result of a wide range of factors including: (1) the nature and sectorial composition of an industrial organization in the economy, including the role of agriculture, government, industry, and the informal sector, and the relatively small size of the indigenous private sector; (2) the cultural milieu of the country including the history, ethnic and racial composition, sociopolitical behavior, and institutional development; and (3) the national character in terms of both social and demographic attributes, and geographic characteristics. This section briefly discusses the relevancy of the special considerations for the transfer of technology, knowledge, skills and expertise for: (1) small-scale enterprises (SSEs); (2) agricultural extension services; and (3) small and island states.

1. Small-Scale Enterprises

Most developing countries have dualistic technological systems made up of the modern and the informal or traditional sectors. The modern sector tends to be highly sophisticated, complex, prestigious, and expensive and uses more advanced technology. Its operations run on a larger scale, and need a relatively high level of technological capacity to operate, service, and maintain. The informal sector to which the SSEs belong, on the other hand, is small by way of employment (1–50 employees), and uses simpler technology, scrap, or unusable materials from the modern sector. It uses mostly local materials, has a very low ratio of capital investment per job, needs limited technological capacity, and has very limited contacts with foreign technology suppliers. Small-scale enterprises (SSEs) also have very limited access to modern facilities and services such as electricity, credit, government services, and modern sector technological and managerial know-how. The SSE sector is sometimes defined in terms of the hostility or lack of support and collaborative institutional arrangements it suffers from other sectors of the economy. For example, in a recent World Bank report, Page and Steel define small-scale enterprises as those ". . . engaged in activities involving barriers to entry in the form of human or physical capital that do not have ready access to institutionalized credit and incentives without special assistance" (1980:13).

Yet, SSEs play a very significant role in the economies of medium- and low-income developing countries (Steel and Evans, 1984). Table 6.1 gives the figures for the relative contribution of large-scale and small-scale enterprises to manufacturing employment in seven low-income developing countries. The figures show that SSEs contribute more than 50 percent of total manufacturing employment for all the countries except Egypt. For

Table 6.1

LARGE- AND SMALL-SCALE ENTERPRISES' SHARE OF MANUFACTURING EMPLOYMENT
(Percentages)

Size (number of workers)	Tanzania 1967	Ghana 1970	Egypt 1966/ 1967	Kenya 1969	Nigeria 1972	Ethiopia 1971	Sierra Leone 1974
Large scale (50 or more)	37.4	15.0	64.0	41.0	14.5	17.3	4.4
Small scale (under 50)	62.6	85.0	36.0	58.9	85.5	82.7	95.6

SOURCE: John M. Page, Jr., and William F. Steel, *Small Enterprise Development: Economic Issues from African Experience*, Washington D.C.: World Bank Technical Paper Number 26, 1984, Annex II, p. 42.

Sierra Leone, the contribution of SSEs to total manufacturing employment was over 95 percent in 1974. SSEs, according to the World Bank report, contribute more than half of the industrial output in Botswana and Burundi, and 8.2 percent and 4.6 percent of GNP, respectively. These figures show the significance of the small-scale enterprises and point to the need to provide appropriate technology to these enterprises and to utilize the sector more effectively as part of a national development strategy for employment, production, and more equitable distribution of technological opportunities.

There are several important considerations for technology transfer to the small-scale enterprises. First, there is an increasing trend for technological displacements whereby the simpler local technology suitable for small-scale enterprises is being replaced by more complex imported technology. For example, in Kenya, traditional roller mills for maize grinding are being replaced by imported modern maize mills. In Tanzania, automatic continuous baking is rapidly replacing simpler traditional baking more in tune with the local technological know-how. This kind of technological displacement raises the required LTC and isolates the small-scale enterprises.

Second, there is technological duality without collaboration. Quite often the duality exists within the same or similar industries such as timber harvesting and woodworking and furniture making; automatic bakeries and small-scale batch bakeries using wood stoves; automatic food processing and packaging cans and slow-speed, locally designed and manufactured ones; and automatic shoe making and handmade shoes. In spite of this dualism, there is little or no contact or exchange of ideas, know-how, goods, or services between the modern sector and the informal sector even within the same industry. Because of the lack of contacts or collaborative institutional arrangements between the two sectors, the SSEs cannot take maximum advantage of the LTC developed by implementing organizations within the modern sector. Moreover, the modern sector organizations cannot produce technological adaptations or innovations suitable for the SSEs in the informal sector.

Third, there is little or no contact or direct linkage between the production organizations such as the individual enterprises, and the nonproduction organizations such as research institutes and government agencies monitoring technology transfer. The large enterprises tend to look down upon domestic suppliers of technological know-how in favor of foreign suppliers, while the entrepreneurs of the small-scale enterprises do not see the relevancy of these organizations to their pressing immediate problems, which often manifest themselves as operational key variances.

A final consideration is that most small-scale enterprises, owned and operated as sole proprietorships or family businesses, are quite conservative and slow to change or adopt new forms of technology. They prefer to move at their own cautious, calculated, slow, and sure pace rather than to rush on to new technological bandwagons. This philosophy contrasts with that of the modern sector enterprises, especially the state-owned enterprises that actively seek out the most advanced technology the world can offer.

These considerations seriously inhibit the development of mutually supportive and beneficial technological interdependence between the two sectors. Yet, experience shows that, in the more technologically advanced developing countries, this interdependence is actively promoted. For example, according to Cooper (1980), local small-scale machine makers in Thailand supply components of can-making plants to modern sector multinational corporations. The International Rice Research Institute in Manila and the Central Leather Research Institute in Madras are two research institutes with a reputation for successful facilitation of technology transfer to the small-scale enterprises of their respective sectors.

Integration of the Formal and Informal Sectors for Technology Transfer. There is a need to break down the communication barriers between the two technological solitudes in order to develop an integrated local technological capacity made up of the relevant organizations from the formal and informal sectors, and the production and nonproduction organizations.

Figure 6.4 provides a conceptual framework for the development of the interorganizational coordinating mechanisms, and collaborative institutional arrangements through which effective technology transfer can be facilitated between the two sectors. There are four direct linkages between the formal and informal sectors. The primary or most important linkages are those with the formal sector implementing agency, a production organization; the local or national institutions for research, training, consulting, and education; and a proposed new government agency for promoting developments in the informal sector. The informal sector, made up of very small individual enterprises or production units, may need to be organized into a larger collectivity such as an association or cooperative that would democratically represent the individual and collective interests of the small-scale enterprises outside the informal sector. Individual small business enterprises can make direct contacts or representations to other organizations in the formal sector if they have the need and capacity to do so.

Figure 6.4 also shows that the production and nonproduction organizations would be, under the proposed framework, directly linked with one another. The formal sector implementing organization would be directly linked with the relevant government agencies for monitoring the technology transfer process, and the research, training, and educational

Figure 6.4

A FRAMEWORK FOR THE EFFECTIVE TRANSFER OF TECHNOLOGY BETWEEN THE FORMAL AND INFORMAL SECTORS

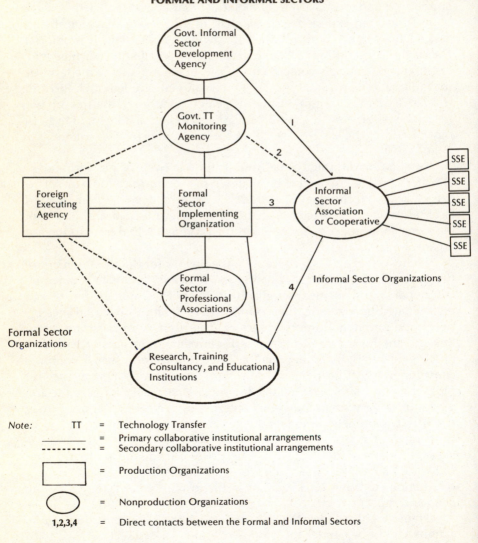

Note: TT   =   Technology Transfer
          _____   =   Primary collaborative institutional arrangements
          ----------   =   Secondary collaborative institutional arrangements

          ▭   =   Production Organizations

          ◯   =   Nonproduction Organizations

          1,2,3,4   =   Direct contacts between the Formal and Informal Sectors institutions for enhancing the organization's LTC. These linkages together would enhance mutual understanding, respect, and perceived relevance among the participating organizations. They would particularly deal with the common problem in developing countries that the implementing organizations have little regard and respect for the local research, training, and educational institutions.

The framework illustrated in Figure 6.4 also shows that the informal sector can take advantage of the services offered by foreign organizations such as the executing agency through its contacts with the implementing organization and other formal sector agencies and institutions. These collaborative institutional arrangements would reduce the time lag between the time technology as acquired by the formal sector, and its availability in usable form by the small-scale enterprises in the informal sector.

In some cases, the informal sector performs its COTs more efficiently than does the modern sector. For example, in Kenya and Bangladesh, the small private transport operators have lower operating costs than the larger national transport companies. What these operators lack and need most is some basic strategic management (SMATs) skills that will enable them to improve the management of their businesses including effective use of new technology. The framework outlined in Figure 6.4 can facilitate this.

2. Agricultural Extension Services

Extension services are common in a wide range of social and economic services such as agriculture, education, health, small business, and community and rural development. From an organizational perspective, the purpose of extension service organizations is to develop a relatively permanent, efficient, and cost-effective organizational delivery system linking producers or providers of techniques, knowledge, or skills with the potential users. It is an effective organizational arrangement for transferring technology and for building an effective LTC within the informal underorganized sector in which production or service delivery takes place. Common among these is the Training and Visit (T&V) system developed by Benor and Harrison in the 1970s and popularized by the World Bank, which has been modified and is now used in over forty countries in Asia and Africa (e.g., India, Thailand, Kenya). It is a highly structured organizational arrangement that links farmers in the informal sector with the research and agricultural management organizations (e.g., the Ministry of Agriculture) in the formal sector.

The structure provides the mechanism for effective communication and practical problem solving between the farmers, extension personnel, researchers, and the ministry of agriculture. These collaborative institutional arrangements (CIAs) promote effective links and interaction among the participating organizations through "regular training sessions and workshops for extension and research personnel, joint participation in planning each season's extension and adaptive and applied research activities, shared responsibility for farm trials, joint field trips to review specific crop problems and to obtain a better idea of actual production conditions, and visits by extension staff to research stations" (Benor et al., 1984:32). These practices are facilitative of effective technology transfer and the development of appropriate LTC consistent with the farmers' needs and sophistry. They can be useful in negotiating and managing the relationships and the technology transfer process between the executing agency and the implementing organization discussed above in Figure 6.1.

The organization of the extension service is designed to ensure that the village extension workers, the most important contact persons with the farmers, "are making scheduled regular visits to farmers, choosing proper extension workers, and are being well trained" (Benor, Harrison, and Baxter, 1984:25). It concentrates on building an LTC for the effective performance of the farmers' critical operating tasks (e.g., cropping, irrigation), while the top echelon of the extension organization (e.g., Director of Extension) takes primary responsibility for most of the farmers' strategic management skills. A recent World Bank Report (1983) explains the success of the T&V system in terms of its exclusive concentration on only extension functions (specialization), simplicity, regularity, and communication. These are some of the attributes of successful industrial organizations.

The organizing concepts and practices of the T&V system, which are consistent with the principles of modern management, can be generalized to other similar situations where there is a need for technology transfer, the strengthening of existing organizational arrangements, and the building of appropriate LTC for the effective performance of the relevant organizations' critical operating and strategic management tasks.

3. Small and Island States

Small and island states are part of a larger group of about 100 developing countries and territories whose unique characteristics give rise to the need for special considerations, not only for technology transfer, but also for other aspects of development administration. These unique characteristics, which include small island, multi-island, and land-locked states, are particularly common, though by no means limited, to the developing regions of the world. Various international organizations such as the World Bank's Group of Twenty-Four (1982), the IMF, the United Nations Conference on Trade and Development (UNCTAD), and the Commonwealth (1986) have all shown keen interest in the problems of small and island states because a large number of their members share these characteristics. For example, of the 49 Commonwealth member states, 27, or over 55 percent, have an individual population of under one million.

The interest in small and island states stems from the assumption that these experience unique organizational and management problems that require special consideration and attention. For example, in 1981 the International Association of Schools and Institutes of Administration (IASIA) established a working group with representatives from the Caribbean and Pacific basins where most small and island states are located. The purpose of the working group was to study the administrative problems facing these states. After several years of study and discussion, the group concluded that "the administrative and management problems of these small states were in many respects unique and different from those of larger countries" (Schaeffer, 1985:23). Other researchers have come to the same or similar conclusions (e.g., Jalan, 1982; The Commonwealth, 1986); however, some scholars (e.g., Srinivasan, 1986) doubt the uniqueness of the problems of small and island states.

Although discussions of problems of small and island states cover a wide range of administrative issues such as public management, decentralization, and human resource management, the discussion here is limited to an examination of the possible effects of these problems on the ability of the state and its constituent organizations, both private and public, to develop and sustain an effective local technological capacity for effective acquisition and utilization of technology. The discussions begin with the definition and scope of small and island states and focus on the effects of their unique problems on the transfer of technology, knowledge, and expertise.

The four measures used most commonly to determine the smallness of a country are total population, surface area, gross national product, and market size. Of these, population is the simplest and most commonly used and attempts made to develop a composite measure of smallness made up of these measures have met with conceptual and methodological difficulties (Jalan, 1982). It is generally accepted that small countries are those with a population of five million or less, and mini-states or micro-states are those with a population of less than one million. An important consideration in the precise definition of smallness is the generally accepted hypothesis that there is a critical minimum size of economies in terms of employment or population and investment or level of income below which a country cannot maintain a positive rate of growth in labor productivity, especially in the manufacturing sector.

Over one-half of the world's countries are either small or very small. From a total of 189 countries, Srinivasan (1986) found that 67 were very small (1.5 million or less), and 33 were small, giving a percentage of almost 53 percent. Out of 62 island economies, almost 84 percent are either very small (46) or small (6). The figures also show that out of a total of 26 landlocked economies, 42 percent of them are either small (6) or very small (5). These figures show that a significant number of countries are disadvantaged either by size or island status, or by being landlocked—each of which creates conditions that inhibit economic development and effective acquisition and utilization of technology. For example, of the 36 least developed countries on the United Nations list, 21 (58 percent) are either small or very small.

All small and island states are not necessarily poor or underdeveloped. Table 6.2 gives a list of UN/World Bank member states with a population of less than one million. The table shows wide variations in economic and social development indicators for these mini-states ranging from the poor countries with GNP per capita of less than $410 U.S. to the very rich ones with GNP per capita of over $10,000 and life expectancy of over 65 years. However, excluding oil exporting and European states, most of the mini-states are relatively poor.

Problems and Their Effects on Technology Transfer.   From the point of view of economics, the most important problem facing small states is one of *small economies of scale.* Small and high cost production systems make it difficult for organizations in small and island states to utilize foreign technology efficiently because such technology is predicated on large size, high volume, and low unit costs. Lall and Ghosh (1982) point out that size affects the development of a local technological capacity because of the lack of a domestic industrial and marketing base necessary for effective acquisition and utilization of technology. Helleiner (1982), in an empirical balance of payments comparative study of small, medium (5-10 million), and large (over 10 million) developing countries, found that population smallness imposes high costs of information and management systems, lower returns on these countries' reserves, and high costs of acquiring foreign capital.

A second problem facing small and island states is one of *concentration.* These economies are concentrated in four important aspects: (1) high ratio of foreign trade to national income; (2) a high degree of concentration on a few export products or services; (3) a high degree of concentration of a few countries to which exports are sold; and (4) a high degree of concentration on a few commodities imported from only a few sources. These problems cause financial and operational problems for small states in their quest for foreign capital. In addition to foreign exchange problems resulting from a small, highly vulnerable export base, there are difficulties in maintaining a wide range of machinery where there is a very small number of each type. As Benedict (1967) points out, these problems, plus the problems of training and staffing necessary to run these machinery, impose limitations and delays on the effective utilization of technology in small states. Few of the organizations in these states can afford to keep stocks of extra spare parts for all the machines they need.

These problems suggest the need for organizations in small and is-

Table 6.2

SELECTED VERY SMALL AND ISLAND STATES WITH A POPULATION OF LESS THAN ONE MILLION

Country	Population (thousands) mid-1983	Area (thousands of square kilometers)	GNP per Capita Dollars 1983	GNP per Capita AAGR, % 1975-83	Life Expectance at Birth 1983
Guinea-Bissau	863	36	180	-	38
Gambia, The	697	11	290	1.4	36
Sao Tome and Principe	103	1	310	-1.3	65
Cape Verde	315	4	520	0.5	69
Guyana	802	215	520	0.5	69
Solomon Island	254	28	640	-	57
Grenada	92	(.)	840	0.9	69
St. Vincent and the Grenadines	102	(.)	860	1.8	69
Swaziland	705	17	870	2.6	55
Botswana	998	600	920	8.5	61
St. Christopher and Nevis	46	(.)	950	2.4	63
Dominica	81	1	980	-0.4	-
St. Lucia	125	1	1,060	3.1	69
Belize	153	23	1,140	3.6	66
Mauritius	993	2	1,160	2.8	67
Antigua and Bermuda	78	(.)	1,710	-0.4	-
Fiji	670	18	1,790	3.4	68
Seychelles	65	(.)	2,400	3.4	-
Surinam	374	163	3,420	4.5	65
Malta	360	(.)	3,490	8.7	73
Cyprus	655	9	3,680	5.5	75
Gabon	695	268	3,950	3.2	50
Barbados	253	(.)	4,050	3.8	72
Bahamas	222	14	4,060	-1.8	69
Iceland	237	103	10,260	2.6	77
Bahrain	391	1	10,610	-	69
Luxemburg	365	3	14,650	3.9	73
Brunei	209	6	21,140	-	-
Qatar	281	11	21,210	-7.0	72
Comoros	368	2	21,210	-0.6	48
Djibouti	399	22	-	-3.6	50
Equatorial Guinea	359	28	-	-	44
Maldives	168	(.)	-	-	47
Vanuata	127	15	-	-	55
Western Samoa	161	3	-	-	65

SOURCE: Adapted from the World Bank, *World Development Report 1985*, p. 232.
NOTE: AAGR = Average Annual Growth Rate. (.) means less than one thousand square kilometers.
- signifies data not available. Some of the data are for periods other than specified and therefore the reader is encouraged to consult the original source.

land states to pull their resources together in managing their interdependencies with the rest of the world. In the example given above, if all utility companies were to get together and approach several world producers of the small generators to make modifications to their technology to suit small and island economic and operational conditions, they would be more likely to succeed than if they did it individually. Regional organizations like the Organization of Eastern Caribbean States (OECS), made up of seven small, relatively poor island states, can be used to promote and facilitate international collaborative institutional arrangements that benefit the national organizations of their members.

A third problem most small and island states face is one of *human resource development and utilization*. These countries typically have very limited opportunities for education, training, and employment. It is very costly for each small state to train its own experts. The more ambitious nationals leave for training and employment opportunities elsewhere, forcing the state to hire foreign experts from abroad who must be paid world market wages. The small nature of the production system also limits the opportunities and effectiveness with which specialists can be utilized. These problems create shortages of technical and managerial skills both of which are necessary for the development of an effective local technological capacity.

Although large developing countries such as India, Nigeria, and Egypt have suffered from prolonged brain drains, it is the smaller states such as Jamaica and other Caribbean Island states that are more affected proportionately by emigration. Emigration affects the demographic composition of the population and causes sociological problems, as young men and women leave and go to work elsewhere, leaving their families behind to fend for themselves. Dependency on outsiders for jobs, markets, technology, capital, and expertise creates a national psychological dependency that perpetuates for these states an image of a "bedroom community" or "playground." Such an image is not good for the confidence, pride, and self-esteem necessary for the development of an effective, independent, and relevant local technological capacity.

Proportionately *high administrative costs* constitute the fourth problem facing small and island states. Establishing and maintaining a full public service with economic, social, security, diplomatic, and administrative functions is costly because of the small size of the population. Moreover, as Benedict (1967) argues, smallness creates overlapping roles so that individual citizens are tied to each other in many ways. Thus, on a small island, almost everyone knows everyone else. Familiarism and particularism do not promote organizational rationality and impartiality. Western technology has built-in assumptions of rationality, universality, impartiality, objectivity, and separation of personal and official transactions (Brunsson, 1985). In small and island states, familiarism creates conditions under which organizational decision making and resource allocation are dictated by considerations of affiliation and appeasement rather than by objective analysis of organizational needs and task conditions. These may compromise the development of an effective local technological capacity drawing from Western technology and management. Foreign executing agencies can play a very significant role in working with the local implementing agency to reduce dysfunctional consequences of familiarism and to build organization and management systems that promote more objective management and utilization of personnel and other organizational resources.

Small and island states also suffer from their own *natural and physical characteristics*. Most of these states are located in the "ring of fire," making them susceptible to natural disasters such as earthquakes, volcanic eruptions, hurricanes, cyclones, and floods. Defense against natural disasters is expensive for any country, let alone the small or island states. Yet, when they occur, they cause massive costly destruction in property and lives. Moreover, many of these states are in remote locations long distances away from the world business centers. Consequently, transport, especially air and shipping, and external communications are expensive. Under these conditions, small and island states find it difficult to compete with larger states in attracting foreign technology at reasonable prices and to develop an effective local technological capacity for the acquisition and domestic utilization of the technology.

Some small and island states such as Singapore and Hong Kong have managed to overcome these problems and have developed an effective local technological capacity and a sustainable industrial base. In addition to having a well-defined domestic technological infrastructure, these countries and their respective organizations spend considerable resources developing and nurturing contacts with the rest of the world. This experience seems to suggest that small and island states can overcome most of their unique organization and management problems by establishing effective working relationships with other organizations both domestically and internationally. According to Benedict, "solutions to many of these problems may be sought in the combination of small countries through regional and international agreements to help their exports and pool their services" (1967:3). Lall and Gosh (1982) also suggest that small states should use multinational corporations more effectively to develop interorganizational coordinating mechanisms and institutional collaborative arrangements in order to manage their disadvantages and to develop the appropriate local technological capacity.

Organizations in small and island states can overcome their management problems through creative applications of interorganizational coordination (IOC) and collaborative institutional arrangements (CIAs). For example, domestically, local employers can develop joint human resource management programs to alleviate staff shortages and poor use of specialists. They can also join hands in undertaking preacquisition investigations before making decisions about what technology to buy, where to buy it from, and which organizations to use as executing agencies. Regional and international collaborative institutional arrangements are the most effective ways of addressing most of the problems and vulnerability of small states. A recent Commonwealth (1986) report has provided several examples of how these might be established in areas of economics, security, and diplomacy. International development agencies can play an important role in fostering these collaborative institutional arrangements. For example, the Canadian International Development Agency (1986) is currently spending over $75 million on the Caribbean Airports Program (CAP) to upgrade operational safety and physical maintenance of twenty-two airports in thirteen Commonwealth Caribbean countries. It is expected that the program will provide a framework for a more permanent collaborative institutional arrangement for airports managements for these small and island states. In 1987, the Commonwealth Fund for Technical Co-operation and the Canadian International Development Agency, as part of the Commonwealth Heads of Government Meeting in Vancouver, funded and organized a six-day Commonwealth Small States Exposition in both Toronto and Vancouver in which thirty-one Commonwealth countries participated to promote trade, investment, and tourism. It is by means of international collaborative institutional arrangements such as these that small and island states can overcome their natural disadvantages, access world technology and markets, and build effective local technological capacities appropriate to the unique character and needs of their organizations' critical operating and strategic management tasks.

Technology Transfer as a Continuing Learning Process.   Learning is a relatively permanent change in behavior that occurs as a result of experience. Learning, at the level of the individual operator or manager, the small workgroup, the organization and its stakeholders, or the country and its constituent communities and institutions, is a continuing integral part of the entire process of technology transfer and the building of effective local technological capacities. Without learning, there can be no development.

Both organization science and development administration provide various social learning models potentially applicable to the technology transfer process. These include the Skinnerian organizational behavior modification (OB Mod.) model (Luthans and Kreitner, 1975); Kolb's (1974) model of adult learning based on individual differences in learning styles; the social learning paradigm (Korten, 1980; Gran, 1983; Thomas, 1983) that emphasizes a participative social learning process for project design and implementation by all stakeholders rather than the "blueprint" pre-planned, top-down hierarchical approach; Argyris and Schon's (1978) double-loop learning model that emphasizes the organization's sustained capacity to detect and correct errors; and the on-the-job training (OJT) model. These models are mutually reinforcing and share common concepts and ideology. They view learning as a continuous participative social process in which the trainees play an active or a proactive rather than a passive role. They emphasize the importance of trainee participation, participative goal setting, giving and receiving of feedback, and proper motivation and incentives. They accent the need for localized training based on the trainee's sociocultural and technological environment and indigenous knowledge systems, and job-related training based on the organization's current and future task (COTs, SMATs) requirements. They view training not only as cognitive learning, but also, and perhaps more importantly, as an experiential process designed to change attitudes, work values, belief systems, and work habits.

Argyris' double-loop learning model, Korten's participative learning process approach, the Skinnerian model, and Pava's concept of deliberations provide useful concepts and methods for facilitating the development of effective learning systems for technology transfer training. The double-loop learning model provides the ultimate criteria for the learning process because it "occurs when error is detected and corrected in ways that involve the modification of an organization's underlying norms, policies and objectives" (Argyris and Schon, 1978:3). Korten's approach provides for the broad-based participative bottom-up process by which lower level participants are involved and committed. Pava's concept of deliberations provides the mechanisms for bringing together different stakeholders for unstructured learning characteristic of the complex strategic management tasks. The on-the-job training emphasizes the practical hands-on experience so necessary for both critical operating and strategic management tasks, and the Skinnerian model provides the motivation and incentives for the trainees to acquire new skills and use them on a continuing basis for solving their COTs and SMATs work problems.

Organizations, however, tend to inhibit the creation of effective learning systems because of the risks involved in questioning the validity of operating norms, policies, objectives, and established cause-effect assumptions. The development of effective learning systems depends on the existence of valid and reliable information, free and informed choice, genuine participation by the stakeholders, commitment to their choices, and a benign and facilitative environment. Information about alternative technologies, potential executing and implementing agencies, the host country's local technological capacities, and changing government policies is expensive to collect and analyze in terms of money, time, and personnel. Consequently, most technology transfer decisions are made with invalid or incomplete information.

Choices of technology are rarely free and informed. To the extent that they are based on satisfying decisions (March and Simon, 1958) and incomplete information, they cannot be truly informed. When an implementing agency has to buy at least 80 percent of the "soft" and "hard" technology from the donor country, it loses that percentage of freedom. Investing in effective learning systems and collaborative information exchange among the implementing agencies can help regain some of the lost freedom.

The application and limitations of various training methods for developing countries have been discussed by Kerrigan and Luke (1987). Table 6.3 summarizes the rated effectiveness of fifteen selected technology transfer training methods for critical operating (COTs) and strategic management (SMATs) jobs. The table shows that the methods most effective for one type of tasks are not necessarily those effective for the other. Apart from on-the-job training, which is potentially effective for both types of jobs, the more mechanical or automated methods such as computer-

Table 6.3

SELECTED TECHNOLOGY TRANSFER TRAINING METHODS AND THEIR EFFECTIVENESS FOR COTs AND SMATs

Method	Effectiveness for:	
	COTs	SMATs
1. On-the-job Training	H	H
2. Apprenticeship Training	H	L
3. Job Rotation	H	M
4. Lecture	M	L-M
5. Audiovisual Techniques	H	L-M
6. Computer-assisted Instruction	H	L
7. Equipment Simulators	H	L
8. Programmed Instruction	M	L-M
9. Business Games	L	M
10. Role Playing	L	H
11. Case Study Method	L	H
12. Coaching	L	H
13. Correspondence School	M	L
14. Overseas Study Tours	M-H	L
15. Employee Orientation and Socialization	L-M	M-H

Note: COTs = Critical Operating Tasks; SMATs = Strategic Management Tasks.
H = High, M= Medium, L= Low indicating the extent to which the training method is effective (H), or ineffective (L) for either the COTs or the SMATs.

assisted instruction (CAI) and equipment simulators are more effective for COTs, whereas the training for SMATs is accomplished more effectively by use of labor-intensive methods such as case studies, and role playing, which also require experienced trainers in clinical or interpersonal skills.

On-the-job training, when properly planned and combined with other on-site and off-site training methods, can be effective for both COTs and SMATs. Lack of knowledgeable, experienced, and motivated local trainers (employees) can limit the effectiveness of on-the-job training. When the expatriates are used as trainers, they can be effective as training operators for COTs but are limited as trainers for SMATs because of their lack of intimate knowledge of the local organizational environment. A recent USAID evaluation of 277 agricultural projects in Africa found that formal training was the principal type of organizational enhancement, whereas on-the-job training was important in only 19 percent of the cases (Rosenthal et al., 1986). Kerrigan and Luke have concluded that on-the-job training "has significant unrealized potential for developing managerial talent" (1987:97) for organizations in developing countries.

Summary

In summary, the real test of effective technology transfer is the extent to which it enables the implementing organization to build a sustainable local technological capacity supported by an effective learning system. That is, the implementing and the executing agencies engage in continuing learning and exchange of information. Technology transfer training should focus on enhancing the implementing agency's capacity to perform its current and future COTs and SMATs. The models presented in the final section of this chapter can facilitate the building of an effective learning system, and the training methods outlined in Figure 6.4 can provide a basis for informed decision about the design and implementation of the necessary training and learning, depending on whether the focus is on the critical operating or on the strategic management tasks.

The chapter has described a process model of international technology transfer involving all participating organizations in the technology exporting and importing countries. It emphasizes the importance of effective technological capacity (LTC). It links technology transfer and the existence of LTC to the efficient and effective performance of the implementing organization's critical operating and strategic management tasks. It also supports the conceptualization of technology transfer as a negotiated transaction involving participative deliberations among stakeholders inside and outside the implementing organizations.

The chapter has ended with a discussion of technology transfer under the three special considerations of small-scale enterprises (SSEs), extension services in agriculture, and small and island states.

CHAPTER 7

Decentralization

This chapter discusses the complex and often misunderstood centralization-decentralization concept in the management of organizations drawing on the literature from both development administration and organization science. It is divided into three sections. The first section defines the concept of decentralization and reviews its different meanings. The second discusses decentralization within the context of organizational critical operating tasks (COTs) and strategic management tasks (SMATs). It includes decentralization within and among organizations, dimensions and contingencies of decentralization, forces for and against decentralization including international pressures, decentralization and state-owned enterprises, and decentralization of service delivery systems in underorganized or isolated communities. The chapter ends with a discussion of the assessment and implementation of decentralization.

I. What Is Decentralization?

A lot of attention is being paid to decentralization in the management of organizations in developing countries, especially in the area of public management improvement. At the same time, the literature shows confusion as to the meaning and purpose of decentralization. Decentralization (or centralization) is not a unitary concept but a shorthand for various forms of structural arrangements by which power and other organization resources are distributed to facilitate the efficient and effective performance and coordination of the organization's critical operating and strategic management tasks.

The definition of decentralization expressed by Cheema and Rondinelli is typical of the development administration literature. They define decentralization to mean the "transfer of planning, decision making, or administrative authority from the central government to its field organizations, local administrative units, semi-autonomous and parastatal organizations, local governments, or non-government organizations" (1983:18). This definition covers a wide range of macro- and micro-level structural arrangements including intraorganizational and interorganizational forms of decentralization. It also emphasizes the transfer of power associated with strategic management rather than operating tasks.

Cheema and Rondinelli's definition illustrates other important aspects of decentralization. For example, they do not consider the question of decentralization or centralization *within* either the central government, or each of the local government units. As several researchers have shown in parastatal organizations (Sarkar, 1984) local administration (Griffin, 1981), and organizations in general (Mintzberg, 1983), merely transferring administrative authority to lower level organizational units does not by itself constitute decentralization or increased participation by members or stakeholders of the organization. Moreover, if a central government agency sends some of its professional or technical staff to local government organizations, it does not necessarily constitute decentralization, and could even enhance central government control and influence over local authorities and the way they perform their tasks.

Representing the organization science literature, Mintzberg defines decentralization in terms of decision making and power distribution when he writes: "When all the power for decision making rests at a single point in the organization—ultimately in the hands of one person—we shall call the structure centralized; to the extent that the power is dispersed among many people, we shall call the structure decentralized" (1983:95). He focuses on intraorganizational decentralization, pushing decision making and control systems to the lowest possible levels within the same organization. It relates to strategic management tasks although operating tasks are easier to decentralize (Child, 1984). The centralization-decentralization process also involves trade-offs that management must make in the light of the organization's own internal attributes such as size, dispersal, technical complexity, resource availability, and information processing capacity, and external environmental task requirements such as clients' system demands. Like all other organizational interventions, the primary objective of decentralization and the guidelines or criteria by which trade-offs should be made is the design of sustainable optimal structural arrangements that enhance the organization's capacity to perform its critical operating and strategic management tasks and to meet the legitimate expectations of its important stakeholders.

It is important to establish the relationship between the organization's internal capacity to decentralize, and its need to perform its operating and strategic management tasks effectively and satisfy the service requirements of its clients. Emphasizing the importance of this relationship, Kochen and Deutsch wrote: "the core of decentralization in a service system is its responsiveness, the shortness of its communication time, and the directness of its channels between servers and clients" (1980:xix). They emphasize the critical operating tasks of a service delivery organization and their effects on the quality of service received by the clients. This is an interorganizational perspective.

In public administration, the capacity of the individual organizations to decentralize their COTs or SMATs may be limited indeed. For example, in most developing countries, functions such as finance and human resource management are centralized within a central agency. The line ministries are therefore dependent on the central agencies (e.g., treasury, public service commission, planning and budgeting) for the performance of these tasks. This reliance affects their capacity to delegate these and other functions either to lower levels in the ministry, or to other organizations outside the government. Attempts to decentralize functions from the central government to local governments when these functions are highly centralized within the central government are not likely to succeed. Moreover, the general profile of organizations in developing countries given in Chapter One is not conducive to decentralization (see Figure 1.1).

II. Decentralization and the Critical Operating and Strategic Management Tasks

In this section, decentralization is discussed in the context of the organization's critical operating (COTs) and strategic management (SMATs) tasks. It provides a conceptual framework for the analysis of decentralization within and across organizations both for COTs and SMATs. It discusses the various dimensions and contingencies of decentralization and their differential effects on the performance of the participating organizations' tasks, by describing decentralization of public enterprises and delivery service systems in various developing countries.

1. Decentralization Within and Between Organizations

Instead of assessing decentralization in relation to unidentifiable or unorganized entities like citizenry, peasantry, or local populace as is often the practice in development administration, we need to delineate and specify the participating organizations or units to which and from which decentralization is being effected. Even if action is required for a relatively underorganized social system such as the family or village, we should conceptualize it as an organization with a hierarchy of authority, task systems, decision-making processes and priorities, and control and reward systems. In development administration there is a tendency to treat the central government and subnational levels of government each as a unitary concept or single organization. In fact, public management is a convenient shorthand for a variety of organizations with different tasks, structural configurations, and management capacities and processes. For example, the central ministry of planning would bear little resemblance in terms of structure or task systems to the ministry of local government and rural development. Naturally, the need, capacity, and strategies for decentralization for each of these ministries would be different.

In order to understand the concept and process of decentralization, we should identify and distinguish among participating, decentralizing, and receiving organizations. *Participating* organization refers to any organization involved in the decentralization initiative or program. This may be a single organization, as is often the case in organization science (e.g., General Motors' divisionalization) or it may be several organizations at different hierarchical levels. An illustration of the latter is a central government that decentralizes the functions of various ministries to organizations at various subnational levels. The *decentralizing* organization is the one relinquishing power, control, authority, or influence over the performance of certain specified operating or strategic management tasks to another organization or organizations. The *receiving* organization is the one acquiring the decentralized power, authority, or control over the same specified tasks. Each of these organizations has its own operating and strategic management tasks that must be analyzed and diagnosed before effective decentralization can be implemented. If decentralization is undertaken within a single organization, these concepts would then refer to units of the same organization at different hierarchical levels. When two or more organizations are involved, as is often the case in public management decentralization in developing countries, the analysis and diagnosis must be interorganizational and therefore involve two sets of COTs and SMATs.

Figure 7.1 illustrates the different types of participating organizations and the possible range of effects on their respective COTs and SMATs. All four organizations depicted by the triangles—ABC, CDE, MNK, and KJL—are participating organizations. Intraorganizational decentralization, shown by the dotted lines, is the simpler form because it is circumscribed within a single organization. Triangle CDE shows the different types of intraorganizational decentralization from the SMATs to the COTs or to the middle, and from the middle to different parts of the organization. Intraorganizational decentralization to the COTs can boost operator morale and improve task performance through increased organizational involvement and commitment. Professional COTs operators expect to receive decentralization within their areas of expertise.

Figure 7.1 also shows three more complex forms of interorganizational decentralization across two or more organizations. First, it depicts the COTs-COTs form, in which the COTs of one organization are decentralized to the COTs of another, that is, they move from the CDE to the MNK organization. This form is appropriate for a weak organization within a chain of interdependent organizations. For example, a crop marketing board takes over the functions of buying and distributing agricultural inputs such as fertilizers or seeds because the government agency responsible for these tasks is unable to do so. Second, it shows the SMATs-

Figure 7.1

INTRA-·AND INTERORGANIZATIONAL DECENTRALIZATION FOR OPERATING AND STRATEGIC MANAGEMENT TASKS

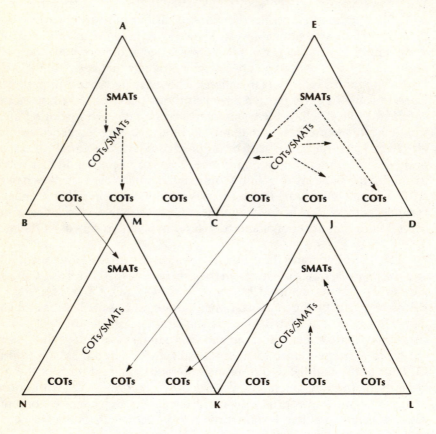

Note: ABC, CDE, MNK, and JKL are four separate organizations.
‑‑‑‑‑‑‑‑► indicates intraorganizational decentralization or centralization.
———► indicates interorganizational decentralization.
       Arrows indicate direction of flow of decision-making power or task performance responsibility.
       COTs = Critical Operating Tasks; SMATs = Strategic Management Tasks.

COTs form, by which the SMATs of one organization are taken over and performed as the COTs of another, that is, the SMATs of the JKL become the COTs of the MNK organization. As an example of this form, a government ministry takes over the strategic management tasks (e.g., corporate planning) of a state-owned enterprise and performs them as its own COTs on a regular continuing basis. Third, the figure delineates the COTs-SMATs form, in which the COTs of one organization are performed by the receiving organization as its SMATs. That is, the COTs of ABC become the SMATs of MNK. As an illustration, a private sector business organization (ABC) has its functions of importing supplies from abroad taken over by a government central agency because such supplies constitute an important strategic input for the country. In general, marketing boards operate in this way because they take over control and performance of some of the COTs and SMATs of the individual farmers.

Figure 7.1 has many implications for understanding and implementing decentralization for organizations in developing countries. First, we must make a distinction between decentralization within a single organization like a ministry of agriculture, and generalized decentralization of all government services involving multiple organizations. Second, interorganizational decentralization involving both COTs and SMATs is much more complex and expensive to undertake than that for only one set of tasks and necessitates the development of the capacity to manage the process by all the implementing organizations. Third, in the design of an interorganizational decentralization program, it is best to start with carefully selected COTs for carefully prepared decentralizing and receiving organizations. Highly centralized organizations cannot implement decentralization easily because they lack the expertise and political will. This deficiency may explain the often reported failures to decentralize public and local administration in most developing countries.

Organizations are often willing to decentralize operating tasks but resist giving up control over strategic management tasks. Even within each of the COTs and SMATs, differences exist in terms of willingness or resistance to decentralize. For example, among the COTs, output tasks such as distribution, sales, market research, and disposal of byproducts are easier to decentralize to other organizations than input tasks associated with acquisition such as staffing, purchasing, and finance as well as transformational tasks associated with the organization's technical core. Among the SMATs, those associated with the organization's core values or mission are the most difficult to decentralize. Accordingly, government agencies are more willing to decentralize or to contract out program implementation than they are policy formulation.

This analysis has implications for privatization of state-owned enterprises. Interorganizational decentralization can constitute the initial stages of privatization; the decentralizing organization gives up control of first the COTs and then the SMATs. Carefully planned gradual decentralization from public agencies to small- or medium-sized indigenous private sector organizations can be developmental and thus provide the receiving organization with the opportunity to develop the necessary management capacity for more complete privatization. Like decentralization, privatization can be brought about as a collaborative institutional arrangement (CIA) among different participating organizations. For example, a crop marketing board responsible for buying, processing, and selling farmers' crops can be privatized through interorganizational decentralization so that different indigenous private sector organizations take over control and performance of the different aspects of its critical operating tasks such as buying, transport, processing, and distribution.

2. Dimensions of Decentralization

This section discusses five dimensions of decentralization and their applications in developing countries. These are devolution, delegation, popular participation, divisionalization, and deconcentration.

Devolution. Devolution can be defined as the "transfer of power to local units of government which operate in a quasi-autonomous manner outside the direct administrative control structures of the central government" (Thomson and Connerley, 1986:12). To the extent that local units of government and the central government can be distinguished as separate hierarchical structures, this then becomes an interorganizational form of decentralization. Because it involves at least two separate organizations, each with its own COTs and SMATs, it is difficult to implement.

In theory, devolution is attractive because it increases local citizen involvement, commitment, and identification with the development initiatives undertaken by the local organizations. It gives the feeling that citizens are getting services that satisfy their needs while at the same time they have some influence over the organizations providing these services. In practice, political considerations are important. Countries that have made extensive attempts at devolution such as the Sudan, Nigeria, and Papua New Guinea all seem to have been motivated by the search for political solutions to regional or ethnic demands for local autonomy. In Algeria, communal popular assemblies were asked to administer the land reform process partly because they were deemed to have the necessary local knowledge and expertise for the task but also because the issue was considered politically too "hot" for the central government.

The Sudan, Africa's largest country with a continuing and debilitating ethnic civil war that has lasted a quarter of a century, has one of the most elaborate devolution forms of decentralization, at least on paper. The provincial governments have wide-ranging powers, including taxation and revenue collection, law enforcement, management of development projects, and overseeing of central government ministries and departments. However, as Rondinelli, Nellis, and Cheema have rightly observed, the crucial goal for the devolution is to "find a way of ending the civil war and to increase the commitment of heterogeneous religious, ethnic, and tribal groups to nation building by giving them a larger part in governance" (1984:21).

In Papua New Guinea, where provincial governments, using grants from the central government, have been given the power to levy and collect taxes and to manage their own development and local social service institutions such as schools and hospitals, and in Nigeria, where state governments have a wide range of statutory local functions such as law enforcement, public works, rural and agricultural development, and water and social services, the underlying motives for devolution are equally political. Politically motivated changes should not be expected to bring about improvements in organizational efficiency or effectiveness.

Delegation.   John Child defines delegation as a form of decentralization "where decision making is passed downwards and outwards within the formal structure, but where there are strict limits imposed on the scope and the type of decisions that can be made without referral upwards" (1984:146). On the other hand, Rondinelli and his co-workers see delegation as the transfer of "managerial responsibility for specifically defined tasks to organizations that are outside the regular bureaucratic structure and that are only indirectly controlled by the central government" (1984:15). Clearly, Child's definition is intraorganizational whereas Rondinelli's is interorganizational. Although Child focuses mainly on management tasks (decision making), in practice, both COTs and SMATs can be delegated.

The advantages of delegation include reduced workload for top management, managerial motivation, management development for junior managers, organizational flexibility and responsiveness to local circumstances and unexpected events, and more effective unit-specific controls and performance measurements. The risk of poor performance and the unwillingness to accept delegated responsibilities by junior officers or managers are some of the dangers of delegation. Delegation can be reinforced and sustained only if junior officers demonstrate the capacity and motivation to perform the delegated tasks to the satisfaction of their superiors.

The literature on decentralization does not offer a theoretical framework or diagnostic tools for determining how far down the subnational levels delegation should go. As a result, while some countries focus their decentralization programs at the provincial or state level, others use the district or village as the operational level. For example, while Nigeria's decentralization program is based on the state as the operational unit, Nepal's is based on the district (*panchayat*) and Tanzania's on the village (*ujamaa*). Sometimes, a country can change its operational level within a relatively short period of time. When it started its decentralization program, Bangladesh used the district (*zillah*) as the most important unit of local government; but, when the military government seized power and introduced martial law, it abolished the district level of government and now uses the subdistrict (*upazillah*) as the operational level for decentralization. The appropriate operational level of decentralization should be determined after careful assessment of the relative capacities of the decentralizing and receiving organizations. It is possible and may be desirable for a country to decentralize at two or more different levels for different regions, ministries, and organizational tasks. This practice is consistent with the concept of selective decentralization, in which different functions or types of decisions are delegated to different levels of the organization.

Popular Participation.   Popular or citizen participation is a form of decentralization because it removes decision making and implementation from the exclusive control of senior management in either the private or the public sector organizations. It differs from other forms of decentralization in that power is decentralized to individuals, groups, and other organizations *outside* the boundaries of the organization being decentralized. It is a common form of decentralization for a wide range of corporate and human services professions including education (Rogers and Chung, 1983), social work, community psychology, urban planning, environmental protection, participatory democracy (Ollawa, 1979), international management (Janger and Berenbeim, 1981), and rural development (Hunt and Truitt, 1971; Uphoff, 1986). It is considered a form of social change through cooperatives, collectives, and nationalized industries (Nash, Dandler, and Hopkins, 1976).

Popular participation legitimizes the participation of outsiders in the decision making and management processes of the organization. Specifically, it allows outsiders to participate in the performance of the organization's strategic management or critical operating tasks. For example, as Rogers and Chung (1983) clearly state, in decentralized school systems, parents, community groups, and civic leaders participate in the educational planning processes (strategic management) and in the actual delivery of programs within the individual schools (operating tasks). In rural development, the local citizens become partners in the formulation and implementation of development initiatives. This is an effective strategy of what Hyden (1983) calls "capturing the peasantry" as willing participants in the development process. It assumes, however, that the peasants or citizens are able and willing to participate meaningfully in the performance of the organization's strategic or operational tasks, and that the organization has the capacity to accommodate these outside demands for direct participation without losing its identity, integrity, or capacity to perform.

Advocates of individual or suborganizational levels of analysis as a strategy for development assume the existence of functioning organizations. For example, in one of their earlier papers, Bish and Ostrom observed that, in making their choices, individuals must have "access to judicial, legislative, and constitutional remedies in seeking redress against officials and governments which violate constitutional rights or rights created under legislative authority of the state and federal governments" (1973:18). Clearly, the public choice approach is based on the assumption of the continuing existence of a functioning organizational infrastructure. Yet this cannot be taken for granted in most developing countries.

Mintzberg (1983) distinguishes between vertical and horizontal decentralization. In vertical decentralization, power moves up and down the formal organizational hierarchy. In horizontal decentralization, power is distributed horizontally across hierarchical levels and ends up in the hands of nonmanagerial personnel such as specialists, advisors, analysts, planners, or even operating staff. In organizations in developing countries in which these roles are not fully developed or adequately staffed, this form of decentralization can be difficult. Instead, in many of these organizations, if horizontal decentralization occurs, power may be passed on to individuals or groups *outside* the boundaries of the organization such as politicians, clients, citizen groups, foreign technical assistants, suppliers, professional associations, or other outside interest groups. Accordingly, the decentralized organization loses its capacity to perform and control its COTs and SMATs. It becomes porous and vulnerable.

Divisionalization.   Divisionalization occurs when a large bureaucratic organization is divided into semi-autonomous units. Each unit or division is given the power and necessary resources to manage its critical operating tasks and to control its strategic management tasks within the confines of its domain. The division's domain may be determined by products, markets, or territory or policy sector. Divisionalization is intraorganizational and is limited to the decentralization of selected SMATs from senior management to the division managers.

In the United States, divisionalization dates back to the 1920s when DuPont de Nemours introduced a new structure using autonomous multidepartmental divisions. It was then popularized by Alfred Sloan of General Motors. It is attractive to management because: (1) it frees senior managers from the routine operating tasks and allows them to concentrate on the more important complex strategic management tasks; (2) it facilitates the creation of semi-autonomous business units, each run separately as a cost/profit center, which allow the divisional managers to exercise entrepreneurship; and (3) it sets the stage for establishing an effective incentive reward system for the division managers and their employees based on the division's absolute and relative level of performance. It is used by large organizations and has been extended by Ouchi (1984), who advocates a societal participative multidimensional form of industrial organization by which American business can recapture its competitive edge against Japanese and other sources of international competition.

Divisionalization can be an effective form of decentralization from the organization's headquarters to the division managers' level. However, it does not necessarily lead to decentralization *below* the divisional level. In fact, not unlike decentralization at the provincial or public enterprise level, divisionalization may have the effect of encouraging the divisional managers to exercise high levels of power and control, and thus to run the division like a highly centralized organization.

Divisionalization is based on at least three premises: (1) availability of enough competent managers to run the division; (2) the division's capability to perform its critical operating tasks without the direct involvement of the senior managers; and (3) the existence of a reliable management information system that provides relevant, objective, and timely performance indicators of each of the divisions, right down to the level of each employee.

These conditions are hard to meet for most organizations in developing countries. Shortage of qualified and experienced managers, especially in Africa and in parts of Asia, have been discussed in previous chapters. In addition, many organizations in developing countries experience difficulties maintaining efficient performance of their operating tasks. Consequently, managers end up being personally involved in routine operating tasks instead of working on the strategic management tasks. Finally, objective performance measurements are hard to attain, especially in the area of public management. Divisionalization works best when accountability can be tracked down to the smallest operating unit.

Deconcentration. Deconcentration can be defined as the handing over of some administrative authority and responsibility down the hierarchy within central government ministries, agencies, or corporations. It involves the shifting of workload and selected decision-making authority from headquarters to lower or field level officials. It is therefore an intra-organizational form of decentralization, as the shifting of workload and decision making takes place within the same hierarchical structure. The main advantage of deconcentration is that it enables the local officials to make decisions and take independent action, accommodating for local conditions but being careful not to overstep the policies and guidelines of the headquarters. The deconcentrated authority can be taken over again by headquarters at any time they are not satisfied with the way it is being handled.

According to a recent World Bank report, deconcentration is one of the most widely used forms of decentralization. In various Asian countries deconcentration has been implemented by means of various approaches, including provision of funds and technical assistance to local authorities to plan and manage their own development.

Table 7.1 summarizes the different approaches, purposes, and probable effects on the local authorities for deconcentration as used by eight Asian and African countries. Although the methods vary in details and scope, they all involve providing the local hierarchical levels with resources such as money, personnel, or authority to build the capacity to manage their own development. The effects are limited to the critical operating tasks of the local authorities' organizations and the control of the strategic management tasks remains with the respective central government organizations.

Table 7.1 also shows the effects of deconcentration on the local organizations' COTs and SMATs for each of the eight countries. In the majority of cases, the intended effects of deconcentration are limited to the organizations' critical operating tasks. Only in the Philippines, Tunisia, and Tanzania do the stipulated effects include some aspects of the local organization's strategic management tasks. For example, in the Philippines, the plans stipulated development of management capacity in the governor's office for the management of local development initiatives. Even here the effects on SMATs are quite limited, and in the case of the *ujamaa* villages, they never materialized (Picard, 1980).

3. Contingencies of Decentralization

By now, we should know that there is not one best way of organizing or managing work. Decentralization is neither good nor bad. All depends upon the contingencies, which can be either internal or external to the organization. Internal contingencies include the organization's: (1) age and size; (2) nature of tasks; (3) technology; (4) internal operational and management capacity; (5) incentives; (6) leadership; (7) management values and organization climate; (8) history of innovation; (9) internal support; and (10) physical dispersal.

Old, small, or very large organizations tend to be centralized. The nature of the tasks performed by the organization also affects decentralization. Organizations or parts thereof performing routine tasks tend to be centralized, while those doing more complex, innovative, and interdependent tasks are more effective with decentralized structures. Simple, routine, standardized technology pushes the organization toward centralization, while complex, changing technology requires a more organic decentralized structure. The internal operational and management systems should be strong with a solid record of performance with adequate organizational slack before an organization can confidently embark on a program of decentralization. The rewards and operational incentive systems for employees at different levels of the participating organizations should be consistent with the desired behaviors in support of the decentralization program.

Table 7.1

DIFFERENT APPROACHES, PURPOSES, AND EFFECTS OF DECONCENTRATION ON COTs AND SMATs

COUNTRY	APPROACH	PURPOSE	Effects on Local Organizations' COTs or SMATs
1. **China**	Creation of production teams and management committees for each of the 53,000 communes and changing farmers' incentive systems through the Production Responsibility System (PRS)	To use a variety of local government management and incentive systems relatively free from central government controls to increase agricultural production, incentive pay, and overall income for the peasant farmers	COTs
2. **Indonesia**	Provision of funds from central government and international donor agencies to the Provincial Development Program	To increase rural productivity and household incomes	COTs
3. **Morocco**	Creation of local communal councils with overall responsibility for local development using funds, technical and professional staff provided by central government	To develop the technical, professional, and management capacity of the councils to take over complete responsibility for economic development and provision of social services	COTs
4. **Pakistan**	Creation and supervision of the *morkaz* councils by the central government	To promote integrated rural development bringing together local agricultural, credit, public works, cooperatives, and private activities	COTs
5. **The Philippines**	Central government provides financial, technical, and management assistance to the provincial governors through the Provincial Development Assistance Program funded by USAID. Creation of regional development councils of the National Economic Development Authority	To develop the necessary development management capacity in the governor's office. To translate national development plans into provincially operating goals. To coordinate activities of other ministries at the provincial and local levels	COTs, some SMATs

Table 7.1 (continued)

DIFFERENT APPROACHES, PURPOSES, AND EFFECTS OF DECONCENTRATION ON COTS AND SMATS

COUNTRY	APPROACH	PURPOSE	Effects on Local Organizations' COTS or SMATS
6. **Tanzania**	Abolition of pre-independence local government and absorbtion of staff into the central government service, and creation of communal *ujamaa* villages. Decentralization of national ministries	To enable *ujamaa* villages to initiate and manage the provision of social services, economic development, and political education	COTs, some SMATs
7. **Thailand**	Funds provided to *tambon* (village) councils to undertake job creation programs	To increase agricultural production and household incomes	COTs
8. **Tunisia**	The central government provides each of the 20 *gouvernorats* an annual grant for economic development and job creation programs that are managed locally through the Rural Programs (PDR)	To reduce the central government's role in rural development to one of supervision and project approval, and to build the development management capability of the *gouvernorats*	COTs, some SMATs

Source: Based on information contained in a World Bank Report, *Decentralization in Developing Countries: A Review of Recent Experiences* by D.A. Rondinelli, J.R. Nellis, and G.S. Cheema, 1984.

Note: COTs = Critical Operating Tasks; SMATs = Strategic Management Tasks for the local organizations.

Leadership is also important for decentralization. Effective decentralization requires strong, competent managers with a high level of self confidence, trust, and achievement motivation. Decentralization requires the managers to take moderately high levels of risk. The prevailing management values and climate in the organization should be consistent with the values and basic assumptions of decentralization. Senior managers should reinforce participation or delegation of responsibilities to lower level employees. Paternalistic and theory X attitudes rather than theory Y or theory Z attitudes are incompatible with the philosophy of decentralization. Experimenting organizations with a history of successful structural, technological, or management innovations are more likely to succeed with decentralization than are those who have no such history. Support from the employees, clients, and the community is important, especially for the initial start-up performance problems.

External contingencies of decentralization include: (1) the nature of the environment the organization operates in; (2) the political climate; (3) community support; and (4) the nature of the client system. When the task environment is stable and predictable, and when the organization's tasks are routine, centralization is the more effective structural arrangement. However, a stable political environment creates conditions for a benign environment, which tends to facilitate decentralization. This condition is particularly relevant for organizations in developing countries. One of the implications for this contingency is that decentralization programs introduced amid internal political strife, or as a possible solution to political conflicts, are not likely to succeed because they would be operating under inappropriate contingencies. The literature from organization science suggests that a stable task environment pushes the organization toward centralization, but experience from development administration indicates that decentralization is best facilitated when the general political environment is rather stable.

4. Forces for and against Decentralization

Both development administration and the more applied literature in organization science promote decentralization on the assumption that it will produce a better organization in terms of productivity, integration, innovation, and self-renewal, and better employees and stakeholders in terms of morale, self-esteem, autonomy, and commitment to the organization's mission. As a result, since the 1970s and increasingly in the 1980s, many governments in Africa, Asia, and Latin America have undertaken various forms of decentralization to state, provincial, district and local governments, local field administrative units, special purpose corporations, nongovernmental organizations, and private voluntary organizations. Likewise, in North America and Western Europe, a significant number of organizations have experimented with various forms of decentralization and employee participation programs. In both cases, the results of these initiatives, especially the long-term effects of decentralization, have been well below expectations. Both a 1982 United Nations report and a 1982 World Bank report concluded that, as far as developing countries are concerned, "the actual impact of decentralization for effective administration has been very limited" (Rondinelli, Nellis, and Cheema, 1984:4). In spite of the disappointing results, efforts throughout the developing countries continue toward further decentralization. This section examines the forces behind these efforts.

The arguments for decentralization can be grouped into five categories. These are: (1) economic arguments; (2) social considerations; (3) political reasons; (4) reasons of organization and management; and (5) international pressures. Each of these is discussed briefly.

Economic Arguments.   By the 1970s it became clear that the centralist megaproject approach to the organization and management of a national economy had not worked. The disappointing results have been responsible for a re-thinking of the whole strategy of managing development and have led to the conclusion that small-scale decentralized projects, close to the people whom they are designed to serve, are more effective than large-scale projects.

Moreover, there has been a shift away from industry or mining as the engine of growth to agriculture and renewable natural resources. Managing agricultural development requires, among other things, the mobilization of large numbers of people, and the provision of a wide range of services not previously available to many dispersed rural communities. Such services like road maintenance, irrigation, extension, and transportation are more effectively provided under decentralized arrangements.

Decentralization can be used as a response to a wide range of structural market imperfections and price distortions that are so common in developing countries. This would enable the receiving organizations to perform their COTs and SMATs more cost effectively because of increased competition.

Social Considerations.   Decentralization is seen as a structural and administrative mechanism to bring about a more acceptable distribution of income, wealth, and opportunity. The evidence, however, does not support the view that decentralized administration brings about better distribution of resources among the citizens. It may, on the contrary, contribute to more uneven distributions. In Sri Lanka, for example, the District Development Councils that are supposed to serve as the operating units for the management of development initiatives in each district are so fragmented and disorganized that it may well be that these Councils are intended only as a political "slush fund" for Members of Parliament. Decentralized decision making can also create conditions for the satisfaction of basic needs (Blunt, 1983; Sandbrook, 1982) and facilitate popular participation in development.

Political Reasons.   It is generally recognized that the centralization-decentralization debate in most developing countries is political in nature. The motivation for decentralization, the implementing strategies, and the interpretation of the results are often colored by political considerations. These include mobilizing, organizing, and utilizing local support and resources for nation building and development and encouraging various interest groups to identify with the national government.

Countries like Sri Lanka, India, Malaysia, the Sudan, Nigeria, Ethiopia, and Guyana with multiethnic or multiracial populations see decentralization as a practical solution to their ethnic and regional strife. As well, decentralization may be used as a way of breaking up powerful interest groups potentially opposed to the governing regime and establishing more balanced power distribution. These may have been the motives in the break-up of the Uganda Development Corporation under Idi Amin, and of Algeria's SONATRAC national oil company (Hafsi et al., 1987). It is also true in countries such as Brazil, Ghana, Nigeria, and Uganda where economic, industrial, and educational opportunities are traditionally concentrated in the south, and for countries like Malaysia, Guyana, Fiji, and the Sudan where the imbalances cut across racial differences.

Organization and Management.   Decentralization can bring about improvements in the performance of organizational tasks in many different ways including freeing up the time of managers, who are often overloaded with routine operating tasks, in order to concentrate on the more strategic long-term management of the organization. Decentralization can also lead to better utilization of resources because the management and maintenance of centrally planned development can be expensive, wasteful, and unresponsive to the changing local needs and circumstances.

Communication is always a problem in large organizations. Decentralization can reduce overload and congestion in the channels of administration and communication and upgrade the quality of bottom-up information coming from the local units to the top of the organization. These steps will then better the performance of both COTs and SMATs by improving the quality of operational and management information available to decision makers.

Decentralization can also provide opportunities for personal and organizational development. If the local unit's organizational and management capacity is low or poor, it can create the basis for building and sustaining a better management capacity by introducing more comprehensive administrative procedures, installing new equipment or technology, changing the structuring of the organization and its coordinating mechanisms with outside organizations, or obtaining better trained and experienced personnel. If the local unit's personnel are lacking in training and experience, decentralization can provide opportunities for on- and off-the-job training and experience.

Finally, decentralization can provide senior managers with the opportunity to manage the individual units each according to its needs and circumstances, instead of applying blanket policies and administrative procedures even if they do not fit. It can accommodate the contrasts and contradictions found in most developing countries by allowing each level of the hierarchy to be organized and managed differently in accordance with its capacity and task requirements. Instead of pushing for decentralization of predetermined functions like finance or accounting as mandated by top management, as is often the case, management can concentrate on delegating different functions to different local units based on a careful analysis of their management capability, the needs of their clients, and the nature of the decentralized tasks, COTs and SMATs.

International Pressures. Governments and individual organizations in developing countries are under direct and indirect pressures to undertake decentralization. The international development and donor agencies including the World Bank and USAID are actively promoting decentralization in all regions of the developing world. For example, through various projects in Asia, USAID is promoting decentralization of finance and management functions in countries as diverse as Bangladesh, Nepal, Sri Lanka, Pakistan, Indonesia, the Philippines and Thailand, which vary widely in their social, economic, and political development and stability, physical and management infrastructure, and capacity.

The decentralist trends in Western democracies may also be exerting pressure on developing countries to follow suit. In Western Europe, for example, various efforts are being made to increase employee participation in decisions affecting their work. West Germany's industrial democracy, France's self-management, and Sweden's work redesign of new factories (Agurén and Edgren, 1980) generate ideas and provide illustrations that are intellectually appealing to policy makers in developing countries. Moreover, in the West, the public service is concentrated at the subnational, state, provincial, and municipal levels, while, for developing countries, the national government controls the majority. The Yugoslav socialist model of employee corporate ownership and participation in the selection of managers is also ideologically appealing to many developing countries and has been emulated, for example, in India, Algeria, and Tanzania. International pressures to decentralize in developing countries are expressed both at the macro national levels (Stohr and Taylor, 1981) and at the more micro enterprise level (Kanawaty et al., 1981). Western academics are legitimizing these pressures largely for ideological reasons.

5. Forces for Centralization

The forces against decentralization of organizations in developing countries are: (1) historical; (2) economic; (3) political; (4) organizational; and (5) cultural.

Historical.   For many developing countries, centralized administration is a direct legacy of colonial administration. Colonial administrations were highly centralized because of a combination of local circumstances and nineteenth century European management styles. Most of the colonial structures were retained and senior administrators of the new nations saw their challenge as sustaining and building on those structures rather than creating new ones.

Economic.   The economic arguments are essentially based on economies of scale. Centralized administration is assumed to create conditions for more effective utilization of scarce resources while decentralization would lead to fragmentation and inefficiency. It is also argued that the expertise and mandate for managing the national economy rests with the central government while the regional authorities have limited management capabilities and only parochial interests. Staff shortages in local administration in countries like Kenya, Tanzania, the Sudan, and Malaysia illustrate the problems of resource limitations. According to this argument, small may be beautiful, but it can also be vulnerable.

Political.   Strong nationalistic political arguments are often made in favor of centralization. Nation building and the enhancement of national unity, especially in young, fragile emerging nations without the traditional institutional bonds to keep the disparate parts together, require a strong central government with centralized administration. National unity is a necessary precondition for meaningful decentralization.

Underdevelopment and its derivatives—ignorance, poverty, and disease—can be regarded as the moral equivalent of war. Managing development in any of the developing countries, especially the least developed ones, is equivalent to managing a permanent crisis. It is therefore appropriate to have centralized administration with strong leadership at the top with a central command post. Decentralization is a luxury that underdeveloped countries cannot afford.

Centralization also favors the regime in power in terms of domestic politics. It provides to those in power the ability to use public funds to reward political allies and punish rivals by controlling the distribution of opportunities, privileges, and access to national development programs. In countries where resources are scarce and alternatives are limited, it can be a very powerful instrument of control by the top officials of the central government. After all, the centralization-decentralization debate is one about decision making and the exercise of power and control over organizational resources.

Organizational.   The organizational arguments for centralization are based on efficiency and effectiveness. Centralization allows ease of control, integration, and coordination within the organization and with other elements in the external environment. Because the senior officials have the experience and the strategic overall picture of the organization to make the best decisions, high-quality decisions can be made at the top. Lower level officials have neither the experience nor the information for the overall strategic position of the organization. Centralization also economizes on the scarce managerial resources typical of organizations in developing countries. In times of crisis, centralization saves time and provides a central focus. Finally, centralization provides enriched and challenging jobs and opportunities for training and experience for the few administrators and managers in senior positions.

Cultural. It has been claimed that centralization is consistent with the cultural traditions and values of most societies in developing countries. This view is supported by the prevalence of patrimonial and patriarchical systems of governance and social organization as well as the belief in the "greatman" theory of leadership whereby absolute powers are vested in the hands of a single chief, king, or president. They also reflect a tendency for personalized leadership so that the office is subservient to its incumbent. When you have a "president for life," or a charismatic leader (House and Woycke, 1987), it is hard to decentralize.

6. Decentralization and State-Owned Enterprises

State-owned enterprises (SOEs) constitute the most widely used form of public management decentralization in developing countries. They are found in all sectors including development of the physical infrastructure like dams and transport, agriculture, mining and manufacturing, marketing, banking, credit and loan, regional and rural development, and social services. The two questions of interest are: (1) to what extent do SOEs provide an effective mechanism for decentralized macro management of the economy with a minimum of government or political interference; and (2) to what extent are the individual SOEs managed as decentralized organizations? The first question attracts most of the attention in development administration, while the second receives very little attention.

Policy makers assume that decentralization can be used to separate important functions away from the slow, bureaucratic and inefficient government departments and into the more business-like public enterprises. As Rondinelli, Nellis, and Cheema observed: "It is assumed that autonomy or semi-autonomy will free the organizations to which functions are delegated from the cumbersome or patronage-ridden personnel regulations, rigid and incentiveless bureaucratic pay scales, and unproductive work habits frequently found in the regular civil service" (1984:15). International donor agencies prefer project implementation through SOEs as opposed to government departments because the former provide for more focused project visibility, evaluation, and accountability, and because they provide conditions under which projects can be treated as "sheltered experiments."

Figure 7.2   **COMMON STRUCTURAL FORMS OF STATE-OWNED ENTERPRISES**

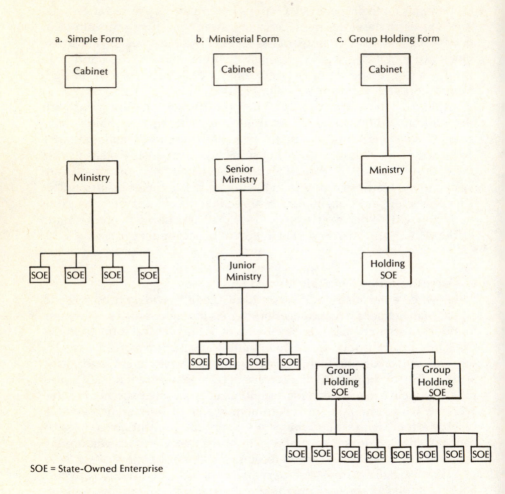

SOE = State-Owned Enterprise

Figure 7.2 shows some of the common forms of SOEs and their structural relationships with the government. The simple form (Figure 7.2a) illustrates, for example, an SOE such as a national airline that reports directly to the cabinet minister of transport. Under the ministerial form, however, the SOE reports to the cabinet through at least two ministerial hierarchies (Figure 7.2b). The group holding form is even more hierarchical in the sense that the individual SOEs report to the minister through several hierarchies of other (holding) SOEs. These different structural arrangements provide different opportunities and constraints for decentralization of the operating and strategic management tasks of the operating SOEs.

Other contingencies being equal, we would expect that control and autonomy from the parent ministry are easier to gain by means of the simple form, as it has fewer hierarchical levels to deal with. Because it has no hierarchical buffers from direct political interference, it might, however, be the easiest victim of ministerial control. We would assume that the ministerial form would lose most of its autonomy as it reports to two ministerial hierarchies, each attempting to exercise its own control and influence. If, however, the junior ministry were more sympathetic or business-like, it might protect the enterprise from undue higher ministerial, political, or cabinet interference. The group holding form is most susceptible to political and bureaucratic interference, as the individual operating SOEs have to exert their authority over layers of corporate, bureaucratic, and political power, control, and influence. With limited control and autonomy, these SOEs cannot adequately perform their operating or strategic management tasks.

Direct government involvement and control over SOEs is often deleterious to the performance of their operating and strategic management tasks. For example, Turok (1984) describes the structure and composition of the board of directors of the Zambia Industrial and Mining Company (ZIMCO), which almost guarantees maximum government and political interference in the management of ZIMCO and its subsidiaries. ZIMCO is a holding SOE with subholding groups of companies, each with its own operating subsidiaries that may be wholly or partly owned by the state. Each of these companies reports to a minister who has functional responsibilities for their operations and provides a link to the cabinet and to the overall national planning. ZIMCO's board of directors is made up of the chairman and managing directors of the subsidiary companies, who are in turn personally appointed by the President of Zambia. Although each subsidiary company has its own board, its composition is heavily weighted in favor of government and party appointments, including permanent secretaries of the relevant ministries, managing directors of holding and subholding companies, and other high-level political appointees. Moreover, interlocking directorships are common, with managing directors of holding companies, like the Industrial Development Corporation Limited (INDECO), the Permanent Secretary of Finance, the Governor of the Bank of Zambia, and the Chairman of ZIMCO, sitting on at least half a dozen boards of other companies. Excessive government control must be one of the factors for the persistent record of poor performance by ZIMCO and its subsidiaries.

Decentralization is important for the effective performance of SOEs because it helps define the optimal level of enterprise autonomy and government control. Governments tend to grant autonomy only when the enterprise has demonstrated a superior record of performance; otherwise it is subjected to close supervision and centralized control both in its COTs and SMATs (Hafsi, Kiggundu, and Jorgensen, 1987). This approach creates a "catch 22" situation. When enterprise performance is poor, it immediately shows in the performance of its critical operating tasks and clients and other stakeholders complain to government. The government responds with further tightening of controls on both the COTs and the SMATs of the enterprise. This does not guarantee that the enterprise's performance of its COTs will necessarily improve. Indeed, it is likely to make matters worse because the government is too far removed from the industry or the firm's business and task requirements (COTs and SMATs). The situation is often aggravated by frequent turnover among board members and the chief executive officer as the enterprise loses time and opportunities adjusting to new leadership.

If SOEs are expected to earn their autonomy by first demonstrating the capacity to perform their respective tasks effectively and to meet the stakeholders' expectations, they must also be given the chance to have appropriate control over the performance of their COTs and SMATs. SOEs must be accorded the tools to manage and the freedom to act if they are to improve their task performance, satisfy stakeholders' expectations, and shake off their poor image as corporate laggards.

7. Decentralized Service Delivery Systems

Decentralization can be useful for developing an effective service delivery system especially in countries where population and opportunities are not evenly distributed. A decentralized service delivery system makes it possible for the organization to reach the maximum number of potential clients without losing the advantages of scale. In developing an effective service delivery system the primary objective is to decentralize those aspects of the COTs that translate directly in services to the clients. The SMATs need not be decentralized unless they translate directly into client services.

Self-service can be used to enhance the effective performance of the COTs for a decentralized service delivery system. It requires that the client perform all or a specified set of tasks associated with the provision of the required service. In developing countries, it can and has been used by family units for services like delivery of produce to markets, collection of seeds, fertilizers, water, and spraying. At the community level, it can also be used for service delivery systems, such as road construction and maintenance, canal drainage, environmental protection, tree planting, forest fire control, and community policing and law enforcement.

III. Assessing the Results of Decentralization

The effects of decentralization in organizations in developing countries are hard to generalize, partly because of the variety of approaches used and motives for decentralization, and partly because there are no systematically controlled experimental studies separating the effects of decentralization from other policy initiatives or environmental changes. It is generally accepted, however, that the overall results of decentralization are disappointing. In Africa, Latin America, and Asia decentralization remains largely an ideal rather than a reality. In spite of the endless efforts made since the 1950s, in spite of the rhetoric and pronouncements from national politicians, and in spite of the pressures from international donor agencies, public management in these regions remains highly centralized with a few civil servants and politicians wielding most of the power and control of the policy making and implementation process.

In Africa, development administration remains highly centralized, even in countries like Tanzania, which had made repeated deliberate efforts to decentralize. As Picard (1980) and others have found, these efforts have neither facilitated popular participation nor led to the development of strong local institutions as instruments of social change and development. The local population does not identify with government organizations because these do not seem to relate to local problems or experiences. Local leadership has little or no effective control or input in the policy-making process. The real centralization-decentralization struggle seems to be between the senior managers and administrators on the one hand, and the specialists or analysts on the other.

In Asia and Africa local governments continue to be highly dependent on the central government, especially for critical resources such as finance and personnel. Even in countries like Indonesia, where decentralization enjoys wider support, grants to the provinces are dependent on central government revenue fortunes. Consequently, continued falling oil prices may affect the government's ability to fund decentralization programs. In Latin America, central government bureaucracies are quite extensive and grow at the expense of local governments. Moreover, there is no conclusive evidence that decentralization, either in public management or in the private sector, necessarily leads to more efficient and effective organizations in terms of COTs and SMATs performance.

Decentralization, however, has had some limited areas of success. It has encouraged central government bureaucrats and politicians to pay more attention to remote, previously neglected poor and weak areas. This interest is particularly important in large countries like Indonesia, Brazil, Nigeria, the Sudan, and Mexico, with many remote impoverished areas. In countries like Tanzania, decentralization may have contributed to the development of a more sensitized and vocal local leadership with increasing capacity to put pressure on the central government to pay more attention to the needs of the local areas. Evidence suggests that local government management capabilities may be improving in parts of Asia and Latin America, and in countries like Nigeria, Morocco, Egypt, and Algeria.

The creation of new organizations to manage development initiatives at the local levels is a potentially positive result. These organizations include, for example, provincial planning boards in Indonesia, development planning committees in Thailand, state planning units in Malaysia, regional development councils in the Philippines, and special purpose development organizations in Pakistan. If they can be assisted to become fully fledged organizations with the capacity to manage development, they can provide the foundation for the development of regional or local representative institutions that would be more responsive to local needs and problems and to which the local population could easily relate.

If the goals of a decentralization program are specific and narrowly defined, and if the scope of the program is limited to reallocating selected functions among units of the central government (selective decentralization), experience shows that such programs often achieve their intended goals. It is perhaps in this context that Montgomery's (1972) account of successful land reform programs must be understood. With clearly defined and properly implemented goals, the decentralized land reform programs led to a number of positive results. Officials increased their knowledge of local conditions, community leaders became more interested in the program and took a more active role, communications between the local authorities and the central government improved, and there was an increase in community solidarity and interest in land reform projects. Decentralization enhances collaborative institutional arrangements among participating organizations.

Discussing Botswana's pragmatism in public sector management, Raphaeli, Roumani, and MacKellar observed:

> The centralization of these functions permits a higher quality in estimating their cost and allows the government to take advantage of bulk purchasing and economies of standardization. Moreover, this centralization functions as a means of ensuring efficiency and control of operations while leaving line managers with adequate flexibility in carrying out their responsibilities. This efficiency is further encouraged by the Tenders' Board which operates without influence or political interference. (1984:3)

Assessing the effects of decentralization is complicated by the lack of carefully planned, controlled field experiments. Such studies are necessary in order to delineate and establish cause-effect relationships among the many forms of decentralization, and among the various organizational and extra-organizational dependent variables associated with decentralization. Naturally occurring field experiments are not easy to find. Policy makers do not look at their policies as social experiments for scientific inquiry. Yet, we know so little about the antecedents, consequences, and contingencies of decentralization, especially in development administration, that an experimental approach would provide usable knowledge. Indonesia, with its large size and a gradual introduction of decentralization to dispersed provinces, provides a natural setting for a comprehensive longitudinal quasi-experimental study of the effects of decentralization.

Such a study would, as a minimum, include both the decentralizing and implementing organizations, and would analyze current levels of performance of their respective COTs and SMATs and their level of centralization or decentralization before introduction of the decentralization program. It would assess the capacity to implement the program for both organizations, focusing on the performance of their COTs and SMATs, and the degree of support and motivation of the stakeholders. It would be longitudinal in design, presumably with control or comparison organizations.

Rogers' (1968) and Rogers and Chung's (1983) longitudinal study of decentralization of the New York City school system provides interesting methodological and substantive ideas for development administration. The study starts with a description of a highly centralized inefficient pathological bureaucracy insensitive to the needs of its client groups. In 1969, the New York City school system was decentralized and, almost 15 years later, the same bureaucracy was revisited to assess the results of decentralization over a relatively long period of time. These are the kind of studies needed for organizations in developing countries (Davis, 1968; Miller, 1975).

IV. Implementation of Decentralization

For purposes of implementation, decentralization should be conceptualized as an organization intervention designed to achieve specific objectives. Whether it is introduced as a national public policy initiative or only as a more circumscribed management technique, it should be subjected to the same rigors of project cycle stages of planning, design, implementation, monitoring, evaluation, and impact assessment. Financial and social costs and benefits must be assessed, and the necessary resources (authority, money, personnel, etc.) should be planned and made available. System readiness, including personnel training and staffing, conflict resolution, stakeholder deliberations, and institutional support, are key to successful implementation. Like other structural organization development interventions, decentralization is a slow and protracted process; its results are long term and uncertain, and it is not suited for all organizations in all countries at all times. It is not a quick fix for temporary management or political difficulties. It requires the active sustained support of major players, both inside and outside the organization.

In their discussion of decentralization in developing countries, Cheema and Rondinelli (1983) recommend that, before embarking on such ambitious programs, each country should independently: (1) determine its desired scope of decentralization; (2) assess existing national, regional, and local operational and management capacities; (3) determine the level of political support at the national and subnational levels; (4) review environmental or community support and constraints; (5) estimate the financial and technical requirements and capacities of the central agencies (e.g., treasury board, public service commission, training institutions); (6) design specific decentralization; (7) mobilize support; (8) create and sustain internal integrating and external collaborative institutional arrangements (CIAs); and (9) establish baseline monitoring and evaluation procedures. It is also advantageous to build a prototype program, especially for countries or organizations with little or no experience with decentralization. The primary objective is to assess and enhance the capacities of the participating organizations in the performance of their respective COTs and SMATs under different structural arrangements.

Centralization and decentralization are ideal-type concepts in the Weberian tradition. They cannot and should not be achieved in their absolutes. The challenge for the practicing manager or policy maker is to strike an optimal but dynamic balance between the center, where formal power, authority, and control are vested, and the periphery, where participants may be weak and underorganized. This approach is similar to Peters and Waterman's (1984) concept of loose/tight properties, whereby companies are both decentralized by pushing autonomy down to the critical operating tasks, and centralized around core values and strategic management tasks. Charles Perrow (1982) calls this the bureaucratic paradox because the efficient organization must centralize in order to decentralize. He also observes that centralization and decentralization must go hand in hand because the failure to decentralize may erode the manager's control. This may explain the often reported experiences of powerlessness by senior managers and administrators in public and private sector organizations in developing countries.

Summary

This chapter has discussed the theory, practice, and forces for and against decentralization in developing countries, and emphasizes that the purpose of decentralization is to enhance the implementing organizations' capacity to perform their respective COTs and SMATs and meet stakeholders' expectations. It differentiates between intraorganizational and interorganizational decentralizations and emphasizes the need to identify the implementing, decentralizing, and receiving organizations and assess their capacity to implement a sustained program of decentralization.

Implementing organizations are those involved in the decentralization effort. Decentralizing organizations are those giving up power, control, and organizations or parts thereof. Receiving organizations are those to whom such tasks are decentralized. If decentralization is intraorganizational, all its players come from different parts of the same organization; if it is interorganizational, it involves two or more organizations.

Decentralization is neither good nor bad. It is an organizational arrangement for performing the organizations' COTs and SMATs which, depending on the internal and external contingencies operating on the implementing organizations, may prove advantageous to the receiving organization and its stakeholders. Management's organizational choice is not whether or not to decentralize, but what (tasks) and how much to decentralize.

The chapter has also discussed public enterprises as a form of decentralization but proposes that, in cases in which performance is below expectations, public enterprises are likely to remain centralized, although this state does not necessarily solve their performance problems. The chapter has concluded with a discussion of the difficulties of decentralization and the need for systematic assessment of the results of decentralization programs and their implementation.

CHAPTER 8

Managing Structural Adjustments

Throughout this book, the emphasis has been on the importance of using the organization as the relevant unit of analysis, diagnosis, and intervention for understanding and managing the development process. Specific attention has been paid to the more significant aspects of development administration such as technology transfer and decentralization. In this chapter, the discussion continues in the same vein, focusing on the more macro aspects of managing structural adjustments and public sector reform.

In the past, interventions based on broader macroeconomic levels of analysis have been unsuccessful because adequate attention was not paid to the specific organizations through which implementation would take place. Strategies of structural adjustments and public sector reform can best be understood and implemented if the problems and suggested remedies are specified right down to the level of the participating organizations such as a state-owned enterprise (SOE), a government department, or regulatory agency. The statement that the public sector is inefficient and ineffective basically translates into specific identifiable organizations that lack the capacity or motivation to perform their respective critical operating tasks (COTs) or strategic management tasks (SMATs) with efficiency, economy, and effectiveness over a sustained period of time.

Discussing problems of public sector management in developing countries, the World Bank's 1983 World Development Report identifies the following six causes of inefficiency: (1) inappropriate macroeconomic policies such as ineffective exchange rates and excessive borrowing; (2) distorted incentives; (3) low-yielding investments; (4) investment delays and rising costs; (5) low capacity utilization; and (6) poor maintenance. Each of these problems can be traced to the responsible organizations within which reform strategies should be anchored.

It is argued here that structural adjustment is essentially a process of identifying, creating, changing, developing, nurturing, and sustaining a wide range of public and private sector organizations for the effective management of the economy and its constituent sectors. The need for improved management discussed in previous chapters is even greater here because structural adjustments create new management challenges for organizations, some of which do not exist and need to be created. An internal IMF review of the adjustment experiences of African countries for the period 1980–83 concluded that "the expected improvements did not materialize mainly because of the limited administrative capabilities of the government to effect the requisite changes" (Zulu and Nsouli, 1985:16). Similarly, a recent sessional paper on Kenya's economic management and growth concluded that the "central government has reached the limit of its ability to manage competently a growing number of parastatals and development projects" (Government of Kenya, 1986:19).

This chapter is organized in four sections. The first section discusses the meaning of structural adjustments and public sector reforms. The second describes selected organizational aspects of structural adjustments including SOEs. The third section introduces privatization as a process of developing effective indigenous private sector organizations, while the last section focuses on the need for establishing domestic and international multisector collaborative institutional arrangements (CIAs) for the effective management and coordination of structural adjustments.

I. What Is Structural Adjustment?

Structural adjustment is broadly defined as a comprehensive restructuring, management, and coordination of a county's public, parastatal, and private sector organizations so as to make them individually and collectively more productive and to contribute more effectively, on a sustainable basis, to the country's development goals. It must be comprehensive, pervasive, and sustainable in order to have long-term positive effects. It requires the active participation and support of local and international organizations and groups. It calls for a significantly different, subtle, and complex role for the government and government agencies. It necessitates a gradual but steady breakdown of monopolistic powers and an elimination of market imperfections, and allows the competitive market forces a bigger influence in the making of economic decisions and allocation of resources to organizations. It demands more effective mobilization, distribution, and use of the country's scarce productive resources such as foreign exchange, public funds, investment capital, and technical and management skills. Finally, it requires continuous systematic coordination among participating organizations.

Although strategies for structural adjustment programs differ across countries, the following elements are common: (1) redefining the role and core responsibilities of the state in the management of the economy; (2) introducing public service reforms for improving national and sectorial economic management; (3) improving management of public service organizations, programs, and projects; (4) establishing more active open participation in international trade; (5) reducing price distortions and market imperfections; (6) promoting the development of the indigenous private sector; (7) improving human resource development and utilization in both the formal and the informal sectors; and (8) assessing the role, structures, and performance of SOEs for improved management, divestiture, or privatization.

1. Ownership, Control, and Management

In theory, it is possible to create effective organization under any system of ownership because the key factor determining organizational performance is not whether it is publicly or privately owned but how it is organized and managed. In practice, most public sector organizations have performed far below expectations, in terms of both economic indicators and social goals, raising questions about their efficacy as positive instruments for economic and social progress. The search is underway for more cost-effective alternative forms of organizational ownership to achieve economic and social development. Preliminary evidence shows that these alternatives can yield better economic results. Even in small-scale agriculture for which organizations are weak and arguments for government interventions are much more compelling, agricultural policy reforms have contributed to improved productivity and rural farming incomes for countries such as China, Thailand, Indonesia, Sri Lanka, the Sudan, Brazil, and Bangladesh as documented by the World Bank's 1986 World Development Report.

Distinction must be made between organizational ownership, control, and management. Ownership is legal title to the organization's assets and earnings, but it also exposes the state to added risks, contingent and noncontingent liabilities. Control is the ability to affect the nature and performance of the organization's COTs and SMATs. Management, on the other hand, is the active and informed participation in the day-to-day running and strategic decisions of the organization. It is not always clear whether government motives for the ownership of certain organizations are justified for their own sake, or whether they are intended as an instrument of control, management, or both. In many cases, especially in international joint ventures, the government may have legal ownership of the enterprise with little or no effective control or meaningful participation in its management. If the government lacks experience in an industry and management expertise and technical know-how for the performance of the relevant COTs and SMATs, it cannot instantly achieve effective control through equity ownership. Effective control can indeed be achieved without ownership or participation in the organization's management. For example, government can have effective control over the behavior of the enterprise through policy, administrative, fiscal, and political instruments, or personal influence without necessarily exercising legal ownership. If control is the prime motive for enterprise ownership, the government should first explore alternative formal and informal instruments of control and influence that may achieve results similar to those attained by ownership, at lower costs.

If the government wishes to exercise control over domestic private sector organizations, it can choose from a wide range of internal formal political or administrative instruments including personal persuasion. Control of multinational corporations (MNCs) requires more complex government internal and international collaborative institutional arrangements. Control can be achieved without ownership, but ownership does not guarantee effective control or management of the organization.

II. Organizational Aspects of Structural Adjustments

Structural adjustment is a nationwide process involving many organizations. Table 8.1 provides a partial list of the major types of organizations involved in the process. This list includes private and public sectors as well as domestic, regional and international organizations. Each of these organizations must perform its COTs and SMATs effectively in order to contribute positively to the reform process. Their individual activities must be effectively coordinated by a central agency. A USAID discussion paper illustrates the problems of management and coordination of the participating organizations when it observed that in Zambia:

> Serious bottlenecks in the management of the co-ordination and implementation of reform are evident. Lack of co-ordination and integration across agencies and sectors, data deficiencies for the monitoring of limited managerial capabilities for the implementation of specific restructuring components, and the absence of systems for managing these processes of restructuring all have impeded the full realization of the goals of the restructuring effort. (U.S. Agency for International Development, 1986b:7)

Accordingly, in order to achieve the goals and objectives of structural adjustments, the participating organizations must be clearly delineated and the performance of their COTs and SMATs enhanced. Table 8.2 gives five of the typical reform objectives and their likely effects on the COTs and SMATs of the participating organizations. For example, redefining the role of the state in economic management affects the COTs of public and private sector organizations through decentralization, downsizing, closures, and creation of new operating units. The effects of the advancement of the indigenous private sector organizations (IPSOs) on the SMATs focus on the development of collaborative institutional arrangements with government and other organizations. Analyzing each of the participating organizations' COTs and SMATs, and improving and co-

Table 8.1

**PARTIAL LIST OF THE MAJOR ORGANIZATIONS IN THE
MANAGEMENT OF STRUCTURAL ADJUSTMENTS**

1. **Public Sector**
   - The executive branch
   - The public service: Line ministries, central agencies
   - The military
   - Local government: State, district, municipalities, villages
   - Political parties/groupings
   - Cooperatives
   - State-owned enterprises

2. **Private Sector**
   - Indigenous private sector: IPSOs, SSEs, local capital markets, village lenders, etc.
   - Foreign-owned: MNCs, others
   - Joint ventures: International, domestic
   - Financial institutions

3. **Regional Organizations**
   - Regional groupings: ASEAN, SADCC, ECOWAS, PTA, OECS, etc.
   - Regional financial institutions: Development banks, currency board, investment agencies
   - Regional management institutes: AMI, ESAMI, CARICAD, ICAP, etc.

4. **International Organizations**
   - The World Bank, IMF. and affiliates
   - International development agencies
   - International investment agencies
   - United Nations agencies: UNDP, UNIDO, ILO, etc.

5. **New Organizations**
   - Privatized SOEs, new IPSOs, joint ventures, SSEs, NGOs, etc.
   - Project development facilities: Africa (APDF), Caribbean (CPDF)
   - Privatization units (public sector)
   - Multilateral Investment Guarantee Agency (MIGA, World Bank).

Note: IPSOs = Indigenous private sector organizations; SSEs = Small-scale enterprises; MNCs = Multinational corporations; ASEAN = Association of South-East Asian nations; SADCC = Southern African Development and Coordination Conference; PTA = Preferential Trade Agreement (East Africa); OECS = Organization of Eastern Caribbean States; ECOWAS = The Economic Community of West African States; AMI = Asian Management Institute; ESAMI = Eastern and Southern Management Institute; ICAP = Central American Institute of Public Administration; CARICAD = Caribbean Center for Development Administration.

ordinating their performance, would eliminate the management problems and help realize the reform goals and objectives.

III. State-Owned Enterprises and Structural Adjustments

State-owned enterprises (SOEs) have received as much bad press in the 1980s as they received good praise in the immediate post World War II period as potential instruments of national economic and social development. The attack has been so vicious and persistent that SOEs have become the cornerstone of the public policy debate on structural adjustments and public sector reform in both the developing and the industrialized countries. Is all this attack justified, or are SOEs victims of circumstances well beyond their control? Is it realistic to expect SOEs to disappear all together from the industrial maps of these countries? What role can or

Table 8.2

SELECTED OBJECTIVES OF STRUCTURAL ADJUSTMENTS AND THEIR EFFECTS ON ORGANIZATIONAL COTs AND SMATs

EFFECTS ON ORGANIZATIONAL:

OBJECTIVES	COTs	SMATs
1. Redefinition of the Role of the State in Economic Management	• Decentralization of operations to local or private sector organizations • Closure or downsizing operations • Creation of new operating units (e.g., IBAS)	• Reformulation of public sector organization missions • Management of downsizing • Decentralization • Management of facilitating rather than regulatory functions • Conflict management
2. Public Service Improvements	• Sustaining of more efficient ITOF • Use of performance incentives • Focus on client need satisfaction • Effective resource utilization	• Improved strategic management capabilities: IOC, CIA, supervision • Development of performance-based management systems
3. Reduction of Price Distortions	• Elimination of administrative/ bureaucratic regulatory tasks • More competitive pricing of critical inputs and outputs • Streamlined operation for maximum efficiency	• More active environmental scanning, planning, and management cost controls
4. Development of Indigenous Private Sector Organizations (IPSOs)	• Development of LTC for performing public/government Tasks • Improved transactions record keeping • Streamlined operations and administration	• Creation of CIA between government and the IPSOs • Creation of new organizations • Increased need for coordination • Management of IPSOs extension services (e.g. credit, management, technology, etc.)
5. Privatization	• Decentralization of government operations to IPSOs • Formation of local and International joint ventures • Increased participation of foreign firms	• Sale of SOEs • Management of foreign capital flows • Economic management by incentives rather than regulations • Development of capital markets

Note: COTs = Critical operating tasks; SMATs = Strategic management tasks;
IBAS = Indigenous Business Services; LTC = Local Technological Capacity;
ITOF = Inputs, Transformations, Outputs, and Feedback.

should SOEs play in the management of structural adjustment and public sector reform? This section discusses some of these questions.

1. SOEs: Victim or Villain?

SOEs are criticized not only on the basis of their record of performance but also for the social and economic problems of the country as a whole (Goyal, 1984). For example, Balassa et al. (1986) blame most of the current problems in Latin America on state capitalism. They argue that the Latin American state has failed as a direct investor or owner of business enterprises. They also found that Latin American SOEs are notoriously inefficient and that they contribute substantially to many of the problems hindering the economic growth of the economy such as public sector deficits, domestic and foreign borrowing, misallocation of resources including credit allocation and commodity subsidies, and inappropriate pricing and incentives. They also believe that regulation, state capitalism, and corruption go hand in hand. Persuaded by recent experiences in Britain, Spain, and France, they call for the Latin American states to eliminate regulation, promote divestiture, and eliminate or restructure most of the SOEs as a prerequisite for renewed economic growth.

Some of this criticism is justified, because, as several studies have shown (Aharoni, 1986; Berg, 1981; Jones and Moran, 1982; Nellis, 1986; Shirley, 1983), the performance of SOEs, no matter how measured, has generally been below expectations. Nor have they been able to act as effective agents of social change especially in the areas of employment, technology transfer, mobilization and utilization of local resources, or more equitable distribution of income, wealth, or opportunities. Specific problems associated with SOEs include poor economic performance, overstaffing, overvalued assets, capital-intensive use of inappropriate import-dependent technology, high debt ratios causing constant drain on the national treasury, and nonresponsive top management unable to identify and take advantage of changing domestic and international commercial opportunities.

It is also true, however, that most SOEs are victims of circumstances beyond their own control. They operate in an economic, political, cultural, and technological context that almost guarantees failure and in which organizational survival rather than profitability or growth is always the first priority of top management. A number of reasons account for this status. First, some SOEs exist in sectors or industries with mandates or structures that make it almost impossible to operate as commercially viable organizations. One of the early justifications for SOEs was to develop business enterprises in sectors or regions of the economy in which private capital would not go, at least for a while. Second, SOEs are highly truncated and highly controlled by various government agencies, and therefore lack the autonomy and flexibility necessary to operate and compete on a commercial basis. Third, they have to respond and deal with multiple tutelages, divided and violently conflicting political groups, turning them into a political or ethnic battleground. In a study of Uganda's Coffee Marketing Board, Bates (1985) found that the SOE was being used as a battleground for the country's deeply divided political and military interest groups who could not sacrifice their own interests for the sake of the then badly needed rational international performance of the state-owned marketing board.

Government intervention in the management of the SOEs can and often is dysfunctional for several reasons. First, it is inconsistent, irregular, and designed to deal with immediate crises. Second, government officials often lack intimate inside industry knowledge and technical expertise to make informed judgments. Third, they often use extra-organizational considerations for making decisions, thus exposing the

SOE to unnecessary environmental disturbances, risks, or threats. Fourth, government intervention tends to concentrate on SOEs in financial or operational difficulties, a choice that, in most cases, simply makes matters worse.

Some SOEs are provided with inadequate human, capital, financial, and management resources; yet they need these to operate as efficient and effective commercial organizations. This may be a deliberate government strategy to control the SOEs by limiting access to needed resources. As an SOE becomes commercially viable, financially independent, and technologically competitive, its ability to fight off excessive government control significantly increases. Resource-dependent SOEs are vulnerable to excessive government control, a condition that in turn leads to poor performance and more calls for control (Hafsi, Kiggundu, and Jorgensen, 1987).

Victim or villain, the record of performance of SOEs as a group justifies raising serious questions about their efficacy as an effective organizational form for managing development. Tony Killick, Director of the Overseas Development Institute, put it bluntly when he wrote: "To an African Government contemplating the creation of a substantial public sector as a means of promoting industrialization, the advise of this writer would have to be: 'don't do it'; there are better ways of stimulating industrial growth" (1983:87). Wade (1985) shares similar views about India.

Indeed, these sentiments are held by many, including Berg (1981) and Nellis (1986). In a recent review of SOEs in Africa, Nellis found that SOEs have made the biggest contributions to their countries' public debts and have proved incapable of servicing the loans they have accumulated over time. In Zaire, for example, the state assumed responsibility for $1.3 billion of SOE debts. Excessive government control has been partly blamed for the poor performance. In Zambia, according to Turok (1984), not only did the president and the prime minister personally make senior appointments for ZIMCO (Zambia Industrial and Mining Corporation Ltd.) and its subsidiaries, they also chaired board meetings.

In spite of the problems facing SOEs and their respective governments, there is still considerable support for their continued existence, especially among nationalists and social scientists. Ghai (1985) symbolizes the counterattack on Berg and the World Bank. He argues that the World Bank's drive for divestiture and privatization is based on misleading conceptions of the performance of the public and private sectors in the economy. Simple calculations of profits and return on investment obscure the diversity of purposes underlying public enterprises and are therefore inappropriate in highly uncompetitive markets. Ghai concludes that it is unrealistic and premature for Africa seriously to consider the development of the private sector built on competitive forces when there are no competitive markets. His solution to the current performance prob-

Table 8.3

STATE-OWNED ENTERPRISES, ECONOMIC GROWTH, AND THE PUBLIC DEBT BURDEN

Country	Year	Number of SOEs	GNP per Capita U.S. Dollars 1984	Average Annual Growth Rate 1965-84	Total Long-Term Debts As a Percentage of GNP 1970	1984	Change (+ or -)
Benin	1982	60	270	1.0	16.0	59.8	+43.8
Botswana	1978	9	960	8.4	17.9	31.3	+13.4
Burundi	1984	51	220	1.9	3.1	35.8	+32.8
Cameroon	1980	50	800	2.9	13.0	31.3	+18.3
Congo	1982	75*	1140	3.7	53.9	76.2	+22.3
Côte d'Ivoire	1978	147	610	0.2	19.1	107.5	+88.4
Ethiopia	1984	180	110	0.4	9.5	29.5	+20.0
Ghana	1984	130	350	-1.9	-	-	-
Guinea	1980	181	330	1.1	47.1	59.5	+12.4
Kenya	1982	176	310	2.1	26.3	53.3	+27.0
Lesotho	1978	7	530	5.9	7.7	24.3	+16.6
Liberia	1980	22*	470	0.5	49.9	77.4	+27.5
Madagascar	1979	136	260	-1.6	10.8	73.0	+62.2
Malawi	1977	101	180	2.3	43.2	63.5	+20.3
Mali	1984	52	130	1.1	88.1	95.9	+7.8
Mauritania	1983	112	450	0.3	13.9	171.2	+157.3
Niger	1984	54	190	-1.3	-	76.7	-
Nigeria	1981	107	730	2.8	5.9	17.0	+11.1
Rwanda	1981	38	280	2.3	0.9	15.1	+14.2
Senegal	1983	188	380	-0.5	15.5	69.4	+53.9
Sierra Leone	1984	26	310	0.6	14.3	34.7	+20.4
Somalia	1979	44	260	N.S.	24.4	90.4	+66.0
Sudan	1984	138*	360	1.2	15.2	77.2	+62.0
Tanzania	1981	400	210	0.6	20.7	69.6	+48.9
Togo	1984	73	250	0.5	16.0	100.1	+84.1
Uganda	1985	130	230	2.9	7.3	20.5	+13.2
Zaire	1981	138	140	-1.6	-	-	-
Zambia	1980	114	470	-1.3	37.5	115.4	+77.9

Source: Compiled from John R. Nellis, *Public Enterprises in Sub-Saharan Africa*, Washington, D.C.: World Bank Discussion Papers, 1986, Table 1, p. 5, and the *World Development Report 1986*, Washington, D.C.: The World Bank, Tables 1 and 17, pp. 180, 212.
GNP = Gross National Product.
*Excludes financial institutions.

lems is one of restructuring and management improvements rather than divestiture and privatization. The ILO also favors internal management improvements (Powell, 1987).

Table 8.3 provides data for twenty-eight African countries in regard to the number of SOEs, economic performance over a twenty-year period, and long-term debt. The data provide some evidence relating to the question of the effects of SOEs on macroeconomic performance as measured by GNP, and the public debt burden. Although the results are mixed, the data show some interesting observations. Low-income countries tend to have more SOEs than those with slightly higher incomes. Most countries with less than $500 GNP per capita such as Ethiopia, Tanzania, Senegal, Guinea, and Kenya have more than 100 SOEs each. Countries like Botswana, Cameroon, and Congo with more than $500 GNP per capita have fewer SOEs. However, the relationship is not perfect as some very low-income countries such as Burundi and Mali also have fewer SOEs.

The data show a stronger relationship between the number of SOEs and the growth rate. All countries with negative average annual growth rates for the 1965–84 period such as Zambia, Zaire, Senegal, Niger, and Ghana also have 100 SOEs or more. Moreover, the two countries with the highest average annual growth rate for the same period—Botswana and Lesotho—have less than ten SOEs each.

The data on long-term debt are equally suggestive. Both in 1970, before the first oil shock and the world recession, and in 1984, countries with fewer SOEs such as Botswana, Liberia, and Sierra Leone also had a smaller long-term debt as a percentage of their respective GNP. Between 1970 and 1984, all the countries shown in the table increased their long-term debts as a percentage of GNP. Of the eight countries with an increase of over 50 points, all except two (Somalia, Togo) have at least 100 SOEs. Countries such as Lesotho, Botswana, Rwanda, and Sierra Leone, each with less than 50 SOEs, have among the smallest increase in their public debt burden over the same period.

These aggregate data do not provide conclusive evidence of the relationships between a country's number of SOEs, slow economic growth, and increasing public debt burden. Nor do they establish direction of causation. They are, however, suggestive of the strength of the links among a country's propensity to use SOEs as agents of economic development, slow economic growth, and rising public debt burden.

2. Why Do Some SOEs Do Well?
Not all SOEs are poor performers or need to be privatized or dissolved. Even in Africa and Latin America, where SOEs have received particularly unfavorable reviews, there are known winners such as the Kenya Tea Development Authority, the Botswana Meat Commission, the Tanzania Electricity Company (Tanesco), Ethiopian Telecommunications Authority,

Ethiopian Airlines, and the Cotton Development Authority of Madagascar (HASYMA). This section discusses some of the factors that account for the relative success of these and similar SOEs.

Again, SOEs are organizations and, as such, in order to understand how and why they do or do not work well, it is necessary for us to examine the organization and performance of their respective COTs and SMATs. SOEs that do well are those whose management capability, local technological capacity (LTC), structures, and control and incentive systems contribute to the maximum performance of their COTs and SMATs. Those that do not do well experience problems performing these tasks. The most ineffective SOEs are those that are both truncated and retarded. SOEs are truncated if they are unable to perform their SMATs effectively either because they have been usurped by the parent ministry or because management is simply incompetent. They are retarded if they have been unable to develop the necessary LTC for the performance of their COTs. Both handicaps are debilitating because they illustrate the extent to which the SOE is unable to perform its essential tasks.

Successful SOEs are characterized by: (1) simple structure and clear objectives; (2) technical competency and industry knowledge; (3) frequent business-like contacts with the parent ministry; (4) proper financial management control; (5) systemic human resource development and utilization; and (6) mutually rewarding domestic and international CIAs. Political promises must be translated into realistic business plans; the SOE must identify and take advantage of commercially beneficial niches in the industry; government stakeholders must be kept informed and continually educated to minimize SOE misuse or abuse; and costs, prices, and the budgeting process should be sound, realistic, and respected.

The SOE should avoid overstaffing, use expatriates and outside consultants selectively, and provide employee incentives that promote learning and performance. As Nellis found with HASYMA of Madagascar, ". . . the company staff are well-trained and highly motivated; the company has managed to attract and retain qualified staff by providing high salaries, substantial fringe benefits and opportunities for career development" (1986:26–27). Likewise, successful SOEs break away from some of the dysfunctional government controls and establish independent domestic and international CIAs similar to those of private business enterprises in the same industry. For example, Ethiopian Airlines would never have been able to stand up to its Marxist masters if its reputation was not a source of national pride and international respect.

In a recent study, Hafsi, Jorgensen, and I (1987) developed a life cycle evolutionary model that describes SOE-government collaborative institutional arrangements in terms of enterprise autonomy and effectiveness. The model can be extended to analyze collaborative institutional arrangements of other major participating organizations in the private sector such as IPSOs and SOEs with government, nongovernment, domestic, and international organizations. These CIAs can help explain and improve the management of the structural adjustment process.

3. Strategies for SOE Reform

The argument that SOEs should necessarily be sold off or closed is both simplistic and unrealistic. Like their counterparts in the private sector, SOEs as complex organizations are created and continue to exist for a variety of rational and nonrational reasons. The rational models are not adequate for explaining all forms of behavior in organizations and, as Brunsson (1985) clearly demonstrates, not only is irrational decision making in organizations common, it is fundamental for understanding and managing organizations in both the public and the private sectors. In the process of judging each case on its own merits, organization science can make a contribution by providing conceptual frameworks, diagnostic tools and expertise, and empirical evidence for informed operational and policy choices.

Table 8.4 provides a range of options potentially available for dealing with SOEs. The three broad strategies of internal management improvements, partial divestiture, and complete divestiture vary on a number of dimensions. While management improvements are limited to internal changes, complete divestiture is more drastic and should reflect a significant shift in the role of the state in the management of the economy. Internal management improvements should be undertaken when there is genuine belief that significant improvements are indeed possible, or when a tactical intermediate step for the more drastic strategies is advisable. The strategy should not be used as a delaying tactic as this is likely to waste valuable resources.

Partial divestiture provides the most commonly used range of reform options in developing countries. These options are attractive to the major actors for a variety of reasons. First, they are aimed at improving the management and task performance of the SOE. Second, they provide alternative arrangements for bringing in foreign capital and expertise with or without equity ownership. Third, they tend to reduce but not to eliminate the overall control of the government in the management of the SOE. Fourth, they provide a framework for various actors to work together through various forms of multilateral arrangements. For example, contract farming, whereby a multinational corporation agrees to buy, process, and market specified quantities and quality of farm produce at preset prices, is commonly used for the production of bananas, other fruits, and vegetables, especially in Central America. According to Glover (1986), these arrangements help bring MNCs together with small growers, cooperatives, peasants, host country governments, and international financing and development agencies. These arrangements enhance the perfor-

Table 8.4

STRATEGIES FOR STATE-OWNED ENTERPRISE REFORMS

1. **Internal Management Improvements:**
   - Critical Operating Tasks (COTs)
   - Strategic Management Tasks (SMATs)
   - COTs/SMATs Coordination
   - Collaborative Institutional Arrangements:
       - Domestic
       - International
       - Technology Transfer
       - Decentralization
       - Human Resource Management

2. **Partial Divestiture:**
   - Contracting
   - Leasing
   - Joint Ventures
       - Domestic
       - International
   - Franchising
   - Management Contracts

3. **Complete Divestiture:**
   - Privatization
       - Employee Stock Ownership Plans (ESOPS)
       - Venture Capital
       - Leverage Buyouts
       - Local/Foreign Purchaser
   - Liquidation
       - Assets
       - Equity
   - Closures
       - Partial
       - Complete
   - Decentralization
       - COTs and SMATs
       - Central to Local Governments
       - Government to Domestic/International Private Sector

Note: COTs = Critical Operating Tasks; SMATs = Strategic Management Tasks; ESOPs = Employee Stock Ownership Plans.

mance of the participating organizations' COTs and SMATs as well as their domestic and international collaborative institutional arrangements (CIAs).

Management contracts are also common especially in large-scale farming and other complex organizations. In Africa, they are used to expedite the process of technology transfer. Major multinational corporations like Booker McConnell, Tate & Tyle, and Lonrho have management contracts with SOEs in Africa. For example, through its affiliate Booker Agriculture International, Booker McConnell manages the Mumias outgrower sugar scheme in Western Kenya. In return, the MNC receives three types of income: (1) a fixed fee for expatriate salaries and related overhead costs; (2) commission on sales of sugar; and (3) a small share of net profits.

The MNC fees should be based not only on the performance of the SOE, but also on the extent to which it facilitates the development of private sector organizations (IPSOs, SSEs) in the economy.

Complete divestiture, which is only beginning to emerge as a policy option for many developing countries, provides a wide range of options that involve changes in the ownership of the SOE. Under privatization, several alternative sources of capital include employee stock ownership plans (Cowan, 1985), venture capital, leverage buyouts, and local (IPSO, SSE) or foreign purchases (see Table 8.4). Leverage buyouts are arrangements whereby the new buyer raises money from a third party, who also takes some equity in the new firm. In Côte d'Ivoire, the International Finance Corporation arranged a leverage buyout of an agro-business SOE. This is an area where both domestic, regional, and international financial institutions and development banks can become more actively involved in the reform process by alleviating problems of obtaining capital for privatization. Opportunities for Employee Stock Ownership Plans (ESOPs) should be more actively promoted because, in addition to providing needed capital and promoting employee participation and commitment to the reform process, they are likely to be attractive in most developing countries for ideological and cultural reasons.

All strategies of SOE reform call for different roles, abilities, skills, and knowledge, especially for government officials and SOE managers. These needs are clearly illustrated by a recent experience in Togo where the government leased a near-defunct SOE steel mill to a foreign entrepreneur on very generous terms. The terms for the foreign entrepreneur included tax-free import of raw materials, 41 percent guaranteed rate of return, lease fees of only $175,000—a sum much less than the continuing government interest payments on the original investment—and the stipulations that the finished products were to cost more than equivalent imports and the firm was not obligated to employ more than the original level of 75 people. To the government of Togo, these concessionary terms were necessary in order to demonstrate to the world that "Togo is open for business again." Moreover, the mill would have closed down and leasing, as opposed to complete divestiture, leaves the government the option to get it back should conditions change. Nevertheless, this case illustrates the need for governments to strengthen their capacity for managing the reform process (Nellis, 1986).

Each developing country should determine its own reform package that combines different strategies ranging from internal management improvements to complete divestiture. Even if the ultimate objective for reform is total divestiture, in the short run it may be prudent to rehabilitate the SOE and turn it into a productive and commercially attractive organization. The considerable amount of pressure coming from international organizations such as the World Bank and U.S. Agency for International

Development serves a useful purpose insofar as it forces governments to rethink and restructure their economies and improve the performance of their organizations.

IV. Privatization

Today, privatization as a strategy for renewed economic growth and development is as popular as nationalization and SOEs were only twenty years ago. One aspect common to both is that we know no more about the theory and practice of privatization and its long-term effects than we did then about SOEs and nationalization. Privatization seems to be driven more by the failure of competing strategies of managing development than its own internal consistency and proved record. The differing ideological assumptions implicit in these competing strategies make any attempts at integration and reconciliation almost impossible. Yet, for a variety of reasons and pressures both from within and outside the developing countries, both privatization and SOEs are likely to continue to coexist for a long time. Activities designed to support or discredit one or the other strategy will, in the long run, prove less useful than efforts directed at the development of integrated knowledge and experience applicable to both. As Bozeman (1987) has argued, what matters is not whether an organization is privately or publicly owned, as both types are subject to varying degrees of political control and authority, but rather the extent to which its behavior in the conduct of its essential tasks is determined by government conduct or market forces. Both privatization and state ownership or control should be discussed in the context of their respective effects on the performance of the participating organizations' COTs and SMATs and on overall national development.

1. What Is Privatization?
In its policy statement, the U.S. Agency for International Development defines privatization as "the transfer of a function, activity, or organization from the public to the private sector," and that ". . . it brings together policy reform, institutional development, and utilization of the private sector" (U.S. Agency for International Development, 1986: June, 2). Drawing from this definition, but broadening it beyond simple transfer transactions across sectors, we can define privatization as a comprehensive economic, social, and political strategy designed to increase competitive market forces and to reduce or eliminate market imperfections by reducing the role of the state and increasing that of the private sector in the ownership, control, and management of the economy's productive resources.

Privatization has economic, social, and political goals and objectives. Its economic goals relate to increased productivity through more effective and competitive mobilization, distribution, and utilization of resources by private rather than public sector organizations. They include liberalizing markets, transferring economic resources from a few public hands to diversified private interests, pruning and improving the public sector, and providing opportunities and incentives for the development of private sector organizations. The social goals are aimed at more equitable distribution of income, wealth, and opportunity. The political objectives are related to the need for more democratization of the political process and the enhancement of individual and collective human rights and freedoms under a free enterprise political system.

2. Why Privatization?

Governments are attracted to privatization for a wide range of reasons including: (1) receipt of immediate cash income or foreign exchange; (2) promise of future cash income and foreign exchange; (3) the need to settle foreign debt; (4) the desire to reduce the role of the state in the management of the economy and to control budget deficits and the debt burden; (5) encouragement of industrial development and foreign investment; (6) development of more active and efficient capital markets; (7) improvement of the efficient performance of economic organizations; (8) promotion of a political philosophy of liberalization, improved human rights, and free market capitalism; (9) achievement of more equitable distribution of income, wealth, and opportunity among the various sectors and groups; and (10) response to and quelling of international pressures.

The objectives and possible outcomes of privatization are so diverse that it is important for a government to articulate its policy objectives before embarking on privatization. It is also necessary to specify the methods and criteria by which the policy is to be implemented and evaluated. This step is particularly important because privatization is a new social experiment for most developing countries and there are very few research data or systematic experiences regarding the entire process and all its possible outcomes and social costs.

3. Preconditions and Methods of Privatization

For privatization to proceed, a number of conditions are necessary. These include: (1) the existence of willing buyers and sellers brought together by a system of near perfect information; (2) an adequate and well-maintained physical, social, and institutional infrastructure, an attractive business climate, and political stability; (3) low common tariffs; (4) prompt and fair enforcement of contracts; (5) elimination or equal application of controls; (6) equal access to credit and foreign exchange on equal terms; (7) elimination of protectionism or market imperfections; (8) establishment of market-based interest rates; (9) reform of employment, investment, tax, and licensing laws to allow more competitive market forces to operate; and (10) political preparedness in order to ensure that potential losers and beneficiaries have been identified and mobilized and that their legitimate concerns and opposition have been dealt with in a manner consistent with the overall policy objectives of privatization.

Whether the transfer involves change in legal status or only decision-making authority, however, it is important that the buyer is free to: (1) restructure the firm; (2) change the firm's products or product mix; (3) change the firm's business or line of activities; (4) use subcontractors and leases; (5) expand, contract, or close down some of the firm's activities; (6) alter terms and conditions of employment and compensation; and (7) make management and operational decisions relating to areas such as financing, cost reduction, production engineering, innovation, staffing, and marketing. In essence, the new owners should have a free hand in the structuring and performance of the organization's emerging or recreated COTs and SMATs.

Four of the most common methods by which privatization can be achieved are: (1) complete divestiture; (2) partial divestiture; (3) contracting out; and (4) partial privatization. With complete divestiture, either the SOE is sold operationally intact to private interests, or it is terminated and its assets are liquidated. Complete divestiture of SOEs is the preferred approach to privatization by the U.S. Agency for International Development because it: (1) relieves the host government treasury of the recurrent cost burden of unproductive assets; (2) ends the need for special subsidies or incentives for unproductive SOEs; and (3) reduces the role of the state in the economy and contributes to greater market allocation of resources.

Partial divestiture can take one of two forms. The host government can enter into a joint venture with private investors with the government retaining only a minority equity position and allowing control to pass on to private hands, and the enterprise to operate as a private entity. Alternatively, the functions of the SOE can be divided into purely public functions that are retained by the government and private functions that are sold off or contracted to private interests. For example, an export crop marketing board may lose the monopoly of buying, collecting, storage, and processing of the crop to private sector interests, but retain export and international marketing functions.

Contracting out of services is increasingly becoming a popular method of privatization in both industrialized and developing countries. In this method, the government specifies the work that needs to be done and sends out requests for proposals (RFPs) to prospective private sector bidders. Each bidder responding to the RFP provides a statement of its understanding of the work that needs to be done, its technical and managerial competency to perform the required work, its financial integrity, and the price it will charge the government for the work. The government can specify additional requirements such as maximum use of local resources, employment of or discrimination against certain regions or groups of citizens, and technical specifications of the work. Examples of service contracts include road and vehicle maintenance, medical laboratory work, fertilizer distribution, and general government services such as printing, production and distribution of utilities, social services, and transport and telecommunications.

Bidding on government contracts and responding to RFPs requires time, money, and expertise, which local IPSOs and SSE organizations may not have as part of their COTs or SMATs. Foreign organizations, especially MNCs, often have an unfair advantage over local competition. It may therefore be necessary to provide special incentives or programs to help indigenous private sector organizations to develop the necessary expertise for the required (RFP) COTs and SMATs for effective participation in privatization. International development and financial institutions, commercial and development banks, United Nations agencies such as UNIDO and UNDP, and national and regional management institutes can play a crucial role in facilitating active participation of the local indigenous organizations.

There has been very little research done on the effects of contracting out on structural adjustments. A recent NASPAA/USAID (Moore et al., 1987) study of the Honduran experience of construction activities in housing, rural primary schools, and rural roads found, however, that contracting out did not yield better results in terms of quality, timeliness, or costs. The indigenous private sector enterprises were not able to perform their COTs more efficiently than the government partly because of their own internal operational and strategic management limitations and partly because the government was unable or unwilling to remove the various bureaucratic obstacles that were causing market imperfections.

Partial privatization also takes at least two forms. It can be achieved when the government retains ownership of the SOE but contracts certain functions such as management, production, marketing, or finance to the private sector on a long-term basis. Management contracting, widely used in large-scale agro-businesses, mining, manufacturing, airport management and maintenance, and hospital administration, is one of the most popular forms of partial privatization. Privatization in the financial area can be accomplished by turning over revenue collection to a private sector agency, or by requiring users to pay full, unsubsidized costs. Kenya's Kenyatta National Hospital is undergoing partial privatization; it is to be managed by a semi-autonomous board responsible for its costs and revenues and free to organize and perform its COTs and SMATs independent of the Ministry of Health. Partial privatization can also be achieved by selling off subsidiaries of a vertically integrated SOE. For example, an airline SOE that also owns hotels, tour operations, and travel agencies, can be partially privatized by selling off or liquidating unprofitable lines of business. Partial privatization can be a short-term interim measure, or part of a country's comprehensive policy of public sector reform. It is not unreasonable to expect that a country's comprehensive program of public policy reform will include use of different methods of privatization with complete divestiture in some sectors or industries and only partial privatization in others.

4. Potential Areas for and Recent Examples of Privatization

Opponents of privatization argue that it is unsuitable for a developing country because of its: (1) lack of a viable and respectable indigenous private sector separate from the government; (2) weak competitive or efficient markets; (3) shortage of capital; (4) unattractive business and investment climate; (5) inability of the small countries to negotiate fair deals with international organizations or MNCs; (6) weak and inadequate infrastructure; and (7) political instability. They further argue that there is no conclusive evidence that, outside the small-scale operations found in the SSE sector, the private sector is necessarily more effective than the public enterprises. Moreover, there is no guarantee that privatization will stop government control or intervention either in the management of the economy or in the individual private sector enterprises. Self-restraint is not a question of policy; instead, it is a matter of discipline and institutional tradition based on belief in the separation and differentiation of power across sectors, respect for private rather than communal property rights, confidence in individuals and organizations outside the government to be economically and socially responsible, and the political and professional maturity of the major actors. Most of these traditions do not exist in developing countries.

Privatization will not be accomplished through a massive inflow of private capital because of unattractive investment climates. The public/private mix is not likely to be much changed by current divestiture because actual cases have been few and their success has been marginal. A number of potential areas where further privatization should take place include: (1) agricultural marketing of inputs (e.g., seeds) and outputs; (2) state trading corporations; (3) agricultural services such as fertilizer distribution in Bangladesh, extension services in Chile and other Latin American states, and sanitary services; (4) supply of water under management contract as in Côte d'Ivoire; (5) construction; and (6) small holder agriculture and social forestry and transportation.

On the privatization of transport services, Berg observed, "there can be little question that in urban transport—and, almost as surely in other transport—small-scale private operators have decisive advantages over public sector producers and over large-scale operators generally" (1985:79). Indeed, studies have shown that private urban transport operators in Buenos Aires, Calcutta, Istanbul, Bangkok, Hong Kong, Nairobi, and Chiegmai, Thailand, make more profits, run more frequently, serve more remote areas, and utilize labor and capital more effectively without subsidies. On the other hand, the large public corporations operate at a loss, depend on continued subsidies, are overstaffed, and provide only limited services.

In spite of earlier skepticism, it is estimated that privatization has been tried in one form or another by at least 50 developing countries and another 50 are seriously considering its applicability to their own situations. Application has not been limited to one continent or region but cuts across all regions of the developing world. A few examples will help to illustrate the point. Between 1974–80, Chile sold about 130 SOEs and received over $500 million. In 1981, Brazil created a commission for divestiture; within its first five years of operation, it sold over 50 SOEs. Jamaica has also established a similar committee through which it has sold public enterprises and leased out hotels. Pakistan denationalized over 2,000 rice, flour, and cotton mills while Bangladesh returned 35 jute and 23 textile mills to the private sector. These cases show that a trend for privatization is being established, although in some instances governments had to sell on attractive terms to interest investors who could as easily have started their own enterprises. Roth (1987) refutes the conventional wisdom that only the public sector can supply certain services in developing countries by describing dozens of examples of traditional public services in education, health, electricity, telecommunications, urban transport, and water supply which are being privately provided in more than 50 developing countries.

The nature and the scope of divestiture and privatization vary by region and country. In general, however, complete divestiture is moving at a slower rate than partial divestiture. In Africa, liquidations and closures have been more frequent. Nellis (1986) reports a 1985 sample study of 15 sub-Saharan African countries which found that 88 closures and liquidations of SOEs took place in the period 1979–84, for example, in Mali, Liberia, Guinea, Madagascar, and Cameroon. In the same period, there were also 23 sales of assets or equity, 20 management contracts, 13 leasing arrangements, and 7 joint ventures in Mali, Senegal, Zaire, and Kenya.

Preliminary evidence points to the fact that most of the activity in divestiture and privatization has been concentrated in marginal areas. Specifically, sales and liquidations have been largely for those SOEs with little or no chance for rehabilitation. As well, governments have been quick to push for divestiture in marginal areas with little consequences for the overall size of the public or parastatal sectors.

All this may change because the U.S. government, through the U.S. Agency for International Development, has made privatization the cornerstone of its international development assistance to the developing countries. It has established a goal of "at least two privatization activities in each mission by the end of the fiscal year 1987, and two new privatization activities every year thereafter" (U.S. Agency for International Development, 1985:3). It has targeted 43 countries: 18 in Africa, 13 in Asia, and 12 in Latin America. It will provide technical and financial assistance to participating countries and has made its economic development assistance contingent on a country's willingness to undertake public sector reform that almost invariably means divestiture and privatization. It has created the Center for Privatization as a conduit organization to help sell and implement privatization in all developing countries. By 1990, the U.S. Agency for International Development alone is expected to generate over 250 privatization activities in different parts of the developing World.

With the U.S. government as the prime mover, and the active support and involvement of the World Bank and other international development and financing organizations, privatization is likely to become the darling of the 1990s in international aid and development.

5. Risks and Limits to Privatization

As privatization is a relatively new approach, there is very little accumulated field experience from which to learn. It is generally accepted, however, that it is associated with certain risks and limitations that developing countries' policy makers should be aware of. These risks are accentuated by formidable obstacles peculiar to developing countries which threaten to prevent widespread application of privatization. Current experiences in the United States, Britain, and France, and the limited success stories, especially in the SSE sectors, may not be generalizable. To avoid unpleasant surprises, countries must proceed with prudence and should be prepared to make policy shifts or change implementation strategies and tactics as they gain more experience. Drawing from Latin American experiences, Morrison observed that: "Orthodox economic liberalization programs undertaken in Chile, Argentina, and Uruguay . . . encountered serious, unforeseen difficulties which undercut the drive to expand exports and made serious mid-course revisions necessary" (1986:9). More recent examples of street riots and political unrest have come from Zambia, Egypt, the Sudan, Ghana, and Pakistan.

One of the risks associated with privatization is that it may be a passing fad. Although international organizations are now actively promoting it as a policy of reform, five years down the road, faced with mixed or discouraging results, they may abandon the policy and leave the participating countries out on a limb. There is also the fear of failure. Public policy makers are concerned that if the private sector were to prove incapable of managing the organizations and providing the goods and services formerly in the public sector domain, the consequences would be disastrous.

Yet, the quality and management capability of the private sector organizations for many of the developing countries remain largely unknown.

There is also concern about a wide range of social and political risks associated with privatization. It has been suggested that privatization benefits the weak but inflicts losses on powerful stakeholders. This situation can be a source of political instability, especially in those countries where the bureaucracy and the military form a joint coalition against the peasantry. In the past, the private sector, especially the MNCs, have been associated with activities dangerous to the political or military security of the country. For example, some of the earlier nationalizations in Zambia occurred in response to perceived security problems associated with South Africa and Rhodesia. In some countries, the private sector is not trusted because it is dominated by a different ethnic, racial, or religious group. Examples include the Chinese in South-East Asia, the Asians in East Africa, the Lebanese in Côte d'Ivoire, and the Jewish people.

The social and economic risks associated with privatization include rising prices of basic needs such as food, energy, water, and transport, and higher levels of unemployment especially among the uneducated youths with little or no industrial experience or portable marketable skills. These problems are most likely to hit hardest in the urban areas, which are also the places in which most political riots and other acts of violence originate. Hofstede (1983) has argued that most people in developing countries support a large public sector for cultural rather than economic or political reasons. He suggests that the individualism embodied in privatization is inconsistent with the collective national culture that characterizes most of the developing countries. If this concept is true, then the whole policy of divestiture and privatization may be perceived by these people as an attack on their fundamental cultural values and beliefs. This is one of the areas sorely in need of further investigation.

Finally, there is the risk of resistance from within. In many developing countries, the public sector bureaucracy (government and SOEs), which would be expected to play a leading role in the conceptualization and implementation of privatization, may be opposed to the policy perhaps out of self-preservation. Over time, these people have institutionalized resistance to change, as can be evidenced by previous policy reform efforts such as decentralization and bureaucratic reorientation. Even those countries with the economic wisdom to accept privatization as a reform strategy, and the political determination to implement it, may fail because of subtle opposition from public sector institutions. This is likely to be the case in countries like Kenya where the same bureaucrats are deeply involved in the ownership and management of the emerging private sector organizations. In Latin America, business executives and politicians draw from different intellectual and cultural external influences with significant ideological differences. The social costs for the weak, the poor, the landless, and the unemployed deserve more serious thought and action.

V. Structural Adjustment as a Form of Collaborative Institutional Arrangements

From an organizational perspective, structural adjustment can be seen as a process of developing and sustaining collaborative institutional arrangements (CIAs) for the effective performance of the participating organizations' COTs and SMATs. These CIAs are advantageous because they involve a large number of organizations, spread the management burden, create an organizational infrastructure where none existed before, generate organizational synergy by enabling local organizations to link up with national and international organizations, and provide a mechanism for the development of a dynamic local technological capacity and shared utilization of scarce resources.

In analyzing structural adjustment and its effects, we must pay attention to the participating organizations and their individual and collective efforts in facilitating or inhibiting sustainable reform for the country. Participating organizations can be classified as: (1) domestic; (2) international; (3) public; and (4) private. Figure 8.1 gives examples of typical organizations in each of the four categories in which the CIAs can be established.

1. Domestic Organizations

These can be public or private, profit or nonprofit organizations. In a discussion of structural adjustments, emphasis is often given to the public sector with little or no attention paid to the private sector and nongovernmental organizations. Indeed, structural adjustment has been presented as a government policy initiative instead of as a comprehensive domestic and international effort aimed at the restructure of internal political economies and international global markets.

Figure 8.1 gives examples of private and public domestic organizations. Private organizations such as the IPSOs/SSEs, local NGOs, cooperatives, farmers, credit institutions, political organizations, and social service agencies play an important role and should be given as much attention as is often given to public sector organizations. Here the discussion is focused on the domestic private sector because of its importance in the management and institutionalization of the reform process.

The Domestic Private Sector.   The domestic private sector is made up of the IPSOs and SSEs. Although a lot of work has been done on the public sector, very little is known about the structure, composition, ownership, organization, dynamism, and constraints facing organizations in

Figure 8.1

COLLABORATIVE INSTITUTIONAL ARRANGEMENTS (CIAs) AMONG
STRUCTURAL ADJUSTMENT PARTICIPATING ORGANIZATIONS

O W N E R S H I P

	Private	Public
Domestic	1 - IPSOs/SSEs - Peasants/Farmers - Cooperatives - Banks and Credit Institutions - Local NGOs - Social Service Agencies - Political Organizations - Church and Citizen Groups	2 - Government Line Departments - Government Central Agencies - Local Governments - Municipalities - Security and Military Organizations
International	3 - MNCs/PSEs - Banks and Financial Institutions - International NGOs/PVOs - Consulting Firms - The Press and Academics	4 - IMF/World Bank and Affiliates - Development Facilities - Development Agencies - Regional Banks - UN Agencies - Regional and International Organizations

L O C A T I O N

Note: IPSOs/SSEs = Indigenous private sector organizations/small-scale enterprises;
MNCs/PSEs = Multinational corporations/private sector enterprises;
NGOs = Nongovernment organizations; PVOs = Private voluntary organizations;
IMF = International Monetary Fund; UN = United Nations.

the private sector. Governments, however, are increasingly beginning to articulate their policies toward the private sector. For example, in a recent sessional paper the Government of Kenya declared that "the underlying aim is to establish an incentive environment under which private participants of all sizes in all sectors can make profits while simultaneously contributing to widely shared development in Kenya" (Government of Kenya, 1986:25).

A sizable IPSO/SSE sector is necessary for privatization because: (1) it provides a proven record of private sector success; (2) it would have the organizational and management capacity and resources to acquire parts of the public sector and to compete with foreign private sector participants; (3) organizations in this sector are inclined to get into export-based industries as a way of protecting themselves against undue government interference; (4) it provides a realistic option for joint ventures and other forms of divestiture with the government (SOEs), or the MNCs; and (5) finally, the big, well-established international IPSO sector organizations could be used to facilitate privatization in other developing countries. For example, foreign capital in Bangladesh might be more acceptable if it came from Indian rather than Japanese or American multinationals. An International Labour Organization (1984) study suggests that subsidiaries of multinationals from developing countries are more responsive to the economic and social needs of developing countries than those from the West.

The role of the SSE sector in promoting structural adjustments has not been given as much attention as it deserves. These small-scale enterprises are particularly attractive because they: (1) conserve scarce resources such as foreign exchange; (2) employ most of the people with minimal capital; (3) depend on personal, family, or clan savings; (4) provide their own skills training at little or no cost to the public; (5) use local resources or byproducts of the formal sector which would otherwise be left unused; (6) derive their strength and vitality from traditional social organizations such as the extended family and tribal kinships; (7) offer unmatched potential for job creation and economic development in remote rural areas as well as those areas of the urban sectors least suited for the medium or large IPSOs or SOEs; and (8) almost replicate perfect market conditions with ease of entry and exit.

SSEs, however, have some limitations as instruments of reform. First, they suffer from small size and underorganization. Second, they lack the technological capacity and management depth to run multipurpose, multiproduct businesses. Third, many of them are so interlocked with family and kinship networks and practices that they may not be able to function as modern commercial enterprises. Finally, they lack the capital, the human resources, or even the desire to expand. Expansion of family businesses in patrimonial societies depends entirely on the family's ability (luck) to raise suitable sons to take over from their father when he retires or dies. Although there is some evidence from countries such as India, Sri Lanka, and Kenya that some family businesses grow up and become modern commercially viable organizations, for the majority of SSEs a small size may be their strength, and growth their undoing. Special nongrowth CIAs may have to be developed specifically for these types of organizations.

In a recent study of entrepreneurial family-owned firms in developing countries, Jorgensen, Hafsi, and I (1986) found that these firms suffer from several market imperfections such as succession problems, extended family demands on the firm's working capital, shortage of managerial talents, and the entrepreneur's extensive participation in civic and community activities. We also found that these firms are structured like an "octopus," with the tentacles of many unrelated businesses. This diversity is necessary in order for the entrepreneur to hedge against business risks and to keep the more educated offspring interested in the firm. Different value orientations between the older and younger family members can hurt the business. The entrepreneur, in addition to running the octo-pus businesses, takes on leadership positions in tribal, community, or na-tional organizations in order to gain a voice in the administrative alloca-tion of societal resources. The son is often busy looking for ways to spend the money.

The October 1986 Nairobi Enabling Environment Conference organ-ized by the Aga Khan Foundation confirmed the efficacy of the private sec-tor's contribution to development, and the need for the development of stronger domestic and international collaborative institutional arrange-ments with the IPSOs and SSEs. More recently, strong arguments have been presented in favor of private provision of public services such as edu-cation, health, electricity, telecommunications, urban transport, water, and sewage (Roth, 1987). This can be brought about only if a country has strong private sector (IPSO/SSE) organizations with strong domestic and international collaborative institutional arrangements.

2. International Organizations

Figure 8.1 shows some of the international organizations that exert pres-sure and facilitate structural adjustments. These include the MNCs, the UN agencies, the World Bank and its affiliates, regional development banks, and the international development agencies.

Multinational Corporations (MNCs).   These organizations can play a leading role in facilitating privatization through equity and nonequity forms of operations. Nonequity forms include subcontracting, contract farming, and leasing and management contracts. The choice between equity and nonequity forms of participation should be made on a case-by-case basis after serious study because quite often MNCs use nonequity participation to reduce their commitment to the enterprise and transfer risks to the local participants. Moreover, local ownership does not neces-sarily mean local control, especially in vertically integrated industries where poor countries without international IPSOs or SOEs cannot pene-trate external markets on their own. Unfortunately, the flow of direct foreign investment is unevenly distributed. For the 1973–83 period, five countries—Brazil, Indonesia, Malaysia, Mexico, and Singapore—re-ceived 50 percent of all foreign direct investments. During the same period 41 low-income countries excluding India and China received only 2 percent.

International subcontracting is another nonequity arrangement by which MNCs can facilitate privatization. This is a contractual arrangement whereby the MNC subcontracts one or several local firms to undertake cer-tain aspects of the production of its finished or semi-finished products. Countries such as Tunisia, Sri Lanka, and Haiti openly promote international subcontracting as the official industrial development strategy, while others such as Morocco and the Philippines accept it more implicitly. International subcontracting was expected to promote industrialization of developing countries through their private sectors by contributing to the local firm's technological development, management capabilities, and access to international markets. According to a recent OECD comprehensive review, however, ". . . the ripple effects of international subcontracting on other sectors of the economy are small and agreements are by and large not very diversified, either from the point of view of "subcontracted" activities or from that of the principals, while their duration is short and often even very short indeed" (Germidis, 1980:21).

International private sector organizations (MNCs/PSEs) have the technology and management expertise that the IPSOs and SSEs need. Therefore, alternative forms of international collaborative institutional arrangements must be found to increase their participation in development through these domestic private sector organizations.

The International Monetary Fund and the World Bank. The activities of these two sister institutions in promoting structural adjustments and privatization are well known. Thus, here I shall only emphasize the point that success of these efforts depends on the quality of organizations both domestic and international available to a particular country. Two recent organizational arrangements specifically created to promote privatization in developing countries, the Emerging Markets Growth Fund and the Multilateral Investment Guarantee Agency (MIGA), are briefly discussed because of their potential implications for managing the structural adjustment processes.

The Emerging Markets Growth Fund was created in the spring of 1985 by the International Finance Corporation (IFC), an affiliate of the World Bank that spends over 90 percent of its investments in the developing countries in the form of loans rather than equity. The purpose of the Fund is to accelerate the growth of capital markets in selected developing countries by investing in their stock markets. With an initial investment of $50 million, the Fund seeks investments in relatively open and developed securities markets in countries such as Malaysia, Thailand, Indonesia, Mexico, Brazil, and India.

If the Fund were indeed to facilitate the development of efficient capital markets in developing countries, its success would have significant effect on the organization, relationships, and management of the IPSOs/SSEs in the private sector including financial institutions. For example, an efficient capital market creates collaborative institutional arrangements in the private sector which link investors with entrepreneurs, reduce the role of the state in mobilizing and distributing investment resources, and allow market forces to determine investment decisions and utilization.

The Multilateral Investment Guarantee Agency (MIGA) was established during the 1985 World Bank-IMF meeting in Seoul. Its purpose is to stimulate the flow of direct foreign investment into the developing countries by issuing long-term guarantees protecting investors against noncommercial risks. The Agency, when fully established, will provide insurance against risks such as currency transfer and inconvertibility, expropriation, nationalization, denial of justice, breach of government contracts, civil unrest, and war. It will also provide technical assistance to developing countries wishing to attract direct foreign investment.

It is expected that MIGA will be able to support US\$5 billion in insurance guarantees by the end of its four-year trial period and that it will generate a net capital inflow of about US\$200 million. These are rather small amounts, but the existence of the Agency within the World Bank-IFC system is likely to have significant effects on the behavior of domestic and international organizations operating in developing countries. For example, governments will have to learn to treat private investment with respect, while private sector investors will have to develop the expertise to manage the rather complex international collaborative institutional arrangements (CIAs) arising from their dealings with the Agency or the Fund. These two organizational arrangements are expected to improve the Bank's current spending of less than four percent on SSEs.

Project Development Facilities.   Various UN agencies such as the United Nations Industrial Development Organization (UNIDO), the United Nations Conference on Trade and Development (UNCTAD), and the United Nations Development Programme (UNDP) participate in the facilitation of privatization using various CIA programs. In this section, two particularly recent programs, the African Project Development Facility and the Caribbean Project Development Facility, created by the UNDP with the participation of other international organizations, are briefly discussed.

In 1986, the African Development Bank, the International Finance Corporation, and the United Nations Development Programme joined in an effort to assist African entrepreneurs in promoting viable medium-sized businesses by establishing the African Project Development Facility. This joint venture followed extensive study that showed that there was great untapped potential in the African private sector and that assistance in project preparation would serve a useful function in bringing together entrepreneurs and lenders or investors. The objective of the Facility is:

> . . . to accelerate private sector growth in Sub-Saharan Africa, to allow the private sector to play an increasing role in the economic development of Africa thereby generating productive employment, improving participating states' balance of pay-

ments through expanded export and bringing about self-sustained growth and development through the creation of medium-sized and smaller enterprises. (UNDP, 1986:4)

The Facility is expected to assist with 90 to 120 projects and contribute up to US$180 million over its four-year trial period and it is expected that most of these projects will come from the agro-industry.

The Caribbean Project Development Facility (CPDF) was jointly created in October 1981 by the IFC, the UNDP, and the Caribbean Development Bank. The objective was to assist small- and medium-sized businesses that are substantially owned by Caribbean citizens to raise funds, both loans and equity, for new productive investment projects. Contributions to its US$14 million budget came from USAID, CIDA, the European Community countries, Sweden, and Switzerland. As of April 1985, the CPDF had completed the preparation of over thirty project proposals having an aggregate investment cost of about US$54 million and had successfully raised approximately US$24 million for these projects. The financial contributions of these international initiatives are quite small but they are significant because of their expected "snowball" effects in attracting direct private foreign investment and because of the impact they are likely to have on the management of small- and medium-sized private sector organizations in these countries. They also provide a timely opportunity to study and to further our understanding of these rather elusive but increasingly important organizations.

Both facilities are examples of international collaborative institutional arrangements designed to promote structural adjustments through the development of the private sector (IPSO/SSE) organizations, and to eliminate some of the structural, institutional, and administrative constraints of industrial cooperation between European firms and African, Caribbean, and Pacific countries (Queyrane, 1985).

Regional Development Banks.   Six of the best known regional development banks are the Asian Development Bank, the African Development Bank, the Caribbean Development Bank, the Arab Development Bank, the Central American Bank for Economic Integration, and the Inter-American Bank. Each of these banks can play a more active role in facilitating the financing and management of structural adjustments and privatization by: (1) directing their funding activities away from general administration to more productive projects in the private sector; (2) working more collaboratively with national and subregional development banks and other financial national and international institutions; (3) establishing rapport with foreign investors and promoting foreign investment in their regions; (4) mobilizing domestic savings and channeling them into local investments; and (5) reorganizing themselves more responsively in accordance with the changing needs of their members' economies, the international economic situation, and the interdependence between the two.

Recent changes in the African Development Bank illustrate the positive role development banks can play in the advancement of the private (IPSOs/SSEs) sector through sustainable CIAs among the participating organizations. During the 1967–82 period, the Bank's lending to the industrial sector was less than 30 percent of its total loans. Moreover, most of the industrial sector lending went to SOEs rather than to the private sector. Following the admission of nonregional members in 1982 and the subsequent expansion of its capital, the Bank made a review of its lending policies and operations aimed at increasing its participation in the region's private sector. Specifically, the Bank's current strategic plan calls for: (1) doubling its lending to industry over the previous thirteen years, giving special attention to agricultural businesses; (2) financing rehabilitation of existing industries; (3) giving high priorities to industries that maximize utilization of local resources and minimize continued dependence on imported inputs; (4) relying more heavily on and collaborating with national development banks and other financial institutions; and (5) giving loans for scholarships for study in engineering, business management, accounting, finance, and law in order to deal with Africa's skills shortages. The Bank is also to investigate the feasibility of establishing a facility for direct financing of private sector enterprises, and the practicality of using barter as a trading mechanism among its member states.

These initiatives seem to have resulted in some positive changes because "50 percent of all loans approved today are now going into productive sectors" (African Development Bank Group, 1984:36). Unfortunately, the Bank's ability to finance privatization is rather limited because it is not organized for small- and medium-sized loans suited for smaller enterprises, and partly because most of the national development banks lack the necessary financial and management capabilities to serve as effective financial intermediaries to the African IPSO and SSE sector. For example, the Bank has operational problems with loan guarantees with the East African Development Bank, and the Banque de Développement des Etats de l'Afrique Centrale (BDEAC). Moreover, the financial and management situations of the National Development Bank of Sierra Leone, BCI in Central Africa, and the BDGEL are so bad that their "capacity to play the role of an effective financial intermediary in the development of their respective states has been seriously impaired" (African Development Bank Group, 1984:59).

The International Development Agencies.   Various international development agencies provide financial and technical assistance that directly or indirectly supports efforts toward structural adjustments and privatization. Several European countries and American and Japanese private sector organizations have individually or jointly created agencies specifically for promoting investments and privatization through IPSOs and SOEs. Examples include the German Finance Company for Investments in Developing Countries (DEG), the Netherlands Finance Company for Developing Countries (FMO), the Industrialized Fund for Developing Countries (IFU) of Denmark, and SIFIDA (Société Internationale Financière pour les Investissements et le Développement en Afrique).

Established in 1970, and owned by Arab, Australian, European, British, Japanese, and North American public and private sector corporations, banks, and international organizations, SIFIDA's primary objective is to foster economic growth and development of independent African countries by investing in productive industries and private sector organizations. As of 1985, it had 114 projects, mostly in the private sector, totaling US$2 billion and over 30,000 jobs in 31 countries. In addition to direct investment and loans, SIFIDA provides advisory services in areas such as project development, economic intelligence, and management assistance, and assists African organizations to gain access to international financial markets. Through its Advisory Unit, SIFIDA is actively promoting privatization in areas such as Benin's agro-industrial sector, Mali's jute bags, Niger's animal feed, and Tanzania's cashew nuts. In partnership with African entrepreneurs, it makes a decent return on investment and pays regular dividends to its shareholders. Collaborative institutional arrangements can be profitable. In the future these are likely to become multicountry and multiorganizational.

Within the United States, there are various organizations capable of providing technical assistance in this area. These include the National Association for Schools of Public Affairs and Administration (NASPAA), the Center for Privatization, and universities such as Harvard. Each of these organizations has different mandates, philosophies, approaches, and capabilities, and it is important for prospective clients to do a complete investigation before choosing where to obtain technical assistance. For example, NASPAA takes a gradual, research-based, long-term approach focusing on the development of the necessary institutional capacity for the client organization to initiate, implement, and sustain reform programs. The Center for Privatization, on the other hand, is more oriented to clients who are virtually ready to embark on privatization. The AID missions have a privatization quota to meet.

Table 8.5 illustrates how an IPSO can improve the performance of its COTs and SMATs through CIAs with domestic and international organizations from both the private and public sectors. For example, in improving its quality control, a persistent problem among IPSOs, it can draw on a government advisory service unit (IBAS), use a local consulting firm or an international private sector firm, or get consulting and technical assistance through an NGO or PVO. For new business development, it can draw on the expertise and resources provided by SIFIDA, MNCs, or the Project Development Facilities. Each of these organizations would in turn

Table 8.5

COLLABORATIVE INSTITUTIONAL ARRANGEMENTS FOR AN EMERGING INDIGENOUS PRIVATE SECTOR ORGANIZATION: AN ILLUSTRATION

Collaborating Institutions

IPSO TASKS:	Domestic				International			
	Public		Private		Public		Private	
	IBAS	SOEs	SSEs	Local Consulting Firm	IMF/World Bank/RDBs	UNDP/PDF	MNCs/PSEs	NGOs/PVOs
I. COTs:								
1. Purchasing		*	*				*	
2. Production	*						*	
3. Quality Control	*			*			*	*
4. Finance					*	*		
5. Marketing	*		*					
6. Export Promotion						*	*	*
7. Training		*		*			*	
II. SMATs								
1. Strategy Formulation				*				*
2. Corporate Planning	*			*				
3. Environmental Scanning	*							
4. Management Development	*			*			*	*
5. New Business Development	*			*		*	*	*
6. Developing LTC	*			*		*	*	*
7. Managing Business Government Relations	*			*		*	*	*

Note: IPSO = Indigenous Provate Sector Organization; IBAS = Indigenous Business Advisory Services; SOEs = State-Owned Enterprises; RDBs = Regional Development Banks; PDFs = Project Development Facilities; PSEs = Private Sector Enterprises; NGOs = Nongovernment Organizations; PVOs = Private Voluntary Organizations.
* Indicates collaboration between the IPSO and the collaborating institution for the performance of the corresponding task.

have its enabling collaborative institutional arrangements. These creative and dynamic domestic and international collaborative institutional arrangements across both public and private sector organizations are absolutely critical for the development of effective indigenous organizations, and the long-term success of structural adjustments and the reform process.

Summary

Managing structural adjustments has been discussed from an organizational perspective and conceptualized as a process of developing domestic and international collaborative institutional arrangements specifically designed for the development and strengthening of domestic public and private sector organizations. Structural adjustment reforms are not viewed as policy initiatives limited to a few public sector organizations, but as a holistic, comprehensive, sociopolitical process requiring the active participation of different types of organizations. Emphasis is given to the need for the development and active involvement of the domestic (IPSO/SSE) and international (MNC/PSE) organizations in collaboration with one another and with public sector organizations.

The chapter has also discussed the nature and drive for privatization and the performance and changing role of state-owned enterprises in the reform process. It concludes that the existence of public enterprises and privatization are not mutually exclusive but can co-exist, depending on the country's policy objectives.

Finally, structural adjustment has been presented as an international collaborative effort whose success depends on the joint participation of a wide range of international organizations. International collaborative institutional arrangements are illustrated by the experiences of multinational corporations, the IMF and the World Bank, regional development banks, project development facilities, and international development agencies. It is concluded that the success and effective management of structural adjustments depends on the development of these domestic and international collaborative institutional arrangements, giving rise to strong and sustainable indigenous organizations in both the public and the private sectors.

CHAPTER 9

A Final Word:
Linking Organizations
to National Development

This book has discussed the management of organizations in developing countries and how they can be effectively utilized as instruments of development. Part One provided a conceptual framework that describes how the organization works by focusing on its critical operating and strategic management tasks. Part Two has used the same framework to discuss selected topical applications such as human resource management and utilization, technology transfer, decentralization, and structural adjustment. The book has shown that these and similar interventions, their prospects and limitations, can best be understood if we use the organization as the unit of analysis. Chapters throughout the book have attempted to link their discussion with more micro or individual levels of analysis (e.g., Chapter Five), as well as the more macro or national levels (e.g., Chapter Eight).

This last chapter fulfills three main objectives. First, it provides an explicit link between the organization and other levels of analysis and intervention that are important for the development process. Second, it shows how developing countries can use organizations as effective building blocks for managing sectorial, regional, national, and even international development by developing a national management infrastructure. Finally, the chapter concludes with a brief discussion of the relevancy of this approach for leadership and sustainability in developing countries.

I. The Development of a National Management Infrastructure

Efforts directed at improving the performance of organizational tasks (COTs and SMATs) are effective only if they are spread over a critical number of organizations, particularly if such efforts are targeted at *strategic organizations*. Strategic organizations are defined as ". . . those macro-level organizations such as the Planning Commission or the cabinet that are directly involved in promoting socioeconomic development. They also include organizations operating in specific sectors that have or take the responsibility for the development of these sectors" (Khandwalla and Rao, 1987:1). When organizational and management improvement interventions are targeted at strategic organizations, and when these are successful over a period of time, the country develops a critical level of national management infrastructure capable of initiating, implementing, and sustaining development programs.

The process of identifying strategic organizations starts with the articulation of a widely accepted statement of national ideology, governance, mission, and direction. This then is operationalized through detailed national, sectorial, or regional development plans. Out of this can be identified a set of strategic organizations that are the organizations charged with the responsibility of defining, implementing, coordinating, monitoring, and evaluating the tasks associated with the successful realization of these plans.

No organizations are intrinsically strategic or nonstrategic. Organizations acquire or lose strategic status depending on the overall importance of their tasks for the achievement of national plans and objectives. When a country makes major shifts in its national plans and priorities, it gives rise to a new set of strategic organizations. For example, Iran before and after the Shah has operated under different sets of strategic organizations. It is the shift from one set to another set of strategic organizations that often breaks or makes national revolutions. Likewise, countries such as the Sudan or Nicaragua, which are experiencing difficulties developing a consensus over national plans and priorities, cannot identify a mutually acceptable set of strategic organizations for national development.

Strategic organizations can be production or nonproduction service organizations. They may be public or private, domestic, indigenous, regional, or international. In China, the Institute of International Economic Management in Beijing has become a strategic organization because of the role it plays in the country's modernization policy, which, in addition to training and socializing young Chinese in international business, also facilitates the development of collaborative institutional arrangements between Chinese indigenous organizations and organizations in other countries (Lindsay and Dempsey, 1985).

The basis for the strategic status of organizations is not always easy to discern. For example, in East Africa sugar factories take on strategic importance well beyond the industry's contribution to the national economy because government support from the *wanachi* depends on a steady supply of sugar at a price they can afford. In Zambia breweries receive a lot of attention from the government, partly because of the excise revenue from beer sales, but also because beer shortages are politically unacceptable.

Once strategic organizations have been identified and agreed upon, they become the building blocks for development of a national, regional, or sectorial management infrastructure for development. National resources and management interventions can then be deployed within and across those organizations to enhance their individual and collective capabilities to perform their respective COTs and SMATs as they relate to national development plans and priorities. Interventions located and resources deployed in nonstrategic organizations cannot contribute directly to the development of this management infrastructure.

Within each strategic organization, there are strategic roles whose accomplishment is crucial for the effective performance of the strategic organization's COTs and SMATs as they relate to the successful implementation of national plans and objectives. In Chapter Six, specific key roles were identified for cooperants and counterparts in the process of technology transfer to the implementing organization (see Figure 6.1). Such roles can be regarded as strategic if they are required for building or sustaining a local technological capacity for one strategic organization, or a network of strategic organizations. Strategic roles should not be confused with strategic management tasks (SMATs), discussed in the previous chapters. Some of the strategic roles are involved in the performance of critical operating tasks (COTs). For example, a tax assessment officer putting in long hours to increase the country's tax collection as part of managing the public debt may be performing a national strategic role, but only an ordinary operating task for the department of finance.

II. Managing Strategic Organizations

Management improvements in developing countries should concentrate on strategic organizations. Drawing from the discussions in the previous chapters, we can create a synthesis that illustrates the development and management of strategic organizations. Figure 9.1 is a matrix presentation of the development and management of a country's strategic organizations once these have been identified and agreed upon. The right-hand side of the figure shows selected strategies for the development and improvement of the management of the strategic organizations which use some of the strategies discussed in the previous chapters. These include human resource utilization, development of local technological capacities, decentralization, various forms of public sector reform, and the development of indigenous private sector organizations.

The left-hand side of Figure 9.1 provides opportunities to shift to different levels of analysis including sectors, regions, communities, organizations, or projects. The important thing to remember is that the elements within each unit of analysis must be strategic as defined above. The four organizational tasks illustrated in the figure are development of domestic and international collaborative institutional arrangements (CIAs), in-

Figure 9.1

**A MATRIX PRESENTATION OF THE DEVELOPMENT AND MANAGEMENT
OF A COUNTRY'S STRATEGIC ORGANIZATIONS**

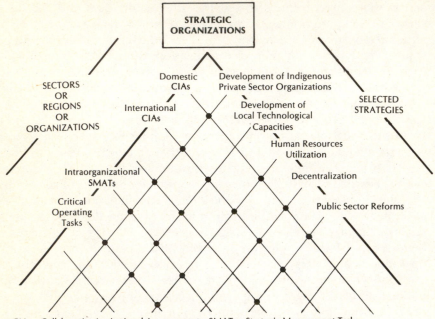

Note: CIAs = Collaborative Institutional Arrangements; SMATs = Strategic Management Tasks.
        The list of topics on both sides of the matrix is not exhaustive.

ternal management improvements, and improvements in the performance of the critical operating tasks. Of course, these can be broken down into smaller units of analysis. For example, domestic CIAs can be subdivided into public and private sector organizations, and COTs can be further divided into input, transformation, and output tasks.

Putting the two sides of the matrix together, we can make a match between the specific management strategies and the organizational tasks through which improvements can be made. For example, if one of the country's development strategies is the development of indigenous private sector organizations (IPSOs), as discussed in the previous chapter, this can be facilitated by building collaborative institutional arrangements between selected IPSOs and other domestic and international organizations. It can also be done by assisting the IPSOs to develop the local technological capacity to perform their COTs efficiently. Likewise, improved human resource utilization among strategic organizations can be achieved by improving internal management or by encouraging the development of collaborative institutional arrangements with like organizations at home and abroad. This analysis can be done for a single strategic organization, a network of strategic organizations, a geographical region, or the country as a whole. It is a versatile conceptual and diagnostic framework.

III. Strategic Organizations and Structural Adjustment

As was discussed in Chapter Eight, structural adjustment is a major macrolevel policy intervention that involves significant changes in the management and task performance of many organizations in many sectors or regions of the country. It was also observed that many developing countries do not have the capacity for sustained implementation and coordination of the various component elements of the program because they lack the necessary organizational and management infrastructure. It is therefore prudent for these countries to introduce improvement programs for the management and operations of their organizations before putting the structural adjustment program in place. It is neither possible nor necessary, however, to develop such programs for all organizations. Instead, the country, with outside assistance, should begin by identifying strategic organizations, strategic groups, strategic roles, and strategic individuals, and redirect available scarce resources toward these strategic aspects of the structural adjustment program. It is also important to realize that major policy shifts such as nationalization or privatization involving strategic organizations are extremely delicate and must be implemented with care and thought.

Table 9.1 provides a partial list of strategic organizations for a hypothetical developing country on a typical structural adjustment program. That an organization achieves strategic status does not mean that all its COTs and SMATs are strategic within the context of the structural adjustment program; thus the table also gives the strategic functions of these organizations. Identifying strategic functions is useful not only for the individual strategic organizations but also, and perhaps more importantly, for the central coordinating agencies such as the cabinet office and the central bank. In coordinating the program, the central agencies need not concern themselves with all aspects of the strategic organizations, but only with the strategic functions, be they COTs or SMATs.

Table 9.1 identifies the strategic organizations by sector because, according to the structural adjustment program, different sectors are expected to play different roles. For example, while the parastatal sector is expected to be downsizing, the domestic private sector should be experiencing growth and development and the public sector should be improving its advisory, monitoring, and coordinating capabilities.

For each strategic organization it is possible to identify strategic roles and staff them with strategic individuals. For example, the secretary to the cabinet, minister of finance, governor of the central bank, head of international security, and secretary to the treasury are some of the strategic

Table 9.1

**SELECTED STRATEGIC ORGANIZATIONS AND FUNCTIONS FOR A COUNTRY
ON A STRUCTURAL ADJUSTMENT PROGRAM**

Sector	Organization	Selected Strategic Functions
Public	Cabinet Office	Overall SAP coordination and supervision
	Ministry of Finance	Fiscal and budgetary management and control
	Ministry of Planning	Overall planning, monitoring, and evaluation
	Ministry of Agriculture	Increased agricultural production
	Ministry of Industry	Promotion of private sector industrial activities
	Ministry of Trade	Export promotion
	Ministry of Defence	Ensurance of internal security
	Central Bank	Debt, monetary, foreign exchange management
	Central Bureau of Statistics	Provision of data on strategic activities
Parastatal	Export Crop Marketing Board	Promotion of agricultural exports
	Industrial Development Corporation	Rehabilitation of productive industries
	National Transport Corporation	Transportation of exports and imports
	National Development Bank	Financing of strategic projects
	National Electricity Board	Supply of power and energy for strategic programs
Private	Indigenous Private Sector Corporation	Increase of private sector participation in SAP
	Small-Scale Enterprises	Increase of industrial and commercial output
	Private Voluntary Agencies	Strengthening weaker or nonstrategic individuals or groups
International	The IMF/World Bank	Conditionality, supervision, funding, CIAs
	UN Agencies	Institutional strengthening of strategic organizations
	Multinational Corporations	Promotion of trade, investment, industrial development, IPSOs
	Regional Development Banks	Financing of private sector strategic projects

Note: SAP = Structural Adjustment Program; CIAs = Collaborative Institutional Arrangements;
IPSOs = Indigenous Private Sector Organizations.

roles for a country on a structural adjustment program and these should be staffed by individuals with exceptional abilities, motivation, commitment, and leadership qualities. Chief executive officers of strategic indigenous private sector organizations should be equally capable.

The concept of strategic roles is useful for linking organizations to development at the more micro individual levels of analysis and intervention. For example, in agriculture, the management of extension service systems such as the T&V system discussed above is effective to the extent that it concentrates on the improved task performance of strategic roles such as the contact farmers, the village extension workers, subject matter specialists, and extension officers and managers. Likewise, the development of small-scale enterprises can be much more selective, focusing only on those making direct contributions to explicitly stated national or local development plans. Moreover, problems of the brain drain and human resource shortages can be put into a strategic context. These are important to the extent that they facilitate or inhibit the recruitment and staffing of qualified nationals for strategic roles in strategic organizations or sectors.

This analysis can contribute significantly to the success of the structural adjustment program. First, it helps to identify and focus on only those organizations and their tasks (COTs or SMATs) of direct consequences for the sustained implementation of the program. Second, it recognizes existing organizational gaps and overlaps so that informed decisions can be made as to the areas where new organizations need to be created, old ones pruned, and new collaborative institutional arrangements established or discouraged. Third, it identifies those organizations outside the country whose participation is required for the success of the program and the specific strategic function(s) they are expected to perform. This step is particularly important for countries such as Kenya, Zimbabwe, Egypt, Pakistan, and Indonesia, which are so popular among international development agencies but whose capacity to deploy them strategically is rather limited. Finally, it allows for a more rational deployment of available scarce resources such as foreign exchange, management expertise, technical assistance, and political leadership and support. These should be directed toward the effective performance of the strategic functions of the strategic organizations.

IV. Leadership and the Management of Organizations

Leadership plays a critical role in the management of organizations and the development of a sustained capacity for the performance of their respective COTs and SMATs. Many developing countries are said to be experiencing a crisis of leadership at both the national and the organizational level. Yet, little is known about the personal attributes and the contextual antecedents or contingencies that facilitate the emergence and effective utilization of high quality leadership in organizations in developing countries. It is known, however, that such high quality leadership is a product of a highly dynamic and mutually interactive influencing process between the leader and his or her attributes, and the context within which the leadership is exercised.

Leadership, however, should not be equated with formal education or management development. Numerous developing countries such as India, Egypt, Nigeria, and Pakistan have many highly educated nationals but still experience serious leadership problems in the management of their organizations. Moreover, while many managers from these organizations have attended management development programs both at home and abroad, they are not necessarily high quality leaders. At best, they become good managers or administrators.

What then is organizational leadership? It is a multidimensional concept that, for organizations in developing countries, includes the following components:

1. The sagacity to identify with and articulate national sentiments, ideology, cultural norms and practices, and development goals, plans, and priorities; and to translate them into a coherent organizational mission, goals, plans, and objectives.

2. The capacity to acquire, organize, and mobilize resources and technical and political support for the development of a sustained management infrastructure for the successful accomplishment of the organization's mission, consistent with national sentiments and expectations.

3. The ability, motivation, and perseverance to remain focused on the organization's mission; and the sustained capacity to perform its COTs and SMATs and to maintain the necessary technocratic and political support both within and outside the organization.

4. The skills, knowledge, respect, and emotional appeal from all stakeholders to develop and maintain the organization's unity, identity, and integrity by protecting its values, vital core, and core technology from undue outside interference.

These attributes are hard to find, and if organizations in developing countries are experiencing leadership crises, it is partly because these organizations demand much more from their leaders than do comparable organizations in the industrialized countries where the management infrastructure is already in place. Efforts must therefore be directed to the search, selection, and development of individuals who can meet this formidable challenge. The sociocultural imperatives within which organizations in developing countries operate require that these individuals should be nationals who have the cultural background and sensitivity to understand and identify with the operative domestic cultural and political ethos (Ratiu, 1987). Expatriates are not suitable for these culturally sensitive strategic roles though they can provide technical and administrative support.

It is also important to recognize that such high level leadership requires a critical mass of people in the country who develop a network of mutual support and work together in discharging their respective strategic functions. One way to do this is to establish regular residential retreats and workshops. For example, in April 1986 the prime minister of India personally participated in a week-long retreat away from New Delhi. The purpose of this management development retreat was to bring together political executives and senior public administrators "to pause, reflect, introspect, think, explore, and examine together what they can do to make development administration more efficient and effective" (Sinha, 1987:82).

Leadership in developing countries tends to be personalized, based on personal charisma rather than proved technical expertise and experience. This pattern is not surprising because charismatic leaders tend to emerge under conditions of institutional failure when there is widespread loss of faith in the established order (House and Woycke, 1987). Many organizations in developing countries are experiencing institutional decay (Kiggundu, 1985b), or demise (McHenry, 1985). Charismatic leadership is also based on the emotional commitment and attachment of the followers rather than the objective attributes of the leader, and this pattern, too, is characteristic of traditional societies. On the positive side, charismatic leaders bring about more success than do noncharismatic leaders, and they are better at articulating mission and ideology and at providing normative appeal and order, by employing symbolism and identifying with cultural myths (House and Woycke, 1987).

To the extent that charismatic leadership is based on personalities, it is not particularly suitable for organizations in need of developing and institutionalizing a systematic management infrastructure. Moreover, it creates problems of succession when the charismatic leader retires or dies. While charisma may be important in the initial stages of nationhood or organizational creation, as the organization becomes more developed with complex (COTs and SMATs) task systems, its need for experienced technocratic managers increases significantly. Accordingly, organizations in developing countries need a dynamic optimum balance between personal charisma and technocratic management expertise among their leaders.

V. Sustainability

Sustainability is the most serious problem facing organizations in developing countries. Even where outside assistance has been generous, organizations continue to experience grave problems due to lack of the capacity to implement and sustain development initiatives. The framework developed in this book can be used to bring about better diagnosis and understanding of problems of sustainability either for a single organization, or for a set of interdependent organizations. It can also be used to develop a strategy for building the necessary capacity for sustainability. This can be achieved by focusing on the necessary improvements for the performance of the relevant organizations' tasks (COTs and SMATs), identifying strategic organizations and working through strategic roles, establishing effective domestic and international collaborative institutional arrangements for these organizations, and developing the appropriate leadership and management infrastructure.

For most international development and funding agencies, sustainability is limited to its capacity to carry on the project and its related tasks after the end of the official sponsorship or technical assistance. This, however, is a narrow view of the issues and problems of sustainability. In general, sustainability is the extent to which the organization develops and maintains the capacity for the effective performance of its COTs and SMATs. At a national level, sustainability refers to the combined capacity of the country's strategic organizations to initiate, implement, and sustain development initiatives. It is a dynamic concept reflecting changes in the internal task requirements of the organization(s), and environmental demands and expectations.

Organizational sustainability depends on the existence of an effective management infrastructure, the development of a local technological capacity for organizational task performance, the effectiveness of existing domestic and international collaborative institutional arrangements, high quality dynamic leadership, and appropriate development and utilization of available human resources.

Chapter Three provides a framework for diagnosing organizations in terms of the extent to which they perform their respective COTs and SMATs. Organizations in Quadrant 4 of Figure 3.4 are those that perform both their COTs and SMATs efficiently and effectively. From this analysis, it can be concluded that sustainability for a single organization necessitates its moving to and staying in Quadrant 4, and for a country, its strategic organizations must be located in the same quadrant. If the strategic organizations occupy any of the other quadrants, organizational and management interventions are available to build and maintain sustainability for these organizations. Developing countries must select those interventions that facilitate the evolvement of a network of mutually supporting strategic organizations in order that their combined contribution to national development is greater than the sum of their individual efforts.

The welfare and prosperity of billions of people in developing countries depend on how well or badly the development enterprise is organized and managed and the long-term results of our individual and collective efforts. This book provides numerous models and approaches for improving the organization and management of development. It identifies the major players in development and the challenges they face in fighting underdevelopment and in bringing about sustainable economic and social development for many people. It provides practical approaches for addressing one of the greatest challenges of our times—improving the well-being of the majority of the people in the world and making the global village, which we all share, a better place for all of us to work and to live in.

Bibliography

Aaker, D. A. (1984). *Strategic Market Management.* New York: John Wiley.

Abramson, R., and Halset, W. (1979). *Planning for Improved Enterprise Performance.* Geneva: International Labour Office.

Adams, W., ed. (1986). *The Brain Drain.* New York: Macmillan.

Adams, W., and Dirlam, J.B. (1968). "An Agenda for Action." In *The Brain Drain.* Edited by W. Adams. New York: Macmillan.

African Development Bank Group (1984). "Policy and Operational Guidelines for the Industrial Sector." ADB/0-01S1/84/01/ENG. Internal Bank Document.

Aga Khan Foundation (1986). The Enabling Environment Conference: Effective Private Sector Contribution to Development in Sub-Saharan Africa. Nairobi, Kenya, 21–24 October, 1986.

Agurén, S., and Edgren, J. (1980). *New Factories: Job Design Through Factory Planning in Sweden.* Stockholm: Swedish Employers' Confederation.

Aharoni, Y. (1986). *The Evolution and Management of State-Owned Enterprises.* Cambridge, Mass.: Ballinger.

Aiken, M., and Hage, J. (1968). "Organizational Interdependence and Intra-organizational Structure." *American Sociological Review* 33(6):912–30.

Albrecht, K. (1979). *Stress and the Manager: Making It Work for You.* Englewood Cliffs, N.J.: Prentice-Hall.

Aldrich, H.E. (1979). *Organizations and Environments.* Englewood Cliffs, N.J.: Prentice-Hall.

Amsalem, M. (1984). "Technology Choice for Textiles and Paper Manufacture." In *Technology Crossing Borders.* Edited by R. Stobaugh, and L.T. Wells. Boston: Harvard Business School Press.

Andrews, K.R. (1971). *The Concept of Corporate Strategy.* Homewood, Ill.: Dow-Jones Irwin.

Argyris, C. (1964). *Integrating the Individual and the Organization.* New York: John Wiley.

Argyris, C. (1968). "Some Unintended Consequences of Rigorous Research." *Psychological Bulletin* 70:185–97.

Argyris, C., and Schon, D.A. (1978). *Organizational Learning: A Theory of Action Perspective.* Reading, Mass.: Addison-Wesley.

Bacon, J., and Brown, J.K. (1977). *The Board of Directors: Perspectives and Practices in Nine Countries.* New York: The Conference Board.

Bakke, E.W. (1959). "Concept of the Social Organization." In *Modern Organization Theory.* Edited by M. Haire. New York: John Wiley.

Balassa, B., Bueno, G.M., Kuczynski, P., and Simonsen, M.H. (1986). *Toward Re-*

newed Economic Growth in Latin America. Washington, D.C.: Institute for International Economics.

Baranson, J. (1981). *North-South Technology Transfer: Financing and Institution Building.* Mt. Airy, Md.: Lomond Publications.

Baritz, L. (1960). *The Servants of Power: A History of the Use of Social Science in American Industry.* Middletown, Conn.: Wesleyan University Press.

Barko, W., and Pasmore, W., eds. (1986). "Sociotechnical Systems: Innovations in Designing High-performing Systems." Special issue of *The Journal of Applied Behavioral Science* 22(3).

Barnard, C.H. (1938). *The Functions of the Executive.* Cambridge, Mass.: MIT Press.

Bates, R.H. (1985). "The Analysis of Institutions." Paper presented to the Office of Rural and Institutional Development, Bureau for Science and Technology, U.S. Agency for International Development.

Baum, W.C., and Tolbert, S.M. (1985). *Investing in Development: Lessons of World Bank Experience.* Washington, D.C.: The World Bank.

Bell, M., Ross-Larson, B., and Westphal, L.E. (1984). *Assessing the Performance of Infant Industries.* Washington, D.C.: World Bank Staff Working Papers, No. 666.

Benedict, B., ed. (1967). *Problems of Smaller Territories.* London: Institute of Commonwealth Studies, University of London.

Benor, D., Harrison, J.Q., and Baxter, M. (1984). *Agricultural Extension: The Training and Visit System.* Washington, D.C.: The World Bank.

Benson, K.J. (1982). "A Framework for Policy Analysis." In *Interorganizational Coordination: Theory, Research, and Implementation.* Edited by D.L. Rogers and D.A Whitten. Ames, Iowa: Iowa State University Press.

Berg, E. (1985). "The Potentials of the Private Sector in Africa." *The Washington Quarterly,* pp. 73–83.

Berg, R.J. (1981). *Accelerated Development in Sub-Saharan Africa: An Agenda for Action.* Washington, D.C.: The World Bank.

Bertalanffy, L.V. (1968). *General Systems Theory.* New York: George Brazillier.

Bish, R.L., and Ostrom, V. (1973). "The Public Choice Approach." Chap. 3 of *Understanding Urban Government: Metropolitan Reform Reconsidered.* Washington, D.C.: American Enterprise Institute for Public Policy Research.

Blau, P.M. (1963). *The Dynamics of Bureaucracy.* Chicago: University of Chicago Press.

Blau, P.M., and Scott, R. (1962). *Formal Organizations.* San Francisco: Chandler.

Blunt, P. (1983). *Organizational Theory and Behaviour: An African Perspective.* London: Longman.

Bowen, C.M. (1971). *Developing and Training the Supervisor.* London: Business Books Limited.

Bozeman, B. (1987). *All Organizations Are Public: Bridging Public and Private Organizational Theories.* San Francisco: Jossey-Bass.

Bresser, R.H., and Harl, J.E. (1986). "Collective Strategy: Vice or Virtue?" *Academy of Management Review* II(2):408–27.

Brinkerhoff, D. (1979). "Inside Public Bureaucracy: Empowering Managers to Empower Clients." *Rural Development Participation Review* I(1):7–8.

Brunsson, N. (1985). *The Irrational Organization, Irrationality as a Basis for Organizational Action and Change.* New York: John Wiley.

Buffa, E.S. (1983). *Modern Production/Operations Management*. 7th ed. New York: John Wiley.

Burns, T., and Stalker, G.M. (1961). *The Management of Innovation*. London: Tavistock.

Bussink, W., Davies, D., Grawer, R., Kovalsky, B., and Pfefferman, G.P. (1980). *Poverty and the Development of Human Resources: Regional Perspective*. Washington, D.C.: World Bank Staff Working Papers, No. 406.

Cady, J.F., and Buzzell, R.D. (1986). *Strategic Marketing*. Boston: Little, Brown & Co.

Cameron, K.S., and Whetten, D.A. (1983). "Organizational Effectiveness: One Model or Several?" In *Organizational Effectiveness: A Comparison of Multiple Models*. Edited by K.S. Cameron and D.A. Whetten. New York: Academic Press.

Canadian International Development Agency (CIDA) (1985). "Review of Training Component of Agricultural Planning Project." Planning Division of the Ministry of Agriculture and Water Development. Prepared by I.K. Singhal, Department of Agriculture, Government of Canada, Ottawa, Ontario.

Canadian International Development Agency (1986). *Development: Transportation and Communications*. Hull, Quebec: Spring–Summer.

Carleton Board of Education (1986). A report from the board meeting of September 22, 1986. General circular published by the School Board's Public Relations Department, Nepean, Ontario, Canada.

Casse, P. (1982). *Training for the Multicultural Manager*. Washington, D.C.: The International Society for Intercultural Education, Training and Research.

Chambua, S.E. (1985). "Choice of Techniques and Underdevelopment in Tanzania." Ph.D dissertation, Carleton University, Ontario, Ottawa, Canada.

Chandler, A.D. (1962). *Strategy and Structure*. Cambridge, Mass.: MIT Press.

Cheema, S.G., and Rondinelli, D.A. (1983). *Decentralization and Development: Policy Implementation in Developing Countries*. Beverly Hills, Calif.: Sage.

Chenoweth, F.A. (1986). *Ministry of Agriculture and Water Development: A Study of the Organization and Planning Process of the Planning Division*. Planning Division Studies No. 22. Hull, Quebec: Canadian International Development Agency, Zambia Desk.

Child, J. (1972). "Organization Structure and Strategies of Control: A Replication of the Aston Study." *Administrative Science Quarterly*, 17(1): 163–84.

Child, J. (1984). *Organization: A Guide to Problems and Practice*. 2d ed. London: Harper & Row.

Clayre, A. (1980). "Some Aspects of Mondragon Co-operative Federation." In *The Political Economy of Cooperation and Participation: A Third Sector*. Edited by A. Clayre. Oxford: Oxford University Press.

Commonwealth (1986). *Vulnerability: Small States in the Global Society: Report of a Commonwealth Consultative Group*. London: Commonwealth Secretariat.

Conway, M. (1984). "Reducing Expatriate Failure Rates." *Personnel Administrator* 29(7):31.

Cooper, C. (1980). *Policy Interventions for Technological Innovation in Developing Countries*. Washington, D.C.: World Bank Staff Working Papers, No. 441.

Cowan, L.G. (1985). "Divestment, Privatization and Development." *The Washington Quarterly* (Fall):47–56.

Crosby, J. (1976). "Personnel Management in a Developing Country." *Personnel Management* 8(9):19–23.

Crozier, M. (1964). *The Bureaucratic Phenomenon*. Chicago: University of Chicago Press.

Daft, R.L., and Steers, R.M. (1986). *Organizations: A Micro/Macro Approach*. Illinois: Scott Foresman.

Dahlman, C.J., Ross-Larson, B., and Westphal, L.E. (1985). *Managing Technological Development: Lessons from Newly Industrializing Countries*. Washington, D.C.: World Bank Staff Working Papers, No. 717.

Dasah, B.Z. (1986). *Report on the In-country Exchange of Skills Seminar in Nairobi, Kenya: July 22, 1986*. Hull, Quebec: Canadian International Development Agency, Briefing Centre.

Dasah, B.Z., and Kiggundu, M.N. (1985). *Report on the Debriefing of the Canada-Kenya Business Forum*. Hull, Quebec: Canadian International Development Agency, Briefing Centre.

Dasah, B.Z., and Kiggundu, M.N. (1986). *Transfer/Exchange of Skills*. Hull, Quebec: Canadian International Development Agency, Briefing Centre.

David, F.R. (1986). *Fundamentals of Strategic Management*. Columbus, Ohio: Merrill.

Davies, D.G. (1980). "Human Development in Sub-Saharan Africa." In *Poverty and the Development of Human Resources: Regional Perspectives*. Washington, D.C.: World Bank Staff Working Papers, No. 406.

Davies, H. (1977). "Technology Transfer Through Commercial Transactions." *Journal of Industrial Economics* XXVI(2):161–75.

Davis, L.E., and Cherns, A.B., eds. (1975). *The Quality of Working Life*. New York: The Free Press.

Davis, S.M. (1968). "Entrepreneurial Succession." *Administrative Science Quarterly* 13(3):402–16.

Davis, S.M., and Lawrence, P.R. (1977). *Matrix*. Reading, Mass.: Addison-Wesley.

de Bettignies, H.C. (1978). "The Management of Technology Transfer: Can it be Learned?" *Impact of Science on Society* 28(4):321–27.

DeFranco, S. (1979). "Employment and the Urban Informal Sector: The Case of Managua." Ph.D. Dissertation, The University of Wisconsin, Madison.

Dewar, D.L. (1980). *The Quality Circle Guide to Participation Management*. Englewood Cliffs: Prentice-Hall.

Donaldson, L. (1985). *In Defence of Organization Theory. A Reply to the Critics*. Cambridge: Cambridge University Press.

Doz, Y. (1986). *Strategic Management in Multinational Companies*. Elmsford, N.Y.: Pergamon Press.

Drucker, P.F. (1967). *The Effective Executive*. New York: Harper & Row.

Dunlop, J.T. (1958). *Industrial Relations Systems*. Carbondale: Southern Illinois University Press.

Dyer, W.G. (1983). *Contemporary Issues in Management and Organization Development*. Reading, Mass.: Addison-Wesley.

Eaton, J., ed. (1972). *Institution-Building and Development: From Concepts to Complication*. Beverly Hills, Calif.: Sage.

Emery, F.E., and Trist, E.L. (1965). "The Causal Texture of Organizational Environments." *Human Relations* 18:21–32.

Engelstad, P.H. (1972). "Socio-Technical Approach to Problems of Process Control." In *Design of Jobs*. Edited by L.E. Davis and J.C. Taylor. Middlesex: Penguin.

Esman, M., and Uphoff, N.T. (1984). *Local Organizations: Intermediaries in Rural Development*. Ithaca: Cornell University Press.

Evan, W.M., ed. (1971). *Organizational Experiments: Laboratory and Field Research*. New York: Harper & Row.

Faucheux, C., Amado, G., and Laurent, A. (1982). "Organization Development and Change." *Annual Review of Psychology* 33:343–70.

Fayol, H. (1949). *General and Industrial Management*. New York: Pitman.

Fehnel, R.A., Freeman, H., Murray, A., and Picard, L. (1985). *Interim Evaluation of Development Support Training Project: USAID/Pakistan*. Washington, D.C.: National Association of Schools of Public Affairs and Administration (NASPAA), Contract No. DAN 0000-1-00-5051-00, U.S. Agency for International Development, Bureau for Science and Technology, Office of Rural and Institutional Development.

Fiedler, F.E. (1967). *A Theory of Leadership Effectiveness*. New York: McGraw-Hill.

Fombrun, C.J. (1984). "The External Context of Human Resources Management. In *Strategic Human Resource Management*. Edited by C.J. Fombrun, N.M. Tichy, and M.A. Devanna. New York: John Wiley.

Fombrun, C.J., Tichy, N.M., and Devanna, M.A., eds. (1984). *Strategic Human Resource Management*. New York: John Wiley.

Galbraith, J.R. (1973). *Designing Complex Organizations*. Reading, Mass.: Addison-Wesley.

Galbraith, J.R. (1977). *Organization Design*. Reading, Mass.: Addison-Wesley.

Germidis, D., ed. (1980). *International Subcontracting: A New Form of Investment*. Paris: Development Centre: Organization for Economic Cooperation and Development (OECD).

Ghai, Y. (1985). "The State and the Market in the Management of Public Enterprises in Africa: Ideology and False Comparisons." *Public Enterprises* 6(1): 15–26.

Glover, D.J. (1986). "Multinational Corporations and Third World Agriculture." In *Investing in Development: New Roles for Private Capital?* Edited by T.H. Moran. Washington, D.C.: Overseas Development Council.

Glueck, W.F. (1982). *Personnel: A Diagnostic Approach*. Plano, Texas: Business Publications.

Goldstein, I.L. (1986). *Training in Organizations: Needs Assessment, Development, and Evaluation*. 2d. ed. Monterey, Calif.: Brookes/Cole.

Gomes-Casseres, B. (1985). "Multinational Ownership Strategies." *DAI* 46(12): A3787, Harvard University.

Goodsell, C.T. (1983). *The Case for Bureaucracy: A Public Administration Polemic*. Chatham, N.J.: Chatham House.

Gould, D.J., and Amaro-Reyes, J.A. (1983). *The Effects of Corruption on Administrative Performance: Illustrations from Developing Countries*. Washington, D.C.: World Bank Staff Working Papers, No. 580, Management and Development Series, No. 7.

Government of Kenya (1986). *Sessional Paper No. 1 on Economic Management for Re-*

newed Growth. Nairobi: The Government Printer.

Goyal, S.K., ed. (1984). *Public Enterprises*. New Delhi: Indian Institute of Public Administration.

Gran, G. (1983). "Learning From Development Success: Some Lessons From Contemporary Histories." NASPAA Working Papers, No. 9. Washington, D.C.: National Association of Schools of Public Affairs and Administration.

Griffin, K. (1981). "Economic Development in a Changing World." *World Development* 9(3):221–26.

Group of Twenty-four (1982). Communique of the Group of Twenty-four, September 3.

Gulick, L., and Urwick, L., eds. (1954). *Papers on the Science of Administration*. 3d ed. New York: Institute of Public Administration.

Gyllenhammar, P.G. (1977). "How Volvo Adapts Work to People." *Harvard Business Review*, July–August, pp. 105–13.

Hackman, J.R., and Oldham, G.R. (1980). *Work Redesign*. Reading, Mass.: Addison-Wesley.

Haddow, P.S. (1982). "The Post-Graduate Training and Utilization of Professional Planners and Economists in the Government of Kenya: Recommendations to the Government and Donor Agencies." A Report for the Ministry of Economic Planning and Development of the Government of Kenya and the Canadian International Development Agency, July, Hull, Quebec.

Hafsi, T., Kiggundu, M.N., and Jorgensen, J.J. (1987). "Strategic Apex Configurations in State-Owned Enterprises." *Academy of Management Review* 12(4): 714–30.

Hage, J., and Finsterbusch, K. (1987). *Organizational Change as a Development Strategy: Models and Tactics for Improving Third World Organizations*. Boulder, Colo.: Lynne Rienner.

Haire, M. (1959). *Modern Organization Theory: A Symposium*. New York: John Wiley.

Hall, I.R. (1976). "A System Pathology of an Organization: The Rise and Fall of the Old *Saturday Evening Post*." *Administrative Science Quarterly* 21(2):185–211.

Hall, I.R. (1984). "The Natural Logic of Management Policy Making." *Management Science* 30(8):905–27.

Hanna, N. (1985). *Strategic Planning and Management: A Review of Recent Experiences*. Washington, D.C.: The World Bank Staff Working Papers, No. 751.

Hardy, C., Langley, A., Mintzberg, H., and Rose, J. (1983). "Strategy Formation in the University Setting." *The Review of Higher Education* 6(4), Summer.

Harrigan, K.R. (1985). "Vertical Integration and Corporate Strategy." *Academy of Management Journal* 28(2):397–425.

Hawes, F., and Kealey, D.J. (1981). "An Empirical Study of Canadian Technical Assistance: Adaptation and Effectiveness on Overseas Assignment." *International Journal of Intercultural Relations* 5(3):239–58.

Helleiner, G.K. (1982). "Balance of Payments Problems and Macro-Economic Policy." In *Problems and Policies in Small Economies*. Edited by B. Jalan. London: Croom Helm.

Hersey, P., and Blanchard, K. (1982). *Management of Organizational Behavior: Utilizing Human Resources*. 4th ed. Englewood Cliffs, N.J.: Prentice-Hall.

Herzberg, F.B., Mausner, B., and Snyderman, B. (1959). *The Motivation to Work*. New York: John Wiley.

Hickson, D.J., Butler, R.J., Cray, D., Mallory, G.R., and Wilson, D.C. (1986). *Top Decisions: Strategy Decision-Making in Organizations*. San Francisco: Jossey-Bass.

Hill, T.M., Haynes, W.W., Baumgartel, H., and Paul, S. (1973). *Institution Building in India: A Study of International Collaboration in Management Education*. Boston, Mass.: Harvard University, Graduate School of Business Administration, Division of Research.

Hinchliffe, K. (1985). *Issues Related to Higher Education in Sub-Saharan Africa*. Washington, D.C.: World Bank Staff Working Papers, No. 780.

Hofstede, G. (1980). *Culture's Consequences: International Differences in Work-Related Values*. Beverly Hills, Calif.: Sage.

Hofstede, G. (1982). "Cultural Pitfalls for Dutch Expatriates in Indonesia." Jakarta, Indonesia: TG International, Management Consultants.

Hofstede, G. (1983). "The Cultural Relativity of Organizational Practices and Theories." *Journal of International Business* 14(2):75–89.

Honadle, G. (1986). *Development Management in Africa: Context and Strategy—A Synthesis of Six Agricultural Projects*. Washington, D.C.: U.S. Agency for International Development.

House, R.J. (1971). "A Path Goal Theory of Leader Effectiveness." *Administrative Science Quarterly* 16(2):321–39.

House, R.J., and Woycke, J. (1987). "A Comparative Study of Charismatic and Non-Charismatic Leaders in the Third World." In *Organizational and Behavioural Perspectives for Social Change*. Edited by P.N. Khandwalla and R.M. Rao. Ahmedabad, India: Indian Institute of Management.

Howell, P., Strauss, J., and Sorensen, P.F. (1975). "Research Note: Cultural and Situational Determinants of Job Satisfaction Among Management in Liberia." *Journal of Management Studies* 12:225–27.

Hrebiniak, L.G., and Joyce, W.F. (1984). *Implementing Strategy*. New York: Macmillan.

Hunt, D.R., and Gufwoli, P. (1986). *Strategic Management: Kenya. A Book of Cases*. Bristol, Indiana: Wyndham Hall Press.

Hunt, R.M., and Truitt, N.S. (1971). "The Poder Project in Colombia: The Successes and Failures of a Pilot Popular Participation Project." *International Development Review* 13(4):14–18.

Huse, E.F., and Cummings, T.G. (1985). *Organization Development and Change*. 3d ed. St. Paul, Minn.: West Publishing.

Hyden, G. (1983). *No Shortcuts to Progress: African Development Management in Perspective*. London: Heinemann.

Ickis, J.C., De Jesus, E.C., and Maru, R.M. (1986). *Beyond Bureaucracy: Strategic Management of Social Development*. West Hartford, Conn.: Kumarian Press.

Ingle, M.D., and Smith, K.A. (1984). "Microcomputer Technology and International Development Management: An Assessment of Promises and Threats." Paper presented at the International Association of Schools and Institutes of Administration (IASIA) Conference, Bloomington, Ind., 30 July–2 August.

International Development Research Centre (1986). *Searching Research: A Path to Development*. Ottawa, Canada: IDRC.

International Labour Organization (1984). *Technology Choice and Employment Gen-*

eration by Multinational Enterprises in Developing Countries. Geneva: International Labour Office.

International Rice Research Institute (1985). *International Rice Research: 25 Years of Partnership*. Manila, Philippines: IRRI.

International Rice Research Institute (1986). *IRRI Highlights: 1985 Accomplishments and Challenges*. Manila, Philippines: IRRI.

Inzerilli, G., and Laurent, A. (1983). "Managerial Views of Organization Structure in France and the U.S.A." *International Studies of Management and Organization*. XIII:97–118.

Jalan, B., ed. (1982). *Problems and Policies in Small Economies*. London: Croom Helm.

Janger, A.R., and Berenbeim, R.E. (1981). *External Challenges to Management Decisions: A Growing International Business Problem*. New York: The Conference Board.

Janis, I.L. (1972). *Victims of Groupthink: A Psychological Study of Foreign-Policy Decisions and Fiascoes*. Boston: Houghton Mifflin.

Jean-Maurice, S., and Hockin, T. (1986). *Interdependence and Internationalism: Report of the Special Joint Committee on Canada's International Relations*. Ottawa: Government of Canada.

Jelinek, M. (1981). "The Need for Organizational Learning." In *Organizations by Design: Theory and Practice*. Edited by M. Jelinek, J.A. Litterer, and R.E. Miles. Plano, Tex.: Irwin-Dorsey.

Jones, L.P., and Moran, R. (1982). *Public Enterprises in Less Developed Countries*. Cambridge, England: Cambridge University Press.

Jorgensen, J.J. (1985). "Managing After the Breakup of the East African Community Corporations." Unpublished working paper, no. 85-14, Faculty of Management, McGill University.

Jorgensen, J.J., Hafsi, T., and Kiggundu, M.N. (1986). "Towards a Market Imperfection Theory of Organizational Structure in Developing Countries." *Journal of Management Studies* 23(4):417–42.

Kahn, R.L., Wolfe, D.M., Quinn, R.P., Snoek, D.J., and Rosenthal, R.A. (1964). *Organizational Stress: Studies in Role Conflict and Ambiguity*. New York: John Wiley.

Kanawaty, G., ed. (1981). *Managing and Developing New Forms of Work Organization*. Geneva: International Labour Office, Management Development Series, No. 16.

Kanawaty, G., Thorsrud, E., Semiono, J.P., and Singh, J.P. (1981). "Field Experiences With New Forms of Work Organization." *International Labour Review* 120(3):263–77.

Kanungo, R.N. (1982). *Work Alienation: An Integrative Approach*. New York: Praeger.

Kanungo, R.N., and Misra, S. (1985). "Declining Work Motivation in India: Diagnosis and Intervention Strategies." Discussion Paper Series, Centre for Development Area Studies, McGill University, Montreal, Quebec, March.

Katz, D., and Kahn, R.L. (1978). *The Social Psychology of Organizations*. 2d ed. New York: John Wiley.

Kaufman, H. (1960). *The Forest Ranger: A Study of Administrative Behavior*. Baltimore: The Johns Hopkins Press.

Kaunda, G.H., and Pendakur, V.S. (1986). "Economic Analysis of the Regional Aircraft Maintenance Centres." Unpublished manuscript, Preferential Trade

Area for Eastern and Southern African States. Ministry of Communications and Works, United Republic of Tanzania.

Kent, T., and McAllister, I. (1983). *Management for Development: Planning*. Lanham, Md: University Press of America.

Kerrigan, J.E., and Luke, J.S. (1987). *Management Training Strategies for Developing Countries*. Boulder, Colo.: Lynne Rienner.

Kets de Vries, M.F.R., and Miller, D. (1984). *The Neurotic Organization: Diagnosing and Changing Counterproductive Styles of Management*. San Francisco: Jossey-Bass.

Khandwalla, P.N., and Rao, R.M. (1987). "International Conference on Organizational and Behavioral Perspectives for Social Development: Report on the Papers, Keynote Addresses, Panel Discussions and Presentations." Ahmedabad: Indian Institute of Management, India, 29 December 1986, to 2 January 1987.

Kidwell, J., El Jack, A., and Ketchum, L. (1981). "Socio-Technical Study for Locomotive Maintenance Workshop at Sennar, Sudan." Volume I. McLean, Va.: Parsons Brinkerhoff CENTEC International.

Kiereini, M. (1985). *Institutions in Rural Development Authority*. Research Essay, The Norman Patterson School of International Affairs, Carleton University, Ottawa, Ontario, Canada.

Kiggundu, M.N. (1978). "The Integration of Task Interdependence in the Job Characteristics Theory of Employee Responses." Ph.D. Dissertation, University of Toronto, Toronto, Ontario, Canada.

Kiggundu, M.N. (1981). "Task Interdependence and the Theory of Job Design." *Academy of Management Review* 6(3):499–508.

Kiggundu, M.N. (1983). "Task Interdependence and Job Design: Test of a Theory." *Organizational Behavior and Human Performance* 31:145–72.

Kiggundu, M.N. (1984). "Participative Work Design and Supervisory Problems." In *Quality of Working Life, Contemporary Cases*. Edited by J.B. Cunningham and T.H. White. Ottawa: Government of Canada.

Kiggundu, M.N. (1985a). "Managing Rural Development: A Comparative Analysis of Institutional Development from Kenya and Mexico." Paper presented at the Joint Meeting of the Canadian Association of Latin American and Caribbean Studies (CALACS) and the Canadian Association of African Studies (CAAS). Montreal, Quebec, 15–17 May.

Kiggundu, M.N. (1985b). "Africa in Crisis: Can Organization Theory Help?" Paper presented at the 45th Annual Meeting of the Academy of Management, San Diego, California, 11–14 August.

Kiggundu, M.N. (1986). "Limitations to the Application of Sociotechnical Systems in Developing Countries." *Journal of Applied Behavioral Science* 22(3):341–53.

Kiggundu, M.N. (1988a). "Africa." In *Comparative Management: A Regional View*, pp. 169–243. Edited by R. Nath. Cambridge, Mass.: Ballinger.

Kiggundu, M.N. (1988b). "The Context and Process of Management in Africa." Unpublished manuscript. School of Business, Carleton University, Ottawa, Ontario, Canada.

Kiggundu, M.N. (1988c). "Managing Structural Adjustment: The Role and Capacity of an African Central Bank." Unpublished manuscript. School of Business, Carleton University, Ottawa, Ontario, Canada.

Kiggundu, M.N., Jorgensen, J.J., and Hafsi, T. (1983). "Administrative Theory and Practice in Developing Countries: A Synthesis." *Administrative Science Quarterly* 28(1):66–84.

Killick, T. (1983). "The Role of the Public Sector in the Industrialization of African Developing Countries." In *Industry and Development* 7:57–83. New York: United Nations.

Kim, L., and Utterback, J.M. (1983). "The Evolution of Organizational Structure and Technology in a Developing Country." *Management Science* 29(10): 1185–97.

Kimberley, J.R., Miles, R.H., et al. (1980). *The Organizational Life Cycle.* San Francisco: Jossey-Bass.

Kochen, M., and Deutsch, K.W. (1980). *Decentralization: Sketches Toward a Rational Theory.* Oelgeschlager: Gunn & Hain.

Kolb, D.A. (1974). "On Management and the Learning Process." In *Organizational Psychology: A Book of Readings.* Edited by D.A. Kolb, I.M. Rubin, and J.M. McIntyre. 2d ed. Englewood Cliffs, N.J.: Prentice-Hall.

Kolodny, H.F., and Armstrong, A. (1985). "Three Bases for QWL Improvements: Structure, Technology, and Philosophy." Paper presented at the National Meetings of the Academy of Management. San Diego, Calif.

Korten, D.C. (1980). "Community Organization and Rural Development: A Learning Process Approach." *Public Administration Review* 40(5):480–511.

Korten, D.C. (1983). "Learning from USAID Field Experience: Institutional Development and the Dynamics of the Project Process." NASPAA Working Paper, No. 7. Washington, D.C.: National Association of Schools of Public Affairs and Administration.

Korten, D.C., and Uphoff, N.T. (1981). "Bureaucratic Reorientation for Participatory Rural Development." NASPAA Working Paper, No. 1. Washington, D.C.: National Association of Schools of Public Affairs and Administration.

Kubr, M., and Wallace, J. (1983). *Successes and Failures in Meeting the Management Challenge: Strategies and their Implementation.* Washington, D.C.: World Bank Staff Working Papers, No. 585, Management and Development Series, No. 12.

Lall, S., and Ghosh, S. (1982). "The Role of Foreign Investment and Exports in Industrialization." In *Problems and Policies in Small Economies.* Edited by B. Jalan. London: Croom Helm.

Lamb, R.B., ed. (1985). *Advances in Strategic Management.* Greenwich, Conn.: JAI Press, Inc.

Lammers, C.J. (1981). "Contributions of Organizational Sociology, Part II: Contributions to Organizational Theory and Practice—A Liberal View." *Organization Studies* 2(4):361–76.

Lammers, C.J., and Hickson, D.J., eds. (1979). *Organizations Alike and Unlike: International and Inter-Institutional Studies in the Sociology of Organizations.* London: Routledge & Kegan Paul.

Lasserre, P. (1983). "Strategic Assessment of International Partnership in ASEAN Countries." *Asian Journal of Management* 1(1):72–78.

Lawler, E.E. (1971). *Pay and Organizational Effectiveness: A Psychological View.* New York: McGraw-Hill.

Lawrence, P.R., and Lorsch, J.W. (1967). *Organization and Environment.* Boston:

Graduate School of Business Administration, Harvard University.

Leonard, D.K. (1977). *Reaching the Peasant Farmer: Organization Theory and Practice in Kenya*. Chicago, Ill.: The University of Chicago Press.

Leonard, D.K. (1986). "The Political Realities of African Management." In *Report of a Preliminary Evaluation Workshop on the Management of Agricultural Projects in Africa*. Washington, D.C.: U.S. Agency for International Development, Special Study No. 33, January.

Levinson, H. (1972). *Organizational Diagnosis*. Cambridge, Mass.: Harvard University Press.

Lewin, A.Y., and Minton, J.W. (1986). "Determining Organizational Effectiveness: Another Look at an Agenda for Research." *Management Science* 32(5):514–38.

Likert, R. (1967). *The Human Organization: Its Management and Values*. New York: McGraw-Hill.

Lindholm, R., and Flykt, S. (1981). "The Design of Production Systems: New Thinking and New Lines of Development." In *Managing and Developing New Forms of Work Organization*. Edited by G. Kanawaty. Geneva: International Labour Office, Management Development Series, No. 16.

Lindsay, C.P., and Dempsey, B.L. (1985). "Experiences in Training Chinese Business People to Use U.S. Management Techniques." *Journal of Applied Behavioural Science* 21:72.

Loubser, J.J. (1983). *Human Resource Development in Kenya: An Overview*. Hull, Quebec: Canadian International Development Agency.

Luthans, F., and Kreitner, R. (1975). *Organizational Behavior Modification*. Glenview, Ill.: Scott, Foresman.

Machungwa, P.D., and Schmitt, N. (1983). "Work Motivation in a Developing Country." *Journal of Applied Psychology* 68(1):31–42.

Manufacturers Life Insurance Company, The (1985). "Our Charter and Statement of Company Aims and Purposes." Toronto, Ontario: Employee Relations, Internal Documents.

March, J.G., and Simon, H.A. (1958). *Organizations*. New York: John Wiley.

Mayo, E. (1933). *The Human Problems of an Industrial Civilization*. New York: Macmillan.

McClelland, D.C., and Winter, D.G. (1969). *Motivating Economic Achievement*. New York: Free Press.

McGregor, D. (1967). *The Professional Manager*. New York: McGraw-Hill.

McHenry, D.E. (1985). "Political Bases of the Dissolution of a Public Corporation: A Nigerian Case." *Canadian Journal of African Studies* 19(1):175–91.

Miles, R.H. (1980). *Macro Organizational Behavior*. Santa Monica, Calif.: Goodyear Publishing.

Miles, R.H., and Cameron, K.S. (1982). *Coffin Nails and Corporate Strategies*. Englewood Cliffs, N.J.: Prentice-Hall.

Miller, E.J. (1975). "Socio-Technical Systems in Weaving 1953–1970: A Follow-up Study." *Human Relations* 28:349–86.

Miner, J.B. (1965). *Studies in Management Education*. Atlanta, Ga.: Organizational Measurement Systems Press.

Mintzberg, H. (1973). *The Nature of Managerial Work*. New York: Harper & Row.

Mintzberg, H. (1979). *The Structuring of Organizations*. Englewood Cliffs, N.J.: Prentice-Hall.

Mintzberg, H. (1980). *Beyond Implementation: An Analysis of the Resistance to Policy Analysis.* INFOR, 18(2):100–38.

Mintzberg, H. (1983). *Structure in Fives: Designing Effective Organizations.* Englewood Cliffs, N.J.: Prentice-Hall.

Mintzberg, H., and McHugh, A. (1985). "Strategy Formulation in an Adhocracy." *Administrative Science Quarterly* 30(1):160–97.

Mintzberg, H. and Waters, J. (1982). "Tracking Strategy in an Entrepreneurial Firm." *Academy of Management Journal* 25:465–99.

Mintzberg, H., and Waters, J. (1985). "Of Strategies, Deliberate and Emergent." *Strategic Management Journal*, pp. 257–72.

Mintzberg, H., Brunet, J.P., and Waters, J. (1987). "Does Planning Impede Strategic Thinking: The Strategies of Air Canada 1937–1976." In *Advances in Strategic Management* Vol. 4. Edited by R. Lamb. Englewood Cliffs, N.J.: Prentice-Hall.

Montgomery, J.D. (1972). "Allocation of Authority in Land Reform Programs: A Comparative Study of Administrative Processes and Outputs." *Administrative Science Quarterly* 11(1):63–75.

Moore, R.J., Swanson, D.A., Lim, G.C., Burke, M.A., Greenstein, J., and Fehnel, R.A. (1987). *Contracting Out: A Study of the Honduran Experience.* Washington, D.C.: National Association of Schools of Public Affairs and Administration.

Moris, J. (1981). *Managing Induced Rural Development.* Bloomington, Ind.: International Development Institute.

Morrison, J.S. (1986). "Public/Private Transitions: A Concept Paper." NASPAA Working Paper, No. 13. Washington, D.C.: National Association of Schools of Public Affairs and Administration.

Mulford, C.L., and Rogers, D.L. (1982). "Definitions and Models." In *Interorganization Coordination.* Edited by D.L. Rogers and D.A. Whetten. Ames, Iowa: Iowa State University Press.

Murrell, K.L., and Duffield, R.H. (1986). *Management Infrastructure for the Development World: A Bibliographic Sourcebook.* West Hartford, Conn.: Kumarian Press.

Mytelka, L.K. (1986). "Stimulating Effective Technology Transfer: The Case of Textiles in Africa." In *International Technology Transfer.* Edited by N. Rosenberg. New York: Praeger.

Nash, J., Dandler, J., and Hopkins, N.S., eds. (1976). *Popular Participation in Social Change: Cooperatives, Collectives, and Nationalized Industries.* The Hague: Mouton Publishers.

Nath, R., ed. (1988). *Comparative Management: A Regional View.* Cambridge, Mass.: Ballinger.

National Association of Schools of Public Affairs and Administration (NASPAA) (1985). "Improving Management in Southern Africa. Final Report to the Regional Training Council of the Southern African Development Co-ordination Conference." Washington, D.C.: NASPAA.

Nayar, B.J. (1983). *India's Quest for Technological Independence: Policy Foundation and Policy Change.* Vol. I. New Delhi: Lancers Publishers.

Negandhi, A.R. (1979). "Convergence in Organizational Practice: An Empirical Study of Industrial Enterprises in Developing Countries." In *Organizations Alike and Unlike.* Edited by C.J. Lammers and D.J. Hickson. London: Routledge & Kegan Paul.

Nellis, J.R. (1986). *Public Enterprises in Sub-Saharan Africa*. Washington, D.C.: World Bank Discussion Papers.

Nicholson, N., Ostrom, E., Bowles, D., and Long, R. (1985). *Development Management in Africa: The Case of the Egerton College Expansion Project in Kenya*. Washington, D.C.: U.S. Agency for International Development.

Niland, J.R. (1970). *The Asian Engineering Brain Drain*. Lexington, Mass.: Heath.

North South Round-Table (NSRT) (1983). "Statement from Istanbul: A Report on the Istanbul Round-Table on World Monetary, Financial and Human Resources Development Issues." Istanbul, 29 August to 1 September 1983.

Oborn, S.R. (1988). "A Summary of the Nordic Evaluation of the Effectiveness of the Human Resource Element in International Development Assistance." Dar Es Salaam, Tanzania: Canadian International Development Agency, Spare Parts Project.

Ollawa, P.E. (1979). *Participatory Democracy in Zambia: The Political Economy of National Development*. Devon, England: Arthur H. Stockwell.

Organization for Economic Co-operation and Development (OECD) (1978). *From Marshall Plan to Global Interdependence for the Industrialized Nations*. Paris: OECD.

Ouchi, W.G. (1981). *Theory Z: How American Business Can Meet the Japanese Challenge*. Reading, Mass.: Addison-Wesley.

Ouchi, W.G. (1984). *The M-form Society: How American Teamwork Can Recapture the Competitive Edge*. Reading, Mass.: Addison-Wesley.

Ozgediz, S. (1983). *Managing the Public Service in Developing Countries: Issues and Prospects*. Washington, D.C.: World Bank Staff Working Papers, No. 583, Management and Development Series, No. 10.

Page, J.M., Jr., and Steel, W.F. (1984). *Small Enterprise Development: Economic Issues from African Experience*. Washington, D.C.: World Bank Technical Paper, No. 26.

Paul, S. (1982). *Managing Development Programs: The Lessons of Success*. Boulder, Colo.: Westview.

Paul, S. (1983a). *Strategic Management Development Programmes: Guidelines for Action*. Geneva: International Labour Office.

Paul, S. (1983b). *Training for Public Administration and Management in Developing Countries: A Review*. Washington, D.C.: World Bank Staff Working Papers, No. 584, Management and Development Series, No. 11.

Pava, C. (1983). *Managing New Office Technology: An Organizational Strategy*. New York: The Free Press.

Pearce, J.A., and David, F. (1987). "Corporate Mission Statements: The Bottom Line." *The Academy of Management Executive* 1(2)(May).

Penrose, E.T. (1952). "Biological Analogies in the Theory of the Firm." *American Economic Review* 42:804–19.

Pereira, D. (1987). "Management Excellence in Strategic Organizations." In *International Conference on Organizational and Behavioural Perspectives on Social Development*. Edited by P.N. Khandwalla and R.M. Rao. Ahmedabad, India: Indian Institute of Management.

Perrow, C. (1982). "The Bureaucratic Paradox: The Efficient Organization Centralizes in Order to Decentralize." In *Organization Development: Progress and Perspectives*. Edited by D. Robey and S. Altman. New York: Macmillan.

Perrow, C. (1986). *Complex Organizations: A Critical Essay*. New York: Random House.

Peters, T.J., and Waterman, R.H., Jr. (1984). *In Search of Excellence: Lessons from America's Best-Run Companies*. New York: Warner Books.

Peterson, B.D., and Pace, W.R. (1978). *Organizational Climate Inventory*. Provo, Utah: Organizational Associates.

Pfeffer, J. (1982). *Organizations and Organization Theory*. Boston, Mass.: Pitman.

Pfeffer, J., and Salancik, G.R. (1978). *The External Control of Organizations: A Resource Dependence Perspective*. New York: Harper & Row.

Picard, L.A. (1980). "Socialism and the Field Administrator: Decentralization in Tanzania." *Comparative Politics* 12(4):439–57.

Plusquellec, H.L., and Wickham, T. (1985). *Irrigation Design and Management: Experience in Thailand and Its General Applicability*. Washington, D.C.: World Bank Technical Papers, No. 40.

Potter, M.U. (1986). "From Zero to Fifty Million: The Organization Explosion." In *Managing High Technology: Decisions for Success*. Edited by J.R. Callahan and G.H. Haines, Jr. Ottawa: Research Centre for High Technology Management, Carleton University.

Powell, V. (1987). *Improving Public Enterprise Performance: Concepts and Techniques*. Geneva: International Labour Office, Management Development Series, No. 22.

President's Export Council (1980). *The Export Imperative: Final Report to the President*. Vols. I and II, December. Washington, D.C.: U.S. Department of Commerce.

Pugh, D.S., Hickson, D.J., and Hinings, C.R. (1971). *Writers on Organizations*. 2d ed. Middlesex, England: Penguin.

Queyrane, P. (1985). "The Constraint on Industrial Co-operation Between Firms in EEC and the ACP [African, Caribbean, Pacific] Countries." Unpublished report, VII/165/85-EN, Commission of the European Communities.

Quezada, F. and Boyce, J.E. (1988). "Latin America." In *Comparative Management: A Regional View*. Edited by R. Nath. Cambridge, Mass.: Ballinger.

Raphaeli, N., Roumani, J., and MacKellar, A.C. (1984). *Public Sector Management in Botswana: Lessons in Pragmatism*. Washington, D.C.: World Bank Staff Working Papers, No. 709.

Ratiu, I., ed. (1987). "Multicultural Management Development." Special Issue of *The Journal of Management Development* 6(3).

Rhee, Y.W., Ross-Larson, B., and Pursell, G. (1984). *Korea's Competitive Edge: Managing Entry into World Markets*. Baltimore: The Johns Hopkins University Press.

Rice, A.K. (1958). *Productivity and Social Organization: The Ahmedabad Experiment*. London: Tavistock Institute.

Rieger, F. (1987). "The Influence of National Culture on Organizational Structure, Process and Strategic Decision Making: A Study of International Airlines." Ph.D. Dissertation, McGill University, Montreal, Quebec, Canada.

Robert, M.M. (1985). *Strategic Thinking: Charting the Future Direction of Your Organization*. Montreal: Decision Precision Process International.

Roethlisberger, F.J., and Dickson, W.J. (1939). *Management and the Worker: An Account of a Research Program Conducted by the Western Electric Company, Hawthorne*

Works, Chicago. Cambridge: Harvard University Press.

Rogers, D. (1968). *110 Livingston Street: Politics and Bureaucracy in the New York City Schools.* New York: Random House.

Rogers, D., and Chung, N.H. (1983). *110 Livingston Street Revisited: Decentralization in Action.* New York: New York University Press.

Rogers, D.L., and Whetten, D.A., eds. (1982). *Interorganizational Coordination: Theory, Research, and Implementation.* Ames, Iowa: Iowa State University Press.

Rondinelli, D.A. (1987). *Development Administration and U.S. Foreign Aid Policy.* Boulder, Colo.: Lynne Rienner.

Rondinelli, D.A., Nellis, J.A., and Cheema, G.S. (1984). *Decentralization in Developing Countries: A Review of Recent Experience.* Washington, D.C.: World Bank Staff Working Papers, No. 581, Management and Development Series, No. 8.

Rosenthal, I., Tuthill, J., Bury, R., and Frazier, M. (1986). *Signposts in Development Management: A Computer-Based Analysis of 277 Projects in Africa.* AID Evaluation Occasional Paper No. 10 for Development Information and Evaluation, Bureau for Program and Policy Coordination. Washington, D.C.: U.S. Agency for International Development.

Roth, G. (1987). *The Private Provision of Public Services in Developing Countries.* New York: Oxford University Press.

Rubinstein, D., and Woodman, R.W. (1984). "Spiderman and the Burma Raiders: Collateral Organization Theory in Action." *The Journal of Applied Behavioral Science* 20(1):1–21.

Sandbrook, R. (1982). *The Politics of Basic Needs: Urban Aspects of Assaulting Poverty in Africa.* London: Heinemann.

Sarathy, R. (1985). "High Technology Exports from Newly Industrializing Countries: The Brazilian Commuter Aircraft Industry." *California Management Review* XXVII(2):60–84 (Winter).

Sarkar, D. (1984). "Workers' Participation in Management of Public Sector Undertakings." In *Public Enterprises,* edited by S.K. Goyal. New Delhi: Indian Institute of Public Administration.

Sasser, W.E., Olsen, R.P., and Wyckoff, D.D. (1978). *Management of Service Operations: Text, Cases, and Readings.* Boston, Mass.: Allyn & Bacon.

Schaeffer, W.G., ed. (1985). "IASIA Working Group Report, 1984." Brussels: International Institute of Administrative Sciences.

Schein, E.H. (1969). *Process Consultation: Its Role in Organization Development.* Reading, Mass.: Addison-Wesley.

Scott-Stevens (1985). "Foreign Consultants and Counterparts: Cross-Cultural Problems in the Transfer of Technical Knowledge." Report submitted to the Indonesian Institute of Sciences, Java, Indonesia.

Sharma, B.R. (1986). *Motivational Crisis in Indian Administration: A Case of Existential Sickness.* New Delhi: Indian Institute of Public Administration.

Shelp, R.K., Stephenson, J.C., Truitt, N.S., and Wasow, B. (1984). *Service Industries and Economic Development: Case Studies in Technology Transfer.* New York: Praeger.

Shirley, M.M. (1983). *Managing State-Owned Enterprises.* Washington, D.C.: World Bank Staff Working Papers, No. 577, Management and Development Series, No. 4.

Silverman, J.M. (1984). *Technical Assistance and Aid Agency Staff: Alternative Techniques for Greater Effectiveness.* Washington, D.C.: World Bank Technical Papers, No. 28.

Sinha, D.P. (1987). "Training at the Top: Building New Administrative Culture— An Ethnographic Account." Edited by P.N. Khandwalla and R.M. Rao. International Conference on Organizational and Behavioural Perspectives for Social Development, 29 December 1986 to 2 January 1987. Ahmedabad, India.

Sivaramakrishnan, K.G., and Green, L. (1986). *Metropolitan Management: The Asian Experience.* Washington, D.C.: Economic Development Institute, The World Bank.

Sloan, A.P. (1963). *My Years at General Motors.* New York: Doubleday.

Smith, K.G., Mitchell, T.R., and Summer, C.E. (1985). "Top Level Management Priorities in Different Stages of the Organizational Life Cycle." *Academy of Management Journal* 28(4):799–820.

Spielman, J.D.B. (1983). "Redefining the Transfer of Technology Process." *Training and Development Journal* 37(10):35–41.

Spitzberg, I.J., ed. (1978). *Exchange of Expertise: The Counterpart System in the New International Order.* Boulder, Colo.: Westview.

Srinivasan, T.N. (1986). "The Costs and Benefits of Being a Small, Remote Island, Landlocked or Ministate Economy." *The World Bank Research Observer* 1(2): 205–18.

Steel, W.F., and Evans, J.W. (1984). *Industrialization in Sub-Saharan Africa: Strategies and Performance.* Washington, D.C.: World Bank Technical Papers, No. 25.

Stewart, F. (1979). *International Technology Transfer: Issues and Policy Options.* Washington, D.C.: World Bank Staff Working Papers, No. 344.

Stobaugh, R., and Wells, L.T., eds. (1984). *Technology Crossing Borders: The Choice, Transfer, and Management of International Technology Flows.* Boston, Mass.: Harvard Business School Press.

Stohr, W., and Taylor, D.R.F., eds. (1981). *Development From Above or Below.* London: John Wiley.

Taylor, F.W. (1911). *The Principles of Scientific Management.* New York: Harper.

Thomas, T. (1983). "Reorienting Bureaucratic Performance: A Social Learning Approach to Development Action." NASPAA Working Paper, No. 8. Washington, D.C.: National Association of Schools of Public Affairs and Administration.

Thompson, J.D. (1956). "On Building an Administrative Science." *Administrative Science Quarterly* 1:102–11.

Thompson, J.D. (1967). *Organizations in Action: Social Science Bases of Administrative Theory.* New York: McGraw-Hill.

Thompson, J.D. (1974). "Technology, Polity, and Societal Development." *Administrative Science Quarterly* 19(1):6–21.

Thompson, V.A. (1964). "Administrative Objectives for Development Administration." *Administrative Science Quarterly* 9(1):91–108.

Thomson, J.T., and Connerley, E. (1986). "Decentralized Finance and Management for Development." A concept paper prepared for the Office of Rural and Institutional Development, Bureau of Science and Technology, U.S. Agency for International Development, April.

Thornton, G.C., and Byham, W.C. (1982). *Assessment Centers and Managerial Performance.* New York: Academic Press.

Thorsrud, E. (1981). "The Changing Structure of Work Organization." In *Managing and Developing New Forms of Work Organization*. Edited by G. Kanawaty. Geneva: International Labour Office.

Tichy, N.M. (1983). *Managing Strategic Change: Technical, Political and Cultural Dynamics*. New York: John Wiley.

Timm, P.R., and Peterson, B.D. (1986). *People at Work: Human Relations in Organizations*. 2d ed. St. Paul: West Publishing Company.

Triandis, H.C. (1972). *The Analysis of Subjective Culture*. New York: Wiley-Interscience.

Trist, E.L. (1975). "Planning the First Steps Toward Quality of Working Life in a Developing Country." In *The Quality of Working Life: Problems, Prospects and the State of the Art*. Edited by L.E. Davis and A.B. Cherns. Vol. I. New York: The Free Press.

Trist, E.L. (1981). *The Evolution of Socio-Technical Systems*. Ontario Ministry of Labour, Occasional Paper No. 2. Toronto: Ontario Quality of Working Life Center.

Trist, E.L., and Bamforth, K.W. (1951). "Some Social and Psychological Consequences of the Long Wall Method of Coal-Getting." *Human Relations* 4:3–38.

Trist, E.L., Higgins, G.W., Murray, H., and Pollock, A.B. (1963). *Organizational Choice*. London: Tavistock Institute.

Truitt, N.S. (1984). "Mass Merchandising and Economic Development: Sears, Roebuck and Company in Mexico and Peru." In *Service Industries and Economic Development: Case Studies in Technology Transfer*. Edited by R.K. Shelp, J.C. Stephenson, N.S. Truitt, and B. Wasow. New York: Praeger.

Tsurumi, Y. (1982). "Japan's Challenge to the U.S.: Industrial Policies and Corporate Strategies." *Columbia Journal of World Business* 17(2):87–95.

Tung, R.L. (1988). "China." In *Comparative Management: A Regional View*. Edited by R. Nath. Cambridge, Mass.: Ballinger.

Tung, R.L. (1983). *Key to Japan's Economic Strength: Human Power*. Lexington, Mass.: D.C. Heath.

Tung, R.L. (1987). "China." In *Comparative Management: A Regional View*. Edited R. Nath. Cambridge, Mass.: Ballinger.

Turok, B. (1984). "Control in the Parastatal Sector in Zambia." In *Law in Zambia*. Edited by Muna Ndulo. Nairobi: East African Publishing House.

United Nations Development Programme (1986). "Africa Project Development Facility." Project Document RAF.85/022/B/01/42: Industrial Development Support Services. Washington, D.C.: United Nations Development Programme.

Uphoff, N.T. (1986). *Local Institutional Development: An Analytical Sourcebook with Cases*. West Hartford, Conn.: Kumarian Press.

U.S. Agency for International Development (1985). "Private Enterprise Development." A.I.D. Policy Paper (Revised). Washington, D.C.: Bureau for Program and Policy Coordination, March.

U.S. Agency for International Development (1986a). "Implementing A.I.D. Privatization Objectives." Washington, D.C.: Policy Determination, DD-14, June.

U.S. Agency for International Development (1986b). "Redesign of Human and Institutional Resources Development Project (Zambia)." Unpublished discussion paper, Project No. 611-0206. Washington, D.C.

Valpy, M. (1986). "Canadians Click in Africa Enterprise." *Globe and Mail*, Wednesday, 29 October, A8.

Vernon, R. (1984). "Linking Managers with Ministers: Dilemmas of the State Owned Enterprise." *Journal of Policy Analysis and Management* 4(1):39–55.

Vroom, V.H. (1964). *Work and Motivation.* New York: John Wiley.

Vroom, V.H., and Yetton, P.W. (1973). *Leadership and Decision-Making.* Pittsburgh, Pa.: University of Pittsburgh Press.

Wade, R. (1985). "The Market for Public Office: Why the Indian State Is Not Better at Development." *World Development* 13(4):467–97.

Wallace, J.B. (1985). "Fostering Management Growth in Developing Countries." *Training and Development Journal,* (January): 67–71.

Wallender, R. (1979). *Technology Transfer and Management in the Developing Countries.* Cambridge, Mass.: Ballinger.

Wasow, B. (1984). "Technology Transfer in the Insurance Industry: American International Group in the Philippines, Nigeria, and Kenya." In *Service Industries and Economic Development: Studies in Technology Transfer.* Edited by R.K. Shelp et al. New York: Praeger.

Weber, M. (1947). *The Theory of Social and Economic Organization.* Translated by A.M. Henderson and T. Parsons. New York: Oxford University Press.

White, L.G. (1986). *Managing Development Programs: Management Strategies and Project Interventions in Six African Agricultural Projects.* AID Evaluation Special Study No. 38. Washington, D.C.: U.S. Agency for International Development.

White, L.G. (1987). *Creating Opportunities for Change: Approaches to Managing Development Programs.* Boulder, Colo.: Lynne Rienner.

Whittaker, J., and Gibson, N. (1987). "Guided Transmission Training: An Effective Multiplier Mechanism." Geneva: ILO MORS Bulletin, 22/87:1–3.

Wiewel, W., and Hunter, A. (1985). "The Interorganizational Network as a Resource: A Comparative Case Study on Organizational Genesis." *Administrative Science Quarterly* 30(4):482–96.

Wildavsky, A. (1972). "Why Planning Fails in Nepal." *Administrative Science Quarterly* 17:508–28.

Williams, D. (1984). "Choice of Technology and Parastatal Firms." In *Technology Crossing Borders.* Edited by R. Stobaugh and L.T. Wells. Boston, Mass.: Harvard Business School Press.

Williamson, O.E. (1985). *The Economic Institutions of Capitalism: Firms, Markets, Relational Contracting.* New York: The Free Press.

Willis, H.L. (1984). "Selection for Employment in Developing Countries." *Personnel Administrator* 29(4):37–44.

Woodward, J. (1965). *Industrial Organization: Theory and Practice.* Oxford: Oxford University Press.

World Bank (1983). *World Bank Report.* Washington, D.C.

World Bank (1985). *Agricultural Research and Extension: An Evaluation of the World Bank's Experience.* Washington, D.C.

World Bank (1986). *World Development Report.* Washington, D.C.

Yoo, S., and Lee, S.M. (1987). "Management Style and Practice of Korean Chaebols." *California Management Review* 39(4):85–110 (Summer).

Young, R. (1983). *Canadian Development Assistance to Tanzania: An Independent Study.* Ottawa: The North-South Institute.

Zulu, J.B., and Nsouli, S.M. (1985). *Adjustment Programs in Africa: The Recent Experience.* Washington, D.C.: International Monetary Fund.

Author Index

Subject Index

Control systems, importance of, 42
Cost-benefit analysis, 138
Council for the Promotion of Education (Mexico), 79, 109
Council of Scientific and Industrial Research (India), 6
Council of Trust for the Indigenous People (Malaysia), 67-68
Counterpart-expatriate relationships, 182
Counterpart-expatriate system, 178-79
Crisis management, 62
Critical operating tasks (COTs), 32-33
  challenges of managing, 39-45
  decentralization and, 230-50
  historical perspective, 33-36
  illustration of, 36-39
  integration with SMATs, 86-95
  local technological capacity for, 207-12
  motivational problems relating to, 171
  operational and strategic variances for, 209-12
  organization performance and, 45-47
  role of boards of directors in, 82-86
  sociotechnical systems approach to studying, 48-49
  technology and, 48-50
  training for, 162
Culture, organization science and, 29-31
Culture Assimilator, 180

Decentralization
  assessing the results of, 250-53
  contingencies of, 239-42
  defined, 228-30
  dimensions of, 234-39
  forces for and against, 242-45
  implementation of, 253-54
  within and between organizations, 230-34
  of service delivery systems, 250
  state-owned enterprises and, 247-50
Decentralizing organization, 231
Decision Processes International (DPI), 93
Deconcentration, 238-39
Delegation, defined, 235-36
Developing countries
  agriculture in, 154
  costs of education in, 151
  managing COTs in, 39-45
  middle management in, 9
  motivational crises in, 168-72
  operating goals in, 71
  organization and management problems common to, 12-13
  organizations in, 7-11
  service organizations in, 50-52
  similarities versus differences in, 11-13
  strategic management in, 59-64
Development administration

(management), 19-21
  areas of integration with organization science, 27-29
  need for integration with organization science, 21-23
Devolution, defined, 234-35
Direct contact, defined, 116-17
Distribution system of service organizations, 54
Divestiture. See Complete divestiture; Partial divestiture
Divisionalism, 237-38
Domestic organizations, 278-81
Domestic private sector, 278-81
Double-loop learning model, 225

Eastern and Southern African Management Institute (ESAMI), 74
Economy, 45-46
Education, underdevelopment and, 151
Effectiveness, defined, 46
Efficiency, defined, 45
Emerging Markets Growth Fund, 282-83
Employees
  dismissing obsolete, 42-43
  training of, 160-65
Employee Stock Ownership Plans (ESOPs), 269
Environmental interdependencies, 76-79
Ethiopian Management Institute, 35
European organizations, strategic management in, 81, 82
Evaluation, of training programs, 164-65
Exchange
  defined, 177
  of skills, 179-80
Expatriates
  determinants of expatriate effectiveness, 180-84
  utilization of expatriate staff, 154, 176-79
Expertise. See Technology, knowledge, and expertise
Extractive research, 22-23

Family-owned firms, 280-81
Flexible bureaucracy, 8

Gender biases, 174
Goals, role in organizations, 103-5

Hierarchies, increasing effectiveness of, 99
Horizontal decentralization, 237
Human obsolescence, 42
Human resource development (HRD), 148, 149-51
Human resource management (HRM), 155-79
  audits of, 158